MW01267630

Honduras

Travel Guides to Planet Earth!

CRITICAL ACCLAIM FOR OPEN ROAD PUBLISHING'S CENTRAL AMERICA TRAVEL GUIDES

Honduras & Bay Islands Guide has been recommended by **Outside Magazine**

"First of its kind, **Honduras ...** includes Honduran history, the people, accommodations, restaurants, transportation, recreational facilities, maps, health concerns, money, climate ... and much more."

Travel Books & Language Center

"If you have to choose one guidebook, Paul Glassman's **Costa Rica Guide** provides a wealth of practical information, with a sharp eye and a sense of humor."

Travel and Leisure

"Belize Guide is *the* book you need. Don't leave home without it. Invaluable."

International Travel News

"... full of well   sightseeing, history, and culture ... S   of prices with plenty of inexpensive   information tips are worth the pric   " -   *Travel Guide Series)*

About the Authors

Jean-Pierre Panet is a travel writer who has bicycled and hiked through North America, Central America, South America, and Europe. He lives in Montreal, Canada.

The updater of this edition, Howard Rosenzweig, first arrived on Honduran shores back in 1984 during a trans-Central America backpacking trip. He now calls Honduras home, residing in the tranquil village of Copán Ruinas with his lovely wife Angela.

Open Road -
Travel Guides to Planet Earth!

Open Road Publishing has guide books to exciting, fun destinations on four continents. As veteran travelers, our goal is to bring you the best travel guides available anywhere!

No small task, but here's what we offer:

• All Open Road travel guides are written by authors with a distinct, opinionated point of view – not some sterile committee or team of writers. Our authors are experts in the areas covered and are polished writers.

• Our guides are geared to people who want to make their own travel choices. We'll show you how to discover the real destination – not just see some place from a tour bus window.

• We're strong on the basics, but we also provide terrific choices for those looking to get off the beaten path and experience the country or city – not just see it or pass through it.

• We give you the best, but we also tell you about the worst and what to avoid. Nobody should waste their time and money on their hard-earned vacation because of bad or inadequate travel advice.

• Our guides assume nothing. We tell you everything you need to know to have the trip of a lifetime – presented in a fun, literate, no-nonsense style.

• And, above all, we welcome your input, ideas, and suggestions to help us put out the best travel guides possible.

Honduras

Guide

Travel Guides to Planet Earth!

J.P. Panet

with
Leah Hart & Paul Glassman

Updated By
Howard Rosenzweig

Open Road Publishing

Open Road Publishing

We offer travel guides to American and foreign locales. Our books tell it like it is, often with an opinionated edge, and our experienced authors always give you all the information you need to have the trip of a lifetime. Write for your free catalog of all our titles.

Open Road Publishing
P.O. Box 284, Cold Spring Harbor, NY 11724
E-mail: Jopenroad@aol.com

6th Edition

Many thanks to all who assisted with this update; Warren in Santa Rosa, Roli in Omoa, Cristina and Matthias in Trujillo, Jorge in Tegucigalpa, Frony in Gracias, Brian in Guanaja, Bob in Copan Ruinas, Brookes in La Paz, Richard at Lake Yojoa, as well as Allan, Lena and Arden. A big thanks to my parents and the Zwicky family who have supported all our Honduran projects both big and small, without hesitation over the years. And, of course, to my wife Angela and son Andre.

Honduras Guide

contents

7. Basic Information   71

8. Sports & Recreation   84

9. Food & Drink   90

10. Best Places to Stay   92

Sidebars
Holidays in Honduras 59
Direct Flights to Honduras 65
Exchange Rate 75
National Parks At a Glance 86
Driving in Tegucigalpa 104
Emergency & Service Numbers in Tegucigalpa 126

Maps
Central America 11
Honduras 17
Central Tegucigalpa 103
Lake Yojoa 141
Pico Bonito National Park 189
The Bay Islands 205
Roatán 224
Copán Ruinas 257
The Ruins of Copán 267

AIDS Warning 155
La Ceiba's Butterflies & Insects 184
Learn Spanish in La Ceiba! 185
The Miskito People 199
Diving High Points & Low Points 210
Beaches & Supplies 232

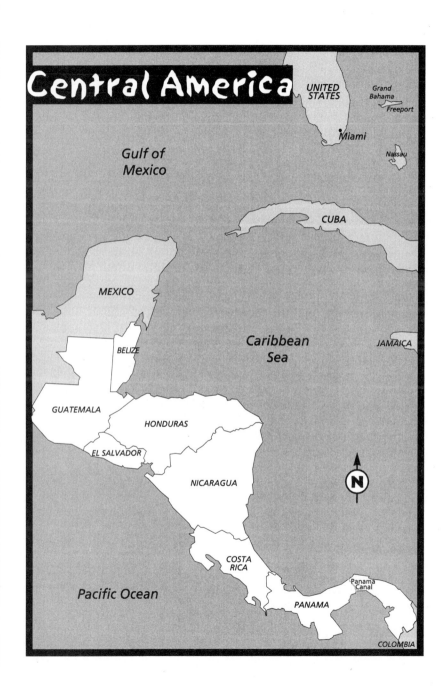

Chapter 1

What does Honduras have in store for you? There are hundreds of miles of pristine, unspoiled, practically deserted beaches. You've got diving wrecks and walls within a swim of shore, along an extension of the longest barrier reef in the hemisphere.

You'll also find the ancient city where the Maya achieved their greatest artistic expression; cloud forest peaks where the elusive *quetzal* can be sighted; remote rivers lined by impenetrable tropical forest; and remains of pirate forts and Spanish forts and English forts that tell of the struggle for dominion and booty along the Spanish Main.

Honduras has it all, and more. And yet, for reasons of politics and economics and bad luck, it has never developed as a tourist destination – which is good luck for you.

Some day, before too long, the all-inclusive resorts will be in place, the gift shops will be everywhere, the charter flights will disgorge their hordes, the tour buses will shepherd groups to the accompaniment of canned patter, and you will have the privilege of putting down your money in order to get away from home and be a cipher.

But for now, you can go to Honduras and be part of the extraordinary. It's an opportunity not to be missed.

Chapter 2

What do you think of when you think of Honduras?
- A banana republic?
- Wars and revolutions, dictators and despots?
- A comic-opera country, the far-off land depicted by O. Henry in *Of Cabbages and Kings*?
- A place that nobody goes to, except, perhaps, to cut another notch in their travel belts?

Let me tell you that if you think of Honduras in any of these ways, you are perfectly correct, at least to some degree. Honduras *has* largely lived from the export of bananas. Honduras certainly *has* had an awful lot of presidents and chiefs of state and influential generals since the Spanish were expelled 170 years ago. There *are* quaint and funny aspects to the country.

But if you think that you might go to Honduras just for the sake of going, let me disabuse you of that notion. Honduras has:

- **Jungly ruins**, where the artistic expression of the ancient, mysterious Maya reached its greatest development.
- Dozens of towns with gems of **colonial churches and monuments**, and a full-fledged Spanish fortress.
- **Pine-clad highlands**, and virtually untouched and unpopulated lowland forests alive with jaguar and tapir.
- Hundreds of miles of **deserted Caribbean beach**.
- **Excellent bird-watching**; a unique tropical botanical garden; swimming, fishing, tennis, golf and all the outdoor sports of a mild climate.

To a greater or lesser degree, other countries in Central America have comparable, little-known attractions that have for well-known reasons of politics and turmoil been ignored or avoided by vacationers and intrepid travelers until fairly recently, and which are now just being discovered and widely publicized.

But Honduras also has the **Bay Islands**, where hamlets barely changed since buccaneer times line the shores, where uninhabited jungled mountains extend inland, where diving along the barrier reef is as good as anywhere in the hemisphere, and where, oddly, the inhabitants speak English.

Personally, I enjoy cycling on roads not too heavily trafficked, with new scenes, new surprises, around every bend. Honduras fits the bill perfectly. One of the best aspects of Honduras is that it is not yet heavily traveled. Yet the facilities are there: good, if not luxurious hotels, a road system that connects most points of interest, well-developed air transport, tour operators, and acceptable conditions of sanitation and health. The inhabitants are ready to greet and help the visitor from abroad, who is still something of a rarity.

And, maybe best of all, the prices for what you get can be very reasonable, even downright cheap, when you compare with other destinations in the Caribbean.

If you go to Honduras now, you will have the satisfaction of having been there before the boom. I think that will happen, but not soon. The touristic development that is now going on is being carried out by families and small companies, and most of the hotels and resorts, especially in the Bay Islands, are wonderfully idiosyncratic, some with pet exotic birds, and mini-zoos, and resident ghosts, and private wrecks for diving. Eating places are sometimes basic, usually wholesome, and sometimes gourmet quality. This is not yet Holiday Inn country, although the first one recently opened in San Pedro Sula.

Here's a quick preview of what Honduras has in store for you:

Tegucigalpa

Central Tegucigalpa, still somewhat colonial-flavored, is small enough that you can get a sense of the city during a walk of just a few hours. There are some fine old examples of colonial and nineteenth century architecture, city squares in which to linger, and pedestrian streets for shopping and observing the flow of city life.

To the North

There is much majestic countryside to be seen during a journey along the major highway, along with **Comayagua**, the old capital where colonial churches still stand; small and little-visited towns where old ways and a slow pace of life still hold sway; and Lake Yojoa, as pleasant a stopping point and vacation area as will be found on the mainland. At the end of the route is **San**

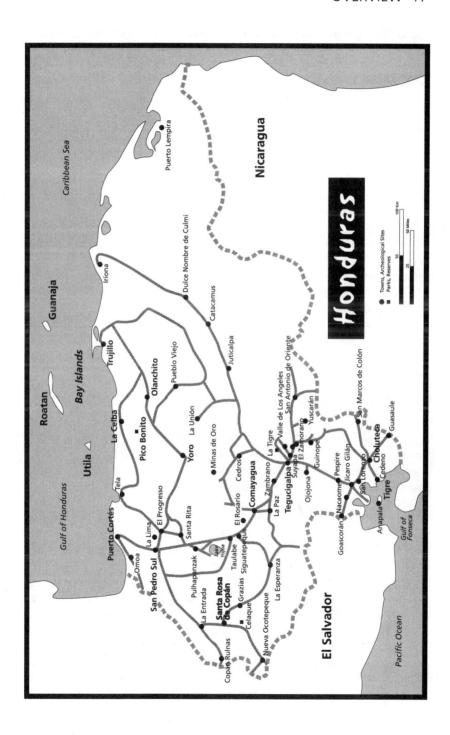

Caribbean Sea

Gulf of Honduras

Roatan

Guanaja

Bay Islands

Utila

Puerto Lempira

Nicaragua

Iriona

Dulce Nombre de Culmi

Catacamus

Trujillo

Pueblo Viejo

Olanchito

Juticalpa

La Cerba

Tela

El Progreso

Pico Bonito

Yoro

La Unión

Minas de Oro

Cedros

San Antonio de Oriente

San Marcos de Colón

Puerto Cortés

La Lima

Santa Rita

El Rosario

Comayagua

Zambrano

La Paz

La Tigre

Valle de Los Angeles

Suyapa

El Zamorano

Yuscarán

Guasaule

Omoa

Taulabe

Siguatepeque

Tegucigalpa

Ojojona

Guinope

Pespire

Jicaro Gilán

Choluteca

Cedeno

San Pedro Sul

Pulhapanzak

Lake Yojoa

La Esperanza

Nacaome

San Lorenzo

Tigre

La Entrada

Grazias

Nueva Ocotepeque

Goascorán

Amapala

Gulf of
Fonseca

Copán Ruinas

Santa Rosa
de Copán

Celaque

El Salvador

Pacific Ocean

Honduras

- ● Towns, Archeological Sites
- ■ Parks, Reserves

| 0 | 25 | 50 | Miles |

| 0 | 50 | 100 Km |

Pedro Sula, the metropolis of the north, and of modern Honduras; beyond are the coastal cities, beaches, and the special world of the **Bay Islands**.

The North Coast

The northwestern lowlands of Honduras — a strip about 50 kilometers wide, backed by mountain ridges for almost 200 kilometers — are the banana republic of Honduras. I don't mean this in any demeaning, stereotyping way. It's just that banana cultivation and commerce in bananas have made this area what it is today.

For the visitor interested in peoples, this is where you'll find the **Garífunas**, or Black Caribs, near Trujillo and Tela, and the **Miskito, Sumo**, and **Paya Indians** along the eastern stretches of coast.

The main attraction of the north coast, however, is **beaches**. There are miles and miles and miles and miles of sandy strip, bordered by palms, as idyllic as any. The most accessible parts, near the ports, have some hotels, and even a few rather good resorts. And if it's isolation that you're after, you do not have to travel very far from any coastal town to find a stretch, away from major roads, where hardly anybody has gone before you.

The North Coast is also the **ecotourism center** of the country. Punta Sal National Park, Punta Izopo and Lancetilla near Tela, Cuero Salado, Pico Bonito, the Cangrejal river near La Ceiba, Capiro y Calentura and Guaymoreto Lagoon near Trujillo together offer a wealth of ecotourism possibilities.

The Bay Islands

More than a stretch of water separates mainland from islands. Mainlanders speak Spanish, while Bay Islanders speak English (sort of). Mainlanders are farmers. Islanders are fishermen and mariners and boatbuilders. Mainlanders are mostly *mestizos*, descended from Spaniards and native Americans. Bay Islanders are largely descended from Africans and Englishmen, from slaves and buccaneers and pirates.

For the visitor, the Bay Islands are a world removed not only from the mainland, but from everywhere else in the universe, a paradise of beach and rain-forested peaks in the sea, with few telephones, clocks, or cares, and some of the best fishing and diving in the hemisphere.

Located about 60 kilometers offshore, the islands are the tips of undersea mountains that extend out from the mainland's Omoa ridge. Their peaks, rising as high as 400 meters (1300 feet), are covered with oak and pine and cedar and dense, broad-leafed undergrowth, and studded with caves and cliffs. Coral reefs virtually surround most of the islands, forming natural breakwaters, and creating ideal, calm pools for diving, fishing, swimming and sailing.

Roatán is the largest of the Bay Islands, with the major towns, though there are also settlements on **Utila** and **Guanaja**. The smaller islands are **Morat, Helene** (Santa Elena) and **Barbaret** (or Barbareta). With more than 60 smaller cays offshore, including the spectacular Cayos Cochinos (Hog Cays), the Bay Islands cover about 92 square miles.

Western Honduras

Western Honduras is mountainous, curving along the borders of Guatemala and El Salvador. It is fairly densely populated for Honduras (though it doesn't seem so), with the highest concentration of Indian inhabitants, some living in villages virtually isolated from modern life.

You'll find the **Copán Ruins** in western Honduras. Copán was the Athens of the Mayan world, where art and astronomy flourished. There were larger Mayan cities to the north, in present-day Mexico and Guatemala, and the structures at Copán are relatively modest compared to those at Tikal and Palenque and Chichén-Itzá. But there are more carved monuments at Copán then elsewhere, and the intricate, swirling, decorative art surpasses not only that of other Mayan cities, but of any other civilization in the Western Hemisphere before the arrival of Europeans.

Southern & Eastern Honduras

In southern and eastern Honduras, there are good views of high plateaus. The vegetation changes to pines, and it is fresh and windy as you gain altitude. From the heights, before long, you can see the Gulf of Fonseca in the distance, as you begin to wind down through hilly and broken terrain toward the Pacific Ocean.

Adventure in the Rain Forest

Honduras is the last frontier of travel in Central America, where an adventuring soul can still be one of the few outsiders to drift along a lazy river bordered by centenary trees, listen to the roar of howler monkeys trooping through the jungle canopy, spot a limpkin wading in the shallows, and wonder at petroglyphs carved by mysterious ancient civilizations.

Diving

Diving is what the Bay Islands are most known for. The sea is calm within the fringing reefs, and there are practically no drift currents along the south side of the islands. And if you like **coral reefs**, you'll find the corals around the Bay Islands spectacular, intact, and very much alive.

The underwater landscape features wandering clefts and caverns, sheer walls, cracks, tunnels, caves and ledges, reverse ledges, and dropoffs of 100 to 200 feet. Walls start as little as twenty feet under the surface, which affords more natural light than is usually available in wall diving.

Fishing

For the most part, sport fishing is something you'll participate in from resorts in the Bay Islands. On the mainland of Honduras, the most famous fishing hole is **Lake Yojoa**, known for bass weighing in at about ten pounds on the average.

National Parks

In just a few years, Honduras has moved into the forefront of Latin America in protecting and preserving its natural treasures. And treasures there are aplenty — over 700 species of birds, 500 piscine species, and flora that includes scores of species of orchids alone.

The **Mosquitia** region along the border of Nicaragua is one of the last largely undisturbed lowland forests in Central America. And there are pockets of highland cloud forest that the magnificent resplendent quetzal, the holy grail of birders, still calls home.

White Water Adventures

Honduras has white water! It's rapid, it's exhilarating, it's ecological, it's adventurous, it's off-beat, it's inexpensive, but best of all, it's warm. There are major rivers throughout Honduras, but rafting operators mainly use those on the north coast, where water levels are most reliable during the rainy season from October to May.

Chapter 3

Honduran Highlands Route

Day 1. Arrive San Pedro Sula, rent a car at the airport or hop the 1st class direct bus with Hedman Alas to Copan Ruinas.

Day 2,3,4. Copan Ruinas, 3 nights. See the Main Site, Sepulturas Site, Maya.

Sculpture Museum, Copan Archeology Museum. Stroll the cobblestoned streets of the quaint and tranquil village of Copan Ruinas. Half day trips to the local hot springs, horse back riding into the neatby hills, birdwatching with an expert bilingual birder, visit the butterfly garden and tropical bird park, lounge by the pool at one of two pools open to the public, hiking in the surrounding hills.

Day 5. Drive to the El Puente ruins, Honduras' second largest Maya site, continue onto Santa Rosa de Copan, spend the night. Visit one of Honduras top cigar factories and stroll the bustling colonial inspired town.

Day 6, 7. Drive or bus it to Gracias. Spend a day hiking in nearby Celaque National Park home to Honduras' highest mountain, soak in the local hot springs and visit picturesque mountain villages.

Day 8. Drive or hop a ride in a truck to La Esperanza, a mountain town which is home to the Lenca Indians.

Day 9-10. Drive or bus it to Lake Yojoa, Visit the newly opened Los Naranjos archeological site, bird watch or fish for bass.

Day 11. Drive or bus to Tela. Visit Punta Sal and Punto Izopo National Parks and the Lancetilla Botanical Gardens.

Day 14. Return to San Pedro Sula.

Caribbean Coastal Route

Day 1,2,3. Arrive San Pedro Sula. Then on to Tela, Punta Sal and Punto Izopo Natl Parks, Lancetilla Botanical Gardens. Wonderful white sand beach, tropical forest, monkeys up close and personal, fresh fish lunch on the beach and one of the world's largest tropical botanical gardens.

Day 4,5,6. La Ceiba, Cuero Salado Coastal Reserve, Pico Bonito National Park. Coastal mangrove swamp, plenty of bird life and monkeys as you weave your way through the mangrove. Pico Bonito offers up plenty of hiking, great birding and views down to the Caribbean. Raft or kayak the Cangrejal River.

Day 7,8,9,10,11,12,13. Fly or ferry to Bay Islands (your choice Roatan, Guanaja, or Utila).

Return to San Pedro Sula.

Note with an extra 2-3 nights, Copan Ruinas can be combined, either at the start or end of any of these trips.

Island Fever Itinerary

Two weeks: Arrive San Pedro Sula, transfer to flight to Bay Islands for diving, beachcombing, munching on fresh seafood, partying and just plainkicking back.

If you want to stay in the main destinations here, stay in Roatan 5 nights, Utila 5 nights, and Guanaja 5 nights.

Return to San Pedro Sula.

Jungle Fever Itinerary

Arrive San Pedro Sula, fly to Palacios, the gateway to La Mosquitia and the Platano Biosphere Reserve, the largest remaining swath of intact tropical forest and jungle in Central America. Home to the Miskito Indians of Miskito Coast fame, the area offers excellent birding and the opportunty to make an Amazon-style jungle river safari in a dugout canoe into the Biosphere.

Day 1. Ibans Lagoon, a beautiful coastal lagoon fringed on one side by the Caribbean and miles of deserted undeveloped beach, and on the other by the towering mountains of the La Mosquitia interior.

Day 2. Travel by launch to the mouth of the Platano River.

Day 3,4,5,6. Head upriver to the small indigenous village of Las Marias whih will serve as your base camp. From here your dugout canoe will take you into the far reaches of the Rio Platano where life has changed little since the arrival of the Spanish pirates and British loggers.

Return to Palacios and San Pedro.

Chapter 4

land & people

As Central America goes, Honduras is a large country, with few people. It has lots of resources, mineral and agricultural and scenic. It has, you might say, limitless possibilities.

But Honduras is a country that has never arrived, or "taken off." For its size, it has few people. Most of the suitable land is unused for agriculture. Minerals are unmined. Forests are cut and not replanted.

In colonial times, parts of Honduras were ruled from different imperial outposts, leaving no sense of nationality, and no tradition of self-rule. Dictatorships and frequent changes in government and competing regimes and foreign intervention have been the norm for most of the nation's independent history, making Honduras, in effect, a country without a government. Boundaries have changed, and part of the country has been controlled by foreigners.

In bare statistical terms, Honduras ranks somewhere near Bolivia and above Nicaragua in terms of national income and wealth per person.

This is all pretty dismal stuff, and yet it would be wrong to put Honduras in the category of national basket cases and depict it as a terrible place. Dictatorships there have been, but in the context of the times, they have never been as severe or sanguinary as in neighboring states.

Poverty is a national condition, but there has never been the extreme divide between rich and poor, nor the large-scale exploitation of the masses, that has characterized countries elsewhere in the region. You'd never guess it, but it was Honduran banana workers who took the lead in the region in improving their conditions. Racial tensions have been few. There has been some land reform, and land is available to those who want to till it. The press has been relatively free, and in the absence of stable and far-reaching national governments, Hondurans haven't done badly at managing their affairs at the local level.

I don't want to make excuses. There *have* been cases of human rights abuses for which the government has been internationally condemned. Honduras was the major base for the Contra War against Nicaragua. But in recent years, the government has been constitutional, elections have been free and fair, and the Central American conflicts that have spilled over the borders of Honduras have receded. The outlook for Honduras is a fairly happy one. And it is a happy place to visit.

Land

Honduras is a fertile country. It rains enough almost everywhere. There are many valleys, with expanses of flat land, there is plenty of sun and rich soil. Everything grows here, from apples and wheat and peaches at the higher altitudes to pineapples down in the wet, hot lowlands.

But Honduras does not have a simple landscape, anything but. It's a bit disordered, even messy. There are mountains here and there, spots of desert, jungle, with no continuation of anything. Nevertheless, it is possible to make something intelligible out of the ensemble.

Honduras covers 112,088 square kilometers (43,644 square miles), about the size of the state of Tennessee, or the country of Bulgaria in Europe. By Central American standards, Honduras is big, second in size after Nicaragua. But this is a sparsely populated land, with just under 7 million inhabitants. El Salvador, next door, has about four times the population density of Honduras.

Honduras stretches between 13 and 16 degrees north latitude, and from 83°15' to 89°30' west latitude. Though its peaks do not reach dramatic heights, it is the most mountainous country in Central America, and most of the land is more than a thousand feet above sea level. Roughly, very roughly, the country is shaped like a triangle bulging on one side. Along the north is the 800-kilometer (500-mile) Caribbean coastline. On the east, an 870-kilometer (545-mile) border with Nicaragua runs south and west from the Caribbean to the Pacific. The distance along the west side of the country is almost as long — 339 kilometers (211 miles) southwest with Guatemala, then 341 kilometers (212 miles) to the southeast with El Salvador, ending at the 145-kilometer (90-mile) Pacific coastline along the Gulf of Fonseca. Apart from this huge chunk of mainland, there are also the Bay Islands off the north coast, and farther out in Caribbean waters, the Swan Islands, or Islas del Cisne.

Mountains cover more than two-thirds of the land thus enclosed. Spread almost haphazardly, they create numerous valleys with small expanses of arable land, mostly isolated one from another. Some valleys, north and east of Tegucigalpa, are broader than the others, covered with savannas. Major ranges are the Merendón and Celaque, running roughly from southwest to northeast, with peaks as high as 2800 meters (over 9000 feet). The Nombre de Dios range, with peaks up to 8000 feet, lies just back from the Caribbean shore, forming the spectacular southern boundary of the department of Atlántida. The Entre Ríos range parallels the Nicaraguan border in the sparsely populated northeast region. The Bay Islands are just a short above-water expression of an undersea continuation of the Merendón mountains.

Mountains not only dominate the topography, they have dominated the history of Honduras as well. In this landscape, with few or no roads for most of the life of the country, regional rivalries flourished, and national unity suffered. Revolts and plots could be repeatedly hatched in the countryside out of earshot of and communication with the capital.

Within the many valleys of Honduras, you can select the climate you desire, for each has its own pattern of rainfall, and temperature, and typical vegetation, depending on altitude, and prevailing winds, and where it is in relation to the coasts, and to what extent mountains can block the passage of clouds. There are some general patterns that apply to the country as a whole, however. The central, southern and western parts of Honduras have a well-defined rainy season, from May though October or November, when prevailing winds bring clouds inland from the coast with great regularity, to shed their water over the mountainous interior. For the remainder of the year, when the winds shift, there is hardly any rain at all. Along the northern coast, where winds blow off the sea throughout the year, rains are more constant, and much, much heavier.

Most settlement was originally attracted to the basin that runs from San Pedro Sula south to Comayagua and Tegucigalpa and the Gulf of Fonseca, actually a series of valleys, with mountain passes in between. This area still has the greatest concentration of population. The bottom lands of valleys and sometimes the slopes are planted to corn, and sometimes to coffee, beans, and sorghum. At the lower altitudes, sugar, rice, tobacco and vegetables are grown. Some of the high plateaus are still forested in pine and oak. Much of the farmland is exhausted, while fertile land elsewhere goes unused. By some estimates, only a fifth of arable land is used for farming.

Eastward and to the north of mountainous Honduras are the great savannas, grasslands where rainfall is limited by the mountain ranges along the coast. Settled sparsely in colonial times, and off the beaten track for many years, they are now home to large cattle ranches.

The two lowland areas of Honduras are around the Gulf of Fonseca in the south, and along the Caribbean, in an irregular strip enclosed by meandering mountains running 40 to 100 kilometers inland. Along the Gulf of Fonseca are settlements that date from well before the arrival of the Spanish conquerors. The natural, seasonally dry landscape of savanna and acacia has given way to fields of cotton and irrigated rice, and cattle ranches. On the other side of the country, the Caribbean coast was virtually uninhabited until the end of the nineteenth century. There, initial Spanish settlements were lost to the dread diseases of malaria and yellow fever, insects, torrential rains, wild animals, endless heat, and impenetrable jungles. Only in the last hundred years has this area been exploited, with the development of banana cultivation, and it is now, in its western reaches, the fastest-growing and most industrialized part of Honduras. Natural vegetation here is as abundant and varied as in almost any other place.

But the economy is still dominated by just a few crops: bananas, coffee, and the African oil palm, cacao, pineapple, melons and other fruit products promoted and exported to the US and Europe. Farther east, the landscape is a waterlogged terrain of mangrove and swamps and lazy rivers, of hardwood and rubber trees and palms and wide sandy bars near the sea, and stretches of scrub Caribbean pine on sandy soil inland, and a few settlements along the rivers. Honduras mahogany of renowned quality, growing sparsely, is cut and shipped out, but few other uses are made of the land.

Honduras is rich in minerals: gold and silver that first attracted avaricious Spanish adventurers; and lead, zinc, tin, iron, copper, coal and antimony. Some of these have been exploited for centuries. There are deposits of gypsum, strata of marble, and limestone, used since Mayan times to make a durable mortar.

Dozens of rivers drain the mountains of Honduras, combining and renaming with their flow as they near the oceans. Major waterways are the Goascorán, Nacaome and Choluteca in the south, and the Ulúa and Chamelecón in the north. Farther east along the Caribbean, the Coco and Patuca were once highways for pirates and English adventurers, and are still major routes in an area where few roads penetrate. Approximately 85% of the national land mass drains into the Caribbean.

Flora & Fauna

The flora and fauna of Honduras is as rich and varied as it's landscape and peoples themselves. No matter where one goes in the country – the Bay Islands, Copan, the interior or the coasts – there is a piece of natural history awaiting to be discovered and enjoyed by the observant ecotraveler.

Honduras is the second largest country in Central America, with mountain ranges covering 85% of its land surface. The ranges run in various directions and have created a large series of valleys of varying sizes. There are also isolated mountains that are termed 'islands;' one example is Capiro y Calentura. In the far east is the vast Mosquitia region, relatively flat and covered with savannas, lowland rainforest and giant lagoons. The interior is filled with pine-covered mountains and cloud forest at higher elevations. Finally, there are the Bay Islands that shine like jewels in the warm Caribbean Sea. All this semingly chaotic mix of geography makes for a very interesting combination of flora and fauna.

Tropical countries have a diversity of vegetation that astounds people from the temperate latitudes, and Honduras is no exception. Here you'll find many of the plants you're familiar with from home, along with "exotica" that you thought could only survive in hothouses.

In your travels around Honduras, you'll mainly see the crops that Hondurans commonly farm for home use and for sale. These include corn, beans, and sorghum at the temperate altitudes toward the center of the country; coffee on mountain slopes; tobacco in warm valleys; and in the hot lowlands, sugar, coconut, manila hemp (*Abacá*), pineapple, cotton, African oil palm, and that signature crop, bananas. Between San Pedro Sula and El Progresso sugarcane and bananas are grown, near Tela there are huge plantations of African palms. Mangos are in season around May. Near Lake Yojoa and La Ceiba pineapples are cultivated. Garden crops and fruits include cassava, common vegetables such as tomato and cabbage, cacao, and tropical fruits such as mangoes, avocados, *zapote*, *anona*, tamarind, guava, papaya, *nance*, and *jocote*.

Outside cultivated areas, Honduras' forests are a treasure trove of tropical variety that has only recently been set aside, in part, as national parks and biological reserves. Atop mountain peaks and along the crests of ridges and cloud forests, the "weeping woods" where abundant moisture allows ferns and vines and orchids (over 700 species of orchids have been identified) and broadleaf plants to thrive at every level, from the rich humus of decaying matter at the ground level, up to the crooks of tree branches, where bromeliadstake their nourishment from passing detritus blown on the wind, and capture the moisture in the air. A nice (and ever growing) collection of orchids can be seen at the butterfly garden in Copan Ruinas. Live oaks and wild avocados are common in most cloud forest areas; the exact plant variety varies according to particular moisture conditions.

Practically beside some of these wonderlands are patches of desert, starved of moisture by nearby peaks that catch the clouds on the prevailing winds. Pines and firs cover vast stretches of highland Honduras below the peaks, and toward the wetter lowlands, mahogany, c*eiba* (silk-cotton), Spanish cedar, and rosewood are typical, with palms along the beaches, and mangroves in the water-soaked coastal areas. Acacias and even cactus are typical of the savannas of the northeast. Within pristine rainforests trees tower over 100 feet tall and are home to hundreds of epiphyticplants (bromeliads, orchids, philodendrons, etc.) as well as thousands of insects, birds and mammals. Native brightly colored heliconias abound throughout Honduras.

Assorted common forest animals typical of Honduras: anteater, armadillo, coyote, deer (white-tailed and brocket), raccoon, kinkajou, coati, turkey, cats (puma, ocelot, jaguarundi, margay, jaguar), opossum, white-lipped and collared peccary, monkeys (howler, spider, capuchin, marmoset), gray fox, gopher, porcupine, tapir, turtles, lizards (iguana, skinks, gecko, etc), snakes (boa, worm, coral, bushmaster, rattlesnake, fer de lance), sloths, cottontail rabbits, rodents (flying squirrel, mice, rats, porcupines, agoutis, paca [tepezcuintle]), skunk, river otter, bats), ocelot, margay, kinkajou and wild pigs. In many protected areas the mighty jaguar still roams free and though rarely seen, their tracks give away their presence.

For the most part forest animals are difficult to find and observe, as many are restricted to areas with extensive forest cover such as La Mosquitia, Sierra de Agalta, Cusuco, Cero Azul Meambar and Pico Bonito national parks. Many are nocturnal and arboreal and it is adviseable not to go out at night unless you are accompanied by a knowledgeable guide. A guidebook to the mammals of Honduras is available (in Spanish) at Lancetilla.

Near and in the water are assorted crocodiles, caymans, turtles (leatherback, Ridley, loggerhead, hawksbill, green), manatees, salamanders, and frogs and toads. In some of the coastal lagoons the serene manatee paddles effortlessly along hyacinth-lined waterways.

There are a total of 116 species of snakes discovered including the boa, fer de lance, tropical rattlesnake, eyelash and jumping vipers, ratsnakes, corals, etc. Few are poisonous, but it is best not to handle any of them. There is a snake exhibit open to the public that displays live poisonous and non-poisonous species, located at the butterfly farm on the grounds of The Lodge at Pico Bonito near La Ceiba.

Another live snake exhibit will open in 2002 at the **Copan Ruinas butterfly garden**. Geckos, iguanas and basilisk lizards are foundthroughout the country as well as many species of toads and frogs. Live iguanas can be seen up close and personal at the **Iguana Farm** at French Harbor on Roatan. A guidebook to the snakes of Honduras (in Spanish) is available at Lancetilla in Tela and at the Insect Museum in La Ceiba.

Fish, aside from game species mentioned in connection with the Bay Islands, include catfish, minnow, cichlid, gar-pike, mud-eel, sea catfish, sharks, guapote (a bass-like river fish), mojarras (cichlids), top minnows (mollies), and black bass introduced in Lake Yojoa; and there are such mollusks as snails, lobster and fresh-water crabs.

For coral and fish watchers, a good reference is *Guide to Corals and Fishes of Florida, the Bahamas and the Caribbean*, by Idaz and Jerry Greenberg published by Seahawk Press and available in a waterproof edition. Natalie's fish-sighting list includes: green moray, spotted moray, barracuda, sand diver, trumpet fish, squirrel fish, fairy basslet, tiger grouper, yellowtail snapper, French and Spanish grunt, porkfish, banded butterflyfish, reef butterflyfish, queen angelfish, rock beauty, French angelfish, yellowtail damselfish, blue and brown chromis, parrotfish, black durgon, blue tang, ocean surgeon, white spotted filefish, hawksbill turtle, coral crab, spiny lobster, spotfin butterflyfish, moon jellyfish, octopus and urchin.

Over 730 species have been recorded to date and birdwatching opportunities abound. The vast array of habitats from sea level to over 8,000 foot peaks found within reserves provide a safe haven for many exotic and migrant species. One endemic species, Honduran Emerald, is found only in dry thorn forest. The highlands are home to Thrushes, Hummers, Warblers, and the Resplendent Quetzal. Wetlands such as Lake Yojoa and Cuero Salado harbor many species of waterfowl and even Jabirus. In the rainforests of the North Coast are found Lovely Cotingas, Motmots, Trogans, Parrots, Hawk Eagles and the Sunbittern. The La Mosquitia region still harbors many endangered species including the Harpy Eagle, Curassow, Scarlet and Green Macaws, plus an array of Antbirds.

Regional checklists for Copan and The Lodge at Pico Bonito (both with nearly 300 species) and the Rio Platano Biosphere Reserve (with more than 350 species) are available through the Naturalist, Bob 'The Buttefly Guy' Gallardo. He resides in Copan Ruinas and offers organized tours lasting from 1-14 days or more. Two week trips can produce up to 300 species. *Tel. 651-4133, rgallardo32@hotmail.com*

Field guides covering all or parts of Honduras include *The Birds of Panama*, 2nd edition, by R. Ridgely & J. Gwynne, and *The Birds of Mexico & North Central America* by Webb & Howell. For migrants: *National Geographic's Birds of North America*.

Opening in 2002 is the **Tropical Treasures Bird Park**, located 2.2 kilometers north of Copan Ruinas. The site will be on 10 acres with towering trees, a river, a coffee plantation and hundreds of macaws, toucans and parrots. Restaurant, coffee roasting and tasting facility, birding trails, and guided tours will be available, and the park will be open daily.

Among typical or notable species (and these are mentioned just to indicate the range of species in Honduras):

The quetzal, an elusive cloud forest trogon in iridescent red and green, with an arc of tail feathers several feet long, which every Central American country claims as its own; nightingale thrush (*jilguero*), black robin (*sinzontle*), wood hewer, clorospinga, hummingbirds (more than twelve varieties), motmots, curassows (*pavones*), chachalacas (wild hen), tinamou, quail, parrots and macaws, toucans, partridge, wrens, grebes, cormorants, pelicans, hawks, falcons, ospreys, vultures, herons, ibises, ducks, swallows, flycatchers, warblers, dippers, orioles, jays, blackbirds, cuckoos, rails, plovers, gulls, terns, pigeons, owls, kingfishers, swifts, mockingbirds, jacana, storks, flamingos, guans, limpkins, sun bitterns, potoos, puff-birds, manakins, honey creepers, finches, sparrows, frigatebirds, boobies, anhingas, egrets, spoonbill, doves, roadrunners, woodpeckers, tanagers, cardinals, turkeys, chickadees.

Insects come in nearly every color and configuration imagineable. Found within forested areas are peanut head bugs, hercules and elephantbeetles, fireflies, silkmoths, giant damsel flies and an array of wasps and ants. Most of the ants inflict painful bites so it is wise to watch where you're standing while outdoors.

In La Ceiba there is a wonderful **Butterfly and Insect Museum** located in La Colonia El Sauce. On display are thousands of preserved insects from Honduras and a few other countries. Educational videos and tours. Contact Robert Lehman at *442-2874* or *rlehman@caribe.hn.*

Some of the world's most beautiful and sought after butterflies are found in Honduras with an estimated 900 species. There are six species of Morphos and five "Owl's Eyes" found in their proper habitats. Transparent "clearwings" are common in the highlands. Tropical swallowtails are abundant around forested areas. Sulfurs, skippers, hairstreaks and metalmarks can be seen around villages. Forested areas shelter the most beautiful and greatest diversity of these flying flowers.

There are currently two butterfly farms open to the public. One is located in Raista, La Mosquitia which was established by former Peace Corps Volunteer Bob 'The Butterfly Guy' Gallardo as Honduras' first butterfly farm. Tours daily. The other farm is located on the grounds of **The Lodge at Pico Bonito** west of La Ceiba, featuring a 4,000 square foot butterfly house. Tours Wednesday through Sunday; *http://hondurasbutterflyfar.tripod.com.*

There are also two live butterfly exhibits that display farm bred specimens. **Roatan Butterfly Gardens** is located near West End, open daily except Saturday. **Enchanted Wings Butterfly House** is located in Copán Ruinas. It is built on five terraces, running water, cascades, a large variety of flowering plants including (an ever growing) collection of orchids. Framed butterfly specimens for sale. In the coming years the garden is to become a full service nature center with serpentarium, insect museum, botanical garden and display of more than 100 species of orchids. Open daily, guided tours, *Tel. 651-4133,* E-mail: *rgallardo32@hotmail.com.*

The best book to identify Honduran butterflies is *The Butterflies of Costa Rica* by P. DeVries.

People

What do you notice first about the people of Honduras? They are friendly and they are helpful. They are easy-going. They are approachable. They are not at all hard to get along with.

To me, this is slightly surprising. For Honduras is a poor country, indeed. Yet in this place, you do not feel the inequalities, the seething social tensions that form a backdrop to a visit to so many other places that are far better off. There are rich people, indeed, in Honduras, but the out-and-out exploitation of the masses that has characterized the history of neighboring countries has been in Honduras less pronounced, if not totally absent.

Nobody in Honduras runs after you on the street to badger you into buying something. Violent crime is not a major problem, and you can feel safe everywhere. Aggressiveness is at level zero. People are quite relaxed, but when you need something, as a visitor, service is not bad at all. There are no lineups and kowtowing to officials as in some other Latin American countries.

There are some odd statistics that illustrate that while Hondurans are poor, they are not desperately off. For example, there are more domestic animals — pigs, horses and mules — than elsewhere in the region. Honduran farmers use animals to work the earth, a luxury for, say, a rural Salvadoran. And they have land to grow the forage to feed their animals.

Another indication of the relatively benign nature of Honduras is that it has attracted immigration, and not just the immigration of slaves and displaced persons and avaricious Spaniards of colonial times. In the last century, freed slaves took up residence in the Bay Islands, and in this century, many Syrians and Lebanese have found opportunity in the developing areas along the north coast.

Hondurans comprise many of the races of the earth. Whites, blacks, Amerindians, Orientals, Lebanese, and every mixture thereof can be found, either as part of the national culture, or as a group maintaining its own separate ways. Spanish is the national language, but American Indian tongues and English dialects are also spoken. Hondurans, as are many of the peoples of poorer countries, are mostly young, mostly country people, and mostly farmers. But there are notable differences between the different groups.

Ladinos

Most of the nearly seven million Hondurans, those you typically think of as Hondurans and who think of themselves as Hondurans, are **Mestizos**, or **Ladinos**, people who have both European and American Indian ancestors. About 88 percent of Hondurans fall into this category. Native Americans are the next largest group, as much as ten percent of the population. Blacks, whites, and assorted other groups and mixtures make up the rest.

Ladinos live everywhere in Honduras, but mostly in the more heavily populated west-central corridor of the country, running from San Pedro Sula to Comayagua to Tegucigalpa to the Gulf of Fonseca. Other groups reside in specific areas, mainly near the perimeter of Honduras.

The Ladinos of Honduras have a heritage similar to that of other Spanish-speaking nations of America. They are overwhelmingly Catholic. They have until recent times been tied closely to the land. Where educational opportunities have presented themselves or been sought after, it has been in the law and arts and literature. The Church, in the absence of other, secular influences, has largely controlled education, officially or otherwise, and sometimes the only way to advance has been to join the clergy. Administrative and governmental skills have been neglected, and commerce was often left in the hands of immigrants from other countries.

Personalismo, the valuation of individuals over ideology and society in general, is a common heritage. Leaders are popular for what they're like, rather than for what they stand for. People are inclined to save their own skins, and those of their loved ones, and altruistic sacrifice for the good of the nation and society is less of a fact than in some other countries.

In Honduran society, family counts for everything. At home, the head of the family is the father, whose word is generally unopposed. Men dominate outside the family as well, still taking the best jobs, and determining which roles are suitable for women. A man's man, a *macho*, is an admired ideal. Extended to politics, strongman rulers who decide rather than consult have been the norm.

Family connections are everything in determining who gets a job, and who gets promoted, and who marries whom. Cronyism is the norm, in business and politics. Who you're descended from, how old your money is, and what your education is determine where you stand on the social ladder. In business, operations can be family-like, and this is not without advantages for workers, who are looked after and helped in difficult times. Family alliances are made through godparent relationships, and endure throughout life in a country where people do not move around from place to place and job to job. Social welfare is an individual, not a governmental, responsibility. Ladino society is difficult for immigrants to penetrate, which is one reason that newcomers such as the Lebanese remain apart, no matter how rich some of them might be.

Overwhelmingly, Ladinos are Catholics, though strict Catholicism is not the norm. This is somewhat odd, for it was the Church that tried to conquer the soul of Honduras for imperial Spain. But, far removed from Spain, colonial Honduras never had enough priests, or money, and even today, much of the clergy is foreign. Pilgrimages to the Basilica of Suyapa near Tegucigalpa and to Esquipulas in Guatemala are made faithfully, but these, as well as village fiestas and exchanges of saints between neighboring towns, are as much social as religious occasions. With a history of Church involvement in politics, sometimes on the losing conservative side, the church and state have been kept separate, and at times, church orders have been legally forbidden.

If Honduras has remained largely Catholic, it may well be from a lack of interest by other religions. This has changed in this century. Methodists have gained converts on the north coast, and more recently, Protestant missions have made gains throughout Honduras. Nevertheless, Catholic holidays, and lip service to Catholic ways, are part of the national culture.

Though families are strong, half of marriages are common-law, due to the lack of priests and the expense of a church wedding. It's understood that people marry within their social class, though beyond this, there's little in the way of formal courtship. In poor families, children by necessity take a role in earning the family living. But when the kids don't have to work, upbringing is permissive, and the kids are spoiled. The late teens are a suitable age for marriage for women. Legal marriages usually endure, at least on paper. When a marriage breaks down, and even when it doesn't, it's accepted that company will be sought elsewhere.

Like other Latin Americans, and most people in traditional societies, Hondurans are very fatalistic. There's a limit as to how much you can do to change your lot in life. So you don't lose out on some of the pleasures, like conversation and passing the time with family, that you might ignore if you were too occupied with trying to get ahead.

Blacks

Blacks have been present in Honduras since the arrival of the Spanish, who soon brought African slaves. Most of these early immigrants, however, blended into the general population, and slavery was abolished with independence.

Blacks who migrated later to Honduras did so as part of distinct groups. Escaped slaves of the British landed on the coast and, in some cases, married natives. Others came from the West Indies to work on banana plantations established by American companies toward the end of the nineteenth century. Gradually, some of these have lost their English language, and blended into Ladino society.

Blacks who came to the Bay Islands, however, have maintained their West Indian ways. Some originally arrived as slaves of British buccaneers, who were intermittently expelled. More permanent settlement started in the 1830s and afterward, as freed blacks, mainly from Grand Cayman but also from other English Islands and from Belize, sought opportunity elsewhere in the Caribbean. On the Bay Islands, they have managed to maintain their own ways, speaking English and holding to their Protestant, largely Methodist religion. Blacks and their former white masters generally live in different communities on the islands. Many make their living as fishermen, boat builders and merchant seamen.

Garífunas

Garífunas, also called **Black Caribs** or **Morenos**, are an ethnic group with both American Indian and African roots, now living mainly along the north coast of Honduras in the vicinity of Trujillo, La Ceiba and Tela, as well as in adjacent parts of Guatemala and Belize. The Black Caribs are descended from the Carib Indians who lived in the Lesser Antilles and on the South American mainland, and from escaped and shipwrecked slaves who found shelter among the Caribs, especially those on the island of St. Vincent.

Rebellious Caribs were deported by the British in 1796 from St. Vincent to Roatán, and in turn were encouraged by the Spanish to leave the islands and settle on the mainland.

Modern Caribs speak their original Antillean language, with ample Spanish and English words thrown in. Many travel regularly to Carib settlements up and down the coast in Guatemala and Belize, and are perfectly fluent in Spanish and many speak English. Though they are mainly African in racial origin, their customs are a mixture of American Indian and British West Indian ways. Formally Catholic, they have many practices that are African in origin. Celebrations of special importance are held on Christmas day and at New Year's, when masked men dance the traditional Yankunu (or John-Canoe) all night. Dancing and mass processions accompany funerals, which are especially important, for the dead can have an important influence on the living. Many other ceremonies are kept shielded from the eyes of outsiders.

Most Caribs live in seaside villages of huts with steep thatched roofs, and cultivate root crops, such as manioc, yams and taro. Many are boat builders and fishermen.

Whites

Whites have been present in Honduras since the Spanish conquest. More whites arrived in the nineteenth century from the British West Indies, and still others from the Middle East. With their varied backgrounds, whites do not form an ethnic group in Honduras, but, rather are components of other groups.

Most of the colonial Spanish settlers intermarried with natives of Honduras, and their descendants form the majority Ladino class, in shadings from white to brown. It is hard for a foreigner not to notice that light-skinned people are generally at the upper end of the social and political ladder.

Whites with quite a different background have inhabited the Bay Islands off and on for hundreds of years. Some of the original settlers were pirates and shipwrecked sailors and British merchants, who were intermittently expelled by the Spaniards, only to return later. Others arrived in the nineteenth century from the Cayman Islands, and for decades kept themselves apart from other, black Cayman Islanders who immigrated to Honduras following emancipation. They have kept their archaic dialect of English even to this day.

Immigrants from the Middle East, or *Turcos* as Hondurans call them, constitute a third group of whites. These are mostly Arabic-speaking Christians from Lebanon, though, to the broad class of Hondurans, Jews, too, count as Turks. Many are involved in small businesses, trade, and *maquilas* (clothing assembly factories for export to the US), especially along the north coast.

Other whites of European and American descent constitute a class apart as in other Latin American nations. Some are Americans and Europeans in Honduras temporarily on aid missions or working on development projects, as volunteers, paid technical advisors, private bilingual school teachers, diplomats or as executives with multinational companies. Though the faces change through transfers, they constitute a permanent and highly visible fixture on the Honduran scene.

Indians

The term **Indian**, or *indígena*, generally refers to Hondurans descended from the peoples who inhabited the land when the Spanish arrived. There have been blood mixtures to some degree among all the Indian peoples of Honduras, and the ways of the Spanish and British have had an influence on their customs. Still, after 500 years of domination by Spain and by independent Ladino governments, many Hondurans maintain ways of life readily identified as Indian, and quite apart from the national culture.

There are several broad groups of Indians in Honduras. Those who inhabited the western parts of the country, the **Lencas** and the **Chortís**, were descended from and related to the Mayas, who had built a great empire in Mesoamerica while Europe was still in the dark ages; and to migrants who came from what is now Mexico. They were largely a settled people, who cultivated corn and squash and beans.

As such, they were relatively easy for the Spanish to control, once initial resistance was crushed. The Spanish relocated them to villages built like the towns they knew from Spain, made them worship in churches, and allowed them to go out and work communal lands and Spanish estates. The Indians continued in many cases to perform the daily tasks to which they were accustomed, but for new Spanish masters who substituted for the former Indian nobility.

The conversion of Indians to Catholicism was allegedly what the Spanish conquest of America was all about, and religion remains stronger today among Indians than among the broader class of Hondurans. Partly, this could be because the natives already had a well-developed religious structure, and Catholicism was overlaid upon it, rather than substituted for it.

Instead of worshipping in caves and at shrines, newly converted Indians worshipped in churches. They honored saints, with attributes roughly similar to those of their old gods and idols. Processions of idols became processions of saints, and images honored in basilicas had a familiar brown cast. If Indians in Honduras, especially in the west, appear to be more religious than their Ladino countrymen, it's partly because it's not, for them, quite the same religion.

In modern Honduras, many Indians have merged into the Ladino, Hispanic, national culture. Sometimes the dividing lines between the two groups are unclear. Different generations of the same family may be more or less fluent in Spanish or an Indian language, or dress in the kind of clothing typical of Indians, or prefer western wear. But even in Ladino culture, Indian heritage is present. Many place names are derived from Nahuatl, the language of the Mexican Indian allies of the Spanish conquerors, and slang words often have an Indian origin.

Of those Hondurans who remain identifiably Indian, more than half are Lencas, who live in the southwestern part of the nation, to the west of

Comayagua, roughly north of the border with El Salvador. Their largest concentration is around Intibucá, the only major town in Honduras with an Indian majority. After the conquest, the Lencas, like other western Indians, were resettled in towns. Their language broke down into local dialects, which are spoken by fewer and fewer people today. But old ways remain. Some Lencas still work communal lands, allotted for lifetime use, instead of owning private property. Some belong to *cofradías*, or religious brotherhoods, devoted to a particular saint. Fiestas in honor of a patron saint have a more serious religious significance than in Ladino towns, and exchanges of saints — *guancascos* — are practiced. Women wear a long skirt and short blouse similar to those worn by Spanish women in colonial days.

Other characteristics that set the Lenca apart are their festival dances, a few remaining handicrafts, such as basket-making and pottery, and the home brewing of *chicha* liquor. While many rural Hondurans use plows and pack animals, Lencas more typically use a digging stick and carry loads on their backs. Unusually, the women as well as men work in the fields. They are said to choose their leaders through consultations of elders, which choices are then confirmed routinely in obligatory elections.

Chortí Indians, another group with a Mayan heritage, live for the most part between the village of Copán Ruinas and the Guatemalan border. Other members of this ethnic group live in nearby mountainous parts of Guatemala. Another remnant group is the **Pipil**, a few of whom live near the border with El Salvador. The Pipil speak a language related to Nahuatl, and it is thought that their ancestors migrated from Mexico to the lowlands of what are now Guatemala and El Salvador. Many of the Pipils who maintained their identity into modern times were massacred in El Salvador in the 1930s.

Indian groups living along the Caribbean shore when the Spaniards arrived were far less settled than those who lived in the highlands of the west and south. Heavy rainfall and soggy lands subject to flooding discouraged the practice of settled agriculture. Abundant game and waterways allowed them to rely on hunting and fishing.

One northern group, the **Jicaque**, possibly of Mexican or South American origin, once inhabited the Caribbean coast, but moved inland to the department of Yoro in the nineteenth century as their lands were taken up by others, especially Black Caribs. Under the influence of missionaries, they settled in villages and began to cultivate corn, much like Indians in the west. Only a few hundred still maintain their language and traditions, such as dress in old-style tunic, and distinctive style of house made of planks tied with vines and roofed with thatch, and old food-gathering ways, such as hunting with blowguns.

Miskitos, Sumos, and **Tawahkas** are three related groups of Indians living in isolated groups along the North Coast and inland regions known as **La Mosquitia**. They share a heritage of hunting and fishing, and cultivation of root crops in shifting agriculture; and languages related to those spoken by

Indians in South America. But racially, the Miskitos are a mixed group, having intermarried with blacks who found their way to the coast as servants and slaves or escapees from the British who once held sway over the area. Another group, the **Paya**, or **Pech**, living in the same area, is thought to have a different heritage.

Without wealth or cultivable lands, the Indians of the coast were ignored by the Spaniards, and it was the English who traded with them, and finally established a protectorate over the so-called Kingdom of Mosquitia. After the region reverted to Honduras, it was largely ignored by the central government.

Miskitos, Sumos and Payas still live mostly in small, self-sufficient settlements, burning and clearing plots for root crops, and moving on when the land is exhausted. Miskitos generally live along the coast, the Sumos upriver. Water transportation is, of course, important in a land mostly without roads, and these tribes have their characteristic *cayucas*, or dugouts, and *pipantes*, boats with flat bottoms. Some fish by stunning their quarry with an extract of jungle vines and bow and arrow.

Other small groups of Indians live in scattered groups. Some, isolated in mountains near the Nicaraguan border, are probably of **Matagalpa** heritage, while others in the northwest near Santa Bárbara are probably of mixed background.

Arts & Letters

With a limited potential audience, arts and letters have never been historically developed in Honduras, though there have been some notable figures. Poet and dramatist José Trinidad Reyes founded the predecessor of the University of Honduras early in the nineteenth century, and brought the first piano to Tegucigalpa.

Modern formal painters include Carlos Garay, Miguel Angel Ruiz Matute, and Alvaro Canales, the last of whom made his reputation in Mexico. Just as appreciated by visitors are the primitive landscape artists of El Zamorano, near Tegucigalpa, such as José Antonio Velásquez and Roque Zelaya. American expat Guillermo Yuscaran has carved out a name for himself as an excellent painter and prolific author. He has written a number of fine books, including a biography of the the great paintor Velásquez and a number   books highlighting the philosophical and cultural journeys he has encountered over the years in Honduras.

Noted poets of this century include Froylán Turcios, a revolutionary as well as writer; Juan Ramón Molina, a follower of Nicaraguan modernist Rubén Darío; and, more recently, Rafael Heliodoro Valle and Clementina Suárez.

a short history

Chapter 5

Honduran history can read like the enumeration of generations in the Bible. From the time the Spanish left until the present, there have been more than 100 presidents, chiefs of state, military rulers, and similarly designated persons-in-charge. Regional chieftain has been succeeded by national savior to be succeeded by a puppet for the country next door. The person at the top has generally ruled without significant limits on his powers by any legislature or courts, and always with an eye to who might want to take his seat. Buccaneers and English traders held sway for years in parts of the country, and the capital shifted back and forth, in colonial times and after independence, until a hundred years ago.

As in other former colonies, much of Honduran history has been an uphill battle to bring together parts of a geographical expression made up of diverse peoples, and swatches of vastly different and uncommunicating territory.

Instability, however, should not be read as necessarily meaning harshness or oppression. Far from it. Generally, nobody has ruled for long enough in Honduras to set up efficient machinery of exploitation and cruelty. Few great riches have led to the advent of avaricious exploiters or enslavement or reduction of natives to serfdom. Honduras throughout its history has been poor, by modern, western standards, but it has not been miserable. Its central government has continued to perform limited functions despite the musical chairs at the top, somewhat like Italy.

Honduras Before the Spanish

Central America is a meeting ground for North America and South America, for the inhabitants and cultural traditions that have crossed back and forth on this land bridge. Before Europeans reached Honduras, the land was populated by groups of people who spoke differing and unrelated languages, and whose ways differed significantly one from another.

It was 10,000 years ago, more or less, that people first came to Honduras. Those early settlers might have been descendants of migrants from Asia across the Bering Strait, or of Polynesians who crossed the Pacific on rafts. The first settlers were probably hunters who lived in simple, perishable dwellings, and in caves. Thousands of years later came people who knew how to plant and harvest root crops, such as cassava, or this knowledge was absorbed from peoples of neighboring lands.

Gradually, in Central America and to the north and south, information and ways were shared by neighboring settlements, or carried to subject peoples on waves of conquest. Cultures, similar ways of doing things, began to develop, and these different ways traveled to and through Honduras. Farming developed, based first on root crops, such as cassava. Pottery-making and other early technologies were discovered.

Those who inhabited the Caribbean coastal areas of Honduras lived in small settlements. When they cultivated crops, it was in shifting areas, burning and clearing and moving as the land was exhausted, which it quickly was, given the torrential rains, and the thin layer of soil that underlay the exuberant rain forest. These inhabitants are thought, by modern studies of the language of their descendants, and of their agriculture, to have been related to Indian tribes of northern South American forests, not least because they practiced head-hunting. The spread of such customs to Honduras might have resulted from migration, or from conquest by distant tribes. No ancient villages or monuments remain from those early inhabitants, but pottery fragments found near the Caribbean coast have been dated as far back as 2000 B.C.

More is known about the native inhabitants of central, western and southern Honduras of pre-Hispanic times, for many were living in settled communities when the Spanish arrived, and others, the ancestors of some of these peoples, erected monumental cities that can still be visited.

In the west and south, geography and politics created more stable and stratified societies than those on the northern coast. Land, more elevated and seasonally dry, was suited to continuing cultivation. At some point, thousands of years ago, some of the peoples of ancient Mesoamerica domesticated wild plants into crops that were regularly sown and harvested. The most important of these was corn, a plant that reliably produced abundant harvests.

With the development of agriculture, all the accoutrements of settled society became possible, and even necessary. When more food was produced than all workers could consume, it became possible for some of the population to become craftsmen, and builders, and administrators. Writing and mathematics were by-products of a society that had time to devote to thinking, and not just surviving. In time, administrative systems had to develop to supervise the division of labor, and the production of food for all the non-farming hands. Hunting and fishing continued, of course, but they were not essential to the survival of the society.

Eventually, the inhabitants learned how to turn clay not just into simple tools and vessels, but into objects of beauty. Their huts evolved into temples. Through war and conquest and trade, the characteristics of different cultures and peoples began to spread across wider areas.

Of the early inhabitants, the Maya were the most powerful and advanced. The Maya dominated what is now western Honduras for at least a thousand years, made numerous significant discoveries and advances, and then faded mysteriously, though their descendants are still present in Honduras and neighboring countries.

People readily identifiable as Mayan, by their pottery and other artifacts that have been found by modern archeologists, began to appear as far back as 1000 B.C. in an area that today includes southern Mexico, Guatemala, and Honduras. Soon after the time of Christ, Mayan settlements began to contain not just houses, but ceremonial structures at their centers. Temples were erected on great platforms throughout the Early Classic period, from 300 to 600 A. D. Some were the tallest buildings in the hemisphere until this century.

Mayan cities, such as **Copán**, in Western Honduras, contained numerous plazas surrounded by temples, multi-roomed structures, ball courts, and what might have been specialized buildings such as sweat baths. The cities were built with the most simple, back-breaking techniques, of rubble carried to the construction site without the aid of wheels or machines, piled into platforms behind retaining walls faced with limestone blocks and plastered over with lime mortar. Limestone was easily worked, and occurs everywhere in Mayan territory. The landscape was also remade as necessary: hilltops were cut off, cisterns constructed, streams diverted, swamps cut by canals for transport and drainage, and built up to create raised gardens. Corn and cassava and yams were planted, and nuts were harvested from the forests.

In the city centers, stelae, or carved stones, were erected in the plazas to record important events, especially those in the lives of royalty. Those at Copán were the most beautiful works of art of any pre-Columbian people. Probably only the nobility and priests could be accommodated in the few, small rooms that could be created under the primitive Mayan arch, or corbel — a single capstone over two walls protruding inward toward each other. Nobility were buried in tombs under temples, which were decorated with painted friezes, and hieroglyphic writing. Games, with death for the losers, took place on ball courts, and captives were sacrificed, at times by decapitation. The different Mayan cities communicated and traded with each other: limestone highways were built through the jungle, inscriptions record the names of far-off cities, and jade from Guatemala and gold from far-off Panama have been found in tombs at Copán. The money of the Maya was probably cacao, or chocolate, still a local product.

The greatest achievement of the Maya was their calendar and arithmetical system, used at first as a guide to planting and harvesting, and eventually, with continuing refinement, as part of a great cosmic and religious system. The Maya understood the concept of zero before it was used in Europe and the Islamic world. They counted using a system of twenty digits, from zero to nineteen, each represented by a series of dots, for units, and bars, for fives.

The basic counting unit of the Maya was the day, twenty of which made up a month. Eighteen months made up a year, with an extra five-day period. There were further units of twenty years, and twenty twenty-year periods. A separate, ceremonial year, or *tzolkin*, consisted of twenty day names combined with thirteen day numbers, making a 260-day year of each of the possible pairs. The combination of any tzolkin day name and a solar day name occurred every 52 solar years. The 52-year cycle, or calendar round, was shared with many other peoples of Central America.

A third time calculation, however, set the Maya apart. This was the **long count**, which tracked the number of days from the beginning of Mayan time, approximately equivalent to 3113 B.C. Long-count dates interpreted by modern scholars are a major aid in deciphering the history of the Maya. Other sophisticated Mayan calculation concerned the solar system. Most notably, Mayan astronomers of the Post Classic period, in Yucatan, calculated that Venus crosses between the earth and sun every 584 days, a fraction of a day off the period calculated by today's astronomers.

Mayan writing, like numbers, gives details about the lives of their cities and rulers. Much of the information that is just now being deciphered comes from places and names and dates inscribed as single glyphs or numbers at Mayan cities. Phonetic syllables that "spell" additional words are currently being decoded, and yielding new information about Mayan genealogy.

For reasons that are still little understood, Mayan cities in Honduras, Guatemala and southern Mexico underwent a sudden and swift decline, starting in about 850 A.D. Temples and stelae were left uncompleted, population declined, and scientific advances halted in the central part of the empire. But in Yucatan, to the north, Mayan civilization continued, influenced by the Toltecs of the central part of Mexico.

In Honduras, the descendants of the Maya survived as separate, remnant nations, alongside groups that migrated from the lands to the north, and others that were either conquered by migrants from Mexico or largely succumbed to foreign influences and rule. Major Maya-related groups are the Chortí and Lenca peoples. The Pipil, of Nahuatl descent, lived along the southwestern mountain slopes, toward the Pacific.

By the time the Spanish arrived, the natives of western Honduras had declined from the levels of achievement of the Maya. There was no central authority ruling over a large area, and interregional trade was limited. Without knowledge of outsiders of other races, there was no solidarity, and warfare occasionally raged not only between nations, but sometimes among people speaking a common language. It was by subduing and subsequently allying themselves with different native groups that the Spanish were able to conquer.

The Conquest

The first encounters between natives and Spaniards in what is now Honduras were peaceful. Christopher Columbus himself sailed along the Caribbean coast in 1502, and in July of that year landed on the island of Guanaja, which he called Isla de los Pinos (Pine Island). Contemporary accounts describe a visit by Indian nobility in a long canoe, bearing cacao beans. Columbus continued his journey, and on August 14 went ashore on the mainland at Punta Caxinas.

Nearby, where present-day Trujillo stands, Bartholomew Columbus celebrated the first Catholic mass on the mainland of America. Continuing along the coast, Columbus gave the name Gracias a Dios to the cape at the extreme tip of present-day Honduras, in thanksgiving for delivery from frightful storms.

It was at the time of this first European visit that Honduras received its modern name, though there are several versions of just whence the name comes. Some say that *Honduras* —literally, "depths" —was applied to describe either the deep seas or low-lying lands of the adjacent coast.

Others say that *hibueras*, the native word for floating gourds, was corrupted into *higueras*, Spanish for fig tree, and later into Honduras; or that the aboriginal name was Ondure. The land was also called the Coast of the Ears, after native ear-plugs; and Guaymura, after a tribe thought to be so named; but Honduras is the name that stuck.

The coast was further explored by Vicente Yáñez Pinzón and Juan Díaz de Solís in 1508, but the land remained largely untouched by the Spanish for a number of years.

Rivalries among various Spanish military leaders led to thrusts into Honduras, finally, from different directions. Gil González Dávila, exploring from Panama, sailed as far as the Gulf of Fonseca, on the Pacific Coast, in 1522. In 1524, González Dávila returned to exert Spanish authority. The Spanish governor of Panama sent another expedition from a base in Nicaragua. Not wanting to lose the initiative to a rival, Hernán Cortés in Mexico authorized an expedition, and when the leader resigned, sent still another force.

It was this last force, led by Cristóbal de Olid, that first conquered Honduran territory for Europeans. After outfitting himself and his 370 soldiers and 100 archers in Havana, and buying 22 horses, he landed on the coast on May 3, 1524, and established a settlement that he named El Triunfo de la Cruz (Triumph of the Cross).

Things did not go well for Olid. He fought with the leaders of the other Spanish groups, and was accused of trying to usurp authority for himself. The internecine struggle ended with the trial, conviction and beheading of Olid. Leadership passed to Francisco de las Casas, a relative of Cortés, who established Trujillo as the head town to replace El Triunfo de la Cruz. This struggle of factional leaders, and the relocation of the capital, was to be a repeating pattern throughout Honduran history.

Distraught at the disorder in his fiefdom, Cortés himself undertook to lead still another expedition to Honduras, this time going overland, through jungles in the Petén region of Guatemala, which hundred of years later would still be largely unexplored. With several hundred Spaniards, and thousands of Mexican Indian allies, Cortés suffered terrible losses, mainly from floods, hunger and disease.

The remnants of his force encountered Spanish stragglers at Nito in the spring of 1525, and moved them farther along the coast to the mouth of the Ulúa River. At Trujillo, Cortés managed to enforce a truce between the warring Spanish captains, and exert his own authority. Satisfied with the state of affairs, he departed in 1526 to deal with other headaches in Mexico. In the same year, a governor, Diego López de Salcedo, was first named.

The boundaries of Honduras were shifting and never clearly defined. A vast territory claimed by the Spaniards lay to the interior, populated by assorted Indian nations, to whom the machinations and rivalries of the Spaniards made no sense. By 1532, Pedro de Alvarado, who had brought the native nations of Guatemala to their knees, was authorized to establish effective Spanish control in Honduras.

After dealing with assorted rebellions elsewhere, and widely accused of having ignored his conquistorial duties, Alvarado finally got around to the task in 1536. He and men acting under his orders founded San Pedro Sula and several other outposts. Alvarado's successor, Francisco de Montejo, turned his attention inland, and ordered a lieutenant, Alonso de Cáceres, to establish a headquarters between the two seas. This was Santa María de Comayagua, founded in 1537, which was to be the capital of Honduras for much of the colonial period.

The Spaniards had battled each other, and disease and rain and hunger, but the native inhabitants of the north coast, isolated in small groups, and evasive, had posed no problems. Now things changed. Spanish penetration of the highlands was brought to a halt and effectively repelled by the Lenca Indian nation, under their chieftain, Lempira. For two years, battles raged between the Spaniards and their Mexican allies, on one hand, and the warriors of Lempira, estimated to have numbered as many as 30,000.

Unable to conquer by force, the Spaniards turned to an old and familiar weapon: treachery. Offering to negotiate a truce, they entered the impregnable fortress of Lempira, and there murdered the native leader, and overpowered the garrison. Within months, the invaders took control of Lenca territory.

Once pacified, Honduras resumed its pattern of administrative indecision and division of authority. For a time, the Audiencia de los Confines, the Spanish colonial authority, was based in Honduras. In turn, the colony was ruled as part of Guatemala, then from Mexico, or Santo Domingo, or Panama, or even directly from Comayagua by a governor sent from Spain. The coastal area was sometimes ruled separately from the highlands, called Higueras. Finally, authority was placed in Guatemala, and Honduras, roughly encompassing the territory of today's nation, became part of the Kingdom and Captaincy-General of Guatemala, which covered the stretch of isthmus from modern southern Mexico to southern Costa Rica.

Honduras was settled in the colonial period, but never to the extent of Guatemala or other Spanish colonies in the isthmus. Discoveries of silver led to the founding of Tegucigalpa as a mining center. And there was some settlement of Spaniards along the land route from Guatemala in the south-west, which already was highly populated by Indians. There was also interest in Honduras as an overland route between the oceans, though that role was to fall to Panama.

The government and society that the Spanish set up in Honduras were based on life in Spain, modified to suit local conditions, with the twin aims of converting the natives and enriching their new Spanish overlords. Spanish-style towns were created: a church and administrative buildings went up around a central square and market. Mercedarians and then Franciscans were authorized to bring the natives into the Christian fold. Local labor was used to build and decorate, under the instruction of master craftsmen from Spain. Indians were forced to settle in the new towns. At first they were apportioned as slaves to Spanish landholders under the *repartimiento* system. Later, under the *encomienda* arrangement, they were tenants on their former land, paying their new Spanish masters through required labor.

Conquered in war, reduced to servitude, ravaged by smallpox, venereal disease, and other ailments brought by the Spaniards, the natives of Honduras suffered a holocaust comparable to the worst of modern times. By one estimate, more than 90 percent were wiped out in the first twenty years of effective Spanish settlement. All this was afflicted by just a few hundred Spaniards, and a few thousand Mexican Indian allies. Occasionally, a voice cried out among the Spaniards, protesting ill-treatment of the natives, such as that of Cristóbal de Pedraza, in the mid-sixteenth century. New laws attempted to protect Indians, as much to preserve the economic base of the empire as from altruism, but avarice and ill-treatment continued as facts of colonial life.

The colony of Honduras remained a backwater. Some cattle were raised and traded, mainly to the mining areas of Honduras; but indigo, cochineal and cacao, the major export crops of the captaincy general, were grown only on a limited scale. Silver, sugar, lumber and tobacco were also exported, along with mules. And slaves went to the West Indies, to replace natives who had perished in the first years of Spanish dominion. Spanish mercantile policy limited trade outside the empire.

It was the early importance of mining that helped to determine the character of Honduras as a society distinct from neighboring colonies, where the Indians stayed on or near their ancestral lands. Those Indians who were forced to work in the mines came from different villages. They spoke different dialects or languages. They were forced to communicate with each other and their masters in Spanish, the common colonial language. In the filth and abuse and violence and dangerous conditions of those early mines, the new Ladino culture was born from the mix and remnants of the old ways, overlain with the new ways of the Spanish.

Far from the mother country, with a small garrison, sparsely settled, vast Honduras was only tenuously held by Spain. As pirate attacks on Spanish convoys increased in the Caribbean, Spain reinforced Puerto Caballos (today's Puerto Cortés), but the long coastline was impossible to defend. Caballos was intermittently taken by pirates, in 1602 and 1639 and 1660, and sacked and burned. Trujillo was captured in 1639, and San Pedro Sula in 1660.

Dutch and British buccaneers sheltered in the Bay Islands, behind the protection of reefs that kept out the larger boats of the Spaniards. British buccaneers, planters, loggers and sailors landed in and occupied parts of Mosquitia in the early seventeenth century. Spain at times tried to dislodge the English, and at other times, admitting its lack of police powers, tolerated their presence, in return for British promises to control piracy, promises which were rarely kept. Only hundreds of persons were involved, just scores at times, but in the business of establishing sovereignty by presence and effective control, the fates of great empires hung in the balance.

By the opening of the eighteenth century, the British had a firm grip on Belize, and protectorates over the Bay Islands and the Miskito Indians on the Honduran coast. Provided with guns and liquor by the English, the Miskito and Sumos attacked any Spanish ships that dared to enter their territory. British forces repeatedly occupied and lost Omoa and Trujillo, and were more firmly established eastward along the coast at Black River (Río Tinto) and Brus.

By the end of the century, as part of the settlement of the American Revolutionary War, the British had mostly been pushed off the mainland, though Spanish control remained weak. Hampered by Spanish mercantile policy, residents of the colony traded illegally, but willingly, through English intermediaries, moving lumber and sugar and gold and silver to and through the Bay Islands and Belize, in exchange for cloth and manufactured goods. At times in the colonial period, most of the trade of Honduras involved smuggling.

Independence

Honduras at the turn of the nineteenth century was a highly stratified society, with a broad base of Indians with few rights. Above them were a few blacks, and the mixed bloods who dwelled in the towns. Those who worked as craftsmen and artisans and provided European-style services had the most prestige.

At the top of the social structure were government officials sent from Spain, and the hierarchy of the Church, who controlled not just the religious life of the people, but also their education, and, through landholdings, a significant portion of the agricultural economy. Below the Spanish officials were Creoles, persons of pure Spanish descent born in the new world. As colonials, they were barred from the highest governmental positions, which were filled by officials sent from Madrid, and could gain lesser positions of prestige only through bribery. Merchants, Creoles and Ladinos, likewise were a class with limited prestige and much dissatisfaction, obliged by Spanish policies to sell and buy goods through illegal channels.

When independence was declared in Guatemala on September 15, 1821, the Creoles and merchants of Honduras went along, and when the forces of the newly independent Mexico under Agustín de Iturbide marched into Central America, influential people in Comayagua acceded to the new union as well, though Tegucigalpa wavered. José Cecilio del Valle, a Honduran who had been educated in Guatemala, went off to Mexico as a representative for Central America.

When Iturbide fell from power, a Central American assembly in Guatemala City proclaimed independence again, and Honduras became part of the United Provinces of Central America, a loose federation with no taxation powers of its own, and a constitution that notably emancipated all slaves and provided for limited voting rights. Honduras was an odd member. Unable to choose between joining as one state or two, it became a single member, with its capital alternating between Tegucigalpa and Comayagua. Dionisio de Herrera became the first Honduran president.

In Honduras, as elsewhere in Central America, conservatives favored privileges for the Church and a strong central government. Liberals, who included those who originally favored independence, wanted a loose federation, and were somewhat anti-clerical. The two factions competed not just in the Honduran and federal legislatures, but on the battlefield as well. Conservatives from the Central American government invaded Honduras in 1826, joining local partisans. **Francisco Morazán**, a prominent Honduran liberal, led the forces that repelled the invasion, and eventually took over the Central American administration in Guatemala. Morazán promulgated laws that cut church tithes and restricted church orders. The result was a series of revolts against his power.

Short of funds, with conservative rebellions flaring in Honduras, and opponents gaining strength in Guatemala, Morazán moved his government to El Salvador in 1833 as the union weakened. By 1838, the states of Central America decided each to go its own way.

The latest stage of "independence" meant little for Honduras. Honduras promulgated a new constitution in 1839, but there was little or no sense of nationhood or nationality. Guatemala and to some degree Nicaragua continued to meddle in national politics and impose and depose presidents. Meanwhile, in a primitive economy that was regionally self-sufficient and traded little with the outside world, where most were farmers, where local plantation owners were the only effective law, the installations of successive regimes meant little. Francisco Ferrera, first president under the independence constitution, went to war against regional leaders, and ruled even after his term of office expired. Juan Lindo ruled from 1847 until the Guatemalans sent him running in 1850. José Trinidad Cabañas succeeded peacefully and legally to the presidency in 1852 — a notable event — but was deposed by the Guatemalans in 1855.

José Santos Guardiola, at least, scored foreign-policy advances against the English. It was Honduras' weakness and disorganization that had allowed Britain to maintain and expand its claim to disputed territories during the early independence period. British subjects from Belize and the Cayman Islands settled the Bay Islands after Spain was no longer a threat, and even threw out the Central American garrison in 1838. Since Britain dominated trade with Central America, taking strong action against the interlopers was a chancy matter.

Financial claims against Honduras led to Britain's short-lived seizure of Tigre Island in the Gulf of Fonseca in 1849. Britain's actions stirred the interest and alarm of the United States, and in the 1850 Clayton-Bulwer treaty, both nations agreed to keep their hands off the Central American mainland. Britain soon violated the spirit of the agreement by declaring the Bay Islands a crown colony in 1852. The Wyke-Cruz treaty with Britain in 1859, during the presidency of José Santos Guardiola, provided for British withdrawal from the Bay Islands, with guarantees for the religious freedom of the islanders. British influence along the coast of Honduras gradually came to an end over succeeding decades.

Unlike most heads of the government, Guardiola was distinguished outside of Honduras as well, for helping to oust the American adventurer **William Walker**, who for a time had taken control of Nicaragua. When Walker attempted a comeback, using the Bay Islands as a base, he was captured by the British, and turned over to the Hondurans, who placed him on trial and executed him in Trujillo.

Guardiola was murdered in 1862, to be succeeded by twenty leaders in ten years, some of them installed or removed by various Guatemalan governments. Constitutions were promulgated in 1865, 1873, 1880, 1894, 1906, and 1924. A country with so many constitutions and governments was, in effect, a country without a government.

Other presidents were only local heroes, particularly Marco Aurelio Soto, who had broad support. Soto allowed secular marriages and separated church and state, expanded the school system, and generally improved public services. Tegucigalpa became the permanent capital of Honduras in 1880, after high society in Comayagua snubbed President Soto's Guatemalan Indian wife.

While British influence was on the wane, that of the United States was increasing. A promoter named Ephriam George Squier, who had once served as U.S.consul, attempted to start up a railroad across Honduras in 1853. No track was constructed until 1871 — money intended for the railroad had a way of going to arms purchases instead — and the railroad never operated. In the process, though, various American business interests learned of and invested in Honduras. Mining was the key attraction at first, and later, banana plantations on the north coast.

Under President Luis Bográn, from 1883 to 1890, Honduras was once again influenced by Guatemala. The last of a string of three conservative presidents was deposed just three years later by Policarpo Bonilla, a liberal, with Nicaraguan aid.

Bonilla oversaw the revision of many laws to streamline administration and encourage foreign investment, and signed Honduras to a union with El Salvador and Nicaragua that never came about. Bonilla was backed by a more formal political party structure than Honduras had previously known.

Succeeding presidents were generals Terencio Sierra and Manuel Bonilla, the latter using a show of force as well as votes to get into office in 1903. Guatemala invaded in 1906, and when Bonilla made peace, Nicaragua invaded the following year and kicked Bonilla out. Bonilla staged a revolt against his successor, Gen. Miguel Dávila, and the presidency was settled on yet another person, Francisco Bertrand, through U.S.-sponsored negotiations.

Bananas

While an elite of politicians and generals from Honduras, Nicaragua, and Guatemala were playing out their power games in Tegucigalpa and regional capitals, it was in the north of the country that the real changes were unfolding, as Honduras was converted into a banana republic.

Around the turn of the century, banana traders in New Orleans began to look into Honduras as a reliable supplier of commercially grown bananas, which were being exported principally from Costa Rica. The predecessor of the Standard Fruit Company made the first shipments. In 1911, the Cuyamel Fruit Company, organized by Sam Zemurray, began operations, followed in 1913 by the United Fruit Company. Honduras soon became the leading exporter of bananas in the world, and bananas were to remain the mainstay of the modern sector of the economy for many years. The banana companies, through their assorted commercial ventures and worker welfare system, were to be, in effect, more important than the government for many Hondurans. In Tegucigalpa, central authority remained shaky. Francisco Bertrand assumed the vice-presidency after an election, succeeded to the presidency, and fled in 1919 after a revolt. New revolts broke out repeatedly under Bertrand's successor.

The elections of 1923 produced no majority for any candidate. With the country on the brink of a new civil war, and Augusto Sandino harassing the U.S. Marines in Nicaragua next door, the United States once again brokered a political solution. New elections were won by Miguel Paz Baraona of the National Party whose leader, Gen. Tiburcio Carías Andino, had gained the most votes in 1923, but, to everyone's surprise, had refused to take power by force.

Carías was a Renaissance man of the times, an intellectual who for a while held his party above his personal ambitions. Carías himself came to power in the 1932 elections. His party allegedly stood for good management, reconciliation, and free elections, but Carías managed to stay in office until 1948, through constitutional amendments. Revolts and opposition flourished at the beginning of his term, but the nation eventually became resigned to his authoritarian rule. Political exiles were encouraged to return home, but those who continued to speak out were subject to arrest.

Early in the Carías regime, Panama disease caused the banana industry to go into a tailspin, and world war cut off trade. During Carías' tenure, the economy diversified somewhat, into mining and ranching and timber exports, and coffee production. Carías selected his successor, Juan Manuel Gálvez, who took office in 1949, his Liberal opponent having conveniently withdrawn. Gálvez cooperated with the Central Intelligence Agency in promoting the overthrow of the populist Arbenz government in Guatemala and restoring the position of the United Fruit Company in that country. After another election which produced no majority, Vice President Lozano seized the government.

While Honduran leaders were helping to meddle in Guatemala, in their own country, banana workers became increasingly dissatisfied and went on strike, and unrest spread throughout the small sector of the economy where people labored for wages. The strike ended with significant increases in benefits for United Fruit and Standard Fruit workers, and recognition for the first time of their right to bargain.

Lozano exiled one of his political opponents, Ramón Villeda Morales, allegedly for helping to foment the "leftist" United Fruit Company strike — certainly not the last time the specter of labor unrest and communism would be used against an opponent. In the end, the army seized power and sent Lozano packing.

Modern Honduras

A constituent assembly brought in a new constitution in 1957, and selected Ramón Villeda Morales of the Liberal Party as president. During Villeda's term in office, the Central American Common Market took shape. Import restrictions were removed, and many products that formerly were imported into Central America began to be manufactured in the region. But most of the new factories went up in Guatemala, El Salvador and Costa Rica, where there were more roads, more shipping facilities, and more sophisticated investors, and Honduras was left behind, in many cases helping to finance the development of its neighbors.

Under Villeda, schools were built and labor rights were strengthened, though unrest continued in the realm of the United Fruit Company. As elsewhere in Central America, a social security system was installed to take care of the medical needs and pensions of a limited number of workers. The border with Nicaragua was finally determined through arbitration, after the neighboring country threatened to invade the newly delineated and sparsely populated Gracias a Dios department. Villeda was turned out of office in 1963 on the eve of new elections by Air Force Col. Osvaldo López Arellano, whose accession was handily "confirmed" by a constituent assembly.

Over the preceding decades, many Salvadorans, crowded by a coffee-plantation economy, had come to settle in Honduras, crossing an ill-defined border and squatting on uncultivated lands. As the numbers of Salvadorans grew, they faced increasing discrimination, and with no documentation, were subject to arbitrary actions by both government and ordinary Hondurans.

In 1969, the situation came to a head with the expulsions of many Salvadorans, and exploded after a soccer match between the two countries. In five days of bitter fighting, El Salvador, then called "the Israel of Central America," drove into Honduras along the Pan American Highway and around Nueva Ocotepeque. The air force of Honduras managed to damage a refinery in El Salvador, but the country was rescued from disaster only by a cease-fire declared by the Organization of American States. A sullen Honduras refused to cooperate further with the Central American Common Market, and despite a peace treaty signed in 1980, hard feelings from the war continue.

López turned the government over to civilians in 1971, but took power again in 1972, this time spouting the reformist populism that was the rage among the military in parts of Latin America. In 1978, a new junta, lead by Policarpo Paz García, seized the government.

Military rule began to wind down once again in 1980, with the convening of a constituent assembly. Still another constitution was implemented in 1982, and Roberto Suazo Córdoba became president. Military buildups in Honduras were significant under Suazo, as the United States poured in weapons in response to the Sandinista victory in Nicaragua. "Contra" opponents of the Sandinistas found refuge and set up bases with American support and

Honduran connivance, and American troops staged maneuvers on a near-permanent basis.

Following a traditionally inconclusive election in 1985, José Azcona Hoyo became president, after the various factions of his party, though not Azcona himself, together gained more votes than the leading Liberal, Rafael Leonardo Callejas Romero. Callejas ran again in 1989. This time he scored a clear victory, and was sworn into office in January 1990.

Callejas came to office facing severe economic problems. The wind-down of the unofficial Contra war with Nicaragua meant a decrease in the flow of military spending from the United States. Export earnings had been stagnant for years, as the price of coffee and other relatively new export crops stayed low, while prices for imported industrial goods went just one way – up. The projected savings in oil imports from the completion of the El Cajón hydroelectric project soon went to pay interest on the international debt.

The uneven balance of trade, a large foreign debt, a weak manufacturing and export sector and a historic legacy of government corruption at all levels have led to a weak foreign investment climate in the country. The uneven balance of trade and waffling about paying a large foreign debt led to an overvalued currency, and, in turn, a decrease in foreign investment.

Other problems faced by the government are continuing ones: poor agricultural management and a lack of infrastructure; inadequate schools, poor technical education, and deficient health care; a population growing almost as fast as production; a lack of roads and railroads, except in the banana country of the north; limited port facilities. These and other problems plagued President Carlos Roberta Reina (of the Liberal Party), and his administration, who came to office in 1994. Reina was a statesman in the classic sense of the word. He struggled hard to bring the rule of law to a nation plagued historically by a lack of a functioning judicial system and endemic corruption.

Reina restrained the formerly all-powerful military, subjecting them to budget constraints and civilian overview and accountability. He paved the way for the modernization of the national police, wresting control from the military and turning the police over to civilian control. In terms of the economy, Reina started the process that will eventually lead to the privatization of Hondutel (the national phone company) as well as the ENEE (the national electricity company). Reina emphasized fiscal responsibility, modernization, and public accountability.

Honduras' current President, **Carlos Flores**, was elected in 1998. Flores was formerly the President of The National Congress. He was educated in the US and first lady Mary Flakes de Flores hails from the US. Flores, who is a member of the Liberal Party, has continued with reforms started by President Reina, among them the privatization of Hondutel and all airports, the conversion of the police to civilian control and national government modernization programs.

Flores' biggest challenge during his administration was to reconstruct infrastructure damage from Hurricane Mitch, jump-start Honduras' storm-battered economy while at the same time continue with a series of social and political reforms. Flores tackled a weak judicial system – oral trials are set to start this year for the first time in Honduran history. A constant headache for the Flores administration was an increase in crime and juvenile gang activity, especially in the major cities. Many public services were privatized; water, garbage collection, electrictiy generation and the management of the nation's four intertnational airports. There was an attempt to sell off 51% of Hondutel, the national phone company, but a buyer was not found who would pay the government's asking price. Tourism infrastructure improved greatly with the opening of new hotels and resorts on the North Coast, Roatan as well as San Pedro Sula and Tegucigalpa.

But Honduras has many material and human resources, it's near potential markets, and her weather and attractions make it a prime candidate for tourist development. With stability returning to the region, the prospects for the nation are promising.

Government & Administration

Honduras is divided into 18 *departamentos* (departments, or provinces), each with its *cabecera* (administrative center, or capital). The departments (and their cabeceras) are: Atlántida (La Ceiba); Colón (Trujillo); Comayagua (Comayagua); Copán (Santa Rosa de Copán); Cortés (San Pedro Sula); Choluteca (Choluteca); Paraíso (Yuscarán); Francisco Morazán (Tegucigalpa and Comayagüela, Distrito Central); Gracias a Dios (Puerto Lempira); Intibucá (La Esperanza); Islas de la Bahía/Bay Islands (Roatán [Coxen's Hole]); La Paz (La Paz); Lempira (Gracias); Ocotepeque (Ocotepeque); Olancho (Juticalpa); Santa Bárbara (Santa Bárbara); Valle (Nacaome); and Yoro (Yoro).

Departamentos are further divided into a total of 289 *municipios* (municipalities, or townships), each consisting of one or several *aldeas* and *caseríos* (villages and hamlets).

Under the current constitution, municipal officials are elected every two years.

The judiciary consists of a supreme court, lower courts, and courts with special jurisdictions, such as labor courts.

The legislature consists of one chamber, with parties represented in proportion to their electoral support. The president is elected by popular vote every four years, and prohibited from succeeding himself.

The major parties are the Liberal and the National, which represent the traditional liberal-conservative split in Central American politics. There are smaller parties as well, such as the Christian Democrats. The president governs in consultation with the council of ministers, or cabinet.

The military continues to have a significant though rapidly diminishing influence on politics and policies. Among recent developments are the election of a civilian defense head and civilian Minister of Security (who is in charge of the civilian national police). A new maximum security prison has been constructed outside of Tegucigalpa to replace the old and decaying dungeon-like Central Penitentiary.

planning your trip

Chapter 6

An eighteenth-century Englishwoman, Mary Lester, wrote a famous (in its time) memoir of travels alone in Honduras, under the pseudonym María Soltera. She commented about the scarcity of food for travelers, the trials of getting around, the difficulty of finding a place to sleep. She brought her own hammock, of course.

Is it all that different now?

I'm happy to say that it is. You can find comfortable lodging and good meals in many parts of Honduras, and not just in the few places on the beaten track for tourists. But you can also end up where there is no decent place to sleep, and no good food to eat, and if you just follow the logical routes on a map, you could easily miss the very best that Honduras has to offer.

Before you go, then, read through this book. Consider a few possible travel strategies:

• Go right to the **Bay Islands**, and spend your vacation diving or fishing in a tropical hideaway.
• Discover unexplored beaches and colonial fortresses along the **Caribbean mainland**.
• Travel the overland routes, to **Mayan ruins** and bass fishing and a tropical botanical garden.
• Stay a while, and experience the pace of life in a Central American capital.

Once you think you know what you're going to do, make any reservations you think are necessary. Consult a travel agent, if you wish, to find a package that suits your plans. In general, resorts in the Bay Islands are accustomed to offering hotel/diving/meal packages; those on the mainland are not. In any case you can perfectly well make reservations yourself, through hotels and resorts directly, or through their agents in the United States.

Climate & Weather

- Temperatures are warm all year, and you can get good weather somewhere in Honduras in every season. But some months are better than others. Or, to put it another way, you can decide what weather you like, and go to the appropriate area of Honduras at the appropriate time.
- Tegucigalpa, along with most of Honduras, has moderate, spring-like temperatures throughout the year. In central Honduras, temperatures get cooler the higher you go. May is the warmest month, but it is rarely uncomfortably hot in the capital.
- It rains for six months of the year in Tegucigalpa and most of central Honduras, from May through October, for a few hours a day, and it is dry on most days during the rest of the year (*verano*, or "summer"). But even in the rainy season (*invierno*, or "winter"), precipitation isn't too high. You can visit Tegucigalpa at any time of year without concern for the weather.
- The south coast along the Pacific has a rainy season, just like Tegucigalpa, but the wet is wetter, and the temperatures are generally hotter. But half of the year is very dry.
- The Caribbean coast on the north, and the Bay Islands, get rain throughout the year. The trade winds that blow from the northeast bump up against the Nombre de Dios mountains that lie just inland from the shore, causing clouds to dump their moisture. Tela and La Ceiba get more than three meters (ten feet!) of rain in a year. Montreal, Houston, and New York get about one meter in an average year. While October through November is the rainiest time, you always have to expect some rain along the coast. But you can expect sunny periods on every day as well. There are occasional tropical storms during the rainiest times along the coast. A major hurricane is a rare occurrence.
- Temperatures throughout the lowlands are hot all year. But right along the water, there is usually a breeze, especially from October through April. Along the Caribbean coast, it is always very humid, so you might need air conditioning for sleeping. Nothing dries, and everything is a little bit rotten.
- Out on the Bay Islands, away from the mountain ridge, rainfall is lower than right along the coast, and though the chart doesn't show it, humidity is lower. January through September are considered good months to visit the Bay Islands. But if you can stand some rain mixed with your sunshine, the rest of the year is okay as well.

What to Take

Before you pack for your trip to Honduras, consider what your trip will be like, and look at the checklist below. You don't want to take anything but what you'll need. On the other hand, you don't want to leave behind any essentials.

If you'll be at one hotel, take as many changes of clothes as you feel you'll need (as long as it all fits in a couple of suitcases), and do the laundry when you get home. Hotel employees at most hotels will be more than happy to hand wash and even iron your clothing at very moderate cost.

The other extreme is incessant travel, a single change of clothes in a carry-on bag, and laundry in the hotel sink every night.

Also consider where you'll be. Casual clothes are the norm for visitors, but there are differences in local standards. If you're just going to the Caribbean coast or the Bay Islands, summer clothing will do. You can wear shorts everywhere along the north coast, but they look a bit out of place in Tegucigalpa or the highlands.

A visit that includes Tegucigalpa, will require some extra packing. You'll need a heavier sweater for cool nights and some mornings. Dressing in layers is suitable. You can peel off your sweater and outer shirt as the day warms. You'll need long slacks, and a plain shirt or blouse. You don't have to dress in a tie and jacket or formal dress for dinner; comfortably casual is de rigeur: a nice pair of jeans or kakhis, a nice button-down shirt, and a pair of loafers will get you in to even the most exclusive restaurant or disco.

Essentials
- passport
- travelers checks
- tickets
- credit card(s)
- soft luggage with a padded shoulder strap is highly recommended over a hard, bulky, heavy suitcase
- some U.S. cash in large denominations. Remember you will get a better exchange rate on cash, especially if you change with street corner *cambistas* or money changers, though nowadays the difference between what you get on the street and in banks is extremely small. So I would recommend changing in banks

Which Clothes?

Take lightweight all-cotton clothing, or loose-fitting, easy-care cotton blends. T-shirts and beach wear are available at reasonable prices in Honduras, but the selection may be limited.

Include:
- hat with ample brim
- a bathing suit

- a few shirts or blouses
- shorts
- comfortable walking shoes. Running shoes will suffice for most purposes, even for jungle walks. Non-slip shoes are helpful on boats.
- socks, underclothes
- sandals or surf shoes (Teva sandals are highly recommended)
- at least one lightweight, long-sleeved top and slacks, in case you overexpose yourself to the sun, and for evenings, when mosquitoes might lurk.
- a light sweater or jacket for cool mornings and evenings, though a heavier one or a jacket will do if you're going to spend much time around Tegucigalpa and at higher elevations. During November-February, temperatures anyplace in Honduras, especially in the evenings, can be cool.
- a raincoat or umbrella if you travel during the rainy months, which vary according to where you're going.

The Business Traveler

Take a light suit or jacket, though a *guayabera* — a light shirt worn outside the pants without a tie — is the more usual "formal" attire along the north coast.

Note: Guayaberas are considered a bit old fashioned in most of today's business circles. A better bet would be a short sleeve button down shirt, khaki trousers, and slip-on loafers. Due to the heat, all of the above should be 100% cotton. Also note that Central Americans place a great deal of importance on the way a person is dressed and personal hygiene. Here people get dressed up to go to the movies, to Burger King, or just to stroll around downtown. The operative words are casual yet stylish. Central Americans frown on a dirty or unkempt appearance. Trim hair, including beard and mustache, and liberal use of antiperspirant and cologne are expected.

Other imortant notes for the business traveller: A firm handshake is expected at all encounters, no matter how well you know the person. When meeting women, especially from the upper class and professional circles, a 'cheek kiss´ is quite common and acceptable. Central Americans will often judge a person by the clothes and shoes they wear, the watch or jewlery they have on, or the kind of briefcase or portfolio they carry. Here appearances mean a lot.

Fishing & Diving

Fishing and diving equipment are available, but the selection is sometimes limited, so you're often better off with your own gear.

If you have them, take:
- mask, snorkel and fins
- regulator, buoyancy compensator, certification card, wet suit (optional), underwater light (optional)
- preferred fishing equipment.

Packing for Other Sports

Take equipment for other sports that you practice, as it is unlikely to be found easily in the country:
• a day bag for carrying purchases, sunscreen, whatever. I prefer a see-through mesh bag — it shows that you have nothing worth stealing. Fanny packs are insecure and undesirable in towns, but fine for the countryside.
• A pen or two, including a felt-tip pen (ballpoints clog up) and paper.

Personal Items

Bring your cosmetics, toiletries, and small personal items, including:
• sunglasses
• your favorite personal kit of aspirin or substitute, sunscreen, sunburn cream, malaria pills, spare prescription glasses, mosquito repellent (most convenient in stick form), etc.

Habits, Hobbies & Vices

According to your habits, hobbies and vices, take your:
• camera and waterproof bag, film (more than you think you'll need), batteries
• camping equipment and flashlights
• personal stereo
• duty-free cigarettes and liquor
• snacks (especially if traveling with children).

For a vacation at the beach or on the Bay Islands bring reading material. Keep your luggage as light as practical, tag your bags inside and out, and pack your indispensable items in your carry-on. And remember that if you don't take it, you might not find it, or you might not want to pay the price. In major cities, you can get most anything you want, including an extensive selection of US products in any large supermarket.

Entrance & Exit Requirements

U.S. and Canadian citizens currently require only a passport to enter Honduras.

As of recently, no visa is required of citizens of: Argentina, Australia, Belgium, Chile, Costa Rica, Denmark, Ecuador, El Salvador, Finland, Germany, Guatemala, Iceland, Italy, Japan, Netherlands, New Zealand, Nicaragua, Norway, Panama, Peru, Spain, Sweden, Switzerland, United Kingdom, and Uruguay.

Citizens of the above countries are initially granted permission to stay in Honduras *for 30 days*. After that period, they must request an extension to remain in the country, just as if they held an expired visa.

Holidays in Honduras

Here are the holidays, both familiar and unfamiliar, to watch out for in Honduras. Banks and businesses will be closed, and you won't be able to make a plane reservation or book a tour, on these days.

January 1	New Year's Day
Moveable	Holy Thursday
Moveable	Good Friday
	(most businesses close all week)
Moveable	Saturday
Moveable	Easter Sunday
April 14	Day of Americas
May 1	Labor Day
September 15	Independence Day
October 3	Day of Francisco Morazán
October 12	Columbus Day (Día de la Raza)
October 21	Armed Forces Day
December 24-25	Christmas Eve and Christmas
December 31	New Year's Eve

Every town also has its own local celebration day. For a complete fiesta calendar, see the miscellany section at the back of this book.

Visas

Visas are not required of transit passengers. When required, visas are issued by Honduran consulates. A visa will usually allow an initial stay of 30 days. To remain longer, you'll have to apply to the immigration department.

Tourist Cards, which can be used in place of a visa by nationals of certain countries, are sold for $2 at the check-in counter by airlines serving Honduras, and by some travel agencies. You can also buy a tourist card upon arrival at an airport in Honduras, but it's safer to have one beforehand. To get a tourist card, you need to show a passport, a birth certificate, or some other convincing evidence of your citizenship. A tourist card is initially valid for 30 days, and can be extended by the immigration department in Tegucigalpa, La Ceiba, or San Pedro Sula.

Special **investors' visas** are issued at no charge to businessmen and technicians for three months and one month respectively, with renewals available to a total stay of six months. Documentation of the purpose of the trip is required.

When you arrive in Honduras, whether by land or air, you *could* be required to show that you have either a return ticket, sufficient funds to cover your expenses, or both. Entry points along the borders with neighboring countries are generally open "officially" from 8 a.m. to 5 p.m. weekdays, but you can cross outside these hours for an extra fee (see below).

Day to day security in Honduras especially where tourists are concerned is quite laid back. Honduras faces a severe shortage of police and immigration officials, so it is likely that once you dispense of immigration formalities at one of the land borders or at the airport, you will never again be asked during your travels to show your documents until you leave the country.

Vaccinations

No vaccination is required unless you're arriving from an area where there is currently an outbreak of some dread disease, such as yellow fever.

Entry & Exit Fees

There´s an entry tax at all land borders of about $2 per person when you enter Honduras. Children are exempt. In addition, there are fees of several dollars to pay for cars, for crossing land borders outside regular business hours, and for assorted other reasons.

The **exit tax** when departing Honduras by air is $25 (about 394 lempiras).

Carry your passport or tourist card with you at all times, and if lost, contact your embassy immediately to obtain new travel documents. A good idea is to photocopy your passport and carry the copy in your money pouch, leaving your passport at your hotel.

Staying On

Most visitors are granted an initial stay of 30 days, though this may be shorter, especially if you enter overland and are short of funds. Extensions of permission to stay are easily obtained for up to 90 days and can be processed at immigration offices in major towns: Comayagua, San Pedro Sula, La Ceiba, Tela, Santa Rosa de Copán, Copán Ruinas and other departamental capitals. With more difficulty and delay, they may be processed in Tegucigalpa, at *Migración, 6 Calle, 11/12 Avenidas.*

Customs

You're allowed to bring in anything reasonable for a vacation trip to Honduras, along with gifts and new personal items up to a value of U.S. $1000. For children, the limit is $500. You're limited to two liters of liquor, and 200 cigarettes or 100 cigars or about a pound of tobacco. Firearms require a permit, and fresh fruits and vegetables should not be carried.

For questions and clarifications about customs, contact: *Dirección General de Aduanas, Avenida Juan Lindo, Colonia Palmira, Tegucigalpa, Tel. 238-*

2566 (Tel. 233-1290 at the airport, Tel. 566-2154 at the San Pedro Sula airport, Tel. 442-0013 in La Ceiba).
If you're going back to the States, you have an exemption of $400 for goods purchased in Honduras, which can include up to a quart of alcoholic beverages and 200 cigarettes. Many handicraft products that you might buy in Honduras are totally exempt from U.S. customs duty.

Canadians can use their yearly $300 exemption, or $100 quarterly exemption, with a cap of 200 cigarettes and 1.1 liters (40 ounces) of liquor.

Whatever you take home, don't include pre-Columbian articles or yaba-ding-dings; coral; fish; or shells. These could be confiscated on your way out of Honduras or into your home country and/or land you in jail or delayed with a court case.

Using Travel Specialists
Specialty Tour Operators
You're best off using the services of a travel agency with whom you've dealt before. However, if the folks near home don't have much to offer or don't have any first hand experience with Honduran travel, which is likely, here are some operators who are very familiar with Honduras.

• **Roatán Charter**, Box 877, San Antonio, FL 33576, *Tel. 800/282-8932, Fax 904/588-4158; E-mail: info@roatan.com, www.roatan.com.* Very helpful people, with a line on everything new in the Bay Islands and the rest of Honduras. The staff at Roatán Charter are truly Honduras experts; they know the country inside and out and are a great help to travelers. Color tour catalog "Honduras & A Little Bit of Belize," videos and brochures available, online tour catalog features scuba and adventure travel, jungle treks, cloud forests, Mayan ruins, white water rafting, kayaking, indigenous cultures. Recommended.

• **Bahia Tours**, 6840 SW 40th St., Suite 208, Miami, FL 33155, *Tel. 800/443-0717 or 305/858-5129, Fax 305/858-5020.* Represents Anthony's Key and other dive resorts and live-aboard boats.

• **Maya Tour**, 2608 N. Ocean Blvd., Suite 108 Pompano Beach, FL 33062, *Tel 800/392-6292, Fax 954/783-7414, Tel 954/942-6262; E-mail: info@mayatour.com, www.mayatour.com.* Maya Tour is the Mundo Maya experts since 1991. Owner Robert Beels has vast experience in Mundo Maya travel and is very knowledgeable. Online brochure of Bay Islands hotels, resorts,cabañas and rentals. Maya Odyssey Tour: 9 days, all inclusive adventure trip, two days in Copán then onto Guatemala and Belize, 15 Maya sites in 9 days, expert guides at each site, $1,799 per person. Quetzal 8 day comprehensive Maya World tour visits three major sites. Copán, Honduras, Tikal, Guatemala, and Palenque, Mexico. Flights between stopovers, $1,499 per person. Honduran ground arrangements, tours, B&B accomodations in Copán. Maya Tours comes highly recom-

mended for professionalism and good value. 9-day Natural Honduras Tour that visits Copan, Celaque National Park Cloud Forest, and on the Caribbean Coast, Punta Sal National Park, Tela and Pico Bonito National Park. 16-page color brochure.
• **Journeys International**, 4011 Jackson Rd., Ann Arbor, MI 48103, *Tel. 734/665-4407, Fax 734/665-2945.* Operates monthly tours that emphasize the marine life of the Bay Islands, and a family tour.
• **Holbrook Travel**, *Tel. 800/451-7111, www.holbrooktravel.com.* Offers guided educational trips to Central America, handles Elderhostel.
• **Solar Tours**, 1629 K Street NW, Suite 604 Washington, DC 20006, *Tel 202/861-5864, Fax 202/452-0905, www.solartours.com.* Strong experience with Central American travel.
• **Far Horizons**, PO Box 91900, Albuquerque, NM 87199, *800/552-4575, 505/343-9400, Fax 505/343-8076; E-mail: journey@farhorizon.com, www.farhorizon.com.* Weekly e-mail trip updates, newsletter, Specialists in archaeological and cultural trips to Central America. Some trips include Copan Ruinas.

Tour Operators in Honduras
Travel agencies in Honduras are mentioned in various parts of this book. But here are a few that you might want to consult from home, in case the above agencies are unable to give you the service you require:
• **La Mosquitia Ecoaventuras**, Avenida 14 de Julio, in front of Parque Bonilla, La Ceiba, *Tel. 442-0104; E-mail: moskitia@caribe.hn, www.honduras.com/moskitia.* Specializes in ten- to fourteen-day low-impact adventures in the vast forests of Mosquitia, including the Río Plátano Biosphere Reserve, with emphasis on birding, wildlife viewing, and non-intrusive contacts with native peoples. This is currently the premier ecotourism tour operator in Honduras. Many years of experience in La Mosquitia. Owner and guide Jorge Salaverdi is well respected for his commitment to the principles of ecotourism and sustainable tourism. Also offered: white water rafting on the Cangrejal River outside of La Ceiba and hiking and jungle trekking through the Pico Bonito National Park. Boating or canoeing trips to Cuero Salado.
• **MC Tours**, *Tel/Fax in San Pedro Sula Tel. 552-4549, 552-4455, Fax 557-3076; in Copan Ruinas, Tel. 651-4453, Fax 651-4297; E-mail: sales@mctours-honduras.com; www.mctours-honduras.com.* MC Tours offers a complete array of mainland and Bay Islands tours, specializing in the ruins at Copán and operating a fine hotel there, the Marina Copán in Copán Ruinas.
• **Mesoamerica Travel**, *Tel 557-8447, 557-3258, Fax 557-8410, E-mail: info@mesoamerica-travel.com; www.mesoamerica-travel.com.* Tour operator specializing in ecotourism in La Mosquitia. Hauke Hoops, Guide/

Biologist and Environmental Consultant leads excellent guided treks into the Patuca region of La Mosquitia, where he heads up a non-profit development organization working to promote sustainable farming practices and the preservation of forest lands.

- **Garifuna Tours**, *Tel/Fax 448-2904 E-mail: garifuna@hondutel.hn; www.garifuna-tours.com.* Since 1994 a Tela institution, specializing in North Coast ecotourism. Tours to coastal National Parks; Punta Sal, Punto Izopo and Lancetilla Botanical Gardens. Copan Ruinas extension with B&B accommodations, transport to and from airport. Highly recommended for commitment to sustainable tourism and excellent service.
- **Omega Tours**, Rio Cangrejal (half-hour from La Ceiba), *Tel 440-0334, E-mail: omegatours@laceiba.com.* Udo, Omegas' guide and owner, hails from Germany and specializes in white water rafting, $31, and kayaking, $37, on the Cangrejal River. Jungle & river hiking, $16, two day jungle hike to 280 foot Bejuco Waterfall, $86, two day raft trips, $85, Class V Ultra Raftin,g $48, horseback riding, $41, Cuero y Salado, $51, La Mosquitia rafting. Free night accommodations at Omegas' rustic jungle river lodge included with all trips; simple rooms, shared bath, pool, great meals.

Getting to Honduras

By Air

Honduras is amazingly easy to get to. To start with, most little countries have only one point of entry by air. Honduras has four. You can land in Tegucigalpa, the capital. Or, if you're just visiting the Caribbean area, you can fly into San Pedro Sula, La Ceiba, or Roatán in the Bay Islands. A short connecting flight takes you from La Ceiba to Roatán, Utila, or Guanaja in the Bay Islands.

Tegucigalpa is currently served by American, Continental, and Taca airlines; and San Pedro Sula by Taca, Continental and several others (see sidebar on next page). Each company has its own peculiar fare structure, offering reductions in some cases in combination with pre-arranged hotel stays or tours. Some travel agents will give you better prices than those quoted directly by the airlines.

If you can get to Cancun, Mexico, on an inexpensive charter, you can also get to Honduras cheaply. There are daily flights between Cancun and San Pedro Sula. Not only is this a low-cost way to get to Honduras, it also saves many of the landings, takeoffs and changes of plane often involved in taking scheduled carriers all the way.

Always try to buy a round-trip ticket before you leave home. You'll usually get a better price, and there are significant taxes to pay if you buy your return ticket in Honduras.

For airline offices in Honduras:

In La Ceiba
- **Isleña Airlines**, *Ave. San Isidro frente al parque central, Tel. 443-0179, Goloson Airport Tel. 441-2521, 441-2522, Fax 441-2527*
- **Grupo Taca**, *Ave. San Isidro frente al parque central, Tel. 443-3720, Fax 443-1913; Airport Tel. 441-2534 Fax 441-2528*
- **Sosa Airlines**, *Ave. San Isidro, Tel. 443-2519, Fax 443-1894 Airport Tel. 441-2512, Fax 440-0692; E-mail: aerososa@psinet.hn, aerolineasosa@edured.net; www.aerolineasosa.com*
- **Atlantic Airlines**, *Edificio Plaza del Caribe, Ave de la Republica, Tel/Fax 440-2343, Tel. 440-2347 Airport 440-1220; E-mail: atlantic@caribe.hn, www.atlanticairlines.com.ni*

In Roatán
- **Aerolineas Sosa**, *Roatan Airport, Tel. 445-1154, Fax 445-1658*
- **Atlantic Airlines**, *Tel. 445-1179,445-0055*
- **Isleña Airlines**, *Roatan Airport, Tel/Fax 445-1550, 445-1387*
- **Grupo Taca**, *Roatan Airport, Tel. 445-1918, 445-1387, Fax 445-1825*
- **Atlantic Airlines**, *Tel. 445-1179, 445-0055*

In San Pedro Sula
- **Aerolineas Sosa**, *8 ave 1 y 2 calle Edif Roman planta baja Barrio, Guamilito S.O., Tel. 550-6545, 550-6548, Fax 668-3128, Airport 668-3223*
- **American Airlines**, *Edificio Firenze Barrio Los Andes 16 ave entre 1 y 2 calle, Tel. 558-0525, 558-0526, Airport 668-3244 thru 51*
- **Atlantic Airlines**, *Tel. 668-7309, 557-8088, 552-7270*
- **Continental Airlines**, *Plaza Versailles Ave Circunvalación, also behind Gran Hotel Sula, parque central, Tel. 557-4141-45, Fax 557-4146, Airport 668-3208, 668-3210*
- **Iberia**, *Edificio Quiroz 2 piso, 2 calle 2 ave., Tel. 550-4609, 550-2530 Airport 668-3219*
- **Lufthansa**, *Edificio Los Alpes 8 calle 15 y 16 ave, Tel. 557-1934, Fax 557-1218*
- **Isleña Airlines**, *Edificio Trejo Marlon Tel. 552-8322, 552-8335, Airport 668-3186, 668-3182*
- **Grupo Taca**, *13 ave N.O., Norte de la Circunvalación Barrio Los Andes, Tel. 550-5262, 550-5264, Fax 550-5269, Airport 668-3333*

In Tegucigalpa
- **Air France**, *Centro Commercial Galleria Ave La Paz, Tel. 237-0229*
- **Alitalia**, *Ave. La Paz, Tel/Fax 239-4246*

- **American Airlines**, *Edificio Palmira, 1 piso, Colonia Palmira Tel. 232-1414, 232-1415, Fax 232-1380, Airport 233-9685, Fax 233-9678*
- **Atlantic Airlines**, *Tel. 234-9702, 234-9701*
- **British Airways**, *Blvd. Comunidad Economica Europea, Tel. 225-5107, 225-5102 Fax 225-0341*
- **Continental Airlines**, *Edificio Palic, Col. Palmira, Tel. 220-0999, 233-7812*
- **Iberia**, *Edificio Palmira, Planta Baja Col Palmira, Tel. 239-4565, 232-4566, Fax 239-1729*
- **Isleña Airlines**, *Galeria La Paz Ave La Paz, Tel. 237-3450, 237-3410*
- **Japan Airlines**, *Edificio Galeria La Paz, Ave. La Paz, Tel. 237-0229*
- **KLM**, *Edificio Naciones Unidas Ave. Chile, Col Palmira, Tel. 232-6410, 232-3885*
- **Lufthansa**, *EdificioPlaza del Sol Ave. La Paz, Tel. 236-7560, 236-7564 Fax 236-7580*
- **Grupo Taca**, *Edificio Interamericana Blvd. Morazán, Tel. 232-0915, 232-7585, Fax 231-1517, Airport 233-2192*
- **Varig**, *Edificio Sempe Blvd. Comunidad Economico Europea, Tel. 225-5102 thru 07, Fax 225-0341*

Direct Flights to Tegucigalpa

American	Miami, Dallas
	• *Tel. 800/433-7300*
Taca	Belize, Guatemala, San Salvador
	• *Tel. 800/535-8780, www.grupotaca.com*
Continental	New York, Houston
	• *Tel. 800/231-0856*

Direct Flights to San Pedro Sula

Continental	Houston, New York, Belize
American	Miami, New York
Taca	Miami, San Salvador
Copa	Mexico City, San José, Panama
	• *Tel. 800/359-2672*

Direct Flights to La ceiba & Roatan

Taca	New York, San Pedro Sula, Roatan
American	New York, Miami, San Pedro Sula, La Ceiba
American	New York, Dallas, Chicago, Houston, Roatan

By Car

I was tempted not to include this section. After all, for most visitors with just a few weeks of vacation, there's no reason to spend up to a week to get to Honduras from home. But if you have extended time, and want to see the sights along the way, and if you love your car, go ahead and start your engine.

But first, drive off to your mechanic for a good inspection and some preventive maintenance. Tune it up, grease it, and replace those bald tires and anything else that's about to go.

Many roads along the way to Honduras are bumpy, and some roads in Honduras are unpaved. Accordingly, you might want to install heavy-duty shock absorbers, and take more than one spare tire. Also useful: a gasoline can, a water container, extra spark plugs, belts, basic tools, electrical tape, and wire. If you plan extensive driving off paved highways, air and gas filters and wiper blades could be useful, along with screens to protect your headlights as well as a nylon tow line.

Unleaded gasoline is now available in Honduras. Gasoline prices are much higher, almost double than those in the United States. In general, it's wise to drive during daylight hours, and to look for a gasoline station when your tank is half full.

While labor for auto repairs is inexpensive in Honduras, parts always cost more — sometimes double the price in the country of manufacture — and sometimes they're not available for your make of car. Don't drive anything too exotic, or in bad condition. Nissans, Toyotas, and U.S. pickup trucks are good choices.

Tourists may enter their vehicles for an initial period of 30 days. Renewals are available through customs offices to extend your stay for up to six months. I recommend that you enter Honduras through Guatemala, rather than via El Salvador.

By Bus

Here's another feat that's possible, though I wouldn't want to go non-stop by bus from North America to Honduras. As part of a measured overland journey, though, it can be fun, and the fare is about $100 from the U.S. border.

Basically, you have to take a first-class bus to Mexico City. This will take from ten hours to two days, depending on where you cross the Mexican border. In Mexico City, catch a bus for the Guatemalan border. There are at least two each day, and the trip takes sixteen hours. Connecting buses take you to Guatemala City, where you catch the Rutas Orientales bus for Esquipulas, then a mini-bus to Agua Caliente on the Honduran border.

Another alternative is to take a bus from Guatemala City to Chiquimula, and from there catch another bus to the Honduran border crossing at El Floridio; from here it is about seven miles to the ruins of Copán. San Pedro Sula may be reached from Agua Caliente via Santa Rosa or from Copán Ruins via

La Entrada. You can also travel from Guatemala via San Salvador and the Pan American Highway to Tegucigalpa.

Getting Around Honduras

By Air
Honduras has a well-developed domestic air transport network. You can't go everywhere, but you can fly the long distances, and continue by bus, taxi, or boat.

Isleña, **Sosa**, and **Atlantic** connect with the Bay Islands and operate along the north coast to Mosquitia. For details, see coverage in Tegucigalpa and other destination chapters.

Fares in all cases are reasonable. A round-trip flight from La Ceiba to Roatán costs $40. A round trip ticket from La Ceiba to Utila costs $40. A round trip ticket from San Pedro Sula to Roatan costs $97.

By Bus
They're not Greyhounds, but on major routes in Honduras, buses are comfortable enough. You'll get a padded seat on something that looks on the outside like a school bus. Standards for leg and hip room might be lower than what you would desire, but for a ride of a few hours from Tegucigalpa to San Pedro Sula, the bus will be tolerable. Luxury first-class buses are now running the following routes: San Pedro Sula-Tegucigalpa (Hedman Alas, Saenz, Viana), San Pedro Sula-La Ceiba (Hedman Alas, Viana), San Pedro Sula-Copan Ruinas (Hedman Alas), San Pedro Sula-San Salvador (Tica Bus), Tegucigalpa-Managua (Tica Bus), San Pedro Sula-San Salvador (King Quality). Service and comfort are excellent and they make a great 'break' from the usual school bus type buses.

As you venture off the main routes, the level of service becomes less desirable. Minibuses and microbuses — vans — serve the less-travelled, bumpier routes, for example, from La Entrada to the ruins of Copán. Seats are small and stiff and crowded together to provide no knee room. Buses may be underpowered, and whine along in low gear at low speed, turning short trips into ordeals. Sometimes, out of greed, or sympathy for passengers who have no other way to travel, the passenger load is beyond reasonable safety limits.

To increase your comfort, wherever you're going by bus, try to start your trip at the terminal point. Line up early to get a reserved seat. Generally, you'll have less bouncing at the front of the bus near the driver, but for safety reasons it is recommended to sit as far to the back as possible. Also, sitting in the back will not afford you the opportunity to look out the front window of the bus, where the drivers' lack of driving skills may pe painfully evident. To be fair, though, most bus drivers are experienced and careful, although once in a while you do get a cowboy behind the wheel.

Bus stops along roads are never marked. Ask the driver to stop where you want to get off. Acceptable tactics for indicating to the driver that you desire to get off include banging hard on the metal interior of the bus, whistling, yelling *alto!* (stop!) or screaming *baja!* (getting off!).

In all cases, bus fares are low. For example, on first-class buses you'll pay about $6 to travel from San Pedro Sula-La Ceiba for a 3-hour trip. The San Pedro Sula-Copan Ruinas trip will set you back $6 for a 3-hour, 198 kilometer trip.

By Car

What's it like to drive in Honduras? Well, you have a good chance of getting lost if you're not careful, if you don't ask questions, and if you don't have a good sense of direction. Road signs hardly exist. You'll see some kilometer posts, stop signs, and arrows to indicate the flow of traffic and one-way streets. But directional signs that tell you where to turn to get to a village or town are practically unknown. Always follow your map carefully, and when you reach a junction, stop and ask for the way to your destination. It's the only way.

The major paved highways in Honduras are the Pan American Highway crossing from El Salvador to Nicaragua in the south; the highway through Tegucigalpa to the north coast; part of the route along the north coast; and the western highway that roughly parallels the border with Guatemala. There are some other paved stretches, but travel off these main routes will often involve unpaved roads either dusty or muddy, according to the season, over winding, unbanked routes that are the descendants of the mule trails that once snaked through the mountains of Honduras. Main roads are now signed, for example the San Pedro Sula–Ocotopeque Road (Western Highway).

But look on the bright side. Only 25 years ago, there were fewer than 100 kilometers of paved road in Honduras, out of a total of 1,000 kilometers of roads. There are now more than 2,000 kilometers of pavement, almost 10,000 kilometers of all-weather unpaved road, and 7,000 kilometers of seasonably passable road. The network is expanding, with paving and construction, and chances are, you *can* get there from here. Today, Honduras has some fine roads, considered by many to be the best in Central America.

When driving in Honduras, take the same precautions you would in any unfamiliar area. Never drive at night, and take it easy when traveling a road for the first time.

You never know what's around the curve and just beyond your line of sight: a horse, a cow, a parked truck, a cyclist, an oncoming vehicle passing on a blind curve, or a pedestrian on the wrong side, sober or otherwise. Potholes, washed out, and eroded sections occur in the most unexpected places on the nicest of roads. Fill your gasoline tank before you turn off any major, paved highway. Sound your horn when approaching a curve, and be prepared to back up when you encounter an oncoming vehicle on a narrow stretch. Many streets even in major cities lack basics such as stop signs, direction arrows, yield signs and construction or hazard warning signs, so drive with caution. Repairs can be accomplished in Tegucigalpa and San Pedro Sula on most familiar passenger cars and pickup trucks. Outside of major centers, you'll probably have to send for parts. Sports cars, turbos, and similar unusual vehicles (for Honduras, anyway) should stay home, rather than face servicing by unfamiliar hands, or a lack of parts. Mechanics are usually available in any decent size town or village. Quality of mechanics and their shops varies. In the big cities you can find modern electronic diagnostic equipment but in most large and small towns, mechanics work in rudimentary shops with dirt floors. Many mechanics are excellent and are experienced at patching up (and sometimes actually fixing) a variety of makes and models.

When driving in cities, exercise caution. Lack of right of way signs, direction signs, stop signs and traffic lights, make for lots of fender benders. Proceed cautiously at all intersections.

San Pedro Sula is excellent for driving, streets are for the most part uncongested and traffic flows at an excellent pace. Tegucigalpa, on the other hand, is a driving nightmare, with lots of traffic, insufficient roads, lack of signs, and a population of one million makes for lots of driving headaches.

Car Rental

Cars are available for rent in Tegucigalpa, San Pedro Sula, La Ceiba and Roatán. I think that taxis are a better way to go, especially if you will be driving mostly in the larger cities like Tegucigalpa or San Pedro Sula. In addition, you can obtain only limited insurance protection in Honduras.

Renting a car is recommended if you are making a long trip with multiple stops along the way, like the **Mayan Mountain Route**, which is San Pedro Sula - Copan Ruinas - Gracias - La Esperanza - Lake Yojoa - San Pedro Sula.

Major rental car companies are Avis, Budget, Hertz, Thrifty and Toyota Rent a Car. Cars can be rented in Tegucigalpa, San Pedro Sula, La Ceiba, Comayagua and Roatan

If you plan to drive on secondary dirt roads or head up into national parks, hot springs, go birdwatching, etc., you should rent a four wheel drive vehicle. They cost a bit more, but are worth it.

By Taxi

Getting around by taxi is cheap — if there's two of you, it's cheaper than taking a bus in North America. A taxi ride just about anyplace in San Pedro Sula for example will run $2-2.50.

By all means, take a taxi! Just make sure that you agree on the fare with the driver before you start out. And on any out-of-town trip, give the vehicle a once-over to make sure that you'll make it to where you're going.

Taxi drivers are a good source of information. They know all the movie theaters, restaurants, and strip joints in town.

Accommodations

In the United States, you often pay for a hotel according to season, with discounts sometimes available if you're an AAA member or have some other affiliation, or if your employer has negotiated a corporate rate. In Honduras, what you pay depends on who you are.

The highest rate is the **rack rate**, which is generally what you'll be charged as a foreigner, whether you make your reservation through a travel agency, a toll-free telephone reservation service, or directly with the hotel from abroad. Usually, the rack rate is the rate I've quoted in this book. The 12% tax is included, unless otherwise mentioned. There is also a 4% tourism tax on hotels rooms, rental cars and tour operators with money raised going to support the marketing efforts of the Honduran Tourism Ministry. This tax may or may not be included on your bill.

The Bay Islands have high and low season rates. The rest of the country, including Copán, does not.

Since Honduras is a poor country, and many rooms are empty outside the high season, **resident rates** are often available to Hondurans, resident foreigners, military personnel, peace corps volunteers, and Central Americans. If you feel that you qualify for a discount under any category, by all means ask for it. Sometimes it takes a little forwardness, sometimes it takes a little fluency in Spanish, but you can often cut your hotel bill just by asking.

Note that this double-rate structure applies only at the high-end hotels. You'll look pretty silly if you ask for a resident's discount at a budget hotel that has mostly Hondurans among its clientele.

Chapter 7

Business Hours

Hondurans are early risers. In a country where many do not have electricity, people get up at sunrise, and don't go out much after dark.

Businesses are generally open from 8am to 11:30am or noon, and from 1:30 or 2pm to 5 or 6pm. Along the hot coast in the north, businesses may open even earlier. On Saturday, businesses keep morning hours only.

Exceptions: Banks are generally open from 9am–3pm Monday–Friday and 9am-11:00am on Saturdays. Government offices are open from 7:30 or 8am until 3:30pm.

Cost of Living & Travel

It costs less to live in Honduras than in North America, and it also costs more. Everything depends on what kinds of goods and services you're buying. For most travellers, Honduras will be a *very* inexpensive destination.

If you take a look at prices mentioned in this book, you'll see that hotels are generally inexpensive. The top hotel in Tegucigalpa has a rate of about $125 double, but modern, comfortable lodgings, usually with a pool, are $50 double or less, tax included. You can usually get a decent meal for $4, though fancy food, when available, will cost more, and imported wine will raise the cost considerably. Locally produced liquors – mostly rums – are inexpensive, at about $3 per bottle; Flor de Caña is highly recommended. If you ever shop for an occasional picnic, you'll find prices for local produce quite low in season.

Most expensive hotels have a **two-tier price system**, with one rate for foreigners, and another for Hondurans. In a way, this is fair, and in another way, it's discriminatory.

You can sometimes get the lower rate during slow periods simply by requesting it. And a few travel agencies in the States are authorized to charge the lower rate to their clients. Shop around.

Public transport is inexpensive. You can cross from the Caribbean to the Pacific by bus for $10. Taxis are cheaper than rental cars. A hop across the Caribbean to the Bay Islands by airplane costs about $40 round-trip.

In the Bay Islands, all costs are somewhat higher than on the mainland. Some hotels charge an inclusive rate of more than $100 per person for lodging, meals and diving. But this is an incredible bargain compared to every other Caribbean locale with near-comparable amenities. And there are clean, modest lodging places that charge much, much less. Utila, for example, has the well deserved reputation as being the cheapest place to eat, sleep and dive in the Caribbean.

It's only if you're going to stay for longer than a vacation that you might find some things expensive in Honduras. Imported food, appliances, cars, and anything not produced or processed in Honduras (or elsewhere in Central America) generally costs one-third more than the U.S. price, with a few exceptions. It can also be surprisingly expensive to rent an apartment or house with the appliances and amenities you might be used to — $1,000 or more per month for a three-bedroom house or apartment in Tegucigalpa or San Pedro Sula. But you can also rent a decent middle class home in a middle class neighborhood for about $300 per month.

In a small town rent is about half as much; outside of the capital, housing costs are lower, and if you can do without built-in closets and American-style bathrooms and kitchen, costs drop. Household workers earn low salaries, and there are no fuel bills for heating.

The moral: rely on local goods and services, and your costs in Honduras will generally be low.

Electricity

Most electricity is supplied at 110 volts, 60 cycles, just as in the U.S. However, some locales operate only on 220 volts, so inquire before you plug anything in. Sockets take standard American-type plugs with parallel blades and no grounding prongs. Always use a surge protector for delicate electronics like, stereo, computer, or television sets. Surges are a constant problem throughout the country

Health Concerns

If you are taking any medications regularly, pack twice the quantity you think you'll need. Brand names in Honduras might be different from the ones you're familiar with. Also prepare a small emergency kit (see below).

It's important to be current with your routine vaccinations, such as tetanus, diphtheria, and polio. Vaccination against typhoid, and gamma globulin as a precaution against hepatitis, are also recommended. There is some malaria in rural areas. Antimalarial pills, such as chloroquine, are taken once a week, beginning one week before and ending four weeks after your trip. Other diseases to watch out for are cholera, which can be avoided by drinking only bottled water and eating thoroughly cooked foods; Leishmaniosis, which is carried by the sand fly (apply plenty of strong insect repellant, especially in the Bay Islands); and dengue fever, another mosquito-borne disease, which can be prevented by liberal application of insect repellant.

If you don't drink the water, and watch what you eat, you shouldn't have any health problems. In general, stick to foods that have been well cooked, and are still hot when served. Fruits and vegetables are okay if they have a peel, or are cooked. But avoid salads, and sandwiches that are decorated with fresh vegetables. Don't hesitate to leave anything doubtful sitting on your plate. Water is not safe to drink from the tap in *any* city in Honduras. Stick to bottled beverages, or take along Halazone tablets or laundry bleach (two drops to a quart, allow to stand 30 minutes). Bottled water is now available all over the country; *Agua Azul* and *Arroyo* are two of the most popular brands.

Your medical kit should include: a sunscreen containing PABA (sunburn can be a problem if you're not used to being outdoors); insect repellent (the best brands, such as Cutter's or Muskol, contain methyl toluamide); condoms (if there is any chance of a new sexual relationship); personal medications; antimalarial tablets; Halazone or bleach for drinking water; sterile pads, bandages, antiseptic soap, and analgesic pills.

For longer stays, consult a public health or travelers' clinic before you go. Useful publications include *Health Information for International Travel* (Department of Health and Human Services), available from the U.S. Government Printing Office, Washington, D.C. 20402; and *Health Guide for Travellers to Warm Climates*, available from the Canadian Public Health Association, 1335 Carling Avenue, Suite 210, Ottawa, Ontario, Canada K1Z 8N8. The **International Association for Medical Assistance to Travellers** may be able to provide a list of English-speaking doctors, in Honduras and other countries, for a small fee. Write to IAMAT, 736 Center St., Lewiston, NY 14092.

In Tegucigalpa and San Pedro Sula, and in any town of any size, there's *always* a pharmacy open at night. Look for a lighted "*de turno*" sign on the outside. "*De turno*" pharmacies are also listed in many newspapers. Prescriptions are not required in pharmacies – if you know what you need and the dosage, just ask for it.

Learning Spanish

The **Escuela de Español Ixbalanque** ("Ish-ba-lan-keh" Spanish school) in Copán Ruinas (site of the greatest Mayan city in Honduras) offers one-on-one instruction in Spanish for four hours a day, five days a week. Students board with local Spanish-speaking families, or have the option of staying at a hotel. Contact: *Escuela Ixbalanque, Copán Ruinas, Honduras, Tel/Fax 651-4432.*

You can also get one-on-one instruction at **Centro Internacional de Idiomas**, Ave. San Isidro, Calle 13, Barrio Solares Nuevos, P.O. Box 476 La Ceiba, *Tel. 440-1557, Cellular Tel. 984-3682; E-mail: cii@laceiba.com; www.worlwide.edu/honduras/cici.* The director is Belinda Linton. Students stay in a hotel or with a local family. Garifuna folklore and dance courses are also offered. The school offers air conditioned classrooms, certified instructors, transfer credit for US universities available, and family or hotel stay.

Try also the **Central America Spanish School**, Ave San Isidro, 12 Street #110 La Ceiba, P.O. Box 1142, *Tel/Fax 440-1707, Tel. 440-1742; E-mail: cass@laceiba.com; www.ca-spanish.com.* All levels, transfer credits available from US universities. Classes available on the island of Utila as well.

Academia de Espanol Guacamaya, half a block north of Central Park, Copán Ruinas, *Tel/Fax 651-4360, E-mail: guacamaya_@latinmail.com; www.guacamaya.com*, offers a 1:1 teacher student ratio, four hours per day of classes, room and board with family, all materials provided and special rates for missionaries. They can accommodate both volunteers and groups. Recommended.

Finally, there's a new school run by Garifuna Tours called **Mango Spanish School**, Tela, *Tel/Fax 448-0338; E-mail:mango@honduras.com, www.mangocafe.net, www.garifunatours.com.* Four hours instruction per day, $89 per week. Lodging available at Mango B&B.

Money & Banking

You pay for goods and services in Honduras in *lempiras*, the coin of the realm, named after the native chief who died fighting the Spanish invaders. The exception is the Bay Islands, where, in some resorts, everything is priced in dollars, and lempiras may not even be welcome.

Lempiras come in bills of 1 Lp, 2 Lp, 5 Lp, 10 Lp, 20 Lp, 50Lp, 100 Lp, and 500 Lp, with the 500 Lp bill worth $31 at the time of writing. The lempira comes in coins of 1 Lp, 50 centavos, 20 centavos, 10 centavos, 5 centavos, 2 centavos, and 1 centavo.

Black Market, Gray Market, Free Market

Honduras has a black market, but it's so open and tolerated, that you might as well call it the gray market, or, even better, the free market.

How do you change money on the free market? Generally, you don't have to look for it, it will find you. Changing in the street is especially useful if you are changing a large amount of money. Remember to take security precautions, such as changing with the street changer inside a bank and then immediately depositing your 'sack' of money into a savings account. Don't forget to close the deal with a handshake.

Exchange Rate

In this book, prices are expressed in U.S. dollars, based on the current exchange rate of **about 15.75 lempiras to the U.S. dollar**. In the case of hotels, especially in the Bay Islands, that quote prices only in U.S. dollars, I give the actual rate in dollars charged by the hotel.

Money changers speak enough English to consummate the deal — more than bank clerks. Some will take travelers checks and their hours are certainly flexible. Street money changers generally don't hold more than the equivalent of $500 in local currency, but additional funds can be procured on a moment's notice. Verify the current official and free-market rates as soon as you arrive. Major cities like Tegucigalpa and San Pedro Sula have a well-defined zone where money changers ply their trade on the street. In Tegucigalpa, it's in front of the Hotel Plaza on the Peatonal (walking street). In San Pedro Sula, you can find it a block from the Central Park in front of fast food row.

We're not encouraging this, but changing dollars on the street is really a quite safe and acceptable practice, and you can always do better than the bank exchange rate by a few centavos.

US dollar savings accounts are easily opened at any bank. Deposits can be in the form of cash, check or travelers checks. Only a passport is required to open an account. Dollar savings accounts are now very popular in Honduras; 42% of all funds deposited in Honduran banks are in dollar accounts. People do this since dollars are a good hedge against inflation and protect savings against the constant devaluation of the Lempira.

Banks

The best rate going these days is usually at the banks. You can change on the street in Tegucigalpa and San Pedro Sula, but the difference in exchange rate is very small. Banks are the safest and most reliable way to obtain funds. Hotels, restaurants, bars and tour operators always give a lower rate than the bank.

Wherever you end up changing money, at a bank or on the free market, you'll find that only U.S. dollars, in cash or travelers checks, have any value. Currencies of neighboring countries can be exchanged at the border, or sometimes at exchange houses, but Canadian dollars, sterling, German marks and other solid currencies might just as well be play money in Honduras. Banks do offer more security for changing money, but shop around; not all banks pay the same exchange rate.

Credit Cards & Funds Transfers

Visa, MasterCard, and American Express are widely accepted at middle- and upper-range hotels in Honduras. Your charge slip will be processed at the bank rate of exchange — certainly no advantage.

For **cash advances** on a Visa card, try any bank displaying the Honducard-Visa symbol. Bancahsa and Bancahorro are authorized to make cash advances throughout Honduras.

Credomatic, *web: www.bancocredomatic.com,* is the main credit card bank in the country handling Mastercard, Visa and American Express. Locations around the country include: Blvd. Morazan, Edificio Interamericana, Tegucigalpa, *Tel 238-7220;* Ave. San Isidro in front of Hotel La Ceiba, La Ceiba, *Tel. 443-0668;* Edificio Crefisa 5ta Ave, 1 y 2 Calle, San Pedro Sula, *Tel 557-4350;* Edificio Cooper, Coxen Hole, Roatan, *Tel 445-1196.* A Copan Ruinas branch on the Central Park should be open by the time you read this.

If you want quick cash from the U.S., your best bet is **Western Union**. They can transfer funds from a U.S. account in 15 minutes. Western Union has offices in Tegucigalpa, *Tel. 231-5353*; San Pedro Sula, *Tel. 552-1288;* and La Ceiba, *Tel. 443-1043.*

It is expensive to send money from the US via Western Union. A better option is to open a dollar savings account in any bank. Only a passport is required, and you can then receive a wire transfer from the US or recieve a direct deposit to your account. This is a good option if you will be staying in the country for any length of time and forsee the need for additional funds and a safe place to deposit them.

Many hotels, restaurants and other businesses, will tack on the commission that they are required to pay to the credit card company to the customer's charge slip. Be vigilant, ask questions and be firm if they try to add an additional 4% or so to your bill. A quick recommendation to the clerk to call the credit card company to verify if they are allowed to charge an extra 4% will usually get the fee removed, as it is illegal to charge you this fee.

Investment Information

For investment information, one source is **FIDE** (Foundation for Investment and Development of Exports), FIDE San Pedro Sula, *Tel 566-3040, Fax 566-3049, dpe@fidehonduras.com;* Tegucigalpa, *Tel. 232-9345, Fax 239-0766, cic@fidehonduras.com;* Miami, *Tel 305/443-3060, Fax 305/444-1610, dghonduras@aol.com, www.hondurasinfo.hn.*

Post Office & Courier Services

Post offices are generally open from 7 a.m. to 6 p.m. during the week, from 8 a.m. to noon on Saturday. There may be some variation in small towns. I should tell you that everything that I've ever mailed from Honduras has arrived safely.

But post offices in Honduras, even in major cities are few and far between. Tegucigalpa, population 1 million plus, has exactly one post office; San Pedro Sula, population of about a half million, also has just one post office!

From North America, you can find express courier service to Honduras from some cities with Hispanic communities. Pick up a Spanish language daily paper and check their ads. Express letter services charge more than the post office, but a fraction of what large courier companies collect.

If nothing else is available in your area, courier companies will deliver letters and documents to Honduras at a minimum charge of about $40 from North America. To send packages quickly from Honduras, your best bet is **Federal Express**, *Tel. 239-1971* in Tegucigalpa, *Tel. 557-6590* in San Pedro Sula, and *Tel. 443-1219* in La Ceiba. **UPS**, *Tel. 557-5840* in San Pedro Sula; *Tel. 239-4287* in Tegucigalpa. **Urgente Express** is a popular and recommended courier between the US and Central America, and **DHL** is also available in major cities.

Retiring in Honduras

Honduras, like several other Central American countries, provides an immigration status for foreigners who would like to live in the country as retirees. And retirement status is one of the easier ways for a foreigner to attain residence.

Benefits

Among the benefits of retirement in Honduras are low-cost medical care, where available; inexpensive liquor, household help, and many other products and services; a benign climate; low construction costs; cable TV with US programming in population centers; and small expatriate communities in several towns with clubs and activities.

Land is quite inexpensive, except in the Bay Islands. It is reasonable to order custom made furnishings and accessories such as wrought iron work. Locally made construction supplies such as bricks, concrete block, adobe roof tiles, floor tiles, wood and iron are all inexpensive. Foreigners can own land with full title.

Dollar savings and checking accounts are easily opened at all major banks. Dollar deposits and withdrawals are accepted.

Under the Honduran law, pensioners (*pensionados*), usually of retirement age, must have a stable monthly income of $600. Annuitants (*rentistas*) require a monthly income of $1000. In addition, retirees' income from abroad is not taxed in Honduras.

Spouses and children under 18 (and children up to 25 who are students) may also qualify as residents, without additional income requirements. The major statutory benefit under the retirement law is that household goods and furniture, as well as a car, may be entered into Honduras free of duty. The car may be replaced, again duty free, every five years, but household goods may enter one time only.

Popular retirement locations are Roatán, Copán Ruinas, Tela, La Ceiba, Trujillo and Lake Yojoa.

Restrictions

Retired residents generally may not work in Honduras, but there are many exceptions and loopholes. Anybody, whether a resident or not, may own an incorporated business. And retirees may be specifically allowed to work if they invest in tourism, housing, industry or agriculture.

Retirees usually must live in Honduras for at least four months a year, but they can stay out of the country if their funds continue to be deposited every month in a Honduran bank, or if they invest a minimum of $50,000 in Honduras.

Leaving the country is more complicated for retirees than for tourists. The Honduras Tourism Institute must certify that the retiree has complied with all conditions of the law. An official identification card, or *carnet*, must be renewed every two years.

Applying for Retirement

Among the documents required by applicants for retirement status are: birth certificate, passport, medical certification, good-conduct certification by local police, a statement that one is not a Communist, affidavit of willingness to abide by the laws of Honduras, six photographs, and proof of income.

Information on the retirement law is available through Honduran consulates. Within Honduras, the retirement law is administered by the Honduran Tourism Institute (Instituto Hondureño de Turismo).

Lifestyle Explorations, 101 Federal St., Suite 1900, Boston MA 02110, *Tel. 508/371-4814, Fax 508/369-9192*, specializes in familiarization trips for prospective retirees and investors. Their program includes sessions with resident foreigners.

You should also pick up *International Living Magazine* (contact: 105 W. Monument St., Baltimore, MD 21201, *Tel. 410/223-2602*). The magazine continually highlights Honduras in their monthly newsletter as an up-and-coming retirement destination. Reports cover specific areas of Honduras with detailed information for prospective retirees and investors.

Tax Assistance for Residents

Help with taxes and other financial matters for foreigners is hard to come by in Honduras. Quality financial and tax assistance for foreign residents is available from **USA Trust** based in Antigua, Guatemala, a full-service trust and tax service company specializing in the needs of overseas Americans. Annual tax forms preparation, setting up a family charitable foundation. Tax, trust and accounting performed by US-licensed financial and estate planners, US and local notaries, IRS licensed tax practitionersand US-licensed CPAs with links to US and local lawyers and paralegals for full document services. Corporate executor and trustee services. Property and business management assistance. CPA services for charities, grantmanagement, nonprofit and for-profit businesses. *Tel 502/832-1471, Fwest2@yahoo.com.*

Shopping

Honduras isn't famous for its shopping, but there are some products that are rather typical of the country, and of special quality.

What you'll see everywhere in Honduras, in gift shops and hotels and markets, is hardwood, especially mahogany, made up into assorted useful and decorative items: bookends, sculptures, oversized salad servers, and lamps.

Straw hats and baskets from Santa Bárbara are of especially good quality, come in many sizes and colors, and are useful during your travels, as well as making attractive souvenirs.

Wicker work is intricate and of excellent quality, especially near and along the north coast, where, along the highways, you will find animals, suspended chairs, rockers, and all kinds of utilitarian and decorative items, many of them, unfortunately, too large to take home easily.

Leatherwork, jewelry, baskets, T-shirts and beachwear and embroidery are also available, along with primitive paintings, which are a special favorite of mine, and of many other people as well.

Honduran crafts are supplemented by crafts from neighboring countries. You can buy fine weaving from Guatemala, and textiles from El Salvador. You should also keep an eye out for more mundane bargains that are offered in *pulperías* (corner stores) and larger outlets: ground coffee, tropical fruit jams, rum, and assorted sauces.

Bargaining is common, but you won't get the big discounts you'll find in some other countries. (Or, to put it another way, asking prices aren't as inflated as in places where tourists abound.) The "right" price in a market may be about 20% less than the first price. In any case, if you walk away and the price doesn't move as a result, you've probably gone as far as you can go.

Honduran cigars are world-famous. Check out *Cigar Afficionado* magazine for their monthly reviews of the world's best cigars. Honduran cigars are always highly rated. The **Flor de Copán Cigar Factory** in Santa Rosa de Copán is world famous for the high quality of its cigars. A tour of the factory can be arranged and cigars can be purchased. A visit to the factory is highly recommended as a side trip from the Ruins of Copán.

Honduras boasts an excellent brand of rum Flor de Cana available in the following presentations: Lemon, Extra Lite 4 years old, Extra Dry 4 years old, Black Label 5 years old, Grand Reserve 7 years old, and Centenario 12 years old.

Woodworkers can make custom pieces from precious woods, quality is excellent and prices low. Bring a photo or catalog to show the carpenter exactly what the piece looks like so they can copy it. Mayan reproductions are of good quality and make fine gifts.

Tuno products, made from the pressed bark of the tuno tree, come from the La Mosquitia region. Miskito women produce a wide variety of beautiful objects, all using natural plant based colors. Nativity figures, sold primarily during the holiday season, are made primarily from dried clay and make wonderful Christmas gifts. Other excellent crafts include custom hand-painted porcelain tiles and rustic dried clay bowls and vessels.

Fine womens´ underwear is a good buy. Honduras is the leading exporter of womens´ intimate garments to the U.S. The Lovable brand is of high quality and available in shops throughout the country...and oh.... how wonderful they look on that special someone! For true afficionados, you could probably arrange a factory tour at the **Lovable plant**.

Taxes

A 12% sales tax and a 4% hotel tax is added to all room and meal bills. On beverages, the tax is 15% and on food it's 12% (these taxes are included on the menu price). Departure taxes for international flights is $25.

Indirectly, you'll be paying import duties on anything you buy. Much of government funding in Honduras comes from taxes on both imports and exports, rather than from income taxes. Innocent items like film and tape cassettes, as a result, sell for double what they would cost in the United States or Canada.

Telephones

The national telephone system, operated by **Hondutel**, serves all major towns and some smaller towns of Honduras.

Calls within Honduras can be made conveniently from hotel phones, or from pay phones where they are available.

You'll find coin telephones — they work with ten-centavo pieces — on the main streets of Tegucigalpa and San Pedro Sula, but nowhere else, for the moment, as most of the country lacks direct-dial service.

In 2000, Honduras had 298,000 fixed phone lines and 152,000 cellular subscribers. There is a waiting list of half a million people for a phone line. Honduras has 5 fixed lines per 100 inhabitants, which is the second lowest in Central America ahead of Nicaragua (3 per 100). Costa Rica has 20 lines per 100. Honduras has 1,300 pay phones (many of which don't work). The Honduran government failed in its attempt to sell a 51% share of Hondutel in 2000.

Celtel is the the only cellular operator at the time of writing. In Honduras, *Tel. 800/223-2323* or on the web go to *www.celtel.net.* Rates are expensive.

The Movil 5 Plan gives 5 minutes, costs $12.50 per month, with additional minutes at 25 cents. The Movil 120 Plan gives 120 minutes, costs $40 per month, with additional minutes at 24 cents. The Movil 250 Plan gives 250 minutes, costs $72 per month, with additional minutes at 23 cents. The Movil 1250 Plan gives 1250 minutes, costs a whopping $300 per month, with additional minutes at 22 cents.

Calling Home

Rates to the US and Canada are approximately $2 per minute during the day, less at night. Collect calls may be placed to the United States, Canada, Mexico, the Bahamas, and all Central American countries except El Salvador. Or you can go to an office of Hondutel, the telephone company, but you'll often face a long lineup and confusing procedures.

Calling the US or Eurpoe from Honduras is expensive, approximately $2 per minute.

USA Direct is available from many public phones (coin deposit required) in Tegucigalpa, and from USA Direct phones at Toncontín airport and certain Hondutel offices. From public phones, dial 8000123 to reach an English-speaking AT&T operator. Use this number as well for calling card and collect calls to the U.S.

Time

Honduras is on **Central Standard Time**, equivalent to Greenwich Mean Time less six hours – so it's the same time in Chicago as it is in Honduras.

Tipping

Generally, you can leave a ten-percent tip in any restaurant, and be considered generous. Many local people will leave less, or nothing at all, especially in small, informal eating places. You can give 10 lempiras (about 70¢) to anyone who carries your bag, more in fancier hotels. Taxi drivers don't get anything on top of the negotiated fare.

Some better hotels and restaurants add a ten-percent service charge to your bill, in which case there's no need to leave an additional tip, except for exceptional service.

Your tipping philosophy should take into account the fact that your waitress or waiter serving you probably has a family or child to support, and probably earns no more than 30-40 Lps per day in salary. Any tip left will go directly to buy necesities for a poor family.

Water

In general, do not trust the tap water for drinking, anywhere in Honduras. There are exceptions to this rule of thumb. You may find clean spring water flowing from the tap in the Bay Islands. But unless you're assured that the tap water is safe, don't drink it.

In most places on the mainland of Honduras, the water is hard — it has a high mineral content. It's not easy to take a shower, and you'll need plenty of shampoo.

Where to Find More Information

The Tourist Office

For a map of Honduras, and assorted pamphlets, try writing to the **Honduras Tourist Bureau** (Instituto Hondureño de Turismo), P. O. Box 3261, Col. San Carlos Edificio, San Carlos, Tegucigalpa, *Tel. 222-2124, 800/222-8687, Fax 238-2102; E-mail: Tourisminfo@iht.hn, hturism@hondutel.hn; www.letsgohonduras.com.* In the U.S., 22100 Ponce de Leon Blvd, Suite 1175, Coral Gables FL 33134, *Tel. 800/410-9608, Fax 305/461-0602, 800/410-9608; E-mail: gohondurastourism@compuserve.com.*

The Tourist Bureau should have beautiful, full color, informative brochures that you can receive upon request.

News Sources in English

Honduras This Week is a gold mine of information about Honduras, and the indispensable tool for keeping up with the latest developments. This weekly paper covers local happenings, profiles villages in the countryside, runs in-depth investigative reports on everything from Tegucigalpa's street children to ecological conflicts to the struggles of indigenous communities to maintain their integrity, serves as an exchange for commercial opportunities in Honduras, and has selective regional and international coverage. New hotels, restaurants and travel services are profiled.

In addition, *Honduras This Week* carries many press-service stories from the States that concern the interests of lesser-developed countries, and are not carried by most U.S. papers. *Honduras This Week* is available in major towns in Honduras, mainly through hotels. To subscribe (for $48 annually in the United States), write to: Apartado Postal 1312, Tegucigalpa, D.C., Honduras, *Tel. 232-8818, 232-0832, Fax 232-2300, web: www.marrder.com/htw/* – or you can e-mail them at *hontweek@hondutel.hn.*

La Prensa is probably the best of Honduras´ Spanish language press. Check out their website at: *www.laprensahn.com.*

A good website with up-to-date Honduras information is *www.hondurastips.honduras.com.*

Books & Maps

Books and maps published in Honduras can be hard to obtain if you're out of the country, but *Honduras This Week* has a reading club, with an order form printed in the back of most issues. Listings included maps, and books on

Honduran history, archaeology, ethnology, and folklore. Most are in Spanish, but some are illustrated and of interest even if your knowledge of the language is limited. They can even arrange to send you the Honduran phone book.

Maps of Honduras and Central America may be available from your automobile club. One excellent detailed map (ISBN 0921463170) is published by **ITMB**, P. O. Box 2290, Vancouver, B.C. V6B 3W5, Canada, and is available at many travel bookstores for $8.95 Canadian or $7.95 U.S. In Tegucigalpa, good maps are available at the **Instituto Geográfico Nacional**.

To get a Honduras Tourist Map through the Internet, contact: *touristmap@honduras.com.*

Another good source for Honduran maps is **World of Maps**, 118 Holland Ave., Ottawa, ON, Canada K1Y OX6; *maps@magi.com, www.magi.com/-maps/.*

It is better to bring maps from the US; you will waste many hours otherwise dealing with the Honduran bureaucracy.

US Consulates & Embassies

Honduran consulates and embassies generally handle trade matters, but in some cases might be able to answer questions about the retirement law or travel in the country. Don´t expect much help from Honduran embassies or consulates abroad.

In **New York**, the consulate is at 80 Wall St., New York, NY, 10005, *Tel. 212/269-3611.*

In **Washington, D.C.**, the embassy is at 3007 Tilden St., Suite 4M, NW, Washington, DC, 20008, *Tel. 202/966-7702; embhondu@aol.com.*

Chapter 8

Cruise Down The Coast
Sail Down in Your Own Boat

The definitive handbook for these waters is *Cruising Guide to the Honduras Bay Islands*, available from Wescott Cove Publishing Co., P O Box 130, Stamford CT 06904. This book includes numerous maps, charts, and customs information that will get you safely to, through, and out of the Caribbean waters of Honduras.

Charter a Sailboat

To have a sailboat waiting for you, contact a travel agency that specializes in Honduras, such as **Roatán Charter**, Box 877, San Antonio, FL 33576, *Tel. 800/282-8932, Fax 904/588-4158.*

For more details, see the chapter on the Bay Islands.

Take a Cruise

The Ukrainian-registered *Gruziya* ("Georgia") sails regularly from St. Petersburg, Florida, to Cozumel, Belize, and onward to Puerto Cortés, Honduras. The five-deck vessel has two restaurants, a casino, pool, disco, and a crew offering an unusual Russian and Ukrainian experience in the Caribbean. Rates for a one-week cruise range from about $1,000 to $2,000 per person, with deep discounts for the third and fourth person sharing a cabin. Contact **Odessa America Cruise Company**, 170 Old Country Rd., Mineola, NY 11501, *Tel. 800/221-3254.*

To arrange diving in conjuction with the cruise, contact **Maya Tours**, 20423 SR7, Ste. 6000, Boca Raton, FL 33498, *Tel. 561/477-4848, 800/ 392-6292, Fax 561/477-4879, info@mayatour.com, http://mayatour.com.* The folks at Maya Tours have a cruise package that includes diving in Mexico, Belize and off Roatán for a package price of under $1,000 per person.

Charter a Boat

Motor vessels without sails can also be secured through **Roatán Charter,** (in the US: *Tel. 800/282-8932*) and through many of the hotels in the Bay Islands.

Diving

Here's an activity that you will enjoy exclusively in the Bay Islands, so see The Bay Islands chapter for more details.

Skin Diver magazine regularly publishes articles covering diving and accommodations in the Bay Islands, and classified and display advertisements for hotels and diving packages. Available at newsstands, or by subscription directly from the magazine at P. O. Box 3295, Los Angeles, CA 90078.

Fishing

For the most part, sport fishing is something you'll do in the Bay Islands. See The Bay Islands chapter for further information.

On the mainland of Honduras, the most famous fishing hole is **Lake Yojoa**, known for bass weighing in at about ten pounds on the average. The few hotels along the lake have limited equipment available for rent. If you own your own gear, it's advisable to bring it along.

A fishing license is required, and is usually obtained in advance through a travel agency – but in practice is not required.

National Parks

Here's another of the surprises Honduras has in store for you. In just a few years, Honduras has moved into the forefront of Latin America in protecting and preserving its natural treasures. And treasures there are aplenty — over 700 species of birds, 500 piscine species, and flora that includes scores of species of orchids alone.

Found throughout Honduras are more than 100 protected areas that fall under an array of categories including national parks, wildlife reserves and refuges, biospheres, etc. For the most part the majority of these biolgically rich areas are just on paper, are difficult to reach and those that are accesible offer few services. However, more areas are falling under the management of local NGO's (non-governmental organizations) who in many cases are striving to promote ecotourism.

National Parks at a Glance

The following parks are among the most accessible and provide some basic services:

• **Celaque** – 5 km west of Gracias. Includes Mount Celaque, highest peak and cloud forest in country, and colonial fort and hot springs. Campsites available. 270 square kilometers.

• **Cusuco** – 20 km west of San Pedro Sula. Includes cloud forest with quetzal habitat, trails. 10 square kilometers.

• **Cerro Azul Meambar** – 30 km northwest of Comayagua. Forest and watershed reserve above the eastern side of Lake Yojoa, with falls and rapids.

• **Pico Pijol** – east of El Progreso. Cloud forest. 114 square kilometers.

• **Pico Bonito** – south of La Ceiba. Includes high tropical forest on Bonito Peak. Trails. 68 square kilometers.

• **Capiro-Calentura** – mountain behind Trujillo, road leads to peak, scenic views.

• **Sierra de Agalta** – Olancho. Includes dwarf forest. Trails and camping. 255 square kilometers. Most pristine and largest cloud forest. 500 bird species. Four-day hike to peak.

• **La Tigra** – 11 km northeast of Tegucigalpa. First national park (established 1980), protecting Tegucigalpa's watershed. Trails, dormitories. 75 square kilometers. Entry through San Juancito past Valle de Angeles.

• **Punta Sal** – 6 km west of Tela. Includes beaches and reefs, trails. 419 square kilometers. Wetland ecosystem, reefs, forest, trails.

• **La Muralla** – 8 km north of La Unión, Olancho. Cloud forest, trails. 16 square kilometers. Visitors center, camping. Lots of quetzals in breeding season.

• **Cuero y Salado** – 20 km west of La Ceiba. Coastal area with river estuaries and navigable canals, includes manatee habitat. Access by boat. 85 square kilometers

• **Laguna Guaimoreto** – East of Trujillo. Includes Lake Guaimoreto. 50 square kilometers.

• **Rio Platano Biosphere** – La Mosquitia. Virgin tropical forest, declared a world biosphere reserve by the United Nations. Extensive lowland rainforest, savannas, wetlands and riverine systems. Over 350 bird species. Access via plane and boat.

Paradoxically, the lack of development has left this ecological bonus intact. Few roads — and poor ones at that— underpopulation, and limited industrial agriculture, except in bananas, have left nature alone in much of the country. The Mosquitia region along the border of Nicaragua is one of the last largely undisturbed lowland forests in Central America. And there are pockets of highland cloud forest that the magnificent resplendent quetzal, the holy grail of birders, still calls home.

But the remaining untouched forests of Honduras are now in danger. Multinational companies are turning envious eyes toward stands of pine and deposits of minerals. Farmers from the exhausted soil of the central part of the country are seeking new lands to clear and plant.

Over a dozen treasure troves of nature are now protected as national parks, reserves and refuges, and many more sites are under consideration for inclusion.

For now, things are in a rudimentary state. Most parks have no trails, camp grounds, guides or guards. But a start has been made, and the establishment of the parks and reserves is holding off loggers and farmers who might otherwise be cutting down the trees and chasing off the animals. And in the not-too-distant future, Honduras is sure to join Belize, Costa Rica and Guatemala as a destination for visitors interested in getting to know tropical life forms beyond the kinds that are attacked with insecticide.

Current information about conditions in National Parks may be available from the following sources:
- **Ministerio de Recursos Naturales** (Department of Natural Resources), Blvd. Miraflores, Tegucigalpa, *Tel. 231-1918.*
- **COHDEFOR** (Forestry Development Corporation), El Carrizal #1, Carretera salida del Norte, Comayaguela, *Tel 223-8810.*

Raft & Kayak the Jungle Rivers

Honduras has white water! It's rapid, it's exhilarating, it's ecological, it's adventurous, it's off-beat, it's inexpensive, but best of all, it's warm.

There are major rivers throughout Honduras, but rafting operators mainly use those on the north coast, where water levels are most reliable during the rainy season from October to May.

The **Cangrejal River**, inland from La Ceiba, rated at Class II to Class V, has some significant rapids, as well as many sedate stretches, where you can take a break from paddling to view the banana fields, riverside forest trailing vines into the water, and colorful tropical birds fluttering into and out of the foliage.

The **Cuero River**, running through **Cuero y Salado National Park**, west of La Ceiba, is a stereotypical lazy jungle river, lined by dense forest and abandoned coconut plantations, perfect for visitors who want to enjoy birding and wildlife observation.

Rafting organizers provide all necessary equipment: raft (or kayak, where appropriate), helmet, life jacket, and paddles. Participants should wear bathing suit and t-shirt or lightweight jogging outfit as protection against the sun, and tennis shoes or surf shoes. Take along a change of clothing for when you're done!

Despite the excitement, there is little danger in rafting the rivers of Honduras. Passengers wear life jackets, and in the case of an occasional capsize, you're soon washed away from any rocks into deeper, safer water.

Four- to six-hour trips out of La Ceiba generally costing about 430 Lps per person are offerred by:

- **Omega Tours**, *Tel. 440-0334, omegatours@laceiba.com*. Offers white water rafting, kayaking. German owners, also run a mountain lodge near Pico Bonito National Park. Restaurant, great food, pool, free nights lodging with all trips, Cuero Salado, La Mosquitia. Specialists in Cangrejal River rafting and kayaking.
- **La Moskitia Ecoaventuras**, *Tel/Fax 442-0104, moskitia@caribe.hn, www.honduras.com/moskitia*. Specializing in La Mosquita river trips, Rio Platano, Cangrejal, Cuero Salado.
- **Garifuna Tours**, *Tel/Fax 448-2904, garifuna@hondutel.hn, www.garifunatours.com*. Sea kayak trips to Punta Izopo National Park near Tela.

Ecotourism

Talk of rain forests, talk of eco-tourism, talk of adventure travel. Whatever you call it, Honduras is the last frontier of travel in Central America, where an adventuring soul can still be one of the few outsiders to drift along a lazy river bordered by centenary trees, listen to the roar of howler monkeys trooping through the jungle canopy, spot a limpkin wading in the shallows, wonder at petroglyphs carved by mysterious ancient civilizations.

Though the pressures of local loggers and land-hungry peasants are inexorable, and more forest has been destroyed in the last few decades than in all the centuries since the Spaniards arrived in the New World, there are more jungles left in Honduras than elsewhere in the region. The forests are protected, at least nominally, in such areas as the **Río Plátano Biosphere Reserve**.

Low-impact tourism by adventurous visitors represents one of the few viable ways to make those lands valuable in a capitalistic world, without destroying their ancient treasures of medicinal plants, animal life, water-storing lowlands, and mangroves where fish breed.

Ron Mader operates an excellent online ecotourism resource and information network. He has the best listing of Honduran environmental groups and information on ecotourism and sustainable tourism available. Contact Ron at his various sites: *www.planeta.com/ecotravel/resources/*

centamdex.html (Central America Travel Providers Directory) *or www.planeta.com/ecotravel/center/center.html* (EcoTravels In Central America)

For questions and comments regarding Honduran ecotourism you can post questions at: *planeta_honduras@yahoogroups.com.*

There are now a number of ecofriendly lodges; **Omega Lodge** (rustic and inexpensive) and **The Lodge at Pico Bonito** (luxurious and expensive) both just outside of La Ceiba, as well as **Finca San Lucas** (rustic and mid-priced) outside of Copán Ruinas. By supporting such lodges, tourists can help show that ecotourism projects such as these can contribute to protecting important ecosystems and at the same time contribute to the development of ecotourt infrastructure.

In 2001 tourism in Honduras approached the $300 million mark, a major stimulus for an economy battered by low commodity prices for such basic exports as coffee, bananas and pineapples. Honduras' potential as an ecotourism destination will hopefully lead to the protection of vitalprotected areas, as well as bring in additional tourism revenues.

food & drink

Chapter 9

As a tourist, you'll probably run across "international food," American cuisine adapted to local tastes and cooking abilities; and food served in the local *style*, without showing off too many local specialties. Your grilled steak (*bistec a la parrilla*), pork chop (*chuleta*) or chicken (*pollo*) might be accompanied by fried plantains (*plátanos fritos*), beans (*frijoles*) and/or rice (*arroz*). Garlic and onion are part of any sauce, and vegetables may include the less-than-familiar *chayote*, or vegetable pear, or *yuca* in place of potatoes. Sometimes you'll get *tortillas*, flat cakes of corn, used in place of bread.

At home, Hondurans enjoy *tapado* (vegetable-meat soup), *mondongo* (tripe soup), *enchiladas* and *tamales* (meat and sauce in tortillas or corn dough), *Pinchos* (shish kebab) cooked on an open charcoal grill (very popluar especially in Copán Ruinas) and black beans. You can partake, too, if you get friendly with the locals, or if you take a meal or two at the bare tables and benches in a local market, where food shops cook up filling, cheap repasts for people of modest means.

On the streets, you can snack on fruits to your heart's content. Peeled oranges and bananas are sold for a few cents each, with or without salt and nutmeg, according to your taste. You'll also find *mermelada de papaya* (papaya marmalade) and other local fruit preserves at every breakfast table.

Along the highways, you´ll occasionally see food and fruit stands, especially on the higway from San Pedro Sula to Tegucigalpa, near Lake Yojoa. Field corn, cooked in the husk over open fires, is especially popular. It's not the sweet corn you might know — it's chewy, and usually quite pale — but it's fresh and delicious.

In the Bay Islands, and among the Black Caribs, or Garífuna, of the northern coast, there are some variations. Seafood of all kinds is eaten more than elsewhere, and coconut invades many a menu item: mixed with rice, or, more usually, in coconut bread.

Soft drinks are sold everywhere in Honduras, probably more than are healthy for the population. On the other hand, carbonated beverages are always safe to drink, while the local water supply may be suspect. Coke, Fanta, Sprite and Canada Dry ginger ale and soda water are major brands, sold for from 50¢ to $1, depending on whether you're consuming at a street stand or in a hotel restaurant. The price is for the contents only. The bottle costs as much as what's in it, or more. If you intend to walk away as you drink, ask for your soda in a plastic bag (en una bolsa) with a straw (con pajilla).

There are local wines in Honduras, made from fruits and imported grape concentrate, but having said this, I'll say no more — they're not worth further mention. And you can find imported California, French and Chilean wines, though by the time they reach your table, with hefty import duties, taxes and markups added on, they'll generally cost at least double what they would in the United States, and sometimes much, much more.

If you're a drinker, moderate or otherwise, this leaves you to choose between hard liquor and beer. Imported liquors, like wines, are pricey. Local rum (ron) is generally quite good.

I can recommenend that you try the local beer. They are light, pilsner type beers, and are consistently cool and refreshing, especially on a hot, tropical afternoon. Salva Vida (Lifesaver), Imperial, Nacional, Port Royal and Holstein are available nationwide. US beers are now being introduced; Budweiser is available.

Honduran rum is of excellent quality and is reasonably priced. I heartily recommend Centenario, which has been aged 12 years – perfect for that after-dinner or before-bed drink.

Chapter 10

San Pedro Sula

GRAN HOTEL SULA, *1 Calle, 3/4 Avenidas NW (P. O. Box 435), Tel. 5529999, Fax 557-6215, 552-7000. 118 rooms. $85 single/$96 double. U.S. reservations: Tel. 800/ 223-6764. No charge for children under 12.*

This is a nine-story building right on the main square of San Pedro Sula. The staff is competent and friendly. The rooms (and the hotel in general) are very clean, the mattresses are excellent, and all are provided with coffee makers. All rooms in the main tower have balconies (I recommend those with a view to the pool, a courtyard work of tiled art, complete with cascades and tributaries), and suites have kitchenettes and sleep sofas. There are also some poolside units. Other amenities include a restaurant, 24-hour coffee shop, newstand, health club and twice daily maid service (extraordinary!).

The Gran Hotel Sula is a trip back in time to the late fifties, when staying downtown did *not* mean staying in a dangerous, decaying area. The hotel is well maintained.

Take the Skandia coffee shop. You can take spin on revolving stools at the lunch counter and order a banana split, club sandwich, and apple pie, and drink of atmosphere that says, this is a *diner!* Of course, if you're not a kid, you can sit at one of the tables. Egg plates, club sandwiches and burgers in the Skandia run $3 and under. For more formal dining, the Granada restaurant overlooks the pool from the mezzanine, and serves filet mignon, shrimp casserole and daily specials for about $7, a lunch buffet for about $6. The cuisine is excellent.

Discounts — significant ones — are available to Hondurans and resident foreigners.

Copán Ruinas

LA CASA DE CAFÉ BED & BREAKFAST INN, *Barrio Las Vegas, three blocks west of Restaurant Llama del Bosque and Tunkul. Write to: Casa de Café, Barrio Las Vegas, Copán Ruinas, Tel. 651-4620, Fax 651-4623, E-mail: casacafe@hondutel.com or casadecafe@mayanet.com; web; www.todomundo.com/casadecafe. 10 rooms. $35 single/$45 double/$53 triple.*

Copán's first B&B offers 10 comfortable rooms in an authentic colonial setting. Wood framed picture windows, lace curtains, handcrafted pine furniture, writing desk, ceiling fan, private hot water bath, garden with spectacular view of the Copán River Valley and distant mountains of Guatemala. Common area has color TV with cable, VHS, reference library with books, magazines, and videotapes on travel, archaeology, and culture in Central America. Breakfast is included in rate – waffles, banana pancakes, country omlettes. Export quality coffee is ground fresh each morning.

The inn is run by a lovely Honduran-American family. English, Spanish and Miskito are spoken. They are a good source of Honduran travel information and can arrange local tours to a coffee plantation, hot springs or horseback riding. This is a very good value for your vacation dollar. Brochure available upon request.

Tela

MAYA VISTA, *two blocks from the beach. Tel/Fax 448-1497, E-mail: mayavista@mail.com; web: www.mayavista.com. Doubles from $18-$32, 2-bedroom apartment sleeps four with living room $50, weekly and monthly rates.*

Owned and operated by a friendly Canadian couple from Québec, Pierre and Susanna Couture. Perched high up on a hill overlooking the town, two blocks up from the beach, with a breathtaking view of Tela Bay below. Six comfortable, breezy rooms, many with a view of the ocean. All rooms with private hot water bath and color TV with cable and ceiling fan.

Above the rooms is a pleasant restaurant/bar with a lovely view of the sea and the town below. Good food at reasonable prices, cooked up by Susanna. Specialties include, fish, shrimp, pastas and breakfasts. Fresh baked cake or pie each day.

Above the restaurant is a lookout tower that rises above the top floor of the hotel. It's a long climb up, but the reward is a spectacular 360 degree view of Tela, Punta Sal National Park, Lancetilla Botanical Gardens and the mountains that rise above it. Pickup at San Pedro Sula airport available.

Trujillo

VILLAS BRINKLEY, *Barrio Buenos Aires. Tel. 434-4444, Fax 434-4269, in the US: Tel. 412/791-2273. 20 rooms. $30 double.*

"The Brinkley" is quite suitable to the old atmosphere of the town, a bay-view complex of cottages in Spanish-colonial architecture on the hills above town, with pool, game room and health club facilities. Arrangements are made for fishing, boating, horseback riding and diving. Restaurant and bar with great panoaramic views. Rooms are air conditioned and two suites have a full kitchenette.

La Ceiba

THE LODGE AT PICO BONITO, *located just outside of La Ceiba, 5 miles from the airport adjacent to Pico Bonito National Park, set in a lovely tranquil spot between the Coloradito and Corinto rivers. Tel 440-0389, 440-0388, Fax 440-0468, Reservations in the US toll-free 888/428-0221; E-mail: picobonito@caribe.hn; web: www.picobonito.com. $165-$220 double, meals extra, 22 rustic yet luxurious cabins.*

This is the finest ecolodge in Honduras. From the welcome cocktail upon arrival, to the gourmet meals served in the wood paneled dining room, to the tastefully furnished cabins, fluffy white towels and private porch where breakfast is delivered, no detail is too small and no request too large for the attentive and well-trained staff.

Trails wind their way throughout the 200-acre property, and there is plenty of wildife, especially birds, to satisfy the most ardent ecotourist. You'll enjoy wonderful views of Pico Bonito, the 8,000-foot mountain the national park is named for, and there's even an observation tower if the view from the ground doesn't suffice. The cabins, surrounded by coffe and cacao trees, are referred to as "rustic elegance," and that is a pretty apt description. Food in the restaurant is first-rate, and the wine list is extensive.

There's a butterfly garden (15-20 species are raised) and serpentarium (Boa, Hognosed Viper, Cascabel, Coral, Timbo and Fer de Lance, the most dangerous snake in Honduras) on the premises. Non-guests have to pay a small admission charge; it's free for guests. Contact James Adams for more information: *sibonxxx@hotmail.com.*.

The lodge features excellent birding, guided hikes into the forest, river swimming, transfers included, tours to Cuero Salado, Cayos Cochinos, river rafting on Cangrejal, Punta Sal, Lancetilla and horseback riding. There's also a swimming pool and spa.

The Lodge is a mmeber of the prestigious Small Luxury Hotels of The World (*www.slh.com*).

Roatán

ANTHONY'S KEY RESORT, *Sandy Bay, Tel. 445-1003, Fax 445-1329, E-mail: akr@gate.net; web: www.anthonyskey.com. 50 units. U.S. office: 1385 Coral Way, Suite 401, Miami, FL 33145, Tel. 800/227-3483 or 305/858-3483, Fax 305/858-5020. 56 cabañas, air-conditioning. Weekly dive packages from $775 to $975 per person, including three one-tank boat dives daily and two night dives per week, dolphin encounter and dolphin dive, and all activities.*

Additional nights $132 to $139 single/$310 double with meals and diving. Non-diving rate, $140 single/$240 double. Children 3 to 11, $45. About 15% lower in summer.

Everything about Anthony's Key can be described in superlatives. The landscaping alone makes it a paradise. The resort flows down a slope, and across to a small cay. Structures, plantings and terrain are all integrated, and there is a great respect for the environment. There are units in the lodge on a hill, bungalows set into the foliage on the slope, and slat houses along the edge of the cay, on stilts in the water, reached by a 60-second boat ride. Macaws and hummingbirds flap and gyre about. Rooms are clean and somewhat sparse, but easy on the senses. Meals are simply prepared, and hearty. The bar is quite expensive.

The emphasis is on diving, as elsewhere on the island, with many boats and good instructors and equipment. Numerous groups come here. The location near the west end of the island allows easy access to diving spots on both shores. (Northers might churn up the sea in front of Anthony's Key, while the south shore remains calm.) Rates are higher than elsewhere, but Anthony's Key has a lot more: horseback riding, weekly beach picnic, swimming with dolphins, a dinner party on the key, island-style entertainment, crab races, tennis, and use of canoes, kayaks, pedal boats and small sailboats are included in the daily rate (non-guests can use the sailboats for a fee).

There are also a wildlife sanctuary with trails on nearby Bailey's Key; the Museum of Roatán, housing an excellent, well-presented display of a variety of artifacts from the mainland and Roatán, admission $4; a decompression chambe; a doctor on-site; and secluded beaches. Fishing can be arranged, and snorkeling equipment is available for rent. Also available: resort diving courses, PADI instruction, underwater photo courses, and videos in which you can star. The souvenir shop has a good assortment of trinkets, and a photography shop offers processing, and rentals of cameras and underwater equipment. There's even the Casino Royal, if you're interested in gambling between dives.

Check their website for special deals.

Guanaja

END OF THE WORLD, *Tel. 991-1257, E-mail: endoftheworld@compuserve.com; web: www.guanaja.com. 5 duplex cabanas. $35 double*

A small, laid back, unhurried, tranquil resort that highlights the best that Guanaja has to offer. Host/Proprietor Brian Rowland is always on hand with plenty of warm Guanaja-style hospitality and treats guests like family. There's superb diving on world class reefs, a wonderful beach a popular restaurant and bar and a fun weekend BBQ. Plenty of activities for the diver and non-diver.

Guests can roam the miles of unspoiled beaches and lush mountains that surround the resor, covered with jungle fauna, birds and animals. Snorkel and dive on the fringing coral reefs right in front of the hotel. Two dives a day and one night dive during the week. Guanaja has many virgin diving sites beginning with shallow lagoon reefs to wrecks, caves, a huge volcano vent system and wall dives. Additional activities include: sailing the Hobie Cat, paddling a canoe from the beach, snorkeling, swimming, fishing, exploring the miles of beaches, island boat tours to the different communities or just relaxing with a tropical drink in a comfortable beach-side hammock. The End of the World is home port to one of the best stocked bars in the Bay Islands, where some of the most infamous local pirates visit. At the beach bar the resident parrot will join you for drinks and is more than happy to pose for photographs.

Panoramic ocean viewsgreet you from the cabanas. Bedrooms are decorated with native stone masks and local artifacts, and all have private bathrooms and a deck area.

Fishing expeditions can be arranged by request, 1/2 or full day, 5-6 person maximum.

Package rates for divers are $799 per person and include 7 nights accommodation, 3 meals, 2 boat dive trips per day, 1 night dive per week, weights, tanks and belts, waterfall trip, use of canoes and round-trip transfers from Guanaja airport. Basic scuba certification $350 per person. Scuba courses run approximately 4-5 days. One day scuba experience course $100 per person.

Package rates for non-divers are $699 per person and include 7 nights accommodation, 3 meals, unlimited snorkeling, use of canoes, waterfall trip and round-trip transfers from Guanaja airport.

Package rates for Kayaking are $1200 per person and include 7 nights accommodation, 3 meals per day, personal kayak, basic instruction, all safety and paddling equipment, professional guide, snorkeling, and round-trip transfers from Guanaja airport. Guided expedition through Guanajas Marine Sanctuary and mangrove lagoons. The kayaking trip is led by former U.S. kayak champion Doug Conners.

Tegucigalpa

HOTEL HONDURAS MAYA, *Avenida República de Chile at 3 Calle. Tel. 220-5000, Fax 220-6000, U.S. reservations, Tel. 800/44UTELL, E-mail: guestser@hondurasmaya.hn or reserve@hondurasmaya.hn; web: www.hondurasmaya.hn. 176 rooms. $130 single/$140 double, $200 to $350 in suites. $13 per extra adult, no charge for children, nominal charge for crib. Visa, Master Card, American Express.*

Located just east of downtown Tegucigalpa, the Honduras Maya is one of the city's landmarks, a high-rise in local terms, at 12 stories, with a trademark sculptured vertical frieze on its main tower meant to reflect the Mayan tradition of Honduras. It's the top hotel in town. Rooms have air conditioning and satellite TV.

Service is more than adequate, the pool is heated, and views are scenic. An on-site health spa includes a sauna and steam bath. There are several restaurants, including a 24-hour coffee shop, convention and meeting facilities, extensive protected parking, and shops and services (auto rental, barber shop, travel agencies, etc.) both on the extensive hotel grounds and in the surrounding neighborhood. There is no charge for local phone calls, a plus if you're in town on business. Also complimentary is the buffet breakfast. Uniquely among Tegucigalpa hotels, the Honduras Maya has a casino, where the gaming includes blackjack, roulette, and slot machines.

t e g u c i g a l p a

Chapter 11

Tegucigalpa as a settlement dates back to 1578, when silver was discovered, on September 29, St. Michael's Day. The town that grew up around the mine was called Real de Minas de San Miguel, in the saint's honor, with "de Tegucigalpa" — "of the Silver Hill" in the *Nahuatl* language — appended to distinguish this San Miguel from many others. In time, Tegucigalpa was the part of the name that stuck.

Throughout the colonial period, Comayagua was the capital, but Tegucigalpa continued to grow in importance, and, after independence, the seat of government alternated between the two major settlements. In 1880, the administration of the country was installed once and for all in Tegucigalpa. Officially, the capital bears the suffix "D.C." for *Distrito Central*," the central administrative district that also takes in adjacent Comayagüela. The city is known as "*Teguz*," pronounced "Tegoose."

Tegucigalpa Today

With more than one million people, metropolitan Tegucigalpa is the most populated city of the country, but it is lacking in some of the attributes of a capital. It really is off the main tourist track. Tegucigalpa has no railroad. The Pan American Highway bypasses the city, and an all-weather road to the north coast was completed only in the middle of this century.

At the end of the 19th century, most economic development in Honduras took place along the north coast, leaving Tegucigalpa with somewhat of a backwater status. The central area, never laid low by earthquakes or volcanic eruptions, has a certain amount of charm imparted by colonial and nineteenth-century architecture. Some of the surrounding hillside neighborhoods are reached by narrow, winding streets, too narrow for vehicles, and by public stairways. The climate, at an average altitude of 1,000 meters (3,327 feet), is rarely too warm.

Still, modern times are catching up. Tegucigalpa has grown at a turbulent pace in the last decades, as people have migrated from the countryside to towns, and from towns to the capital. Slowly, cobblestoned streets are being covered over with asphalt. Anonymous concrete-and-glass structures are replacing venerable homes with walls several feet thick. Red-tile roofs and Italianate and colonial decorative elements are disappearing.

Tourism in Tegucigalpa is barely a fledging industry. There is little to recommend for the international traveler. Most tourism in Tegucigalpa is business-related. Most sites of interest to tourists are quite remote from Tegucigalpa: Copán Ruinas, Gracias, Tela, La Ceiba, Bay Islands.

Arrivals & Departures

Arriving By Air
International airlines serving Tegucigalpa are:
- **American Airlines**, Edificio Palmira, 1 piso, Colonia Palmira. *Tel. 232-1414, 232-1415, Fax 232-1380, Airport 233-9680/85, Fax 233-9678.* To Miami, New York.
- **Atlantic Airlines**, *Tel. 234-9701*
- **Continental Airlines**, Edificio Palic, Col. Palmira. *Tel. 220-0999, 233-7812.* To Houston.
- **Iberia**, Edificio Palmira, Planta Baja Col. Palmira. *Tel. 239-4565, 232-4566, Fax 239-1729.*
- **Lacsa (Grupo Taca)**, Edificio Interamericana Blvd. Morazán. *Tel. 232-0915, 232-7585, Airport 233-2192, Fax 231-1517,* Los Jarros Bldg., Blvd. Morazán, *Tel. 311525*
- **Isleña**, Galeria La Paz Ave, La Paz, *Tel. 237-3410, 237-3450*

Toncontín Airport
Toncontín Airport is just five kilometers south of downtown Tegucigalpa. It isn't much of an airport. The runway is exxtremely short and amazingly enough was built on top of a mesa. Landings at Toncontín are quite an experience. The landing gear seems to touch the hills as well as nearby houses that surround the approach to the runway. Upon touchdown of the landing gear, the jet immediately applies back thrust and brakes due to the fact that the runway is very short. As the plane slows down, it is customary for passengers to break into spontaneous applause.

A tourist card is given at entry, good for 30 days. It can easily be extended up to a total of 90 days. If you need anything, go to the departure area (if it's open). Entry formalities, like everything else at the airport, are minimal.

Getting to Town from the Airport
Once you go outside the terminal, you'll find a hubbub of **taxi drivers** and money changers — disconcerting, perhaps, as your introduction to Honduras, but not dangerous in any way. There's a fixed tariff of about $5 to go from the airport to any location in the capital. Or, you can walk to the main road a couple of hundred meters from the terminal and pick up a regular city taxi for about half that price. **City buses** to town also pass regularly. It's inexpensive enough to reach the airport from town by taxi, but the Loarque or Río Grande bus will also take you. One central stop is on 6 Calle (Av. Jérez) in front of Super Donuts.

Airport **hours** are 5:30am to 8pm. There's an **airport bank**, but you might as well change your money with the fellows out front. The **post office counter** is open from 8am to 3pm, and is one of the fastest ways to send anything home.

Hondutel, the national telephone monopoly, has an airport outpost. There are also AT&T USA Direct phones, which you can pick up to reach an operator in the States.

Budget has a car-rental counter, and there are other companies as well.

Departing By Air
Isleña Airlines, *Tel. 237-3410*, flies to the Bay Islands and to La Ceiba as well. **Atlantic Airlines**, *Tel 234-9701*, flies to the Bay Islands, La Ceiba, Managua, Belize and Guatemala City. One local air taxi service is **Sosa Airlines**, *Tel. 235-5107, 239-0757, 441-2512*

Departing By Bus
There's no central bus terminal in Tegucigalpa, but many buses for suburban and distant destinations leave from private stations in Comayagüela.
TO COMAYAGUA, SAN PEDRO SULA: **El Rey Express**, 1/2 cuadra del anexo de Banco Central, *Tel. 237-8561*. Buses to San Pedro Sula from 5:30am - 6:30pm. **Hedman-Alas** is better than most other companies at 11 Avenida, 13/14 Calles, Comayagüela, *Tel. 237-7143*. Leaves every half-hour from 6am to 5:30pm from Tegucigalpa to San Pedro Sula. Luxury Class service leaves Tegucigalpa at 6am, 8:15am, 10am, 2pm, 4:15pm. Luxury 1st class buses are very comfortable, with bathroom, movie, air conditioning. Connect in San Pedro Sula for Hedman Alas 1st class direct bus to Copan Ruinas, leaving San Pedro Sula at 7am, 9:50am, 2:30pm. Hedman Alas comes highly recommended for service and comfort. Hedman Alas is the only bus line that can take

you from Tegucigalpa to Copan Ruinas. Connect in San Pedro Sula for Hedman Alas 1st class direct luxury bus to La Ceiba, leaves San Pedro at 6am, 10am, 2pm, 6pm. **Saenz Primera**, Centro Commercial Perisur, Comayagüela, *Tel. 233-4229*. Sáenz is one of the only bus companies to accept reservations by phone. Departs Tegucigalpa at 6am, 8am, 10am and 2pm, 4pm, and 6pm Highly recommended, costs a bit more than other buses but worth it. Buses are equipped with bathroom, stewardesses, snacks, airline style seats, and TV monitors. Two movies are shown during the 3 1/2 hour trip. **Viana Clase**, Oro Blvd Fuerzas Armadas, *Tel. 235-8185*. 1st-class luxury class buses leave at 6:3am. 1:30pm, 6:15pm. Connect in San Pedro for Viana bus to La Ceiba.

   TO JUTICALPA AND OLANCHO DEPARTMENT: Empresa Aurora, 6 Calle, 6 Avenida, Comayagüela, every hour; and **Rutas Olanchanas**, 8 Calle, 6/7 Avenidas.

   TO DANLÍ: **Discua Litena**, near Jacaleapa market, *Tel. 230-0470*, five kilometers from downtown in southeast Tegucigalpa.

Other Honduran & Foreign Destinations By Bus

   Bus service for other destinations is given with descriptions of various other towns. To reach **Guatemala** by bus, you can travel via San Pedro Sula and Santa Rosa de Copán, then onto Ocotepeque and the border at Agua Caliente. A better option, though, is to travel to Copán Ruinas (there are direct buses from San Pedro Sula at 7am, 9:50am, 2pm, 2:30pm and 3pm) and then cross the border at El Florido, seven miles away, and then proceed to Chiquimula in Guatemala where connections can be made to Guatemala City. Otherwise, cross through El Salvador.

   For **El Salvador**, take a bus for El Amatillo from the Belén market. For **Nicaragua**, take a bus from the Mi Esperanza station, *6 Avenida, 24/25 Calles, Comayagüela, Tel. 382863*, as far as Guasaule, on the border.

   TICA Bus, Barrio Villa Adela, Comayaguela, entre 5 y 6 avenida, calle 16, *Tel. 220-0579, 220-0590*, has daily departures to Nicaragua, Costa Rica, Panama, Guatemala, Mexico. Buses are very comfortable with bathroom and air conditioning.

Orientation

   It is easy to get disoriented in Tegucigalpa. The city does not have straight streets like those of San Pedro Sula, except at the very center. It's more like the pattern of a souk in the Middle East. The topography of the valley is far from flat, and you have small hills everywhere. The city is divided into units called b*arrios* and *colonias* (neighborhoods and suburbs), each of which is more or less homogeneous in its social class.

   Downtown is Tegucigalpa proper, or *Barrio El Centro*, and across the Choluteca River, connected by four bridges, Comayagüela, the poorer and flatter part of town, with few significant buildings or governmental operations. Everything of any importance occurs in Tegucigalpa, which runs northward up the slopes of Mount Picacho, and wraps around the eastern side of Comayagüela.

Streets wind this way and that through and between the different barrios and colonias, straightening out for a while, then snaking along and up a hill again. The same street will have different names, both traditional and numbered, and one or the other version will be posted.

The first step in finding any location, if you're not familiar with the city, is to ask for its *barrio* or *colonia* (neighborhood or district) and find that area on a map. Barrios are generally older or more centrally located than colonias. Once you're in the general area, ask for the street that you're seeking. Sometimes, an address will be given as a street name with a house number. Sometimes, you'll get the name of the street, and the nearby cross streets.

For example, the Hotel Istmania is at 5 Avenida, 7/8 Calles (between 7 and 8 Calles, or streets). These are the lucky cases. As often as not, though, an address will be given simply as a location relative to a well-known landmark: *media cuadra del Hotel Honduras Maya* (half a block from the Hotel Honduras Maya). Ask for the hotel, and you're halfway there. Now, start looking!

Trying to find places in Tegucigalpa is bound to get you out and meeting people, but after a while, you'll probably want to rely on a taxi driver to help you out. Fortunately, taxis are inexpensive.

Beyond the city, within easy range by day trips, are such villages as San Antonio de Oriente, Valle de Angeles, Lepaterique, Santa Lucia and Ojojona which, despite their proximity to the capital, remain quintessentially rural places, with no industry to speak of beyond local handicraft specialties.

Getting Around Town
Car Rental
If you are going to rent a car, think first about hiring a taxi (see "Taxis," below). Not only is it cheaper, but roads are bad around Tegucigalpa, with many potholes, and traffic is crazy (though it doesn't move too fast, at least), and traffic signs are only an afterthought.

Generally, you will be substantially responsible for damage (such as hubcaps, floor mats, etc.) to a rented vehicle, even if you buy local insurance, which provides only limited coverage. Verify if your automobile insurance from home or your credit card will provide any additional coverage (such coverage is gradually being eliminated).

Among US-based car-rental companies are:
- **Budget**, at the Hotel Honduras Maya and at the airport, *Tel. 235-9531, 233-6927, Fax 233-5170.*
- **Avis**, Hotel Honduras Maya, *Tel. 2320088,* and airport, *Tel. 2339548.*
- **Hertz**, front of Hotel Honduras Maya, *Tel. 2390772, Fax 2320870,* airport *Tel. 2343784.*

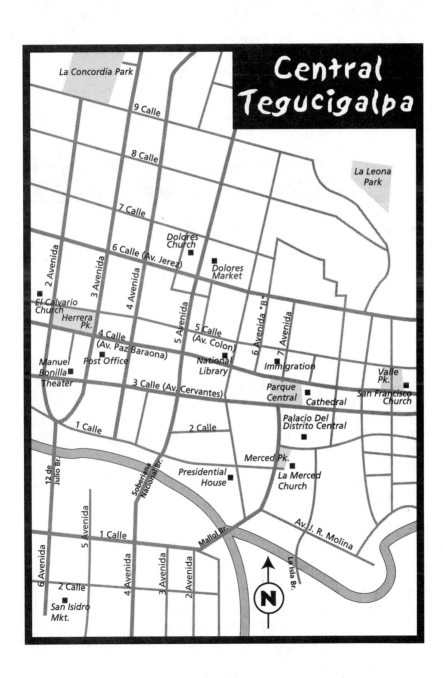

Central Tegucigalpa

Driving in Tegucigalpa

Driving can be a problem in Tegucigalpa, especially at rush hours — about 7am to 9am and 3pm to 7pm. It's not that there are a lot of cars. There just aren't enough streets, and those that exist are narrow and potholed. There are only a few routes to and through downtown, and they are often gridlocked. This explains why bus terminals are on the periphery of Tegucigalpa or in Comayagüela.

Right turns are allowed on red lights, but proceed with caution. Road signs hardly exist, and if you have a choice of driving or not driving, I think you will have a better time not driving.

• **Toyota Rent A Car**, Col Palmira. *Tel. 235-6694, 235-6783; www.123.hn/trac*

By Bus

Buses have set routes, are frequent, and are very cheap. The name of the destination or route is displayed on the front of the bus. Ayudantes (fare collectors) call out the destination. This, however, will be useless for most visitors, as it gives no idea of the route the bus takes as it winds from one hillside neighborhood down and up to another through Tegucigalpa's irregular geography.

Local buses can be crowded. Many of the points of any interest to visitors are in the small downtown area, and those that aren't can be reached inexpensively by taxi for under $2.50 (see Taxis below). If you're staying at a hotel away from the center, such as the Alameda, ask the staff for guidance as to which bus will take you into the city and back out, if you don't want to take a taxi.

Fares on buses are low, the equivalent of about 13¢. Bus drivers and fellow passengers are very helpful.

By Taxi

Taxis are everywhere in Tegucigalpa. They're inexpensive for a run around downtown, $2.50 for a ride to any place on the outskirts of town, $3.50 from the airport or $2.50 in a regular cab. I highly recommend taxis as an alternative to the crowded and confusing service provided by public buses. They're also easier on your nerves than renting a car for local excursions, and usually cheaper, at about $6 per hour for time actually used.

Since taxis are not metered, it is essential to agree on the fare with the driver before you get in. Try to find a taxi that looks as if it has been well maintained. Some are frighteningly dilapidated.

Collective taxis – *collectivos* – go to set destinations on set routes. You share a cab with three or four other passengers. Very reasonable fare, about 45¢. It's cheap, fast, and convenient. Each collectivo route has a set starting point, so you will need to search out the spot.

Tourist Office

The tourist office in Tegucigalpa is located in the **Europa building**, east of downtown in Colonia San Carlos (Calle República de México, Avenida Ramón E. Cruz), *E-mail: Tourisminfo@iht.hn; web: www.letsgohonduras.com*. They have no hotel information, other than a list, but they sell attractive posters as well as maps. As for buses, they will tell you where to catch them, but they have only a sketchy idea as to schedules. If you don't expect much, you won't be disappointed.

To reach the tourist office, take any eastbound Lomas bus from the main square, and get off at Hospital San Felipe. Walk one block west, then left one block on Av. Ramón E. Cruz.

My experience is that you will do better to ask for information when you first arrive at the airport, or by inquiring at your hotel desk, or any travel agency. There is currently no downtown information office.

The best, most complete source of up to date information is *Honduras Tips* magazine, available free all over Honduras at tourist locations. Most reliable businesses advertise their services, including hotels, restaurants, and tour operators. Contact the magazine at *hondurastips@honduras.com* or go to their website: *www.hondurastips.honduras.com*.

Where to Stay

Where should you stay? As far as the neighborhood goes, for most visitors, the choice is easy. Almost all hotels, in every price range, are in a one-kilometer square of central Tegucigalpa and adjacent Comayagüela. The exceptions are the pricier establishments, which are located in the pricier areas of the city.

As elsewhere in this book, the rates mentioned below for hotels include a 12% room tax. There is also a 4% tourism tax. The above taxes may or may not be tacked onto your bill or may be included in your rate, so it's best to inquire.

Some of the larger hotels will offer discounts if you present your business card, or ask for the special rate. I don't guarantee that this will work for you, but this has certainly been the case recently, when occupancy rates at the better hotels have not been that high.

Better Hotels

HOTEL HONDURAS MAYA, *Avenida República de Chile at 3 Calle. Tel. 220-5000, Fax 220-6000, U.S. reservations, Tel. 800/44UTELL, E-mail:*

guestser@hondurasmaya.hn or reserve@hondurasmaya.hn; web: www.hondurasmaya.hn. 176 rooms. $125 single/$140 double, $200 to $350 in suites. $13 per extra adult, no charge for children, nominal charge for crib. Visa, Master Card, American Express.

Located just east of downtown Tegucigalpa, the Honduras Maya is one of the city's landmarks, a high-rise in local terms, at 12 stories, with a trademark sculptured vertical frieze on its main tower meant to reflect the Mayan tradition of Honduras. It's the top hotel in town. Rooms have air conditioning and satellite TV.

Service is more than adequate, the pool is heated, and views are scenic. An on-site health spa includes a sauna and steam bath. There are several restaurants, including a 24-hour coffee shop, convention and meeting facilities, extensive protected parking, and shops and services (auto rental, barber shop, travel agencies, etc.) both on the extensive hotel grounds and in the surrounding neighborhood. There is no charge for local phone calls, a plus if you're in town on business. Also complimentary is the buffet breakfast. Uniquely among Tegucigalpa hotels, the Honduras Maya has a casino, where the gaming includes blackjack, roulette, and slot machines.

CAMINO REAL INTER-CONTINENTAL, *Ave Roble, frente al Mall Multiplaza. Tel 231-1300, 231-1400. From the US or Canada. call toll-free 888/ 567-8725. E-mail: tegucigalpa@interconti.com; web: www.interconti.com/ honduras/tegucigalpa/hotel_tegic.html. 157 rooms and suites. $175 double.*

This is Tegucigalpas' newst luxury hotel. Fine service, excellent restaurant, all amenities, from color TV to hair dryer, safe-deposit box, in-room movies, complimentary outdoor parking, free airport shuttle and much more. For business travelers there's a complete bilingual Business Centre. The location is great: just 15 minutes from the airport, a few blocks away from Boulevard Morazan, and right in front of Honduras' best shopping mall.

HOTEL PLAZA SAN MARTÍN, *Colonia Palmira on Plaza San Martín, P. O. Box 864, Tel. 232-8268. 110 rooms. $90 single/$75 double/$115 triple, $170 in suites. American Express, Diners Club, Visa, Master Card.*

One of Tegucigalpa's major hotels, one block from the Hotel Honduras Maya. A Mayan-inspired building with a slightly sloping facade, terraced to the roof. Rooms are plainly furnished but quite comfortable, each with a balcony, refrigerator, sitting area, television, phone, and central air conditioning. Facilities include coffee shop, restaurant, bar, exercise room and indoor parking, but no pool.

HOTEL PLAZA, *4 Avenida at 4 Calle (P.O. Box 175), Tel. 237-2111. 83 rooms. $38 double/$85 triple. American Express, Visa, Master Card.*

Centrally located on the pedestrian mall of downtown Tegucigalpa, opposite the post office, the Plaza offers good-sized air-conditioned rooms, all with queen-sized beds, and televisions with U.S. programming. Some of the standard rooms have sofa beds as well. Possible negative points for some visitors will be the lack of a swimming pool, and of shops inside the hotel, though most required services are available nearby. There are two restaurants here, including an all-night coffee shop, the Papagallo. Protected parking.

Note: One of the best places in Tegucigalpa to change money at the favorable street rate is in front of the Hotel Plaza.

Moderate Hotels

HOTEL EL PRADO, *3 Avenida, 8 Calle, Tel. 237-0121, Fax 237-2221. 68 rooms. $74 double/$100 triple plus tax. American Express, Visa, Master Card.*

Located near the back of the Cathedral. Rooms are air conditioned and have televisions. Coffee shop and piano bar, protected parking. Courtesy morning coffee and afternoon iced tea. Somewhat comparable to the Istmania, but larger.

HUMUYA INN, *Tel 239-8962, 239-2206, 235-7275, 235-7276, Fax 239-5099, humuyain@david.intertel.hn. $75 single/$85 dbl/single suite $85/dbl suite $95.*

Humuya Inn is a nine guest room and five efficiency apartment establishment located in Colonia Humuya. All guest rooms include air conditioning, direct dial telephones, cable TV, and individually decorated rooms. Breakfast is included and served on the patio overlooking the garden and fountain. The nnn is decorated in colonial style. Owned and managed by American Scott Crook, an excellent host. Five minutes from the airport. Highly recommended for the quality of service and personalized attention to guests needs. Considered by many to be the finest B&B in Tegucigalpa. Two thumbs up!

Budget Hotels

HOTEL GRANADA I, II, III, *Avenida Gutemburg 1326, Granada I Tel, 237-2381, Granada II Tel. 237-4004, Granada III Tel. 237-0843. 46 rooms. $9 single/$12 double.*

At the eastern end of downtown, this is a good buy with a relatively quiet location. Additional rooms are available in two newer annexes one block away next to Cine Aires-Tauro *(Tel. 220597)*. Hotel Granada (old building) is a favorite of Peace Corps volunteers and backpackers. Helpful front desk staff. This is the most popular hotel in town for budget travelers.

HOTEL MCARTHUR, *8 Calle, 4/5 Avenidas, Tel. 237-5906 or 238-0414, Fax 238-0294. 24 rooms. $36 double.*

The Hotel McArthur is located a block up from the Dolores church in a central location. Clean, comfortable rooms have air conditioning and cable television, and there is a coffee shop and swimming pool on-site. Recommended.

We wouldn't advise that you spend the night at a hotel in Comayagüela if you can avoid it – the streets can be dangerous and solitary at night. Comayagüela is also not centrally located to tourist attractions, restaurants, nightspots, etc. You are better off staying at one of the more centrally located hotels near downtown.

Furnished Rooms
Occasionally you will find furnished rooms at assorted price levels are available for persons on long-term stays. You'll find ads with offerings in *Honduras This Week*. Some of the establishments offering rooms are foreign-owned, include breakfast in the rate, and are located in attractive residential neighborhoods.

Local Spanish newspapers are a good bet for long-term lodging. The Humuya Inn has five lovely efficiency apartments that are rented on a long-term basis. Owner Scott Crook from the US is an excellent host and will set you up like a king. See previous listing for Humuya Inn.

Where to Eat

I can't say that Tegucigalpa has all the gourmet delights of a major capital. There isn't enough of an audience for fine cuisine to be very common. But if you attune yourself to what's available, you won't be disappointed – not at all.

Eating places in Tegucigalpa fall into several broad categories.

Basic restaurants serving the working-class population are most common. Food is simple, and the attraction is more price than quality. For most visitors, local hole-in-the-wall diners are not worth mentioning by name. But feel free to try any that look clean, for a cheap meal of rice and beans and some stewed meat or chicken, along with local color.

It is in the *comedores* that you're most likely to encounter home-style Honduran specialties: *tajadas* (ta-HA-das), deep-fried sliced plantains; *baleadas*, beans in a flour tortilla, distant cousins of the northern Mexican burrito; *mondongo*, beef tripe stew; *nacatamal*, similar to Mexican tamales, corn dough stuffed with pork and rice and raisins and olives and sauce, and steamed in a banana leaf.

Fast food restaurants are the rapidly expanding sector of the industry in Tegucigalpa, serving standardized hamburgers and chicken and pizzas at reasonable prices, along with quick service or self-service. For visitors, these outlets offer something predictable.

Steak and Seafood Houses are what most Hondurans have in mind when they have the money and want to dine out. Seafood can be more expensive than you might expect, as Tegucigalpa is far from the sea, while steaks are a bargain. In either case, you won't be disappointed by the quality of the food.

Hotel restaurants generally serve American-style food, which they call "international cuisine" or *"cocina internacional."* Hotel coffee shops and restaurants have more extended hours than other eating places. Quality, especially for items other than standard steak and seafood, will usually be higher than at independent restaurants. One or two budget-priced items appear on most hotel menus.

There are also a few **ethnic** restaurants, mainly catering to foreign communities and employees of international agencies, and one or two genuine **French** restaurants have operated from time to time.

In general, you can count on spending from $4 to $10 for a full meal at most of the restaurants mentioned below (unless a specific price range is mentioned), not including an alcoholic beverage. A soft drink generally costs about 50 cents, a beer about $1, but a glass of wine or a drink with imported liquor will increase your bill considerably.

Downtown

LA TERRAZA DE DON PEPE, *5 Calle (Avenida Colón), downtown, opposite the "Pequeño Despacho."*

The specialty is charcoal-grilled meats — *"carnes a la parrilla"* — which are as tasty as you'll find in Tegucigalpa. But you'll also come here for the old-time ranch atmosphere. Large, friendly, and relaxed. About $5 for most main courses.

BURGER HUT, *next to the church of La Merced (2 Calle, 8 Avenida).*

This is one of many, many fast-food places. And you can also get the real thing at:

BURGER KING, *has an outlet on the Peatonal mall downtown, as well as a couple of outposts in outlying areas.*

RESTAURANTE Y PIZZERIA NINO, *on Callejón Dolores near 5 Calle.*

This is a small establishment owned by a Honduran-Italian family, with not only an assortment of pizzas, but hearty soups and pastas (the latter at up to $5) and saltimbocca, calamari and other specialties (up to $8).

PIZZA BOOM, *Avenida 6, Calles 6/5.*

A step up from your usual pizzeria, with a fireplace and fountain. About $8 for a family-size pizza. They have a branch on Morazán Blvd. at the Guadalupe church.

PIZZA HUT, *off Plaza Morazán.*

The real thing, always packed full of people, which you can take as a real recommendation. The speed of service leaves other eateries in Tegucigalpa in the dust. The food is attractive. Aside from regular and pan pizza in assorted varieties, including vegetarian, there are sandwiches, lasagna, spaghetti, and salad. The most expensive item, the giant super-supreme combination pizza, is just over $10. They have other branches around town.

MEDITERRÁNEO, *Adjacent to Pizza Boom near Plaza Dolores.*
Inexpensive Honduran home cooking with a Greek touch, provided by the owner.
CAFÉ EL PARADÍSO, *now in a new location two blocks from the Hotel Granada.*
This is where ideas are hatched and debated over coffee in a variety of guises, and sandwiches, croissants and cakes, at a dollar or so per item. In keeping with the atmosphere, books and paintings are on display and sale as well.
CAFÉ MARBELLA, *located a half-block from the downtown peatonal-walking street.*
Usually crowded with businessmen and journalists sipping coffee.
SALMANS BAKERIES, *all over the city.*
Salmans offers great fresh baked baguettes (the best in Honduras), pastries, sandwiches, and pizza.

Boulevard Morazán

For fast food, head to **Boulevard Morazán**, the strip that runs east from downtown Tegucigalpa. Follow 3 Calle onto Avenida República de Chile, past the Hotel Honduras Maya, then turn left (east) onto Morazán. There must be about 30 outlets on this street, modern and clean-looking, with names familiar and almost familiar.

For good Honduran fare, try **El Patio**, on Blvd. Morazán, famous for its Honduran country atmosphere and huge portions of grilled meats. Another good Honduran restaurant, also on Blvd. Morazán, is **La Hacienda**, *Tel. 236-8686, Fax 236-6296.* Come here for steak and seafood; they regularly serve crab, either in garlic or sautéed, as well as jalapeño shrimp and standard kebabs and steaks cooked over the coals. A children's menu is available. About $6 for main courses, $3 for sandwiches. There's a piano bar, Monday Night Football on a giant screen, 2-for-1 happy hour Sunday through Wednesday, live music Tuesday through Saturday.

Salsa serves light meals of Tex-Mex food: tacos, burritos and quesadillas, with soft drinks and pie for dessert. .. and rhythm. **Taco Loco** has similar items. For real Mexican cuisine, go to **Restaurant Guadalajara**. *All three places are located on Blvd. Morazán.*

For Chinese food, you can head to the same area for a choice of eateries. Example: The **China Town Palace** has the usual extended Cantonese menu, with some Szechuan items, including shark-fin soup, shrimp with bamboo shoots, hot spicy chicken, and assorted combinations. About $7, more for shellfish or one of the house specialties.

Jack's Steak House, on Morazán at Las Lomas shopping center, is a branch of the long-established restaurant of the same name in San Pedro Sula, and has submarine sandwiches and a salad bar.

El Arriero, *h*alf a block south of the Hotel Honduras Maya on Av. República de Chile at no. 516, specializes in steaks and seafood grilled in Uruguayan fashion, as does **El Novillero**, on the same street. Figure at least $10 for a full meal at any steak house – a bargain for what you get.

Right in the Hotel Honduras Maya, you'll find the relatively formal **La Veranda** restaurant, where the cuisine is reliable, and, though high-priced for Honduras, not at all a bad value for what you get. Specialties include steak Diane, duck á l'orange and paella for $10 and up, and there are also snapper in parchment and surf 'n turf plates for less. A top-notch hotel restaurant like this one is used to serving less than full-course meals, so if you're on a budget, have no qualms about trying a chicken-and-goat-cheese salad for just $4, or a pastry and coffee for a couple of dollars, with shelter from the hustle and bustle of the streets at no charge.

Higher on the price scale, **Alondra**, on República de Chile, opposite the Honduras Maya, *Tel. 2315909*, serves a continental menu, and caters to groups. Expect a tab of $20 or more, with a drink.

El Bistro, Sendero San Juan (off Av. República de Chile one block below the Hotel Honduras Maya), is a French-operated establishment with light European bistro fare that includes salads, quiche, and ratatouille at lunch, and chicken cordon bleu and fondue bourgignonne in the evening, served in large portions. For a good restaurant, the prices are reasonable, at about $6 for lunch, $7 for a main course at dinner. The tab will rise considerably if you order wine.

Also serving French food is **Café du Monde**, near the Hotel Plaza San Martín and the Honduras Maya, on Avenida Juan Lindo.

Panoramic Dining Views

For a meal with a panorama, ask for the road (or take a taxi) to **El Hatillo**, above the city to the north, where **La Cumbre**, located 7.5 km on the road to El Hatillo, *E-mail: invercum@david.intertel.hn,* serves German and Honduran food and drinks. Considered by many to be one of the finest restaurants in Honduras. Closed Mondays.

Seeing the Sights

Downtown

Central Tegucigalpa, still somewhat colonial-flavored, is small enough that you can get a sense of the city during a walk of just a few hours. There are some fine old examples of colonial and nineteenth century architecture, city squares in which to linger, and pedestrian streets for shopping and observing the flow of city life.

A good place to start your excursion is the main square, or **Parque Central**, also known, more formally, as **Plaza Morazán**. On the east side of the square is the twin-towered **Cathedral of Tegucigalpa** (or Cathedral of San Miguel), the construction of which was started in the middle of the eighteenth century. The facade of the cathedral is noted for its inset, or engaged, columns with horizontal grooves — "accordion-fold" or "cushioned" or "pleated" columns — and pillars in the form of mermaids. While the Cathedral is similar in many respects to others of the period in Central America, the pleated columns are a peculiarly Honduran characteristic that occurs here, and on some of the churches in Comayagua. Inside, the Cathedral is decorated with an elaborate pulpit, altarpieces, decorative and functional pieces plated in gold and silver, and paintings of saints, some of which pre-date the building. Part of the collection constitutes a museum of colonial religious art, open weekday afternoons from 2:30pm to 6pm, and on Sundays from 10:30 am to 12:30pm.

South of the Cathedral, across 3 Calle, is the **Palacio del Distrito Central**, which houses the municipal government of Tegucigalpa and Comayagüela. On this site stood the old *cabildo*, or town hall, where the Declaration of Independence of Central America was ratified on September 28, 1821.

4 Calle (or Avenida Paz Baraona by its old name), along the north side of the Central Park, is a *peatonal*, or pedestrianstreet. The peatonal is a great place to stroll and soak up the daily life of the *capitalinos* (as Tegucigalpa redisents are known). To the west, it constitutes the main commercial area of Tegucigalpa, lined by all kinds of shops and eateries, as well as the principal banks of the country, and several hotels. Nearby is the **Villa Roy Museum** on Barrio Buenos Aries, open 8:30am to 3:30pm Wednesday to Sunday, with displays on ethnography, pre-Hispanic history, natural science, and archaeology.

At 5 Avenida, another branch of the mall runs northward, to the twin-towered **Iglesia Los Dolores** (Dolores Church), containing, as does the Cathedral (which it predates by about twenty years, to 1732, though it wasn't completed until 1815), gold-plated altars. The pilasters on the facade are decorated with rosettes, and windows are finished with busts of angels on top and depictions of fruits underneath — altogether, with its unique ceramic decoration and balustrade, this is a more elaborate treatment than on other temples in the city. It is said that the construction of the church was financed by former slaves who made a fortune in mining.

Farther west, across 3 Avenida and then south down a side street, is **Teatro Manuel Bonilla** (Manuel Bonilla Theater). Every Central American capital has one grand, significant performance area, and this is Tegucigalpa's, completed in 1912. The facade is neoclassical, while inside, there is an ornate double horseshoe tier of seating above the main floor, a copy of a contemporary theater in Paris.

Continuing to the west, then one block north along 2 Avenida, you'll come to **El Calvario Church**, dating from 1746.

Farther afield, on the edge of downtown, four blocks north along 2 Avenida, is **Parque La Concordia (Concordia Park)**, a block-sized square that contains small-scale replicas of Altar Q and Stela C of Copán, as well as a model of a temple at Chichén Itzén in Mexico. This is meant to be a small botanical garden as well, with assorted non-Maya statuary, pools, and plantings. Couples frequent the Bridge of Sighs and hold hands alongside the Lake of Love.

Back toward the center of downtown, along 5 Calle, at 6 Avenida, you'll encounter the **National Library and Archives**.

Walking back to the Central Park, then south along 7 Avenida (Calle Bolívar), you'll come to a small square called **Parque Merced**, after the **Iglesia La Merced** (Merced Church) on its east side. This church dates from the seventeenth century, and includes some colonial paintings and an elaborate altar. On the plaza you'll find the **Galeria Nacional de Arte**, open 10am–5pm Tuesday through Saturday, and 10am–2pm on Sundays. The museum has exhibitions of rock art, pre-Columbian cermaics, colonial paintings, religious art and 20th century Honduran painters.

Also on the park is the greenish building that once housed the National University, now removed to a suburban site on Boulevard Suyapa. The university was founded in 1847 as the Academia Literaria by José Trinidad Reyes, and for some years was located in Comayagüela. Farther south is the **Palacio Legislativo**, or **Congreso Nacional** (Legislative Palace, or National Congress), a campus sort of building that dates from 1955, and is quite peculiar among the older and more elaborate governmental edifices in the city.

Walking down toward the river, you'll see the **Puente Mallol** (Mallol Bridge), the oldest bridge in the city. Construction was started in 1818. Back up along 6 Avenida, you'll reach the well-guarded, fortress-like former **Casa Presidencial** (Presidential Palace), at the corner of 1 Calle, completed in 1919. The massive, light-pink, wedding-cake Moorish-Italian architecture, with a dome at one end, ogive arches, and keyhole openings, overwhelmingly defensive, says much about the turnovers of government through the years. Air conditioners, rarely used, jut out incongruously. There's an interior courtyard, but for now, it's not open to casual visitors. It was near this site that the first silver discoveries were made in Honduras.

The executive offices have been moved to the Civic Center in suburban Miraflores; the old palace has been renovated and meticulously restored to its former grandeur for the **Museo de la República** (Museum of the Republic). Highlights here include portraits of former presidents. Open 8:30am–4:30pm Monday through Saturday.

Back at the Parque Central, go east along 4 Calle to 10 Avenida to reach the **Church of San Francisco**. This is the oldest of the churches that remain in Tegucigalpa, started in 1592 (by Franciscans, of course), and greatly altered starting in 1740, when Mudéjar elements characteristic of southern Spain were added to the original simple structure. Inside are gold-plated altarpieces and colonial paintings. Next door is the building that formerly housed the San Francisco monastery.

Other museums in this area include the **Museo del Hombre**, Ave. Cervantes, at the site of the old Supreme Court building; the **Museo Historico Militar**, in Parque Valle; and **Sala Bancatlan**, Blvd. Miraflores, which is a private gallery of contemporary Honduran art and pre-Hispanic artifacts.

Comayagüela

In Comayagüela, southwest of downtown Tegucigalpa, you'll find few high-rise buildings, only numerous bus stations, a few cheap hotels, and assorted other nondescript concrete commercial and residential structures, along with several sights that are not as historically interesting as those in Tegucigalpa proper, but every bit as rewarding for visitors who are interested in the way the broad class of Hondurans lives.

Comayagüela is a working-class area. Small businesses of every sort flourish, and if you need a piece of galvanized steel cut and hammered to a certain shape, or shoes made to measure, or a sack of feed, chances are you can find just the right merchant or craftsman here.

The heart of commercial Comayagüela is the **Mercado San Isidro (San Isidro Market)**, the largest in the city. Here you can find everything, and you can bargain for anything. Yet it's not a frenzied place at all, in fact, it's very calm, and not dangerous (though, as in any market, you should keep valuables out of sight, and money in a hidden pocket).

If you don't find what you're looking for at the San Isidro Market, try the **Artesanías (Handicraft) Market**, held on weekends adjacent to **Parque El Soldado (Soldier Park)** at 4 Avenida and 15 Calle, toward the south end of Comayagüela. Aside from the goods, the park itself is pleasant, with caged birds, and luxuriant vegetation. Soldado Park commemorates those who died in the 1969 war with El Salvador. Just north is the **Obelisco (Obelisk)**, which was erected to commemorate 100 years of independence. Adjacent is the headquarters of the Honduran Armed Forces, with the requisite fatigue clad soldiers stationed out front.

Also in Comayagüela, on 6 Calle, between 2 and 3 Avenidas, is the **Escuela Nacional de Bellas Artes (National School of Fine Arts)**, some walls of which are painted with frescoes illustrating Mayan themes.

Southeast of Downtown

East of Comayagüela, and south of downtown Tegucigalpa, the hill called Juana Laínez juts up alongside the road from the airport. At the top is the **Monumento de la Paz (Peace Monument)**. A walk or taxi ride up to the top will give you a panorama of Tegucigalpa and the surrounding hills. The monument itself is a double-vision image of a flying saucer and complementary rings, set on concrete pillars. I'm not sure of the imagery, but it certainly isn't warlike.

At the foot of the hill is the **National Stadium**. A large fruit and flower market operates here on Friday and up to noon on Saturday.

North of Downtown

North of downtown is the peak called **El Picacho** (1310 meters), one of several mountains surrounding the city. Picacho is included in **Parque Naciones Unidas** (United Nations Park). First of all, before you go to Picacho, ask at your hotel about current conditions — a fire recently did severe damage to the vegetation on the hill, and regrowth is under way. Also, take a sweater.

Tegucigalpas' newest monument is the **Cristo del Picacho**. Inaugurated in 1998, it resembles the Christ that rises above Rio in Brazil.

There are several ways to get here. From downtown, you can walk due north, following 9 Avenida. Once you cross 6 Calle, the streets — many of them cobbled — become more winding and narrow. You pass through the neighborhood called La Leona, where some of the large, old houses have been restored to their past glory. The streets give way to paths, and with some help from passersby, and an eye toward the summit, you should be able to make it to the top. Or, you can go up in a taxi for about $5 round trip, including a wait of a half-hour.

The main reward of a visit to Picacho is the view to the whole valley spread out before you. You get a good orientation to the city. And by looking around, you'll understand why it was that your plane made a couple of sharp turns before touching down at Toncontín Airport, which is on a small plateau, one of the few flat pieces of land in this valley.

You'll also find a small zoo, in decrepit state with the animals badly cared for, and some reproductions of Mayan ruins, including pyramids. In the absence of regular maintenance, the park has become something of a ruin itself. There are also outdoor grills, in case you want to cook your lunch. The area is crowded on Sundays.

Also north of downtown, the **Instituto Hondureño de Antropología e Historia** (Honduran Institute of Anthropology and History) has a museum housed in a mansion, Villa Roy, built in 1936 by President Julio Lozano, and given to the state by his widow in 1981. It's really all quite limited. Part of the building is conserved as a monument to itself, and to the ex-president and his first lady.

Other exhibits illustrate the lives of the Jicaques, Lencas, Chortís, Miskitos and Sumos, native peoples whose ancestors occupied the land before the Spanish arrived. And there are exhibits of fossils and colonial life. In any case, it's a quiet place with nice gardens, and good views of the city. Closed Monday and Tuesday, open from 8 am to 3:30 pm other days, small admission charge.

Take a taxi, or ask for directions from your hotel if you're walking. It's on Calle Morelo, off 3 Avenida, seven blocks north of the post office downtown. You can stop here on the way to United Nations Park.

Nightlife & Entertainment

Bars

You're in the wrong town if you're looking for exciting nighttime entertainment, but there are several places where you can enjoy a quiet drink without hassle.

There are two main areas for nightlfife. First is Blvd. Morazán, where you'll find some of the city's best restaurants and bars. The second is the Blvd. Juan Pablo II, where you'll find an array of lively and noisy discos and bars.

Within the **Hotel Honduras Maya**, the bars serve snacks with drinks, and if you go at around 5:30 in the evening, you'll find the offerings fairly substantial.

Downtown, the **O'Henry Bar** of the Hotel Plaza, 4 Avenida at 4 Calle, has a happy hour from 6 to 7 pm daily except Sunday. Music often plays, and snacks are served with the drinks.

Tobacco Road Tavern, 1120 Av. Barahona La Plazuela, *Tel. 237-3909 (tobaccoroad@optinet.hn),* next to Parqueo Hotel La Ronda, is a fun place. It's a good place to meet people, there's an e-mail café, you can buy cigars, there's a book exchange, they can arrange tours. Happy Hour is 5:30–7, and Tuesday is Ladies Night.

Iguana Rana, Blvd. Morazán, *Tel. 235-7644*, is open 'till 3 am, with snacks, wings, burgers, ribs, fajitas. Pleasant place on the main nightlife strip. This place hops on the weekends.

Popular nightspots include: **Oui**, a combination of of bar, disco and karioki bar, located on Blvd. Juanl Pablo ll; **Rock Castle Pub**, pool tables, disco, popular, on Blvd Juan Pablo ll; **Arenas Sports Cafe**, very popular, located across the street from the National University on Blvd. Suyapa.

Gambling

The two available extremes are lottery tickets, sold for about 50 cents and up by street vendors; and the **Casino Royal** in the Hotel Honduras Maya, with roulette, blackjack, poker, and slot machines. Foreigners only (with passport) are allowed to enter casions in Honduras. Hondurans will be denied entry.

Movies

Look for advertisements for movies in the daily papers, and in *Honduras This Week*, which lists the original English-language title. Most of the films are from the US, and are shown in English with Spanish subtitles. Ads never give addresses, so ask at your hotel or your taxi driver as to where any cinema is located. Admission costs a bit over $3; all movie theaters charge the same price. You'll find a *simpático* atmosphere in movie houses. Going to the movies is a major form of entertainment in the major cities. Well dressed young couples crowd modern cinemas, especially on weekends.

Late Night Diversions For Men

The following nightclubs feature scantily clad young women dancing up a storm. Many will accompany you to your hotel room, but beware, Honduras has quite an AIDS problem, so you would be better off passing on this type of intercultural exchange. Ask your taxi driver or hotel front desk clerk to find out the hot nightclubs at the moment.

Shopping

What you will find when shopping in Tegucigalpa, and in Honduras in general, is quite limited: leatherwork, wood carving (especially in mahogany, including boxes and statuettes), furniture, hammocks, leather bags, beadwork, silver and gold jewelry, baskets, pottery, and clothing items. And, oh yes, cigars. The wood carvings are the most typical souvenirs of Honduras, and if you have some use for an oversized set of salad servers, well, this is the place to find them.

For the most fun shopping, you should head to the markets. **The Artesanas** (Handicraft) **Market** is held on weekends at Parque El Soldado in Comayagüela. Also in Comayagüela, nearer to downtown, is the **San Isidro market**, where you'll find not only handicrafts, but hundreds of simple utilitarian items that seem to date from a past age.

Aside from the markets, almost every hotel has a souvenir shop, where, of course, you'll pay more for anything. And there are dozens of other stores, among them:

Tienda del Artesano, facing the south side of Valle Park (No. 1001). This shop is operated by ANAH (Asociación Nacional de Artesanos de Honduras), a national guild of craftsmen, and has a selection of everything made by artisans in Honduras. Hours are 9 am to 6 pm during the week, to 4 pm on Saturdays.

Tikamaya, on 3 Calle at 10 Avenida, by Valle Park.

Candü, opposite the Hotel Honduras Maya, on Avenida República de Chile has some interesting paintings, and a stock of maps of Honduras and Tegucigalpa. There are other souvenir shops in the immediate area — this is where the money is in Tegucigalpa.

Mundo Maya, in the Hotel Honduras Maya, and also in Colonia Palmira, also provides travel information.

Honduras Souvenirs, in the Lomas del Boulevard shopping center on Blvd. Morazán, also has an assortment of gift items.

Lesanddra Leather, in the Los Castaños shopping center on Blvd. Morazán, has more finely made leather items than you'll find in handicraft stores or markets.

Mall Multiplaza, Blvd. San Juan Bosco next to Instituto San Miguel *(www.multiplaza.hn)*, opened in 1998, is Tegucigalpas' first true US style mall, food court and all the fixin's. Open 10am-8pm.

For the best selection of handicrafts in a lovely colonial, mountain village setting, head to the town of **Valle de Angeles** (for more information, see pages 120).

Excursions & Day Trips

Where can you go on day outings from Tegucigalpa? Day trips, either on your own by bus or in a rented car, or on a tour, generally take in:

• **Valle de Angeles**
• **San Antonio de Oriente**
• **La Tigra Rain Forest**
• **El Zamorano**
• **Ojojona**

I'll describe these places in more detail in the following pages. If you'll be heading to the north coast, you can stop on the way at:

• **Zambrano**
• **Comayagua**
• **Lake Yojoa**

You can also go to the above spots on day outings from Tegucigalpa. They're covered in the next chapter of this book. And along the southern highway, on the way to the Gulf of Fonseca, is **Ojojona**.

The major site to visit on mainland Honduras is the archaeological zone of **Copán**. Because of the way the mountain ridges and roads run, most travelers reach Copán overland from San Pedro Sula, in the north of Honduras, or from Guatemala. And of course, you can reach the **Bay Islands** from Tegucigalpa by plane, or by a combination of bus, plane, and/or boat.

In the pages that follow, you'll find the major excursions from Tegucigalpa.

SUYAPA

The religious capital of Honduras for the overwhelmingly Catholic major-ity, **Suyapa** is a suburb of Tegucigalpa, about eight kilometers east of downtown. The attraction for pilgrims is a six-inch statue of Christ, imbued with miraculous powers, which, according to tradition, was discovered in a corn field in 1743, and, no matter how many times it was moved, returned to its original place. The image was credited with the cure of a captain of the grenadiers, who organized the construction of a church in its honor.

The original church that housed the image could not handle the religious traffic, so a new basilica was started, a neat structure with two bell towers, generous vertical fluting, two triangular pediments balancing the arch directly over the door — it all could have been built from blocks or by a skilled baker of birthday cakes.

The faithful arrive at all times of the year, but especially for the **Feast of the Virgin** on February 2, and during the following weeks.

Suyapa rates as an attraction for those with an interest in the religious ways of Honduras, or for those with some extra time. If you go, catch the number 31 bus from the San Isidro market in Comayagüela, or take a taxi for about $3.

SANTA LUCIA & VALLE DE ANGELES

The round trip to these two towns will take a half-day in a car, by taxi, or on a tour, or a full day by bus if you go to both places. The bus leaves from near San Felipe Hospital, about two kilometers east of downtown on Avenida La Paz, a continuation of 6 Calle, at 7 Avenida. (Take a Lomas bus from Plaza Morazán to Hospital San Felipe; walk one block east, one block south on Av. República Dominicana, then one block east on Calle Bustamente y Rivero, an unpaved street. Departures are about every hour.)

A tour costs about $10 per person, a taxi about $20. The road is paved all the way, and in excellent condition.

Santa Lucía

Santa Lucía, at an altitude of 5,000 feet set in lovely pine forest, is 17 kilometers from Tegucigalpa on a 2.5-kilometer spur from the main road, a small, picturesque village, its main street paved with cobblestones. Santa Lucía was once an important mining center, early in the colonial period, but as the mines were worked out, it became a backwater. In the area of Santa Lucía, flowers are grown for sale in Tegucigalpa.

There's a colonial church, with old paintings and a statue of a black Christ that is said to have been a gift of King Philip II, sculptured in Spain more than 400 years ago. A shop sells handicrafts, and there are pleasing views of tile-roof houses and hills and patches of corn all around. There is pleasant walking in pine-covered hills with lovely views of the sprawling metropolis of Tegucigalpa below.

If you want to stay overnight, try the **Hummingbird Haven B&B**, P.O. Box 1293, Tegucigalpa, *Tel/Fax 221-0071*, $53/double. Susan Tompkins is your friendly proprietor. When you get hungry, wander over to **Parillada Miluska**, *Tel. 237-0472*, for Czech and German cuisine and pastries in a nice garden setting.

Valle de Angeles & Vicinity

Eleven kilometers onward, **Valle de Angeles** is a larger colonial-style town of whitewashed, lime-plastered adobe houses with red tile roofs, massive wooden lintels, and porches with roofs supported by rough wooden posts. Valle de Angeles is cooler than Tegucigalpa (bring a sweater), and is a quiet, clean and friendly town.

Valle de Angeles is without question the best place in the country to buy Honduran crafts. An excellent selection of crafts from all over Honduras is available at good prices.

There are restaurants on the main street and central plaza, and assorted boutiques selling the leather, wood and ceramic articles for which the town is known. You might be able to visit the school where some of these crafts are taught. **Lessandra Leather** is one of several shops with luggage and purses made for the tourist trade, located in front of CDI Center, Valle de Angeles, *Tel. 231-1295, Fax 232-8625.* The store also has a Tegucigalpa location, on the second floor of the Los Castaños Shopping Center on Blvd. Morazán.

La Casa del Chocolate is a tea room where you can buy home-made cookies for consumption with hot chocolate.

More formal is **Posada del Angel**, a comfortable inn where you can take a break from walking around the village. Rooms are available for under $15 double, *Tel. 362-233.* Another nice inn is **Tres Pinos B&B**, Valle de Angeles, *rubio@david.intertel.hn*, 200 meters outside of town on the road to San Juancito.

The **Restaurante Turístico Valle de Angeles**, *Tel. 762-148,* set in the pines on a hill above town, serves Honduran home-style cooking — grilled meats, fried plantains, beans, enchiladas, mountains of tortillas — which is difficult to find outside of private homes, at a tab of up to $6. Open from 10 am to 6 pm, closed Monday.

And there are other establishments offering inexpensive country cooking, as well as a branch of the **Don Quijote** Spanish restaurant.

About two kilometers before you get to Valle de Angeles is **El Obrero** park, a piney area outfitted for day use with charcoal grills and a pool. It's well maintained, and if you negotiate with the guard, and perhaps provide a tip, you can also camp out. There's a small entry fee. Also near the park entrance is an American Adventist hospital.

San Juancito, north of Valle de Angeles, was once an important gold and silver mining center, and is now a quaint backwater of faded wooden houses once brightly painted, many roofed in shingles made of recycled tin fashioned from scrap metal — all quite a contrast to the whitewashed adobe houses with red baked-clay tiles of other mountain villages. San Juancito declined in importance soon after Honduran independence, but its fortunes revived when an American company took over the **El Rosario** mine and others nearby, just over a hundred years ago, and operated them into the fifties. The remains of the El Rosario mine, about two kilometers from the village, are littered with old mining equipment.

LA TIGRA NATIONAL PARK

Above San Juancito, **La Tigra** is a cloud-forest peak where the wonderland of vegetation that once covered much of the high part of Honduras still survives in parts and is regenerating in others. Covering 238 square kilometers, La Tigra National Park protects a watershed that supplies almost half of Tegucigalpa's water. Seventy-five square kilometers are an absolute reserve, the remainder a buffer zone.

Arrivals & Departures

A bus to San Juancito and La Tigra leaves the San Pablo market in Tegucigalpa daily at 10 am Take the Colonia 21 bus from the main square to reach the market. From San Juancito, it takes about an hour at a slow pace on an ascending trail to reach the administrative office of the park, in a former mining camp, where basic lodging is available. Without reservations (by telegram to Parque Nacional, Campamento Rosario, San Juancito), it's best to come during the week with a sleeping bag. Arrangements can also be made to sleep in private houses.

A second route to La Tigra is north from Tegucigalpa by the El Picacho road through El Hatillo to Jutiapa, where there is another visitors' center.

Seeing the Park

Elevations in the protected area are as high as 2290 meters. As many as half of the plant species present in La Tigra are considered rare in other parts of Honduras.

La Tigra's botanical bounty is due to its location near the continental divide, and the prevailing winds that bring rain through much of the year. Broad-leafed plants, vines, mosses, bromeliads and orchids and ferns live not just on the ground, but on the trunks and branches of trees, taking up water from the air and from the ground, sending out huge leaves to take advantage of what light filters through the canopy, and roots to absorb nutrients from decaying plant matter. In parts of the park below 1800 meters, there are also pines more typical of lowland Honduras.

Birds make their nests in the trees and are attracted to the flowers that are always in bloom; the quetzal, iridescent red-and-green with an arc of tail feathers several feet long, is regularly seen, along with the goldfinch and green toucan. Animals that inhabit the park include tapirs, jaguars, ocelots, monkeys and mountain lions, many of them only at the highest and least accessible elevations.

The integrity of all this bounty is threatened by the encroachment of farming. "Park" does not indicate a pristine and inviolable area of nature in

Honduras; more than 10,000 persons live within La Tigra's boundaries, cultivating corn, beans and coffee, some of it within the central zone. Much of the park consists of recovering forest — the original forest was largely leveled to supply the fuel and construction needs of the New York and Honduras Rosario Mining Company. The company even tunneled through La Tigra mountain to reach untouched forests on the western slope. Rusting mining equipment is still scattered through the park.

A network of trails is planned for La Tigra. For now, facilities for visitors are quite limited. If you go to hike, wear sturdy shoes, and take along some food. Only the most basic accommodations are available at San Juancito, or you can return to Valle de Angeles or Tegucigalpa.

Bring along a sweater — it's windy and relatively cool at La Tigra. Hiking shoes are useful, though any comfortable old shoes will do. Make sure you stay on the trails. Not all are well-marked, so if you lose your way, re-trace your steps until you find trail markings again.

If you want to stay overnight, your closest choice is **La Estancia Mountain Hotel**, 14 km from Tegucigalpa near La Tigra Park, *Tel. 211-8651, 2118653.*

Management of the park has been in the hands of a private foundation, **Amigos de La Tigra**, a non-profit ecological foundation, since 1992. For more information, contact AMITIGRA, *Tel. 232-6771, 232-5503.*

SAN ANTONIO DE ORIENTE & EL ZAMORANO

San Antonio de Oriente is yet another old mining town, founded around 1660, and often depicted by José Antonio Velázquez, once the town barber and mayor, and a primitive artist of world renown. Velázquez painted in great detail the town's white, twin-towered church, and sometimes included San Antonio's personalities and animal denizens.

A few kilometers past the turnoff for San Antonio de Oriente, on the highway toward Danlí, is **El Zamorano**, where the **Pan American Agricultural School** is located. The extensive installations and experimental plantings are worth a visit if you're interested in farming, or in seeing spectacular landscaping with effusive displays of tropical flowers. The main buildings are constructed in colonial style of locally quarried stone, with beams of cedar and pine. The farm covers about 5000 hectares.

The Pan American Agricultural School was opened in 1942 under the directorship of Wilson Popenoe, sponsored by the much-maligned but sometimes beneficent United Fruit Company. Teachers have included famed naturalist and essayist Archie Carr. The school attracts student farmers from all over Latin America. Arrangements can be made to stay on the premises. The school operates a store in Zamorano, where its cheeses, preserves and fresh vegetables are sold.

Uyuca Biological Reserve, on the grounds of the school, covers a couple of square miles or watershed for nearby communities.

El Zamorano is 40 kilometers from Tegucigalpa, five kilometers down a side road, at a pleasant altitude of 700 meters. The dramatic drive out takes you through a pass at 1550 meters, with surrounding, higher mountains.

OJOJONA

Ojojona is yet another picturesque hill town with cobbled streets, white houses with red-tiled roofs, and colonial churches — three of them, in fact, with paintings that date from before independence. Ojojona is also known for its pottery, especially water jugs made in the shape of roosters. Other local craft specialties are woodcrafting and leatherwork.

Ojojona sits on a small plateau among mountains. The name of the town means "greenish water" in Nahuatl, the language of the Mexican Indians who accompanied the Spanish conquerors. The original town, now called **Pueblo Viejo**, stood three kilometers from the present site.

Ojojona is located 30 kilometers from Tegucigalpa, on a spur (at kilometer 24) from the main highway for the coast. Buses for Ojojona leave from 4 Calle, 8/9 Avenidas, Comayagüela, about every hour. There is an inexpensive pension in town with clean rooms, the **Posada Joxone**,which also serves meals.

Santa Ana, a nearby village, has a couple of colonial churches. **Lepaterique**, (**Tiger Mountain**) to the west, is also picturesque. The **Montaña Yerba Buena Biological Reserve**, just north of the town, has swimming pools.

Practical Information
Banks

Street money changers can be found in Tegucigalpa, but in case you don't notice them, the best place to look is in front of the Hotel Plaza on the Peatonal mall downtown.

All major banks are downtown.

Contact **Credomatic** for Visa and Mastercard advances, Blvd Morazon Edificio Interamericana, 1st floor, *www.bancocredomatic.com*.

Books, Newspapers, & Magazines

English-language books, magazines, videos, music and CD-Roms are sold at **Metromedia**, Edificio Casa Real Ave. San Carlos, Colonia San Carlos, *Tel/ Fax 221-0770*. Their selection is the best in the entire country. You can also trade used books here. This is a new location, with an expanded selection of books and vidoes, and a cafe.

A smaller selection of English-languate books is available in the **D.T.P. Bookstore** (which stocks mostly Spanish-language material), Miramonte shopping center, *Tel. 239-1081.*

A newspaper and book outlet on the lower shopping level of the Hotel Honduras Maya carries the *Miami Herald, USA Today, Time,* and *Newsweek.* There are also stands at the **Hotel Plaza San Martín**, and, less well stocked, at the Hotel Alameda and at the airport.

Honduras This Week is an excellent English-language newspaper published weekly, distributed free at major hotels and sold at some newsstands. Coverage is mainly of local, regional and international political developments, and the movie schedules, and advertisements for hotels, rentals, restaurants and travel services, will interest many visitors. To subscribe (for $48 annually in the United States), write to: Apartado Postal 1312, Tegucigalpa, D.C., Honduras, *Tel. 232-8818, 232-0832, Fax 232-2300, www.marrder.com/htw/* – or you can e-mail them at *hontweek@hondutel.hn.*

Churches

Catholic and **evangelical** churches with services in Spanish are everywhere in Tegucigalpa, of course. A mass in English is celebrated on Sundays at 11 am at the Instituto San Francisco, Barrio Country Club, *Tel. 327-498.* The **Jewish community** gathers on Friday evenings at 7 pm *at the Hotel Alameda.*

For services and other spiritual attention in English, you might try:
• **Central Baptist**, Colonia Soto, 8 Avenida, 2 Calle, *Tel. 2378615.*
• **Church of Christ**, Barrio Guanacaste, one kilometer below U.S. embassy (by the basketball court), *Tel. 237-6180.* Sunday service in English.
• **Latter-Day Saints** (Mormon), Avenida Juan Lindo, Colonia Palmira, *Tel. 232-3521.*
• **Episcopal Church**, Colonia Florencia, *Tel. 232-0353.*
• **Union Church**, Lomas del Guijarro, *Tel. 232-3386.*

Consulates & Embassies

Call first before visiting an embassy or consulate, in order to obtain office hours, and to get directions. Among the representatives of foreign nations are:
• **Belize**, Colonia 15 de Septiembre No. 1703, Comayagüela, *Tel. 2323191*
• **Canada** (consulate only), Los Castaños building, 6th floor, Boulevard Morazán, *Tel. 231-4545*
• **Costa Rica**, Colonia El Triángulo, *Tel. 232-1768*
• **El Salvador**, Colonia Ruben Dario
• **France**, Avenida Juan Lindo, 3 Calle, Colonia Palmira, *Tel. 236-6800*
• **Germany**, Paysen building, Blvd. Morazán, *Tel. 232-3161*
• **Guatemala**, Colonia Las Minitas, 4 Calle No. 2421, *Tel. 232-1580* (Consulate, Colonia Palmira, Avenida Juan Lindo, *Tel. 232-5018*)
• **Italy**, Colonia Reforma, Avenida Principal No. 2602, *Tel. 236-6391*
• **Japan**, Colonia San Carlos, Entre 4 y 5 calle, *Tel. 236-6825*

• **Mexico**, Colonia Palmira, Calle del Brasil, *Tel. 232-6471*
• **Netherlands** (consulate), Colonia Lomas del Mayab, Calle Copán, *Tel. 231-5007*
• **Nicaragua**, Colonia Tepeyac, *Tel. 232-6471*
• **Panama**, Palmira building, Colonia Palmira, *Tel. 231-5441*
• **Sweden**, Colonia Miraflores, Avenida Principal No. 2758, *Tel. 232-5935*
• **Switzerland**, Colonia Alameda, 4 Avenida, 7 Calle No. 1811, *Tel. 232-9692.*
• **U.S.**, Avenida La Paz. *Tel. 323-120 to 9*
• **United Kingdom**, Palmira building (near Hotel Honduras Maya), *Tel. 232-3161*

Laundry
There's a coin-operated (or more exactly token-operated) laundry near downtown. **Mi Lavandería** *(Tel. 237-6573)* is in Comayagüela on 2 Avenida (Calle Real) between 3 and 4 Calle, opposite the Repostería Calle Real (a sweet shop). They're open every day, including Sundays, and they'll also do your laundry and dry cleaning on a drop-off basis. There are other establishments scattered through Tegucigalpa that will do your laundry at a piece rate if you want to save a few dollars over your hotel's charges.

Maps
The most easily available map is the *Mapa Guía Turístico,* sold at many hotel newsstands in combination with a succinct Spanish-language country guide. Basic maps are available at the **Tourist Office** (see "Tourist Office" section earlier in this chapter).

For anything more detailed, you'll have to go to the **Instituto Geográfico Nacional**, Barrio La Bolsa, in the SECOPT office, *Tel. 337-432.* They have the most up-to-date tourist maps of Honduras and Tegucigalpa, available for a couple of dollars each after official processing of your request; sectional topographical maps of the country on a scale of 1:50,000; geological maps; and regional maps. But it is better to bring your own maps from the US, as you will waste lots and lots of time and may come away empty handed.

Some of these will be useful if you plan on doing any extensive bicycling or hiking. And you can look at an excellent detailed topographical map of Tegucigalpa for exactly five minutes — unless you have special permission from the high command of the army.

Post Office
The **central post office** is on the pedestrian mall (Calle 4, Peatonal) at 4 Avenida, opposite the Hotel Plaza. Hours are from 8am to 8pm.

The service is reliable, at least for letters mailed from this location. But remember: this is the only post office in the entire city!

Telephones

You can make international telephone calls, with persistence, from **Hondutel**, 5 Calle at 4 Avenida. The lines are long, and once you get to the front and order your call, you have no idea if you'll get through. A far better way is to call from your hotel, if it offers long distance service, even at a surcharge; or from a private phone, if you can get your hands on one.

International direct dialing is available from all phones, all over the country. Rates are high. If you're calling the States, the cheapest and easiest way is to dial 8000123 for **AT&T's USA Direct** service. Using USA Direct, you may call collect or charge to your phone card. They have English speaking operators and superfast connections.

From a pay phone, drop in a coin before dialing. There are dedicated USA Direct phones at the Hondutel office.

Emergency & Service Phone Numbers
- **191**– Long distance in Honduras
- **192**– Telephone number information
- **196** –Time of Day
- **197**– International long distance
- **198**– Fire
- **199**– Public security (police)

Water

Officially, the U.S. embassy says the water is *not* safe to drink from the tap. Drink bottled beverages and soda water. In any case, water is a scarce commodity in Tegucigalpa, and if you're not staying in one of the better hotels (which have pumps and storage tanks), you could well find nothing more than a dribble when you turn on the tap.

Weather

In terms of temperature, Tegucigalpa, like much of Honduras, has just one season, a sort of moderately warm summer. Average daily high ranges from a maximum of 86°Fahrenheit (30°Centigrade) in April to 77°F (25°C) in December and January. Average low temperature runs from a maximum of 6°F (18°C) in June to a minimum of 57°F (14°C) in January and February.

Rainfall, however, can run to extremes. The dry season in Tegucigalpa lasts from November through April. Average rainfall in November is just an inch and a half (38 mm), and drops to a trace by March. On most days in the dry times, there's hardly a cloud in the sky. Rain picks up quickly in May — May and June have the heaviest annual rainfall, 7.1 and 7.0 inches (180 and 177 mm) respectively. July and August see a drop to 2.8 inches (70 mm), then rainfall increases somewhat in September and October before tapering off again.

Even in the rainy season, however, Tegucigalpa is not a hard place to take: usually, fewer than half the days in any given month have any noticeable rainfall.

During the months of low rainfall in Tegucigalpa, especially past February, everything is dry — the air, the yellowed grass, the dust that blows up constantly from unwatered and unpaved streets on the frequent gusts of wind. The breeze can make the temperature feel cooler than it really is. But a light sweater is as much as you'll need to keep warm. The higher elevations nearby will require a bit more covering.

t o t h e n o r t h

Chapter 12

North from Tegucigalpa is the heartland of Honduras, the connecting rift valleys between the Caribbean and the Pacific that first attracted Spanish settlers, where Honduran culture was forged as invaders and natives met and contested and finally merged, where even today the population of Honduras is concentrated. But this was a well-developed area even before the Conquest. A culture known as the **Yarumela** flourished near Comayagua more than 1500 years before Christ. Marble pieces decorated with human faces have been found from a culture called the **Ulúa**, which existed after the fall of Mayan civilization.

For all its importance to the country, it is a measure of the underdevelopment of Honduras that much of this route was, until recently, off the beaten track. Only a dirt track, interrupted by a ferry over **Lake Yojoa**, connected the two major cities of Honduras for most of the last hundred years, and only in the last twenty years has it been possible to drive this route on a paved highway. Elsewhere in Central America, the lack of roads was compensated by railroads, but in Honduras, there was nothing.

For the visitor, there is much majestic countryside to be seen during a journey along the major highway, along with **Comayagua**, the old capital where colonial churches still stand; small and little-visited towns where old ways and a slow pace of life still hold sway; and Lake Yojoa, as pleasant a stopping point and vacation area as will be found on the mainland. At the end of the route is **San Pedro Sula**, the metropolis of the north, and of modern Honduras, and beyond are the coastal cities, beaches, and the special world of the **Bay Islands**.

From Tegucigalpa

The northern highway climbs and winds for about ten kilometers out of the capital, affording pleasant views of Tegucigalpa, with its valleys and hills, and of the surrounding peaks. At kilometer 18, the road begins a descent, down to and into a long valley.

The stretch of highway from Tegucigalpa to San Pedro Sula is in excellent shape. The four hour drive affords magnificent scenic views of the changing landscape. It's a lovely drive.

Balneario San Francisco is a swimming and picnicking area located one kilometer off the northern highway, at kilometer 20. It's nothing special, but if you're meandering through, you can make the detour. There are several warm-springs pools (only one of which is currently in use), picnic areas, a basic restaurant, and soccer fields. Accommodations are available at a small hotel.

By kilometer 23, you're climbing again, into the mountains in which the town of Zambrano is located. At km 35, restaurateur, hotelier, and guidebook writer Jorge Valle-Aguiluz has opened Honduras' finest country hotel: **Caserio Valuz**, 1.5 km from Camino de la Catarata Escondida, near the town of Zambrano, *Tel. 898-6755, E-mail: caseriovaluz@hotmail.com*. Wonderful accommodations, great food, beautiful setting. You can exchange work for room and board. Highly recommended.

Half a kilometer after Zambrano, is **Aurora Park**, a picnicking and camping area in pine forests. There's a small lake, with rowboats for rent, and a little zoo. Simple food is available. There are modest fees to pay for day entry and overnight stays. Beyond, the road descends in a serpentine fashion for 15 kilometers, down into the Comayagua Valley at kilometer 60. Along the way you see many adobe houses, and poor country people selling vegetables. At the lower altitudes are coffee plantations.

At kilometer 75, you pass the **Enrique Soto Cano military base**, also known as **Palmerola**, with its permanently detached Joint Task Force Bravo, part of the U.S. Southern Command. The road is in perfect condition. Comayagua is at kilometer 87.

Comayagua

For more than 300 years, **Comayagua** was the capital of colonial and independent Honduras. But "capital" is a grand term for what was, in fact, just the major settlement and administrative center of a backwater colony of little importance in the imperial scheme, or in the world in general. Tax collectors for the empire and the republic were based here, legislatures of important personages met and made laws, and a stream of presidents succeeded each other. The first priests built primitive churches, and modified them into more permanent structures as the capital and society became more stable, if not exactly wealthy.

It was in 1537 that Santa María de Comayagua was founded by Alonzo de Cáceres, as a strategic base for the Spanish conquerors, midway between the two oceans along the major trading routes of the Indian nations of Honduras. The traditional part of the name, Comayagua, which has endured, probably derived from the Nahuatl *comal*, the clay pan for cooking tortillas, though it could have been a corruption of the Lenca words for "well-watered plain."

The first settlement was short-lived, but the town was re-founded in 1539, after the Indians of the region were conquered and resettled under their new masters. Thereafter, Spanish encampments and headquarters shifted with Indian revolts and campaigns of pacification. For a time, Gracias, in the mountains to the West, was the seat of colonial administration. In 1543 the settlement became Villa de Valladolid de Concepción de Comayagua, when it was named as the seat of the Audiencia de los Confines, the colonial government of the isthmus.

In accordance with standard instructions laid down by King Ferdinand V in 1513, and applied in all Spanish settlements in the New World, a *plaza mayor*, or main square, was laid out, surrounded by the most important structures: the church, the governor's house, the cabildo (town hall), and the Casa Real; with a grid of streets extending outward. The first cathedral of Honduras was inaugurated in 1585. As the town grew, the main square was relocated, and new, larger administrative buildings replaced the rudimentary structures of the early days. The hospital of San Juan de Dios was established in 1590, and was the seat of the inquisition. It was flattened in the earthquake of 1785. A university, the first in Central America, was founded in 1632. A new cathedral was completed in 1715.

But the colonial period was the heyday of Comayagua. After independence, congresses met alternately in Comayagua and Tegucigalpa. The city was burned by the invading army of Guatemala in 1827, and, as Honduras settled into an existence as a satellite of other Central American countries, Comayagua never re-assumed its preeminence.

In 1880, Comayagua received its final deflation. President Marco Aurelio Soto, whose Indian wife was snubbed by the Comayagua's high society, snubbed Comayagua in turn, and moved the government permanently to Tegucigalpa. People moved away too, and Comayagua became just a stopping point on the overland mule trail to the Caribbean coast. And its churches and few governmental buildings, no longer much attended or used, remained fairly unaltered, so that today, parts of the town constitute a museum of nineteenth-century Honduras.

Arrivals & Departures

By Bus

Comayagua is about an hour's drive from Tegucigalpa, or 90 minutes by bus. Most San Pedro Sula buses (from Tegucigalpa) stop along the highway, a kilometer from the town center. To catch a bus to Tegucigalpa or San Pedro Sula, walk or take a taxi to the Texaco station along the highway. One yellow bus shelter is located on each side.

Buses also operate to Villa San Antonio hourly from 9am to 3pm; to San Sebastián at noon and 1pm from near the market. Buses to La Paz leave from the Texaco station about every fifteen minutes. There are slower buses to Tegucigalpa from the center of town.

From Tegucigalpa, catch buses for Comayagua and San Pedro Sula at Empresa El Rey, 6 Avenida and 9 Calle, Comayagüela (departures every hour or more frequently, from before dawn to 10:30pm). Fare is less than $3. Buses are comfortable and uncrowded.

Orientation/Getting Around Town

Comayagua has a population of about 30,000. The altitude of about 300 meters makes it warmer than Tegucigalpa, but it's not a sweltering tropical town.

To reach the market, follow the street that passes in front of the Cathedral, toward the south, past the colonial museum. Local fiesta days are February 2 through 11 in honor of the Virgin of Lourdes, December 8 (Immaculate Conception), and December 12 (Virgin of Guadalupe, especially celebrated by Indians of the surrounding area).

Where to Stay

SANTA MARIA COMAYAGUA, *Tel 772-7872, $50 double.*

The best hotel in town. Rooms have private bath, hot water, cable TV and air conditioning. There's a pool, bar, and the good El Portal eestaurant.

HOTEL QUAN, *Barrio Abajo, Tel. 772-0070, Fax 772-2585; E-mail: hquan@hondutel.hn. 29 rooms. $6 single/$24 double with private bath and fan; $20 double with t.v. and air conditioning. Accepts Visa.*

A more than adequate hotel for the price, especially in the air-conditioned rooms. You'll get hot water, cable TV, cafeteria and laundry service. From the end of the Boulevard, go half a block north.

HOTEL IMPERIAL, *Barrio El Torondón, Tel. 772-0215. 22 rooms. $8 single/$12 double.*

A two-story hotel with a few colonial details on the façade. Simple rooms. Well protected, though the street here is not well lit.

HOTEL NORYMAX, *Tel. 772-1210. $13 double.*

Clean and pleasant, charming balconies. Nice, modest rooms, and quiet. Small handicraft store. Washing machine available. Restaurant for breakfast. A good buy.

Where to Eat

VILLA REAL, *located behind the cathedral, Tel 772-0101.*
Lunch and dinner, Honduran and Intl cuisine, excellent service, bar, lovely garden, colonial atmosphere
MANG YING.
Chinese fare. One of the most popular restaurants in town, open 10am -10pm.
TATIS PIZZA, *Ave 4 Centenario near the entrance to the city.*
Pizza, chicken, spagetti, open daily except Monday 11:30am-10pm. On Friday and Saturday nights there's a disco from 9:30pm till 3am, reported to be the best disco in town.
PALMERAS, *located on the Central Park.*
The oldest restaurant in town, typical Honduran cuisine, breakfast, lunch, dinner.
COMIDA RAPIDA VENECIA, *a block from Central Park.*
Buffet style cafeteria food. Open Monday-Saturday 6:30 am - 8pm.
EL TORITO, *located on the San Pedro Sula-Tegucigalpa highway.*
Come here for the best steaks in town.

Seeing the Sights

What remains of colonial architecture in Comayagua dates mainly from the eighteenth century. The rustic churches and palaces of the early Spanish administrative center were repaired, expanded, rebuilt and relocated as the town and colony matured. A new flurry of building followed earthquake damage in the middle of the eighteenth century. But independence brought conflicts between government and church, and endemic civil turmoil. Construction fell off, and the architectural fashions of the late colonial period lived on.

The florid rococo style in Spain, known as *Churrigueresque,* had its own peculiar expression in the Americas in the eighteenth century, taking into account local conditions. Heavy, thick-walled, ground-hugging structures were built, on the theory that they would vibrate less and so suffer more limited damage in earthquakes. Decorative detail — flutings, plaster decorations of flowers, saints placed in niches, metal and wood grilles — relieved the heaviness of the buildings. Columns set into walls are especially characteristic of Comayagua and Honduran colonial architecture.

Many of the buildings of Comayagua fell into disrepair, as the population declined following the definitive relocation of the capital. Some eventually were replaced by nondescript structures. But, with time, many of the principal buildings of the old capital have now been restored. These, and the cobbled streets and red tile roofs that predominate, lend to Comayagua the air of a city from the past.

The rich cultural and historical heritage of Comayagua is being preserved by a joint project of the Honduran Institute of Anthropology, the Municipality of Comayagua, and the Spanish Cooperation Agency. Through their efforts the Central Park and many surrounding buildings have been restored to their former glory. Neons signs have been removed and replaced by small appropriate signs. The park in front of La Merced Church is being restored and work will start soon on the Cathedral.

In the next few pages you'll find the principal colonial buildings and museums of Comayagua.

Church of La Merced

The **Church of La Merced** was started in 1550 under Bishop Cristóbal de Pedraza. Tradition has it that the church was built on the site of the first mass in Comayagua. It was consecrated as the first Cathedral of Comayagua in 1561 and remained the principal church for fifty years. The square on which it stands was, at the time, the main plaza of the city, the location of the market and of all notable public events.

Originally a rudimentary structure of mud on a framework of sticks, with a thatched roof, La Merced was reconstructed around 1590, of stone and adobe. In 1644, it received an altarpiece as a gift from Philip IV of Spain. To judge by the building seen today, the present structure largely dates from the early 1700s. One of the two bell towers was demolished after it was damaged in earthquakes in 1774.

La Merced is a relatively simple structure, recalling mission churches in the southwestern United States, with a fluted border outlining the curving edge of the façade, and a single niche above the door, containing a sculpture of the Virgin of Mercy. Above it, a circular window illuminates the choir. The cupola of the surviving short bell tower is pierced by a lantern-like projection. Inside, the church is largely bare, but for the carved altar.

Cathedral of Comayagua

Three blocks north of the Merced Church, and one block west, is the **Cathedral of Comayagua**, or **Iglesia de la Inmaculada Concepción** (Church of the Immaculate Conception).

The growth of Comayagua by the end of the sixteenth century had led to the enlargement of the urban plan, and relocation of the *plaza mayor*, or main square. All the important buildings of the town had to be moved as well. The new cathedral, constructed under Bishop Gaspar de Andrade, had three naves, adobe walls, and a tile roof. It was not well built, however — a 1699 report describes the Cathedral as being in a terrible state, needing total reconstruction. By 1708, still another Cathedral was completed on the site. This one was, and remains, the most impressive ecclesiastical structure of the old capital.

The multi-tiered façade of the Cathedral is especially rich in decoration and detail. Two niches to either side of the door contain figures of St. Augustine and St. Jerome. St. Gregory and St. Ambrose are placed in niches on the level above, while on the third level is the figure of the Immaculate Conception, flanked by St. Joseph and St. John the Baptist. Above them rises Christ, with His hands extended. Palms and grapes are depicted in low relief throughout, and characteristically Honduran engaged columns climb the entire height. Unfortunately, all of this is white on a white background, and stands out only when the sun strikes in such a way as to create an interplay of light and shadow.

Alongside the Cathedral is the bell tower, jutting forward and supported by buttresses, with arched openings in four tiers, and crowned with a cupola covered by two-toned ceramics. The smooth walls contrast the detail of the Cathedral facade. The tower clock, crafted by Moors in Seville 800 years ago, reposed in the Alhambra of Granada, before it was donated to the original Cathedral of Comayagua by Philip II. It is quite possibly the oldest working clock anywhere.

Inside (enter by the side door if the main door on the square is closed), the Cathedral is a formal, three-nave structure with a floor plan in the form of a Latin cross.

Pillars allow natural light to flood the main nave. Formal pews, numerous altarpieces, mosaic floor and paintings are a sharp contrast to the bare, country-church aspect of the other colonial monuments of Comayagua. The Cathedral holds some of the treasures of colonial art in Honduras. The pulpit and three retables are richly carved—one retable, in a side chapel, dedicated to the Holy Sacrament, has a wrought silver front. Solid silver accessories were gifts from Philip IV. The many paintings include the Martyrdom of St. Barth by Murillo, and there are notable statues of saints.

Other Cathedrals & Museums

The **Colonial Museum**, opposite the Cathedral at the southeast corner of the main square, is located within the Episcopal Palace built in 1735. It houses a display of religious objects and exhibits on indigenous cultures, the pre-Columbian period, and the colonial period. Open Monday-Saturday 9am -noon and 2-4:30pm. Closed Sundays and holidays. Entry Lps 15.

The **Regional Museum of Archeology** is located in the building that was the house of government when Comayagua was capital of the republic. One-story, attractive, it reflects simpler times when the administration of an entire country, such as it was, could be carried out from what today would barely contain a municipal bureaucracy. The museum houses the most complete exhibition of Lenca culture in the world. Part of the museum houses a a school where young people are taught to restore historical structures using traditional techniques. The results of their work may been seen throughout the historical center of town.. It's located off the street that runs in front of the Cathedral, one block to the north. Hours are Tuesday to Sunday 8am-4:30pm. Entrance fee is Lps 20 for foreigners.

La Caxa Real (or "Caja," in modern Spanish), begun in 1739 and finished 1741, was the depository for royal taxes. The building suffered in earthquakes, and now only the front wall remains. If nothing else, its naked state, bare of the plaster and decoration of restored edifices, illustrates colonial construction techniques. Massive stone blocks, bricks, and rubble from older buildings were piled and mortared to form walls up to a meter in thickness.

Of the old **City Hall** of Comayagua, rebuilt in colonial style in 1880, on the north side of the main square, only the façade remains.

The **Column of the Constitution** dates from 1820, the eve of Central American independence. The name of the monument refers to nothing local, but to the 1812 Spanish constitution, which was an inspiration for liberal thinkers in the Spanish colonies. Locally, it's called **La Picota** ("the gibbet"), since the gallows and stocks of the town were adjacent.

Another important church, that of **El Señor Cruxificado de los Reyes** (Crucified Lord of the Kings), once stood just a block to the north of the main square. Destroyed by earthquake in 1809, there were plans to rebuild it on a site where it would compete less with the Cathedral for worshippers; but as administration and the position of the church declined after independence, the plans lay unfulfilled.

The **Church of San Francisco** was constructed starting in 1574. The Franciscans were the second religious order in Comayagua, after the Mercedarians, and erecting this church was their first task, and a continuing one. The building was renovated numerous times — in fact, this is the second site of the church. Damaged in a mid-eighteenth century earthquake, its roof crashed down in 1806. In another earthquake, in 1809, the bell tower collapsed. The current bell tower is three stories high, of the original four stories. The side facade features a Renaissance-style pediment over the door, inset with a niche containing an image of St. Anthony. Another niche contains an image of St. Francis. The monastery next door contains a bell cast in Alcalá in 1464, possibly the oldest church bell in the Americas.

In the northern part of Comayagua, the **Church of Caridad Illescas** is one of the lesser churches of the town, as it was meant to be. This was a neighborhood parish, serving Indians and mixed-bloods who were required to come here for indoctrination. Construction was started in the early nineteenth century, and not completed for another hundred years.

Basically in baroque style, the Church of Caridad Illescas has a pediment over its main door, and, characteristic of Comayagua churches, a round window toward the top of the façade. The decoration along the top is more flamboyant than that of the earlier Merced church, but the general aspect is simple. As is the case elsewhere in Comayagua, the bell tower once stood higher. Inside, there are several colonial retables and sculptures.

The **Church of San Sebastián**, six blocks south of the Merced church, was founded in 1558, also by the Mercedarians. Poorly built, it was reconstructed, probably in the mid-eighteenth century. The building was taken over as a headquarters by the invading anti-clerical army of Guatemala in 1827. The bell towers were rebuilt only in 1957.

Comayagua is home to a truly unique **Easter Week celebration**. Beginning with Palm Sunday and ending on Easter Sunday, the city becomes the spiritual capital of Honduras. Colorful sawdust carpets with intricate designs are laid out overnight on Holy Thursday in preparation for the processions of Good Friday.

Sports & Recreation

Climbing and **hiking** have some enthusiasts in this area. If you're interested, ask for the **Alianza Francesa** (Alliance Française), which has a mountaineering club. Nearby (13 km away) is the **Parque Nacional Montaña de Comayagua**, where you can go hiking in the cloud forest. The park is administered by Ecosimco, a private non-profit group. Their office is on the highway toward La Libertad, *Tel 772-4681*.

Excursions & Day Trips

La Paz, 21 kilometers to the southeast of Comayagua, is the capital of the department of the same name, which stretches southward to the border of El Salvador. Poor roads connect La Paz with regional towns. La Paz probably originated around 1750, as an outpost of Comayagua, serving the few Spanish haciendas in the area. The **La Paz Cultural Center**, in downtown La Paz, has exhibits of Lenca culture and crafts; it's open every day. **Ajuterique** along the road from Comayagua to La Paz, is an older town that dates from 1650, and has a colonial church. The name probably means "turtle hill."

Situated in the Comayagua Valley about an hour and a half north of Tegucigalpa and 20 minutes south of Comayagua, La Paz sits flanked on the northwest side by striking mountains. The weather can be classified as hot with the occasional breeze all year long. The main economy is cattle ranching and some agriculture.

La Paz has two very nice central parks to sit and relax in. Scattered around town are a number of *comedors* and bakeries. Next to the Texaco station on the Avenue de los Pinos is comedor **"San Antonio"** that seves full meals, including meat and salads for a reasonable $3, only open for lunch. Across the street from Hondutel and one block up is **"Samich"** where you can find the best burgers in La Paz. Across the street from the bus station, in front of the hospital are two comedors, one painted red and the other painted blue. Both serve great fast foods including baleadas, enchiladas and tacos all for about $1 each. One block from the market is the **Hotel Alis**, *Tel. 774-2125*, that has decent accommodations for $4 and $7 with bath. There are a number of banks in La Paz but many will only change cash and not traveller's checks. Buses leave all day going to Marcala ($1, two hour trip), Comayagua (50 cents, 20 minute trip) and Tegucigalpa ($1, two hours from the soldier statue in the center of town).

There are a number of interesting sites around La Paz that are worth seeing. In the town of **Yarumela** are some forgotten **Mayan temple ruins**, just the tops are visible. There are a number of **thermal water bathing sites** in and around La Paz. There is one straight up the main road and a little bit out of town, and another on the road from Cane to San Sebastian. The owner of these "Agua Termales," Asterio Suazo, has a wonderful set-up with hammocks, changing rooms and a small bar/restaurant. Asterio is always willing to fry up a fresh fish from the nearby lagoon for anyone who is willing to kick back and enjoy a relaxing lunch.

On the highway from La Paz to Marcala there are a number of nice coffee-producing mountain towns. **San Pedro de Tutule** is a beautiful town. Farther up the road two hours out of Tutule is the Lenca village of **Guajiquiro**. From here, you can hike up into the **Reserva Biologica Guajiquiro**, which covers 67 square kilometers of pine and cloud forest. The highest part of the reserve sits at about 2,200 meters.

Both La Paz and Ajuterique are easily reached on shuttle buses that run several times an hour from the highway bus stop outside Comayagua. There are also buses from the center of Comayagua, and fixed-route taxes from the highway junction. Buses operate also from 8 Avenida, 11/12 Calles, Comayagüela *(Transportes Flores, Tel. 237-3032)*.

These towns make for worthwhile short excursions if you're interested in detouring from the usual tourist path. To continue to more remote towns to the southwest, such as **Marcala**, you'll have to pack your luggage along, as buses run less frequently and the trip is longer.

El Rosario, about 20 kilometers north of Comayagua on a branch of the old road northward, was a great silver-mining center for several centuries. Another road northward heads to coffee-growing country on the way to La Libertad. A branch to the northeast crosses pine forest to reach the colonial villages of **Esquias** and **Minas De Oro** ("Gold Mine," named for obvious reasons), each with a colonial church.

By sturdy vehicle or by infrequent bus, you can continue through to the highway that runs inland from San Pedro Sula to Trujillo. In the northern part of the zone live some Jicaque Indians, who migrated from the coast and took up stable farming only in the last century.

Ten kilometers southeast of Comayagua via a track that departs from the paved highway, **Tenampua** is the fortress where Honduras' Lenca nation held out under their chieftain Lempira against the Spaniards. Easily accessible to the curious for centuries, and unprotected, nothing much of interest remains, but for some deteriorated walls.

Archaeologists both professional and amateur excavating over the years have found mounds with four layers of superimposed construction, as well as a ball court. The site is naturally protected by steep slopes, but great walls, as high and as wide as five meters, roughly built of uncut stone fitted as closely as possible, and terraced on the side of the defenders, block the easiest routes of access.

Practical Information

There are several banks in Comayagua, including **Bancahsa**, Calle del Comercio; **Banco Atlántida**, Calle del Comercio; and **Banco de Occidente**, Calle de Comercio. For car rentals, contact **Budget Car Rental**, *Tel 772-9212, www.budgethonduras.com.*

North of Comayagua

The main highway continues through the warm, fertile **Comayagua Valley**. From kilometer 94, there is a steep climb, to a pass at kilometer 105, on the continental divide. On one side, waters flow toward the Caribbean; on the other, toward the Pacific. The descent is to the **Siguatepeque plateau**, which is forested with pines, the Honduran national emblem.

Siguatepeque, "Hill of Women," is four kilometers off the highway, from a junction at kilometer 114. There is a good American Adventist hospital here, and, at 1140 meters, the climate is relatively cool. If you're hungry, stop at **Pizzeria Venecia**, known for its excellent pizza; **Restaurant La Betania**, on the main highway near the National Forestry School (good buffet); and **La Granja D'Elia**, also on the main highway (near the turnoff to La Esperanza), which is a grocery, bakery, restaurant, and serves an excellent buffet – it's very popular with travelers from San Pedro Sula to Tegucigalpa. From the highway junction, another road cuts to the southwest, to the towns of Intibucá and La Esperanza. Buses operate to Siguatepeque from 8 Avenida, 11/12 Calles, Comayagüela (Transportes Maribel, *Tel. 237-3032).*

At kilometer 115 is the National Forestry School (ESNACIFOR) There are more climbs to the village of **El Socorro**.

Near kilometer 131, you can see from the road a large kiln, where people burn lime for use in mortar, an activity that has gone on since the time of the ancient Maya. Modern cement still has not replaced old methods. You also see small-scale sugarcane mills — *trapiches* — emitting great plumes of smoke. The view in this region is spectacular, out to multiple peaks, and pastured hills and mountains. Unexpectedly, in the midst of a tropical country, it looks as if you were in Switzerland.

At kilometer 137 right on the main highway, a km before **Taulabé** after an abrupt descent, you can visit the caves called Tarule, or Taulabé. There are stalactites and stalagmites, and, if you look straight up, bats. A boy will guide you through at no charge, though you should leave a few lempiras as a tip. The cave is 12 km long, but only 400 meters of it are lit and accessible to visitors. Young guides are available, to walk you through the cave and point out the many interesting formations.The cave is open from 7am to 5pm. The cave is located 20 km south of Lake Yojoa.

The road is very good this way, but watch out for unexpected potholes. There are many small shops and eateries, where you can stop for a drink, and a plain, home-cooked meal.

Northwest of Taulabé, via a branch road, is **Santa Barbara** (population about 16,000), a regional center that dates from the late colonial period. There are several inexpensive hotels, like the **Boarding House Moderno**, *Tel. 643-2203*. Palm hats woven here are sold all over Honduras and in neighboring countries. The village of **La Arada** near Santa Barbara produces fine *junco* handicrafts. Their intricately woven baskets come in a wide variety of sizes and shapes and beautiful bold geometric designs. The baskets are woven exclusively by the women of the village. Junco products may be purchased at various women's waving cooperatives in the village. Prices at the coops are excellent, because you purchase directly from the weavers.

Lake Yojoa

At kilometer 153, you get your first spectacular view of **Lake Yojoa** (yo-HO-ah), surrounded by mountains. One of the beauty spots of mainland Honduras, Yojoa has clear waters, and, for a mountain lake of its size and depth (175 square kilometers, up to 40 meters deep), its waters are surprisingly warm. The altitude along the shore is about 600 meters.

Yojoa is best-known, perhaps, for its bass. These are not indigenous — they were stocked, years ago — but they have taken well, and the lake is now a sport fishing center. Anybody can swim, of course, and the few hotels usually have boats and water-skiing equipment available for rent.

Arrivals & Departures
By Bus

Buses on the Tegucigalpa-San Pedro Sula route will let you off at either the Motel Los Remos or at the turnoff for the Motel Agua Azul, near kilometer 164. From the latter point, buses run along the north shore of the lake about every half-hour.

Orientation

Lake Yojoa lies beside the main north-south highway, which follows its eastern shore. From the road, you'll see marshes, and trees growing out of the water, draped in Spanish moss. It is a true paradise for birds. From kilometer 165 (about 80 kilometers from San Pedro Sula), a branch road traces the northern shore, and it is mainly along this route, and right at the junction with the main highway, that you will find the few lodging and eating places and boating facilities that serve visitors.

A highlight of your trip to the lake will probably be a visit to the myriad fresh fruit stands on the roadside. Pineapples, mangos, papayas, bananas, coconuts, sugar cane, all freshly picked around the lake, are for sale. For tropical fruit lovers, you will immediately notice the difference between these fruits and those you find back home – juicy and sweet beyond description.

From the western shore of the lake, a secondary road reaches San Pedro Sula by way of the falls of Pulhapanzak. Hills and mountains overlook the lake, the highest being Mount Marancho, to the west.

Weather & Climate

The Lake Yojoa region gets copious amounts of rain, from clouds trapped by **Mount Marancho**, or Santa Bárbara (2744 meters). September, October and November are the rainiest months around Yojoa, though most of the rain falls at night. February through June are dryer.

During these months, farmers burn the land to ready it for the next crop season. Sometimes, you cannot see the mountains for all the smoke.

Around Lake Yojoa

The lake itself is largely fed by underground streams. It acts as a natural humidifier — everything around is green, and you can feel the moistness. If you spend any time in the area, inspect your camera lens for fungus. Two islands poke out of the lake. The larger is near the south end.

The flat lands around the lake, well-watered and well-drained, afforded good access by roads, are intensively farmed. Sugar cane, coffee and pineapple are the main crops. Coffee especially is grown — the abundant water means that the coffee bush and the trees that shade it can both prosper.

Shade allows for a slow ripening of the coffee bean, and a maximum development of flavor. Gradually, the fruit of the coffee (the *cereza*, or "cherry") turns from green to red, at which point it is ready for picking. The outer skin is removed by simple machines, then the coffee is dried in the sun, which causes the "parchment" layer to flake off. Further drying is accomplished with hot air blowers fueled by oil. The beans then are classified by size and quality. Different sizes and types go to different markets. Italians get small beans sorted by hand. Mechanically sorted coffee ends up in the States (though experts say that the shape has no effect on the taste).

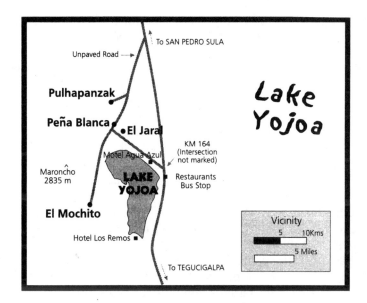

You can visit the coffee dryer at **Peña Blanca** village (see "West of Lake Yojoa" section below), and the coffee plantation at the Adventist school on the road to El Mochito from Peña Blanca. Or ask any farmer in the area for permission to look around. People are very friendly.

The expansion of agriculture in the rich lands around Lake Yojoa has some notably unfriendly effects. The forests on the slopes of Mount Marancho and nearby are legendary for their wildlife. But as trees are cut, some of the jaguars, pumas, ocelots, deer and bears are, in fact, becoming nothing more than legends. There is also concern that agricultural runoff and mining are poisoning the lake's waters. **Fundación EcoLago**, *Tel. 237-5028 or 238-2507, Fax 237-0822*, works to protect the lake's ecosystem. You can also get information about them at the Hotel Agua Azul.

There is also good birdwatching at the lake; 373 species of birds have so far been recorded.

Where to Stay

HOTEL AGUA AZUL, *located along the north shore of Lake Yojoa, about 3.5 kilometers from the junction at kilometer 166. Tel 992-8928, Tel/Fax 991-7244 in San Pedro Sula, Fax (San Pedro) 553-4823. 21 units. $19/double in regular rooms, and up to $25 for a "chalet" (cottage) with six beds.*

Rooms are simple, with old furnishings, but comfortable, and the water from the taps is hot. Maybe I should call this a well-kept fishing camp. The hotel makes arrangements for bass fishing and boating and water skiing. And the bird watching in the area is excellent. The gardens and landscaping are a fantasy world, and everything is quiet, but for the forest noises, and the nocturnal burps of giant frogs. And there's a new pool, if you don't want to jump into the lake.

If you're just passing through for the day, the Agua Azul's shaded lake-view terrace is a good place to try black bass, available here as a filet (you can get it bones and all from any number of roadside stands). They also have a full menu of steaks, chicken and sandwiches, with nothing over $6.

Guides are available for forest hiking and bird watching. The hotel runs fishing trips for $12/hour and inlcudes everything; there's a four-person maximum. The owner of the hotel would also like to pass on to you his special fishing tip: the best bass fishing is to be had five days before and after a full moon!

LOS REMOS, *a cluster of motel units and cottages at the south end of the lake, where the road from Tegucigalpa reaches the shore. Tel. 557-8054 in San Pedro Sula, 19 rooms. $19 double.*

This is not a luxury place by any means: the rooms are bare, there's a smell of damp in the air, and the pool is not well maintained. But everything is clean, and the balcony of the restaurant offers good views. The owners will make arrangements for fishing and boating. There's a launching ramp, in case you're towing your boat. The hotel is currently remodeling; hopefully it will be finished by the time you arrive – but call first to make sure.

HOTEL FINCA LAS GLORIAS, *Km 9, La Guama, Carretera a Pena Blanca, Tel 566-0461, Tel/Fax 566-0462, E-mail: info@hotellasglorias.com; web: www.hotelfincalasglorias.com. 35 rooms. $41 double.*

Set in the midst of a sprawling coffee plantation, this hotel has a lovely lakeside setting. There's a pool and restaurant. Rooms are in individual cabins, with air conditioning, cableTV, and hot water.

HONDUYATE MARINA, *Km 161 on the San Pedro Sula-Tegucigalpa Highway. Tel 990-9386/9387, 982-2338, Fax 232-2324, E-mail: kjoint@datum.hn. 6 cabanas. $42 unit.*

The only seriuos marina on the lake, with sailing, waterskiing, waverunners, and a restaurant specializing in fresh farm raised tilapia. Delightful lakeside atmosphere. Run by an expat couple, Richard and Liliana Joint.

Where to Eat

You can eat reasonably at the above hotels and the marina. Try the lake fish, of course. There are also numerous eateries where the bus stops along the highway, but be careful about them.

The West Side of Lake Yojoa

The road from kilometer 164 to Peña Blanca, on the west side of Yojoa, is one of the nicest in Honduras (in my opinion), with good views to the lake and the surrounding peaks. You will see sugar cane and pineapple plantations.

The village of **El Jaral** is off the road, and was once of considerable importance. It was there that the ferry across Lake Yojoa docked, in the days before the highway between Tegucigalpa and San Pedro Sula was completed. Farther on is **Peña Blanca**, where the paved road ends. The view is attractive from the main street. The village derives its name from the white peak, or outcrop (*Peña blanca*), that can be seen by looking to the west. Buses run between Peña Blanca and the main highway about every half-hour.

The **Hotel Maranata** in Peña Blanca charges $5/double for clean, basic rooms. Also in town are the **Hotel Manolito** and **Comedor El Cruce**, offering simple inexpensive rooms and meals. Just outside of town you can go swimming at the **Balneario El Nacimiento** (a *balneario* is a natural river-fed swimming pool).

El Mochito, to the southwest of the lake, is currently a mining center for lead, copper and silver.

There is an extensive archaeological site at **Los Naranjos** which is of great importance and is currently being readied for tourists. It is recommended to visit it with a local guide, as trails are a bit off the beaten track.

Pulhapanzak Falls

About 11 kilometers to the north of Peña Blanca, via a rough road, the **Pulhapanzak Falls** drop down to a natural pool, a great place for swimming. The site is a park. Groups from San Pedro Sula crowd the facilities on weekends, but on weekdays you'll have the place to yourself. The entrance fee is Lps 3. There is a restaurant and camping is possible.

To reach the falls by public transport, take the bus from Peña Blanca that runs to San Pedro Sula. One passes about every hour. Ask the driver to let you off at Pulhapanzak village. Or, if you're starting from San Pedro Sula, take the bus for El Mochito. It's a slow ride with many stops.

The falls are a kilometer from the village. There are lots of undiscovered Mayan ruins, but to inexperienced eyes they look like hillocks covered with vegetation. Farmers around the lake have discovered numerous Mayan artifacts, though there has been little intensive exploration of the local ruins.

Mount Marancho & Santa Bárbara National Park

It is possible to hike to the top of **Marancho** (also known as **Santa Bárbara** mountain), but this is a task for expert adventurers. According to Michael Bell of the U.S. Peace Corps in Honduras, hikers should:
• be experienced

- have a topographical map, obtainable from the Instituto Geográfico Nacional in Tegucigalpa, and a good compass
- carry plenty of water
- have overnight camping equipment; and
- carry a machete to clear trails when necessary. The ascent, for people in good condition, takes 15 hours — that's a two-day excursion.

Rainfall is high at the top of the mountain, and vegetation is largely as it was created by nature, due to the difficulty of access. You will walk where no human has gone before, and see vegetation and animal life that looks as if it came from a prehistoric world: giant vines dangling from trees and twisting through vegetation, and huge transparent butterflies. At some places, the ground-level layer of living and rotting vegetation is a meter thick. This is all a very special experience.

Santa Bárbara National Park, covering 130 square kilometers, includes the Yojoa basin, as well as Mount Marancho with its cloud forest, and several caves. The core area covers 5500 hectares. A buffer zone comprises 7500 hectares in which agricultural activities and wood-cutting are controlled. Mount Marancho and its underground sink holes, caves and hollows feed Lake Yojoa and numerous streams, forming one of the major watersheds of Honduras.

For information on visiting the park, contact: Associación Ecologia Corazon Verde in Santa Barbara or the office of COHDEFOR in Santa Barbara.

North from Yojoa

From the Yojoa junction (kilometer 164), the main highway rises for several kilometers. You see pineapple plantations, newly established in this area. From kilometer 169, the road begins to descend toward the hot lowlands, winding gently all the way. Many stands sell bananas, oranges and pineapples, all fresh of course, and in the case of pineapples, cut to order.

At kilometer 184 is **Flores**, a wide spot in the road at the junction for **Santa Rita**, 15 kilometers away, on the Comayagua River.

Upriver from Santa Rita is **El Cajon dam**, a huge (for Honduras) hydroelectric project. Placed into operation in 1985, the dam is the tallest in Central America (over 700 feet), and one of the highest in the world, forming a lake covering almost 100 square kilometers snaking and branching through Central Honduras in the valleys of the Comayagua, Sulaco and Humuya rivers. The electricity produced is more than can be used in Honduras, and much is sold to neighboring countries. The dam can only be visited with official permission from the state electric company.

From Flores, you descend another three kilometers, then follow a mostly straight road through the lowlands to San Pedro Sula, crossing the **Chamelecón River**, a brown, muddy, unnavigable river of rapids.

San Pedro Sula

One of the oldest cities in Honduras, **San Pedro Sula** is also the newest, the center of industry and trade in the fastest-growing part of the country, with a population of over 400,000. San Pedro Sula is just 246 kilometers from Tegucigalpa, and a continent away.

Tegucigalpa has venerable governmental buildings and institutions of learning. San Pedro Sula has factories. Tegucigalpa is where the Mestizo culture of Honduras was formed. San Pedro Sula, if not polyglot, is multicultural, with evident African and Levantine strains.

Tegucigalpa, in the mountains, has hills and winding streets. San Pedro Sula, in the lowlands, is flat. Tegucigalpa has buses. San Pedro Sula has buses *and* a railroad. Tegucigalpa developed as the isolated capital of a backwater. San Pedro Sula knows no limits. In the Honduran context, it is Chicago.

Beginnings

This old-new city's roots go back to June 27, 1536, when it was founded as Villa de San Pedro de Puerto Caballos by Pedro de Alvarado, one of the maximum leaders of the Spanish onslaught. The traditional name for the valley, Sula, (from the Aztec for "birds") was added in short order.

San Pedro was for a time a military headquarters, but the center of Spanish power soon moved to the highlands. The outpost near the coast was destroyed by pirates in 1660, and intermittently attacked by Indians and Sambos (mixed-bloods of part-African descent) allied with English pirates. Much later, in 1892, the town was almost abandoned in the wake of a yellow fever epidemic.

But that was the low point. A railroad reached San Pedro Sula from the coast in the 1870s, part of a transcontinental system that was never completed. Bananas were planted widely by American companies, low-lying lands were drained, port facilities were constructed nearby, malaria and tropical diseases were conquered or controlled by chemicals and medicines, and San Pedro Sula began to attract new residents not only from the highlands, but from outside the country. West Indians came to work on the banana plantations, and Lebanese arrived to smooth the flow of trade. Factories were established to produce cloth and processed foods and construction materials for the local market.

All this development occurred in relative isolation from Tegucigalpa: a paved road to the capital opened only in 1971.

Modern San Pedro Sula

San Pedro Sula is a clean, modern, growing town, yet it is still manageable. Prosperity is obvious, and everything looks efficient. There are no beggars, or few of them. And strangely, there is no visible military presence, which can make you feel uncomfortable if you've become used to seeing soldiers around, as you will in some other parts of Honduras.

Downtown San Pedro Sula is small and mostly uncongested, reflecting the rapid growth of the city after the period of motorization. There are pockets of wealthy suburbs, and little evidence of grinding poverty.

There is also very little in the way of points of interest or attractions, except for some annual feasts and celebrations. But San Pedro Sula is *the* starting point for excursions to many other places. You can fly right in from abroad, stay in good accommodations, and continue by road to the ruins of Copán and to points along the coast, on day or overnight trips.

San Pedro Sula is a lot more informal than Tegucigalpa in dress as well as attitude. San Pedro Sula is about business and commerce. Its buidlings are new and the people have migrated from other places.

San Pedro Sula is quite hot from April through September, with temperatures above 100°F a common occurrence and stifling humidity. Light, all-cotton clothing is recommended. The months from November through March, on the other hand, are quite pleasant.

Weather

The dry season (*verano*) lasts from December through April; March and April are the hottest and driest months. The rainy season (*invierno*) last from May through November. The wettest months are August and September. During the months of October through February, temperatures are quite pleasant, days are warm and evenings, comfortably cool.

Arrivals & Departures

By Air

- **Aerolineas Sosa**, 8 ave 1 y 2 calle Edificio Roman planta baja Barrio, Guamilito S.O., *Tel. 550-6545, 550-4558, Airport 668-3128, 668-3223*
- **American Airlines**, Edificio Firenze Barrio Los Andes 16 ave entre 1 y 2 calle, *Tel. 558-0524, 558-0526 Airport 668-3241 thru 50*
- **Continental Airlines**, Plaza Versailles Ave Circunvalación, also behind Gran Hotel Sula, parque central, *Tel. 557-4141-45, Fax 557-4146*, Airport *668-3208, 668-3210*
- **COPA**, Centro Commercial Prisa Blvd Morazán, *Tel. 553-2640, 553-2626, 553-2666, Airport 668-2518*
- **Iberia**, Edificio Quiroz 2 piso, 2 calle 2 ave., *Tel. 550-4604, 550-2530 Airport 6683217*
- **Lufthansa**, Edificio Los Alpes 8 calle 15 y 16 ave, *Tel. 557-1934, Fax 557-1218*
- **Isleña Airlines**, Edificio Trejo Marlon *Tel. 5528322, 5528335, Airport 668-3186, 668-3182*

• **Grupo Taca**, 13 ave N.O., Norte de la Circunvalación Barrio Los Andes, *Tel.*
550-5268
• **KLM**, 4 calle entre 10 y 11 ave N.O. Edificio Villa San Martín Barrio Guamilito,
Tel. 557-3907, 557-3908, Fax 557-3910

And if you're looking for helicopter transport throughout Honduras, including Copan Ruinas, Bay Islands, La Mosquitia, and more, call **TAESA**, *Tel. 553-3101, ext. 112, or Tel/Fax 552-5212.*

The Airport
  Ramón Villeda Morales Airport is located about 12 kilometers east of San Pedro Sula, off the road to La Lima. A taxi will take you out for about $6. Buses for La Lima will leave you more than a kilometer from the terminal.

By Bus
  At least three bus companies provide hourly or near-hourly service between Tegucigalpa and San Pedro Sula. The ride on a first class bus takes about 3 1/2 hours and costs about $6.
  Transportes Sáenz runs truly first-class coach service between San Pedro Sula and Tegucigalpa, with airline-style seats, movies, snacks, stewardesses, bathrooms, pillows. Reservations are accepted for the 3 1/2 hour non-stop service. All other buses make a 1/2 hour stop along the way. Hedman Alas is also highly recommended for excellent first class bus service. First bus leaves San Pedro 5:45 am, last bus at 5:45 pm.
  The routes and bus lines are:
  SAN PEDRO SULA TO TEGUCIGALPA: Empresa Hedman-Alas, 3 Calle, 8/9 Avenidas NW, *Tel. 553-1361*, hourly, with newer buses than those of other companies; **Transportes Sáenz**, 8 ave entre 4 y 5 calle S.O., *Tel. 553-4969, Fax 553-1361*, buses leave San Pedro Sula and Tegucigalpa simultaenously at 6am, 8am, 10am, 2pm, 4pm, and 6pm; and **El Rey Express**, 9 Ave 9 y 10 Calle, *Tel 550-8355*, express service every hour. **Viana Clase Oro**, Ave Circunvalacion, behind Wendy's, *Tel 556-9261*, at 6:30am, 9:30am, 6:15pm, luxury buses.
  TEGUCIGALPA TO SAN PEDRO SULA: **El Rey Express**, half-block from Central Bank annex, *Tel 237-8561* every hour or more frequently from before dawn to 10:30pm. Also **Hedman-Alas**, 11 Avenida, 13/14 Calles, Comayagüela, *Tel. 2377143*. First bus leaves 6am, last bus at 5:30pm. **Transportes Sáenz**, Centro Commercial Perisur, Blvd. Toncontin, *Tel. 233-4249, Fax 233-4294*, buses leave Tegucigalpa and San Pedro Sula simultaenously at 6 a.m, 8am, 10am, 2pm, 4pm, and 6pm. **Viana Clase Oro**, Blvd Fuerzas Armadas, *Tel 235-8185*, departures at 6:30am, 1:30pm, 6:15pm.

TO PUERTO CORTÉS: Empresa Impala, 2 Avenida, 4/5 Calles NW; and **Empresa Citul**, 7 Calle, 5/6 Avenidas SW, *Tel. 553-0070*. Buses operate about every 20 minutes until 6 p.m; it's about a 45 minute trip.

FROM THE TUPSA/CATISA STATION: From the Tupsa station, 2 Avenida, 5/6 Calles SW, every five minutes to **La Lima** (the banana capital) and **Progreso**. Change buses in Progreso for **Tela**; or take a La Ceiba bus to the Tela junction, and a taxi into town (less than a dollar for the taxi ride). Buses leave every hour for La Ceiba. Caution is advised when arriving or departing from this terminal. Youngsters have been known to grab travelers' belongings and then beat a hasty retreat. Your best protection is to be alert.

COPÁN RUINS:

- **Toritos y Copanecos**, 6 Ave 8 y 9 Calle, *Tel. 553-4930*, has buses going to Santa Rosa de Copán. To reach the Ruins of Copán, take this bus as far as La Entrada (two hours), where you can pick up another bus for Copán Ruinas, 64 km and almost two hours onward. San Pedro Sula - Copán Ruinas using Torito bus takes 5 hours. The best way to get to Copán Ruinas is via the direct buses that leave San Pedro Sula daily.
- **Transportes Gama** leaves San Pedro Sula at 7 am and 3 pm. Ticket Lps 50, three hour trip. Bus stop is in the parking lot next door to Hotel Palmira, *Tel. 5522861*. The bus leaves Copán Ruinas at 6 am and 3 pm daily. *Bus stop is at the old bridge at the entrance to town, Tel. 6514421*. Ticket Lps 50.
- **Transportes Casasola** has direct bus service from San Pedro Sula to Copán Ruinas. Buses leave San Pedro Sula at 8am and 2pm. Lps 50, three hour trip. The bus leaves Copan at 7am and 2pm.
- **Hedman Alas** has 1st class direct buses daily, bathroom, movie, highly recommended. Buses leave San Pedro at 6:45am, 9:50am and 2:30 pm daily. Buses leave Copan at 5:30am, 10:30am and 2:30pm. Three hour trip, Lps 100. Connections with super deluxe buses on Hedman Alas to Tegucigalpa and La Ceiba, *Tel. Copan Ruinas 651-4106, San Pedro Sula Tel. 553-1361, 557-3477*. Hedman Alas is the only bus running between San Pedro Sula and Copan Ruinas with its own bus terminal in San Pedro and Copan.
- The owner of **Hotel Patty** has a nice new Peugeot minivan; he makes express charter trips to San Pedro Sula, Tela, and La Ceiba from Copán Ruinas, *Tel. 6514021*.

SANTA ROSA DE COPÁN: Every hour with **Toritos y Copanecos**, 6 Ave 8 y 9 Calle, *Tel. 553-4930*.

TO GUATEMALA: You can continue by bus from Copán Ruinas to the El Floridio border crossing or take a bus to Santa Rosa de Copán, then continue by bus to the border past Nueva Ocotepeque; **Transportes Congolón**, 8 Ave

9 y 10 Calle, *Tel. 5531174*, runs the San Pedro Sula - Ocotepeque route. It is a short hop from there to the Honduran/Guatemalan border at Agua Caliente. **TO SAN SALVADOR & GUATEMALA**: **King Quality**, 6 Calle 7 y 8 Ave, *Tel 553-4547*. Luxury bus to El Salvador and Guatemala at 6:30am.

Departing By Train

A slow, cheap train leaves in the morning for Puerto Cortés and Tela (with a change of train en route) from the station near 1 Avenida and 1 Calle. For information, *call 553-1879 or 553-2997*. If you're a train buff, hurry up and climb aboard before the service is discontinued.

Orienation/Getting Around Town

The central area of San Pedro Sula is divided by 1 Calle (running east-west) and 1 Avenida (running north-south) into four quadrants, or zones: *Noreste* (*NE*, or Northeast), *Noroeste* (*NO*, or Northwest), *Sudoeste* (*SO*, or Southwest) and *Sudeste* (*SE*, or Southeast). Streets are numbered, and addresses in the central area always give the quadrant, using the Spanish abbreviation. (For convenience, I will use the English NW and SW for Northwest and Southwest).

Calles run east-west, *avenidas* run north-south. 4 Avenida downtown is a pedestrian mall (*peatonal*). Avenida Circunvalación is the ring road around the central area. There are also various *colonias*, or suburbs.

Car Rental
• **Avis**, 6 Avenida, 1 Calle NE, *Tel. 553-0888, Fax 553-3718,* Airport *668-3164/ 66*
• **Budget**, 1 Calle 3 y 4 Ave, *Tel. 552-2295, Fax 553-3411, Airport 668-3179; web: www.budgethonduras.com*
• **Dollar Rent a Car**, 3/4 Calle, 3 Avenida, NO, *Tel. 557-0820, 552-7626, Airport 66-83211*
• **Maya Rent a Car**, 3 Avenida, 7/8 Calle NW, *Tel. 552-2670, Airport 668-3168 thru 70*, and at the Hotel Copantl
• **Toyota Rent a Car**, 3 Ave 5 y 6 Ave, *Tel. 552-5498,* Airport *668-3174, E-mail: trac@123.hn; web: www.123.hn/trac.* Recommended, good rates.
• **Hertz**, Airport *Tel 668-3156/57, Fax 668-3155*
• **Thrifty**, Airport *Tel 668-3152/53, E-mail: thrifty@david.intertel.hn*

Where to Stay

CAMINO REAL INTER-CONTINENTAL, *Colonia Hernández y Blvd. del Sur, Multiplaza Mall, Tel. 553-0000, Fax 550-6255, sanpedrosula@interconti.com, www.interconti.com. Deluxe Room $190, Junior Deluxe Suite $300, Junior Suite Club $350, Presidential Suite $600. 150 rooms, 6 junior suites, 1 Presidential Suite. Weekend discount $90 for Deluxe Room. Corporate rate $145. Azulejos*

Restaurant, Scenario Bar, Room Service, Laundry and Valet, Mini Bar, in room safe, business center, Executive Club, Travel Agency, Child Care, Outdoor pool, gym, sauna, spa, 3 function rooms.

This is it, finally a true, world class 5 star hotel in Honduras. Comfortable, well-appointed rooms with king size bed, picture window, writing desk and all the amenities. Excellent service throughout the hotel. The Business Center offers fax, audio-visual equipment, cellular phones, photocopying, secretarial assistance, domestic and international phone services, private meeting rooms, document translations, computers, e-mail, internet, coffee, concierge and courier services.

Restaurant Azulejos offers up excellent food at surprisingly good prices. There is a wonderful breakfast buffet each morning for only $8. A typical Honduran breakfast with all the fixings runs $5 and an American breakfast $6. A la carte, there is Danish at $1, Pancakes $1.50, Waffles $1.50, OJ $1, Café con leche $1. Great food at great prices. There is room service 24 hours. For true burger aficionados, the burger at Azulejos is the best, most delicious this writer has tasted this side of the RioGrande; it comes topped with cheese, bacon and a side of fries – at $3, this has got to be the deal of the millennium! Non-guests are welcome to dine in the restaurant. There are theme nights as well, Wednesday is Spanish Night, Thursday is Mexican Night, Friday is Seafood Night and Saturday is Grill Night. The buffets cost $14. Sunday brunch is $13.

GRAN HOTEL SULA, *1 Calle, 3/4 Avenidas NW (P. O. Box 435), Tel. 5529999, Fax 5576215, 5527000. 118 rooms. $85 single/$96 double. U.S. reservations: Tel. 800/223-6764. No charge for children under 12.*

This is a nine-story building right on the main square of San Pedro Sula. The staff is competent and friendly. The rooms (and the hotel in general) are very clean, the mattresses are excellent, and all are provided with coffee makers. All rooms in the main tower have balconies (I recommend those with a view to the pool, a courtyard work of tiled art, complete with cascades and tributaries), and suites have kitchenettes and sleep sofas. There are also some poolside units. Other amenities include a restaurant, 24-hour coffee shop, newstand, health club and twice daily maid service (extraordinary!).

The Gran Hotel Sula is a trip back in time to the late fifties, when staying downtown did *not* mean staying in a dangerous, decaying area. The hotel has been well maintained.

Take the Skandia coffee shop. You can take spin on revolving stools at the lunch counter and order a banana split, club sandwich, and apple pie, and drink of atmosphere that says, this is a *diner!* Of course, if you're not a kid, you can sit at one of the tables. Egg plates, club sandwiches and burgers in the Skandia run $3 and under. For more formal dining, the Granada restaurant overlooks the pool from the mezzanine, and serves filet mignon, shrimp casserole and daily specials for about $7, a lunch buffet for about $6. The cuisine is excellent.

Discounts — significant ones — are available to Hondurans and resident foreigners.

HOTEL COPANTL SULA, *Colonia Las Mesetas (P. O. Box 1060), Tel. Tel 5567108, Fax 5573890. 205 rooms. $90 to $95 single/$140 double. U.S. reservations, Tel. 800/328-8897, Fax 512/341-7942.*

This is the *other* large hotel in San Pedro, located on the southern outskirts of the city on the way from Tegucigalpa, across the street from the Camino Real Inter-Continental. It's clean, quiet and modern, with a soaring, dark, multi-story lobby, bar, disco, and country-club facilities that include an Olympic-size pool with diving blocks, pool snack bar, four tennis courts, handball courts, sauna and whirpool, exercise equipment, and massage service.

Of the several restaurants, the Pergola, on the seventh floor, is a grill room with reasonably priced fare — steaks, chicken and shrimp brochettes for $7 and less. The ground-floor coffee shop is informal, features quick service, and is frequented by locals as well as hotel guests — a good sign.

Rooms are less attractive than the public areas, on the small side, with a hard feel and less-than-top-notch taste in furnishings, but they're air-conditioned and carpeted, and have color televisions. Shops and services include car rental and travel agencies, and if you need it, there's a casino with card games, slot machines and roulette. A free shuttle bus runs every half hour to downtown during daylight hours on weekdays and till noon on Saturday, otherwise you'll have to take taxis or have a car if you're going anywhere in town. When the hotel is not full, ask for the corporate rate, the military rate, the resident's rate, or some other discount. Overall, the hotel is overpriced for what you get and is not centrally located.

HOTEL BOLÍVAR, *2 Calle, 2 Avenida NW No. 8 (P.O. Box 956), Tel. 553-3224. 70 rooms. $28-$30 single/$26 double. American Express, Visa, Master Card.*

A good, middle-range hotel, a modern building with an excellent central location and attractive grounds, though it could be better maintained and service could be improved. Cable TV offered. Orientation to interior courtyard and pool makes it relatively quiet in most rooms, despite traffic outside. Protected parking.

HOTEL EJECUTIVO, *2 calle 10 ave S.O., Tel 552-4289, Fax 552-5868, Ejecutivo I - Older Annex across the street, $31 double, Ejecutivo II - Newer Main Building, $38 double.*

My favorite mid-range hotel in San Pedro, secure, clean, comfortable, air conditioning, restaurant, reasonably priced. Good breakfast included in rate. Good central location. One block from Holiday Inn and El Fogoncito (a great Mexican restaurant).

MICROTEL INN & SUITES, *on Blvd to airport, Tel 559-0300, E-mail: microtel@netsys.hn. $52 double.*

All the bells and whistles you'd expect at this US franchise hotel. Pool, free transport to downtown, convenient to airport, Larsons' Restaurant on premises.

Businessman Hotels
HOTEL TERRAZA, *6 Avenida, 4/5 Calles SW, Tel. 550-3108. 42 rooms. $10 and up single/$20 double.*

Restaurant, bar, air-conditioned rooms, good central downtown location, functional and good value.

HOTEL COLOMBIA, *3 Calle, 5/6 Avenidas SW, Tel. 553-3118 or 557-5345. 25 rooms. $17 single/$16 double.*

Where to Eat
I have found good eating in some of the better hotels, especially the two noted below:

GRAN HOTEL SULA, *1 Calle, 3/4 Avenidas, NW. Tel. 5529999.*

On the first floor, you'll find the 24-hour Skandia diner, with good, simple meals for just a couple of dollars. On the second floor, the more formal Granada restaurant offers a buffet at noon for about $10, and full dinner at night, and, sometimes, entertainment. The cuisine is genuinely continental, and excellent, aside from which it is a very good value. Even Peace Corps volunteers, who stay in $7 hotels, come out to dine at the Gran Hotel Sula. The lobby kiosk is the best (and one of the only) places in town to find a good selection of US newspapers and magazines.

AZULEJOS RESTAURANT, *in the Camino Real Inter-Continental, Colonia Hernández y Blvd. del Sur, Multiplaza Mall, Tel. 5530000.*

One of the finest, most excluisive restaurants in San Pedro Sula. Excellent food, wonderful service, great ambience, good value, reasonably priced. Breakfast buffett daily $8, Sunday Brunch $14, Wednesday is Spanish Night, Thursday Night is Mexican Night, Friday is Seafood Night, Saturday is Grill Night, $14. A la Carte menu, burger $3, club sandwich $2.50, Fresh fish $7, pastas $4. Tax and service not included. Great prices, great food and great service. Highly recommended.

Fast Food
PIZZA HUT, *1 Calle (Boulevard Morazán) and 4 Avenida, NW, Circunvalación; and downtown on the peatonal just off the Central Park.*

Great pizza, absolutely the best (and one of the only) salad bars in town! Reasonably priced. Always crowded, a great place to watch the city life of San Pedro Sula through the large picture windows.

BURGER KING, *on the ring road, Av. Circunvalación, two blocks south of 1 Calle, and downtown on the peatonal just off the Central Park.*
The King wins the battle of the burgers in San Pedro Sula hands down for service.
MCDONALD'S, *next door to the Cathedral.*
WENDY'S, *on the Circunvalación and downtown on the peatonal just off the Central Park.*
CHURCH´S CHICKEN, *1 calle, near the stadium.*

Chinese
Chinese restaurants with standard Cantonese fare include the **Copa de Oro**, 2 Avenida, 2/3 Calles SW No. 4; **Lucky**, 3 Calle, 3/4 Avenidas, just south of the main square; the **Central Palace**, 4 Calle, 6/7 Avenidas No. 43, SW; **China Town**, 5 Calle, 7 Avenida SW; and **Taiwan**, 5 Avenida, 2/3 Calles, NW.

Other Fare
Most restaurants catering to middle-class residents are located on the outskirts, especially along Avenida Circunvalación, the ring road.
DON UDO'S, *Blvd. Los Proceres, just off the Circunvalación. Tel. 552-5225.*
One of the finest restaurants in San Pedro Sula, with an outdoor deck, bar, and a gourmet food store with European meats, cheeses, and wines. Open for breakfast, lunch, and dinner. The proprietor is Dutch.
LA ESTANCIA, *6 Calle, 12 Avenida NO, Barrio Los Andes.*
A good beef restaurant, serving steaks cooked over an open wood grill, Uruguayan style.
PAT'S STEAK HOUSE, *out of the way at 5 Calle, 17 Avenida SW (on the ring road, in the vicinity of the Hotel Copantl Sula). Tel. 5530939. Reservations recommended.*
This is your best choice if you're looking for a thick cut of beef or a surf 'n turf combo. $10 and up for a meal. Owned by an American, it's often full.
LAS TEJAS, *along the curve in the ring road at 9 Calle, 16/17 Avenida.*
Serves grilled meats to a hacienda theme.
JOSÉ Y PEPE'S, *Circunvalación at 6 Calle SW.*
Steaks, seafood, and Mexican specialties. They have a more pleasant branch above town *in Colonia Palmira, at Avenida República de Panamá 2027.*
TGI FRIDAY'S, *Blvd. Los Proceres, a couple blocks up from the Circunvalación.*
For those of you requiring a hit of home. Great bar, efficient service. Happy Hour is from 4:30 to 7pm One of the best restaurants in town.
LA ESPUELA, *Circunvalación, Barrio Los Andes.*
Excellent Honduran cuisine in an open air, candlelit setting, with strolling mariachis in the evenings (they take requests) serenading your table. Note:

there are two La Espuela's; the older one with the address listed above is the preferred one.

RESTAURANT VICENTE, *1/2 Calle, 7 Avenida, Tel. 5521335.*
Good Italian cuisine since 1962.

PIZZERIA ITALIA, *1 Calle, 7 Avenida.*
Same owners as Restaurant Vicente above. Best pizza in town at reasonable prices. Funky decor.

CHEF MARIANO, *9/10, Calle 16 Avenida, Barrio Suyapa in the Zona Viva just off the Circunvalación.*
The only restaurant in town specializing in North Coast Garifuna specialties.

RESTAURANTE ITALIA, *1 Calle, 8 Avenida.*
Excellent Italian food and the absolutely, positively best ice cream this side of Ben & Jerry´s.

EL FOGONCITO, *1 Calle, 11 Ave, Blvd Morazon, in front ofHoliday Inn, Tel 553-3000.*
I recommend this place for great Mexican food, wonderful ambiance and central location. They have a good bar too.

Cafés

A good downtown cafe frequented by everyday folks is **Espresso Americano**, located on the peatonal right on the newly renovated Central Park. It's a great place to cool off from the San Pedro heat. Big picture window for people watching. Good coffee. Highly recommended.

Seeing the Sights

If I told you there were sights to see in San Pedro Sula, in the usual touristic sense, I would be pulling your leg. Despite San Pedro's long history, all of the city is modern, and there are no notable parks or museums or public institutions. Even the **Cathedral**, with its neo-colonial appearance, is a post-war structure.

You can, however, stroll the streets and get a sense of the commercial life of the town, or shop for handicrafts; though the city is hot for much of the year, especially from April to October, without the cooling sea breezes of the coast. If you're not here for business, you will use San Pedro as a base for visits to Copán, banana country, and the coast to the north. See below ("Trips from San Pedro Sula") for more details.

For an in-town excursion, you can go up to the **Mirador Caprí** (viewpoint) west of the city. This is just a parking area and a Coke stand on a hill, about four kilometers from downtown. Take a taxi ($5 or less) or your own car. There are no buses. On a clear day you can see for miles, to the mountains that look over Lake Yojoa to the south.

The **San Pedro Sula Museum of History and Anthropology**, 4 Calle 3 Avenida (three blocks from the Gran Hotel Sula), *Tel. 557-1496*, is highly recommended. This is one of the finest museums in the country. Housed in an exquisitely renovated school building, the museum features exhibits of pre-Colombian, Colonial, and post-Colonial periods, with an emphasis on San Pedro Sula and its environs. Outdoor cafeteria, gardens, auditorium, library, wonderful gift/crafts shop with excellent pieces from all over Honduras, reasonable prices. The museum purchases crafts directly from the artisans, ensuring good value and that the artisan receives a fair price for their work. Hours are 10am-4pm Tuesday through Sunday. Admission Lps 5.

The **Centro Cultural Sampedrano**, 4 Calle 3 Avenida, has a public library with newspapers, books, and magazines in English. Air conditioned, a good place to cool off and catch up on the news. They offer English classes, an art gallery, exhibitions, and theater productions.

Nightlife & Entertainment
Nightclubs

In Honduras, **nightclubs** usually refer to bars where mostly young males go to partake of alcoholic drinks and watch young, extremely scantily clad women dance up a storm. For those used to such places in the US, you will find Honduran nightclubs refreshingly different.

In the States, it's all about money; strip clubs are big business. In Honduras, the emphasis is more on good clean fun and 'a night out with 'the boys.' On the downside is the fact that most of the pretty young women dancing for you are there due to economic necessity. Most are from poor families and their earnings from dancing go directly to support their families. Although some dancers will offer to return to your hotel with you, the AIDS epidemic requires that a policy of 'look, don't touch' be employed. Ask your taxi driver or hotel front desk clerk for the latest hot strip club of the moment.

Bars
SHAUKI'S PLACE, *18 Ave, 8 Calle.*

Shauki, a Honduran of Arab descent, presides over the bar and always has a handshake for new and old clients alike. English spoken. A speciality of the

AIDS Warning

San Pedro Sula has a very high AIDS infection rate. This is not the place to seek companionship from the world's oldest profession or engage in casual or unprotected sex. Aids testing is recommended prior to any new, local encounter and caution is the watchword. San Pedro Sula is not the place to take risks.

house is fried bull testicles (yes, you read correctly), usually consumed as an appetizer with a couple of cold beers. Not for the faint hearted!

SEÑOR FROGS, *Blvd. Los Proceres, between 19 and 20 Calle, S.O.*
Pool tables, karaoke, large screen TV, 4 bars, disco, restaurant.

JOHNNY´S BAR, *4 Ave, 8 - 9 Calle.*
A unique 1950's-era lounge. Ecclectic music from the owners personal lp collection. The neighborhood is not the greatest at night, so better to hop a taxi. Highly recommended for hardcore lounge lizards.

TGI Fridays has an excellent bar that has become theplace for young San Pedro Yuppies to while away the evenings. **Applebees**, **Ruby Tuesdays** and **Fogoncito** have great bars that hop at night. For the older set, the **Gran Hotel Sula** and the **Camino Real InterContinental** both have very nice, classy bars.

Gambling
San Pedro Sula's only casino is in the **Hotel Copantl**. Entry is restricted to foreigners only.

Golf
La Lomas Golf & Country Club, *Choloma*, and **La Lima Country Club**, *La Lima*. Both are open to the public.

Movies
What the heck, they're cheap. Newspapers don't give the addresses of the cinemas. **The Tropicana I and II** is at 7 Av, 2 Calle SW; **The Aquarius** at 11 Avenida, 2 Calle NW; **Plaza de Sula** (five screens); **Metro** (triplex); and **Geminis I and II**. All theaters are within walking distance of each other. Cinemas are very popular, especially on weekend evenings, with new films starting on Fridays. Movie theaters are clean, modern, and reasonably priced. Films are in English with Spanish subtitles.

Shopping
The **Mercado de Artesanías Populares**, 6 Calle, 8/9 Avenidas NW (also known as **Guamilito Market**), sponsored by the tourist office, has a variety of sculptures in wood, straw items, pottery, hammocks, silkscreen prints, and primitive paintings. Guamilito is the best place in town to see a wide variety of souvenirs at good prices in an authentic market setting. Bargaining is encouraged.

Casa del Sol, in front of Guamilito Market and at Multiplaza Mall, has an excellent selection of Honduran crafts. The best art gallery in San Pedro Sula is **Maymo Art Gallery**, 2 Calle 6/7 Avenida SO, *Tel. 530-318*. They specialize in Honduran painters and do custom framing.

There are three malls in town. **Megaplaza**, on the road to the airport; **Metroplaza**, on the road to Puerto Cortez, has movie theaters and a food court; and **Multiplaza**, on the road to Tegucigalpa, next door to the Camino Real InterContinental. With a food court, the Multiplaza is the most luxurious of the three.

Excursions & Day Trips
West of San Pedro Sula
Cusuco National Park is 20 kilometers west of San Pedro Sula, located in the Merendon Mountain range. The park has a visitors center, dorm facilities and camping is available.

The park takes in a section of just 10 square kilometers of cloud forest on **Tilineo Peak**, divided into a central absolute reserve and a surrounding buffer zone of recovering forest, where agriculture is subject to controls to protect the central area. Quetzals are said to be readily sighted in April and May. Other wildlife includes toucans, and monkeys. Conifers grow at the higher levels.

Nature trails are in the works, and a visitors center has been set up in the village of Buenos Aires. Acess is via a roundabout route, south from San Pedro, then west and to Cofradia and on to Buenos Aires, a 2-3 hour trip. For information, contact: **Hector Rodrigo Pastor Fasquelle Foundation** (they manage the park), 1 Calle 5 Avenida NO (located above Pizzeria Italia), *Tel. 553-3397, E-mail: fehrpf@globalnet.hn.*

North of San Pedro Sula
Lake Ticamaya, about one by two kilometers, is a relatively shallow body of water that attracts herons and other water-loving birds. It lies southeast of **Choloma**, off the highway north from San Pedro Sula. The many maquila factories are the big thing here, where clothing for export to US markets are assembled. You can golf here at **Las Lomas Golf & Country Club**, *Tel. 553-3106, Fax 557-2040.* The club is also a hotel with a pool and restaurant, conference center, and bar.

East of San Pedro Sula
The road from San Pedro Sula to the east, toward El Progreso and the coast, is straight and flat — but watch out for banana peels! Past the airport, nine kilometers out, is an industrial zone. Then you enter banana country.

Practical Information
Banks
For street money exchange, go topedestrian mall, just off the Central Park. Don't take the first offer — rates vary by quite a bit even within the park. From appearances, nobody's worried very much about security. Dexterous traders flip inch-thick wads of 100-lempira notes in your face with one hand as you pass, and display a calculator in the other as they call out the exchange rate of the day.

There are many banks downtown, dollars can be exchanged at any of them at the same rate.

Credomatic handles Visa, Mastercard and American Express, 5 Ave 1 y 2 Calle, *Tel 557-4351*. For cash advances. **Multiviajes**, 2 Calle 2 y 3 Ave, is an all purpose travel agency and is also the representative for American Express in San Pedro Sula.

Churches
- **Latter Day Saints**, Bancatlan building, 3 Avenida, 1 Calle NW, *Tel. 552-8152*
- **Episcopal**, El Buen Pastor, 23 Avenida, 21 Calle, Colonia Trejo, *Tel. 552-2140*
- **Mennonite**, 2 Calle 1507 NE, *Tel. 552-7821*
- **Second Baptist Church**, 4 Avenida, 10/11 Calles SW, *Tel. 553-4039*

Consulates
- **Belgium**, 6/7 Avenida 4 Calle, *Tel. 553-2702*
- **El Salvador**, Edificio Rivera y Compañia, 704, 3 Calle, 5 Avenida N.O., *Tel 553-4604*
- **Germany**, 6 Avenida NO Av. Circunvalación next to the Texaco station, *Tel. 553-1244*
- **Guatemala**, 8 Calle, 5/6 Avenidas No. 38, Barrio Guamalito, *Tel. 553-0653*
- **Italy**, 5 Avenida, 1/2 Calles NW, Constancia building, *Tel. 552-3672*
- **United Kingdom**, 10 Calle, 13 Avenida, *Tel. 557-2046*
- **US Citizens Service Office and Consular Agent**, Banco Atlantida Building, 8th Floor, *Tel 558-1580*. Open Monday, Wednesday and Friday 1-4pm.

Couriers
Federal Express, Edificio Rivoli Plaza, Avenida Circunvalación, 2 Calle S.O. *Tel. 5576590, 5576591, Fax 5576581, fdxopsap@netsys.hn*.

Fiesta
The big local celebration is on June 29, in honor of Saints Peter and Paul. The festivities run for an entire week — at least.

Film
One store well stocked with a variety of film is **Kodak Express**, on the peatonal. They can also do quality same day processing.

Immigration
The immigration office is located on the Calle Peatonal, just off the Central Park. It's open Monday through Friday, 7am–4:30pm

Post Office
The post office in town is located at 3 Avenida, 9 Calle SW, No. 75.

Telephones

Hondutel is at 4 Avenida, 4 Calle SW. Emergency numbers in San Pedro Sula are the same as in Tegucigalpa:
- **123** – AT&T USA Direct
- **191** – Long distance in Honduras
- **192** – Telephone number information
- **196** – Time of Day
- **197** – International long distance
- **198** – Fire
- **199** – Public security (police)

Tours & Travel Agencies

The usual destinations for day trips from San Pedro Sula are the ruins of Copán, Lake Yojoa, the fortress of Omoa on the Caribbean, banana plantations, Tela, and the Lancetilla botanical garden; but there are other possibilities, including Comayagua and even Tegucigalpa.

For the latest travel and tour information, pick up *Honduras Tips* magazine. Among the travel agencies in San Pedro Sula are:
- **Garifuna Tours**, *Tel/Fax 448-2904*. E-mail: *tours@honduras.com, web: www.garifunatours.com*. Trips to North Coast National Parks, Copan Ruinas. Recommended.
- **Mesoamerica Travel**, Edificio Picadelli, local No. 206 1 y 3 ave, 11 calle S.O., *Tel 557-0332, 552-3898, Fax 557-6886, info@mesoamerica-travel.com*. Trips to La Mosquitia led by biologist and La Mosquitia expert Hauke Hoops. Punta Sal, Cuero y Salado, Copan Ruinas, Cusuco.
- **Mundirama Travel Service**, Edificio Martínez Valenzuela (American Express representative), 2 Calle SW, 2/3 Avenidas, *Tel. 553-0490*.
- **MC Tours**, *Tel. 552-4549, 552-4455, Fax 557-3076*, Copán Ruinas Office: *651-4453, Fax 651-4297, E-mail: sales@mctours-honduras.com; web: www.mctours-honduras.com*. Tela, La Ceiba, Trujillo, Bay Islands, Omoa, Lake Yojoa. Specializing in escorted trips to Copán Ruins where they operate the luxurious Hotel Marina. Trip catalog available.
- **Vitour**, 2 Calle 2 y 3 Ave, 1/2 block from Hotel Bolivar, *Tel 557-3808, E-mail: vitour@sigmanet.hn; web: www.vitourhn.com*. Recommended travel agency.

Approximate prices of trips from San Pedro Sula are:
- **Banana plantation** tour, $30
- **Lake Yojoa** and **Pulhapanzak Falls**, $65
- **Cusuco National Park** overnight, including camping, $160
- **Copán Ruins** and **Pulhapanzak Falls**, $75 and up for a day trip, $130 and up overnight
- **Telamar beach resort/Lancetilla Botanical Garden**, $65

- **Omoa**, $65
- **Tegucigalpa** and **Valle de Angeles**, $105 ($140 overnight)
- **Trujillo**, $140 overnight.

If you speak some Spanish and can negotiate with a taxi driver, you can arrange some of these trips for a group of four for considerably less.

La Lima

Two kilometers past the airport is the turn for **La Lima**, capital of bananas. You are surrounded by bananas for as far as you can see. In La Lima, turn right, and you will cross a bridge over the brown Chamelecón River. Alongside is another, pedestrian bridge. Above, **Chiquita** on the water tank watches over. The head office of Chiquita, United Brands, is here.

Past the bridge, on the left side, are the banana company operations, which you can visit if you arrive between 7am and 10am, or from 12:30pm to 2:30pm It is all impressive. I have eaten bananas all my life, yet until I went to La Lima, I was in the dark about the basics of cultivating this fruit and transporting it to markets worldwide.

Well, the guides will show you everything. Bunches of bananas are covered with plastic to protect the fruit from insects. Plants at different stages of maturity are color-coded. Branches laden with bananas are supported with a special tool while they are hacked off the plant with a couple of expert strokes of a machete. The whole mature plant is then cut down, but for a single shoot that will grow up to replace it. The stem of bananas, meanwhile, is transported to the processing plant, where fruits are washed, separated into bunches, sorted, and washed again. Chemical treatment retards ripening, then the fruit is packed and weighed. Blemished fruits go their separate way, to be processed into baby food. As industrial tours go, this one is off-beat, and well worth taking.

Also in town is the **La Lima Country Club**, open to the public, with golf, tennis, and a swimming pool available.

Beyond La Lima, just two kilometers before Progreso, there is a smaller banana processing plant on the left side of the road. With a small tip, you can arrange to visit it, and it takes less time than to see the one at La Lima.

Buses operating on the route to Tela will take you to La Lima for less than 50 cents. While you're out this way, you can also view the classic two-level arrangement of banana towns: standardized housing for the field laborers, which, though it is better than what most people would otherwise inhabit, is still visually dreary and sterile; and pools, golf courses and attractively designed and landscaped residential bungalows for the upper ranks of employees.

El Progreso

Just before **El Progreso**, you cross the **Río Ulúa**, no more attractive than the Chamelecón. El Progreso is a transit town, as much for bananas as for people, on the shortcut from Tegucigalpa to Tela. The bus stop for Tela is two blocks from the main square.

You may visit the **IMAPRO** crafts factory and Turicentro located just outside of Progresso on the road to Tela, *Tel. 6661200, 6664700*, where they make handmade mahogony doors and chests and a variety of crafts.

Department of Yoro

Most travelers will head north from El Progreso to Tela, La Ceiba (takeoff point for the Bay Islands) and, possibly, Trujillo. These places are covered in the next chapter. To the east, however, is an area little visited and lightly populated, the **department of Yoro**, covering the long valley sheltered from the coast by a ridge of mountains. Some of the residents are the remaining Jicaque Indians who were displaced from the coast by migrations of Black Caribs, and, under the influence of missionaries, adopted settled corn agriculture, much like the Indians of western Honduras.

Capital of the area, the town dates from 1578. The name derives from the Nahuatl for "center." Many place names in Honduras are in the language of the Mexican Indians who accompanied the Spanish conquerors.

An odd phenomenon is said to recur every year between June 14 and 25 in **El Pantano**, just over a kilometer to the southeast of the center of Yoro, when a fierce combination of downpour, thunder, lightning and winds leaves in its wake a scattering of stranded fish. This **rain of fish** has given rise to many theories as to its causes. One is that fish from the Atlantic, at the end of their life span, sense and follow an extreme low-pressure system up the Aguán valley to Yoro, and jump ashore when the storm is at its worst.

Elsewhere in the Department of Yoro

Montaña de Yoro National Park, covering 155 square kilometers of rain forest south of Yoro, is adjacent to Torupane reserve of the Jicaque Indians. A 3 or 4 hour hike from Yoro, access by foot or horse only, for the adventurous. For more information, contact Amigos de Montaña de Yoro Office, Central Park above the library.

Ayapa Volcano, south of Yoro, holds caves with pools inhabited by blind fish.

Olanchito, 243 kilometers from San Pedro Sula, is the center of one of the fastest-growing agricultural areas of Honduras, along the Aguán River. The town was founded in 1530, moved to a new location, and never flourished until recent times. Accommodations for visitors are available at the **Hotel Valle Aguán**. There are frequent buses to La Ceiba. **Tocoa**, to the east, is a bustling commercial center

Parque Nacional Pico Pijol, 41 km from El Progresso, access via the village of Morazan. There's a cloud forest at higher elevations, natural swimming holes, and waterfalls with a natural rock slide. Located about a 1/2 hour drive and a 10 minute walk from Morazan. There is a bus, but it is much quicker to hitchhike. Information on Pico Pijol National Park at their office on the Central Park in Morazan.

Cuevas de Tigre, located about 15 km outside of Yoro near the village of La Rosa. There's a natural pool for swimming, and it's possible to swim under the rocks and enter a cave. There is also a dry entrance for those who prefer climbing. Be prepared for cold water. Beyond La Rosa, about 20 km away, is the village of **Luquigue**, a quaint farming village which is the site of the first Missionary Catholic Church built in Honduras. The church is built from adobe with walls 5 feet thick. No accomodations here, and only one bus per day from Yoro.

Another pretty feature in the area are the **Natural Bridge Caverns**, a two hour hike from San Antonio. The river flows through a cave which is fed by a hot spring which falls from the ceiling.

Chapter 13

the north coast

The northwestern lowlands of Honduras — a strip about 50 kilometers wide, backed by mountain ridges for almost 200 kilometers — are the banana republic of Honduras. I don't mean this in any demeaning, stereotyping way. It's just that banana cultivation and commerce in bananas have made this area what it is today.

Farther east, toward the border of Nicaragua, where the land is poorly drained and mostly uncultivable, things are much as they were 100, 200, even 300 years ago. Hardly a road penetrates the marshes and forests, transport is mainly by boat, and Indian bands live in scattered groups.

Just 130 years ago, the northwestern coast was also a lightly inhabited area, where remnant towns dating from colonial days held on precariously, amid drenching rains, enervating heat, swarms of insects, yellow fever, thick undergrowth, and assorted other maladies and negatives.

The North Coast's History

Christopher Columbus was probably the first European to sail along the northern coast of Honduras, during his fourth voyage to the Americas, in 1502. Puerto Caballos, Omoa, and Trujillo were established as towns in succeeding decades, and if the government and mining and agriculture all functioned inland, it was at least necessary to maintain a presence along the coast in order to protect the lifeline of Honduras and neighboring colonies: the Spanish sea lanes.

But even these fortified positions declined in importance after independence. English ships, once forbidden, became the major carriers of trade. And the fractious

United Provinces of Central America were no serious opposition to the English navy, or to merchants under its protection who set up outposts along the shore. Honduran military concerns were elsewhere: in the repetitive wars within Central America, and in rebellions within Honduras itself. The coast was ignored.

The Banana Industry

And then bananas happened.

Wild bananas, offshoot of a plant that originated off the coast of Africa, grew in the Honduran lowlands, and a commercial, edible kind came to be cultivated in small quantities, after bananas were first exported from Costa Rica in the 1870s. But the banana business stayed in Costa Rica, from where all the refrigerated shipping was controlled by the **United Fruit Company**.

Around the turn of the century, merchants based in New Orleans began to look at Honduras as an alternative to the United Fruit monopoly. The **Standard Fruit Company** was organized in 1899 to plant and ship Honduran bananas. The fabled Sam Zemurray, an immigrant to New Orleans, founded the **Cuyamel Fruit Company**. United Fruit itself moved in soon after, and eventually bought out Zemurray (who was to come out of retirement later to manage the enlarged company to greater and greater market penetration).

The banana companies cleared land and drained swamps. Port facilities were expanded to receive banana ships, and rail lines were extended to carry the fruit to port from all over the lowlands. With virtually nothing to rely on in the way of governmental services, the banana companies established their own medical and social benefits, and paid wages above local standards to insure a steady supply of labor. Immigrants were attracted to work on the banana plantations, not only from central Honduras, but from the West Indies as well. Lebanese and Syrians became fixtures in commerce. Research centers were established to study new crops, and plant pathogens.

Honduras soon became the largest exporter of bananas in the world, and remained the leader well into the 1940s. Decaying colonial outposts revived, and what was a remote corner of the nation became its most dynamic area. Today, all of the large towns of Honduras after Tegucigalpa are on or near the north coast, along with all of the railroads, and most of the better highways.

Uneven Progress

The progress of the north was not, of course, uniformly smooth. In the 1930s, Panama disease attacked the plantations, and some were abandoned, or planted in Abacá (manila hemp). It was only with rotation of planting areas, the replanting of new strains over a period of time, and the application of large amounts of pesticide that the industry was saved.

Meanwhile, the banana companies, and especially United Fruit, came under attack for meddling in local politics, for restricting their investments to the coastal area, and for not building a railroad to the interior, as once promised. Things came to a head in 1954, when banana workers refused to work on Sundays without double pay. Other salaried workers joined in. So novel was the strike that it became a Central American issue, with the government of Guatemala taking the side of the workers. The dispute was settled with wage boosts and such "radical" benefits as paid vacations. Collective bargaining was legalized, and Honduras had its first effective labor unions.

Over time, Honduras' share of the world banana market declined, as the banana companies expanded to other countries. Eventually, seeking to lessen its exposure, United Fruit diversified into cattle-raising, pineapples and palm-oil production, and began to buy its bananas from independent farmers. But bananas and the banana companies remain the engine that drives the economy of the north coast, and of all of Honduras.

Banana Tours, Indigenous Peoples, & Beaches

All this, of course, is background for the visitor to the north coast, though there *are* aspects of the banana trade and associated ventures that are well worth looking at even for casual visitors. The tour of banana company operations at La Lima, mentioned in the previous chapter, is one example; the Lancetilla Botanical Garden, near Tela, is another.

There are also attractions for the visitor interested in peoples. The **Garífunas**, or Black Caribs, near Trujillo and Tela, and the **Miskito** and **Sumo** and **Paya Indians** along the eastern stretches of coast, are little known, and little understood, outside their territories.

The main attraction of the north coast, however, is **beaches**. There are miles and miles and miles and miles of sandy strip, bordered by palms, as idyllic as any. The most accessible parts, near the ports, have some hotels, and even a few rather good resorts. And if it's isolation that you're after, you do not have to travel very far from any coastal town to find a stretch, away from major roads, where hardly anybody has gone before you.

Puerto Cortés

Puerto Cortés is the major port of Honduras, and one of the largest in Central America, with modern container facilities, stretching for five kilometers along a bay near the mouth of the Chamelecón River. Located 57 kilometers from San Pedro Sula and 303 kilometers from Tegucigalpa, it's a hot and humid place, with more than 100 inches of rainfall every year, though some sea breezes relieve the heaviness of the climate.

Puerto Cortés dates from the first days of the Spanish conquest. An expedition led by Gil González Dávila, in danger of sinking during a storm, jettisoned 17 horses in great secrecy, to avoid revealing to Indians the mortality of the strange animals. The Spaniards called the place Puerto Caballos ("Port of Horses"), and so was it known until 1869. Puerto Caballos was the major port of colonial Honduras, and for Guatemala as well. In came wine and oil from Spain, and out to the metropolis went indigo, silver, cacao and cochineal. When pirate depredations disrupted trade – the city was sacked in 1591 and 1596 – the principal depot for trade was moved up the coast to Omoa, where a major fortification was erected.

The modern city of Puerto Cortés dates from 1869, when it was founded on swampland across the bay from the old Spanish port, as the terminus of a new interoceanic railway. The railway never got very far, but Puerto Cortés prospered anyway, as a banana port, and later as a center for oil refining. Oddly, it was also the base of the Louisiana lottery from 1893 to 1895, after a run-in with the U.S. Post Office.

Arrivals & Departures

By Bus

Lodging and eating places are limited; consider taking a local bus for the day to Puerto Cortés from San Pedro Sula. Impala leaves every hour from 6am-7pm from 2 Avenida, 4/5 Calles NW (**Empresa Impala**, *Tel. 553-3111*). Citul leaves every 15 minutes from 5am-8pm from 7 Calle 5/6 Avenidas SW (**Empresa Citul**, *Tel. 553-0070*). In Puerto Cortés, the Impala station is at 3 Avenida, 3 Calle. Local buses will take you along the coast to Omoa and Pinalejo (see below).

By Train

A narrow-gauge banana-era train runs between Puerto Cortés and Tela. Trains leave Puerto Cortés Friday and Sunday at 7am, a four-hour trip. The train returns leaving Tela at 2pm, arriving in Puerto Cortés at 6pm.

By Sea

Puerto Cortés is a port, and you are within your rights to insist that it is possible to continue to somewhere by sea. Indeed you can, but patience is required. Large canoes sometimes leave for the Carib towns of Lívingston in Guatemala and Punta Gorda in Belize. Boat service, however, is very irregular – if there are not enough passengers the boat will not leave port.

This can be a soaking voyage even in mild seas. Boats sail to Belize from La Laguna by the fish market, under the new bridge south of Puerto Cortés. There is an immigration office there.

It is a four hour trip by bus to the Guatemalan port of Puerto Barrios. The Honduran border crossing at Corinto is open from 6am to 8pm. The last bus from Corinto leaves at 5pm.

Orientation/Getting Around Town

Of interest are the old Spanish fort at Omoa, just up the coast, and the beaches nearby. Local buses will take you to the Garífuna villages of Travesía and Baja Mar just east of Puerto Cortés. There are few facilities. A Garifuna dance and music festival is held in Baja Mar each year.

For use of a beach with services (restaurant, boats, horseback riding), try the Hotel Playa or the Costa Azul. Other nearby beaches include Coca Cola El Faro, Cienguita, Masca and Omoa Beach.

Maya Rent A Car has an agency at 3 Avenida, 2/3 Calles, *Tel. 5550064, Fax 5550218.*

Where to Stay

HOTEL MR. GGEER, *2 Avenida, 9 Calle. Tel. 665-0444, Fax 655-0750. 30 rooms. $22 double.*

No, I didn't misspell the name. This is a modern hotel, the best in the port, with restaurant and bar, air conditioning, and carpeted rooms with television. A buffet lunch is available most days.

HOTEL PLAYA, *Barrio Cienaguita. Tel. 665-1105. 25 rooms. $91 double.*

This hotel is on the outskirts of Puerto Cortés, four kilometers toward Omoa, then half a kilometer down a side road. Rooms in motel-style low-lying wings, practically on the water, have hardwood panelling, TV, air-conditioning, phone, and a double and single bed; and there are larger apartments. Landscaping and public areas are somewhat harsh in aspect. The hotel is mostly patronized by families from San Pedro Sula on weekend getaways.

Elsewhere around Puerto Cortés, you'll find pleasant beaches along the road to the west. And not far from downtown, in the opposite direction from the port, there's one acceptable hotel, the **Costa Azul,** *Tel. 665-2260, Fax 5552262,* at the El Faro beach area, $37 double.

Where to Eat

You will find no unexpected surprises for your tummy at either **El Torito** (*The Little Bull*), which specializes in red meat, and **Playa Azul** (*Blue Beach*), which serves sea creatures.

Practical Information

Banks include **Bancahsa, Banco Atlántida** (2 Avenida, 3/4 Calles), **Banco de Occidente** (4 Calle, 2/3 Avenidas) and **Lloyds Bank** (2 Avenida, 3 Calle).

Omoa

Omoa dates from late in the colonial period, when the captain-general of Guatemala ordered the founding of a new port, in 1752. The purpose was not only to protect insecure Spanish sea lanes and control smuggling, but to halt the advance of the British, who already had outposts in Belize, the Bay Islands, and at Black River (Río Tinto) in Mosquitia.

Situated east of the mouth of the Motagua River, at a deep harbor, Omoa was well situated to serve not only the commerce of indigo from Guatemala, but of silver from Honduras as well, and it remained the major port on the coast for many years.

A major port required a major defense, and in 1759, work was started on the construction of the **Castillo de San Fernando (Castle of San Fernando)**, named for the saint of King Ferdinand VI of Spain, who ordered its construction. The task was monumental. With no suitable building materials nearby, stone was brought from Santo Tomás de Castilla on the Bay of Amatique in Guatemala. As Indian laborers died off, they were replaced by black slaves. Omoa became known as the graveyard of Honduras. By 1775, the castle was considered complete. It was also ready to be attacked.

In 1779, Spain was again at war with England, this time as an ally of the newly independent United States. On October 16, Omoa was assaulted from land and sea by a mixed English force of regular troops, Baymen from Roatán, and Sambo, Miskito and Carib allies. After four days the fortress fell, and with it, several hundred prisoners, along with two ships full of cargo. In November, Spanish forces mounted a counter-siege, and managed to oust the invaders, frustrating a British plan to control the coast and drive on through Nicaragua.

Omoa stood unchallenged thereafter, functioning as a gateway for trade, though the British managed to dig in at less defended points on the coast. Eventually, Omoa lost its importance as a port, and the fortress was used for a time to house political prisoners. Until well into this century, it served as the nation's foremost penitentiary. Despite its age, the fortress of San Fernando, solidly built, remains in excellent condition. Triangular in shape, it is roughly 200 feet on a side, with walls 12 feet thick and 18 feet high. It is Honduras' largest colonial fort.

Offshore, ships are known to have foundered with Spanish treasure, and at least one wreck with a trove of gold coins was found, in 1972.

Omoa is a typical sleepy Central American coastal village. Not alot going on here, but then again that's part of its charm. It's quite untouristy and uncrowded during the week, however, on weekends the place fills up with day tripping Honduran families packed into pickup trucks out for an afternoon of fun in the sun. The village is a good place to belly up to some good seafood, crash in a reasonably priced hotel, and just hang around soaking up the village atmosphere.

Yax Pac Tours works out of Roli´s and Bernies Place, which is Omoas' best tourist hotel, *Barrio La Playa, Omoa, Tel/Fax 658-9082, yaxpactours@globalnet.hn, www.yaxpactours.com*. Swiss expat Roland 'Roli' Gassmann organizes good quality tours at a good price throughout Honduras and Guatemala (see Roli's & Bernie's Place, below).

Arrivals & Departures

Local bus service is available on **Transportes Omoa** from the center of Puerto Cortes to Omoa and Omoa beach. The bus stop in Puerto Cortes is at 3 and 4 Ave, 3 Calle.

From Omoa, it is possible to travel overland to Guatemala. To go from Omoa to Puerto Barrios, take the bus to Tegucigalpa, 1 hour. From Tegucigalpa there are 4 buses per day to Corinto or take a pickup (available all day). From Corinto take a pickup, 4 km to the paved road on the Guatemalan side of the border. From the border there are mini buses all day to Puerto Barrios. Total trip time from Omoa to Puerto Barrios is 4 hours.

To continue your journey along the Honduran Coast to Tela, La Ceiba, Bay Islands and Trujillo, you have to return to San Pedro Sula where there are good connections for direct buses and flights to the coast and islands.

Where to Stay

HOTEL ACANTILADOS DEL CARIBE (Caribbean Cliff Marine Club), *3 km east of Omoa. P. O. Box 23, Chivana, Omoa, Tel. 665-1461, US toll-free 800/ 327-4149. 18 units. $59 double. Visa, MasterCard.*

New and attractive stone-and-stucco cabanas facing the sea on a grassy hillock dotted with pines and bushes. Each unit has a porch and hammocks. There is no pool, nor television, but this is the best hotel in the area, with air-conditioned rooms, private beach, bar, and restaurant.

HOTEL BAHIA DE OMOA, *Tel 658-9076. 4 rooms. $16 double.*
Dutch-owned. Air conditioning, private bath.

HOSPEDAJE CHAMPA JULIETA, *Tel. 658-9174, $10 double.*
Inexpensive rooms.

Aside from Acantilados, mentioned above, the safest places to eat near Omoa are the stands on the beach, which offer fried fresh fish and Carib-style conch-and-coconut soup for a couple of dollars and up. A full meal of fried fish with all the fixins' will run about $7.

ROLI´S & BERNIE´S PLACE, *50 meters from beach on the main road, buses do not stop in front. Tel/Fax 658-9082, E-mail: Roli@yaxpactours.com English/German spoken, 4 double rooms for $8, Dormitory with 8 beds for $3, camping $2.*

Mountain view terrace, with 8 hammocks and camping space in a large shady yard. Free use of bicycles and ocean kayaks. Kitchen, BBQ, table tennis, darts, guitar. internet, fax, telephone and laundry service. Home-made bread every Saturday. Considered by many to be the best backpacker place in Omoa. Free map ofOmoa available - and always the most up to date Honduras travel information provided by Roli himself, the Swiss owner. He also runs tours to Guatemala and throughout Honduras *(www.yaxpactours.com).*

HOTEL FLAMINGO'S, *on the beach, Tel 658-9199, Fax 658-9288, 10 rooms, $30 double.*

This is the only hotel in Omoa on the beach, withair conditioning and cable TV.

Where to Eat

Omoa Beach offers a great variety of restaurants and *comedors* right on the beach, all serving great seafood dishes. Excellent food at **El Paraiso de Stanley**, which is well known as ' the ' gringo hangout around these parts. After a big meal here, what better than to stretch out on one of Stanley's hammocks with a sea view? Also recommended is **Los Flamingo's**, which boasts the only terrace in town with a sea view. **Comedor Amalu** is a local eatery with typical Honduran dishes.

Seeing the Sights

The **Fortress of Omoa**, *70 kilometers from San Pedro Sula, is open to visitors weekdays from 9am-4pm.* A nominal admission charge is collected at the visitors center alongside, an old building with displays that include maps, illustrations regarding Honduran history, cannon, cannonballs, and an anchor.

The fortress is massive, and yet, oddly, it has today the air of a blinded giant, surrounded as it is by pasture and banana fields. A utilitarian work, it is bare of decorative detail, topped by ramparts, with a lower outer wall with corner turrets.

Arched chambers line the interior courtyard, some of them replastered and restored. Certain of the chambers were used as lodgings by Spanish officials, others as kitchens, a chapel, a prison, a gunpowder store. One contains hundreds of cannonballs.

Visitors can walk on the ramparts, where rusting cannon lie, and look out over the fields toward the now-somewhat-distant sea.

Adjoining the fortress is the lagoon. Variations in water level, or perhaps seismic movements, cause its waters to turn sulfurous during the dry season, poisoning many fish.

Sports & Recreation

Centro Ecoturístico La Bambita is a 325-hectare tropical forest area for hiking, horseback riding, birding and wildlife observation.

Excursions & Day Trips

There are two small waterfalls called **Los Corros**, a 45 and 60 minute walk respectively. Both of them have natural pools where you can swim in the fresh clear mountain water. See Roli at Roli's place above for a map.

Masca, a small Garifuna village, has miles of unspoiled beaches. There are basic accommodations as well as two thatched roof 'champas' serving seafood and drinks. There is a new hotel in on the beach, **Villa del Mar.**

Tela

Ninety km east of San Pedro Sula, and one km off the main Progresso-La Ceiba highway, Tela is an ex-banana port town of clapboard houses that give it an aspect of a forgotten Caribbean port. The beaches are quite attractive, and though the waters are not as crystalline as those off the Bay Islands, and there are some currents, they are as nice as you'll find on the North Coast. In fact, there are rather ambitious plans to take advantage of the area's tourist potential with a resort complex to be called **Tela Bay**, to be called Tela Bay, but as of yet it is simply a plan on the drawing board and nothing has been done to implement the mega-project.

A spur of mountains rises to 2000 feet just inland, backed by the higher peaks of the **Nombre de Dios** range that forms the southern boundary of Atlántida department.

Tela was, for a time, the principal port of the United Fruit Company. But Panama disease and the relocation and rotation of banana plantings led to Tela's decline. The banana company residential compound has been converted into a resort, and the former United Fruit Company experimental station is now a unique botanical garden.

Security

As with any city or large town, personal security is an issue. The following recommendations will make your stay an unforgettable one. Don't walk along the beach from Tela to Ensenada or Triunfo de La Cruz; robberies on this lonely stretch of beach have been reported. Don't go out on the beach at night especially on solitary stretches. Don't walk around or go to the beach with backpacks, jewlery or camera equipment. You are best off leaving all valuables with your hotel. Lonely stretches of beach are wonderful, but remember you will increase your risk of being robbed.

Near Tela, the Hotel Telemar has a beautiful stretch of beach and is very secure.

Arrivals & Departures

By Bus

From San Pedro, take a bus from the Tupsa/Catisa station, 2 Avenida, 5/6 Calles SW, for Progresso, and change there for the bus to Tela. Buses leave every 15 minutes for El Progresso. However, you should take the direct bus to La Ceiba (same bus station), and tell the driver you want to get off at the entrance to Tela. From there it's a short 1 km taxi ride to the beach or your hotel, Lps 6 per person.

Note: This is a busy, crowded bus station, so watch your belongings carefully in and around the station.

Garifuna Tours in Tela, *Tel/Fax 448-2904, E-mail: tours@honduras.com, web: www.garifunatours.com,* runs a good shuttle service with a nice air-conditioned minibus to San Pedro Sula for $10, La Ceiba for $10, and Copán Ruinas for $29.

Buses leave from the terminal in Tela, two blocks east of the main square. Service to El Progresso is every half-hour. Another option is to hop a taxi (Lps 6) to the Texaco station on the main El Progresso-La Ceiba highway and catch the direct bus to San Pedro Sula. Bus service to La Ceiba is at least every hour. The trip to both El Progresso and La Ceiba takes about two hours from Tela.

To the Garifuna village of Tornabé, a bus departs every hour till 3 pm, Lps 5. To the Garifuna village of Triunfo de La Cruz, every hour till 5pm, Lps 4. Direct bus from Tela to Tegucigalpa, Empresa Cristina, Lps 80.

Another option is the Hedman Alas 1st class direct bus from San Pedro Sula to La Ceiba. Simply pay the fare to La Ceiba and tell the driver you want to get off at Tela. **Hedman Alas**, Barrio Guamilito 7 y 8 Ave, 3 Calle, San Pedro Sula, *Tel. 553-1361.*

By Train

A slow moving train operates from Tela-Puerto Cortés on Friday and Sunday, leaves Tela at 2pm. It's a 3-4 hour trip. The Puerto Cortés-Tela train runs Friday and Sunday at 7am.

Getting Around Town

A door to door taxi any place in the greater Tela area costs Lps 8 per person.

Where to Stay

VILLAS TELAMAR, *P. O. Box 47, Tela Nueva, Tel. 448-2196, Fax 448-2984, E-mail: telamar@simon.intertel.hn; web: www.villastelamar.com. 120 rooms. $57 double, $97-$175 for villas with up to four bedrooms and eight beds. U.S. reservations, Tel. 800/742-4276. Visa, MasterCard, American Express, Diners Club. Children up to 12 no charge.*

Much advertised, Villas Telamar is a resort, but in an off-beat kind of way, more like a sheltered residential enclave for banana-company families, which is what, in fact, it once was. It's clean and adequate and a good deal, though not an elegant destination — you won't find the carefully tended luxuriant tropical vegetation of some Bay Islands resorts, for example, nor crass diversions from pure relaxation.

Accommodations are in clapboard cottages set above ground on stilts to catch the breeze, surrounded by picket fences. Rooms have air conditioning, and you have the option of choosing an apartment with kitchenette, or a bungalow with up to eight beds and kitchen. Rates vary by type of accommodation, and how close you are to the water.

Facilities for all members of the family include two pools, tennis courts, an honest restaurant (grilled fish and shellfish, mainly), white sand beach with orderly rows of palms, golf, play areas, and a small, offbeat zoo, with felines, crocodile, toucans, and monkeys, among others.

This is a good place to catch the air of romance of old-time tropical travel, not luxurious in the modern sense (there are no uniform rooms with wall-to-wall carpeting, for example) but civilized, with the necessary amenities and details, and class: highly polished hardwood floors, towering ceilings and equally towering potted plants, wicker and rattan and mahogany furnishings, ample staff . . . ahh . . .

In addition to tennis on-site, fishing, golf and water skiing can be arranged. Horses are kept in Telamar's stables.

MAYA VISTA, *two blocks from the beach. Tel/Fax 448-1497, E-mail: mayavista@mail.com; web: www.mayavista.com. Doubles from $18-$32, 2-bedroom apartment sleeps four with living room $50, weekly and monthly rates.*

Owned and operated by a friendly Canadian couple from Québec, Pierre and Susanna Couture. Perched high up on a hill overlooking the town, two blocks up from the beach, with a breathtaking view of Tela Bay below. Six comfortable, breezy rooms, many with a view of the ocean. All rooms with private hot water bath and color TV with cable and ceiling fan.

Above the rooms is a pleasant restaurant/bar with a lovely view of the sea and the town below. Good food at reasonable prices, cooked up by Susanna. Specialties include, fish, shrimp, pastas and breakfasts. Fresh baked cake or pie each day.

Above the restaurant is a lookout tower that rises above the top floor of the hotel. It's a long climb up, but the reward is a spectacular 360 degree view of Tela, Punta Sal National Park, Lancetilla Botanical Gardens and the mountains that rise above it. Pickup at San Pedro Sula airport available.

HOTEL GRAN CENTRAL , *five blocks from the beach, three blocks from the Central Park. Tel. 448-1099, E-mail: grancentral@hotmail.com. Double $35, 4 persons $40, weekly and monthly rates.*

Opened in 1999, Frenchman Luc Bernard and his wife discovered an old, weathered banana port-era hotel and have transformed it into an oasis of sorts in downtown Tela. Four apartments with full kitchen, ceiling fan, air-conditioning, balcony. Finely furnished and tastefully decorated at a very reasonable price. The downstairs portion of the hotel houses a a classical dance studio (with classes taught by Mrs. Bernard) and a future bar/restaurant.

In Honduras it is quite rare to come across a quality restoration of any sort, no less a tourist hotel. More often than not, old structures are simply razed to the ground to make way for modren concrete ones. The efforts of the Bernards'should be acknowledged and supported by tourists in order to hopefully spur additional restoration projects of important historical buildings. Recommended.

HOTEL SHERWOOD, *on the beach, Tel. 448-1065. $33 double, $40 double in new wing. 40 rooms.*

All rooms with ocean view, family owned and operated. Air conditioning, color TV with cable, hotwater, new wing with balcony and tub, new lobby, beachfront restaurant, new bar, pool.

CESAR MARISCOS, *on the beach, Tel 448-2083, E-mail: info@hotelcesarmariscos.com. $44 double, 10 rooms.*

Rooms have air conditioning and color TV with cable. The restaurant has received high marks for its seafood. Comfortable rooms, ocean view. Recommended.

MANGO B&B, *1 block south of Central Park, Tel/Fax 448-0338, E-mail: mango@honduras.com, web: www.mangocafe.net. $22 double, 10 rooms.*

Rooms come with fan, hot water, bath, cable TV. Breakfast included in fee. Run by the friendly people at Garifuna Tours.

Where to Eat

There are assorted basic eateries around the main square and beach, and fast-food places in New Tela.

RESTAURANTE LUCES DEL NORTE, *half-block from the beach.*

Excellent seafood, fried fish fillet accompanied with fried plantains, salad, bread $5. Whole fried fish dinner $4 – finger lickin'good. Excellent breakfasts. Recommended.

HOTEL MAYA VISTA, *two blocks from the beach. Tel. 448-1497.*

An excellent family-run restaurant, fish, shrimp, pastas, breakfasts. Wonderful panoramic view from their deck. Home-baked cake or pie daily. Recommended.

CESAR MARISCOS, *on the beach.*

The original restaurant was well-known for its excellent seafood dishes. Recommended.

CASA AZUL BAR & RESTAURANT ITALIANO, *one block from the beach. Tel 448-1443.*

Run by a Canadian. Pizza, Spagetti, Lasagne, salads, meatballs, burgers, cappuchino, nice bar. Opens at 4pm, popular gringo hangout in evenings. Recommended.

MANGO CAFE, *downstairs from the Garifuna Museum. Tel. 448-2856, E-mail: mango@honduras.com, web: www.mangocafe.net.*
Italian, Honduran and Garifuna specialties: lasagna, pastas ,fish. Happy hour 6-7 pm Monday through Friday with two-for-one beers. Nice relaxing riverside atmosphere . Good food. Recommended. Info on ecotrips. Internet access is available here for $2 per hour. They also offer a Spanish School, 4 hours instruction per day,1:1 student teacher ratio, homestay, all meals, for $99 per week. Recommended.

TUTY´S RESTAURANT, *in front of Garifuna Tours.*
Good reasonably priced breakfast, *licuados* (shakes), Honduran breakfast $2. Good place to have breakfast while you´re waiting for your 8am departure to Punta Sal National Park with Garifuna Tours.

Nightlife & Entertainment

Tela moves to a distinctively Afro-Caribbean beat in the evenings. A recommended dance spot is **Gecko's Discoteque** in Tela Nueva, located between the center and Telemar, three blocks after the bridge on Calle Principal.

Casa Azul has a nice bar and restaurant that opens at 4pm. It's a popular hangout for travellers and expats, one block from the beach. Cesar Mariscos and the Hotel Sherwood next door have new bars on the beach, and are both recommended. **Maya Vista** has a lovely restaurant deck with a view of the bay.

Excursions & Day Trips

Garifuna Tours, P.O. Box 74, Tela, Central Park Office, *Tel/Fax 448-2904; E-mail: tours@garifuna.com, web: www.garifunatours.com.* Garifuna Tours are the **Tela Bay** ecotourism experts. Tela Bay extends from Punto Isopo to Punta Sal, some 44 km of beautiful white sand beaches and important ecosystems. Their tours are highly recommended for professionalism and value. Internet access is available here for $2 per hour.

Their **Punta Sal National Park Tour** features wonderful pristine, white sand beaches, azure, crystalline waters, jungle hike, hidden bays, snorkeling, expert naturalist guide, excellent opportunities to view troups of monkeys close up, good birding, terrific fried fish lunch cooked up by the local caretaker's wife for $3. Access via fast launch, 1 hour. Considered by many as Honduras' number one North Coast Caribbean national park. Tour leaves Tela at 8am from office of Garifuna Tours and returns at 3pm, $19 per person.

Punta Izopo National Park tour: kayaking through the mangrove canals of the Rio Platano and Rio Hicaque Lagoon. Tour departs 8:30am from Garifuna Tours office and returns 3pm. Transfer to the Garifuna seaside village of Triunfo de La Cruz, where kayaks await; while paddling view monkeys and bird life. Lunch on the beach at Triunfo de La Cruz. $16 per person.

Los Micos Lagoon tour: located within Punta Sal National Park, over 342 species of birds have been recorded. From Tela , transfer by Jeep to Los Micos, passing through the lovely, picturesque Garifuna village of Tornabé and the rustic beachfront hamlet of Miami. Transfer to outboard powered canoe for the Lagoon tour. Yummy fried fish lunch available in Miami. Tour leaves Tela at 8am from Garifuna Tours office and returns at 4pm, $20 per person.

Direct Shuttle Service with air-conditioned van to San Pedro Sula, Airport, 1 hour trip, $10; to downtown San Pedro Sula, 1 hour 15 min. $13; to La Ceiba, 1 hour, $10; Copán, 3 1/2 hours, $29.

Practical Information

There are several banks downtown. At the time of this writing, none of the banks in Tela accept US dollars (cash nor travelers checks). It is better to change money with the proprietor of your hotel. Street money changers may try to shortchange customers in Tela.

There is a Casa de Cambio on the same street as Hondutel. There is an ATM at Banco Atlantida in front of Telemar. You can get a VISA cash advance at Banco Atlantida.

For Tela info online: *www.tela-honduras.com.*

Lancetilla Experimental Station

Just four miles south of Tela is the **Lancetilla Experimental Station**, a wonderland of tropical effusiveness and variety. At 40 square km, Lancetilla is the largest botanical garden in Central America.

United Fruit established this center in 1926, as part of a program to diversify its plantings in Central America. To reach Lancetilla, take the road from Tela out to the San Pedro Sula highway. The Lancetilla turnoff is about a kilometer out of Tela. Follow the dirt road for three and a half kilometers to the entrance. It's also a pleasant walk from Tela of about an hour, however it is recommended to take a taxi.

The amphitheater of hills around the Lancetilla site protects it from the worst extremes of tropical weather, while the elevated situation provides natural drainage for the copious amounts of water that drop from the sky and flow from the surrounding mountains. By the time the property was turned over to the government of Honduras in 1974, following extensive hurricane damage and rising costs, over a thousand varieties of plants had been established. Some of them were notable success stories. The African oil palm has supplanted bananas on many United Fruit plantations; and eucalyptus and teak have also shown themselves to be comfortable here.

But the longtime director of the gardens, famed botanist Wilson Popenoe, to whom they are dedicated, did not limit plantings to crops with commercial potential. Ornamental plants have also been an important feature from the beginning, and these, in turn, attract a great variety of birds.

Among the many, many species of trees at Lancetilla:

Mahogany, which occurs naturally in the surrounding hills, is notably non-gregarious: one mahogany tree is isolated from the next in the forest or on a plantation. Mahogany wood is used for carving, and for furniture.

Teak, also used for furniture and dishes.

Bamboo plants, examples of different types gathered from all over the world. Some are more than 50 years old, and over 50 feet tall.

Nutmeg trees, which come as male-female pairs.

Cinnamon trees in several varieties.

Strychnine trees, which you cannot even touch without serious consequences, including, possibly, death. If you go out in the morning, you can see the bodies of birds that pecked at strychnine trees and dropped dead on the spot. Only certain ants can consume this tree.

A tree native to Africa produces a fruit that can be eaten only during four days a year, when cyanide compounds are absent. The rotting fruit is deadly. (Could this be the original forbidden fruit?)

Another tree produces a delicious fruit after 35 years of growth, under the best of conditions — obviously not a candidate for commercial plantations. I'm also told that there are coca plants in the park, which you might recognize by the parallel veins in their leaves.

The orchid collection can also be viewed, and plants are available for purchase.

Everything at Lancetilla is labeled with color-coded tags: *yellow* for ornamental, *red* for fruit, *green* for timber, and *black* for poisonous.

The garden is open from 7:30am to 3:30pm weekdays, 8:30am to 4pm on Saturday and Sunday, closed on Monday except for the nursery. There is now an admission fee of $4. You should arrive an hour before closing at the latest in order to see anything.

I recommend that you go in the early morning, about 6am, if you're on foot, in order to beat the heat, and to see all the birds that congregate in the trees along the way, toucans and many other parrots, motmots, oropendulas, and the Central American curassow, among others. There are more than 300 species, in fact, which can be seen in the area and in the park. It boasts the largest collection in the world of Asian fruit trees. A checklist is available at the visitors' center.

There is a restaurant at the entrance of the park, or you can picnic in designated areas. A map is given to visitors, but you should look into guide service when you arrive. There is no fee for a tour, but a tip is appropriate. Not all guides speak English.

San Juan & Tornabé

Several small **Garífuna** villages lie along the coast not far from Tela. **San Juan** is four kilometers to the west, and **Tornabé** is another three kilometers beyond. Both are reached by local bus from Tela.

The Garífunas, or Black Caribs, speak a language all their own, which is said to be of Amerindian origin, though some of their vocabulary can be recognized as coming from Creole English. Their houses are of bamboo and thatch, and blasting out from them is reggae music. They are interested in visitors, not least to be included in their photos.

You can join the Garífuna in a lovely seafood lunch or dinner. There are a number of thatched roofed comedors on the beach that serve up an excellent fried fish cooked in coconut oil and the requisite fried plantains, shredded cabbage salad, and pickled vegetables. Other specialties include shrimp, lobster, conch chowder and fresh baked coconut bread.

Buses leave for Tornabé every hour till 3 pm, 40 cents fare, or you can take a collective taxi from the main square for less than a dollar. From Tornabé, continue on to the small beachside hamlet of **Miami**, a wonderful idyllic spot on some of the best white sand beach in Central America. Thatched roof cottages – no accomodations or restaurants – but you may be able to have a woman cook up some fresh caught fish or shrimp for you. It's a two hour walk from Tornabé or a short drive down the beachfront track. Plans are in the works to turn the stretch of beach from Tornabé to Miami into a major tourism center called Tela Bay. See it now though, in its pristine state, before the developers move in.

Where to Stay

There is a small hotel on the beach in Tornabé called **The Last Resort**, *Tel. 984-3964, $32 double.*

Punta Sal Marine National Park

Punta Sal Marine National Park, adjoining the Garífuna villages at the west end of Tela Bay, is a protected area of beach and sea that includes reefs, wrecks, beaches, swamp, wet savanna, coastal lagoons, and cliffs – a varied combination in a small area. Punta Sal is now officially known as **Jeanette Kawas National Park**, in honor of the slain environmental activist who was gunned down in her Tela home.

Wildlife in the park includes ducks, manatees, caimans, and various species of monkey. The park stretches inland over more than 400 square kilometers. Spectacular white sand beaches, blue water, reefs, tropical forest, cliffs, rock formations, lagoon, excellent hiking and snorkeling. This is one of

the nation's most spectacular national parks. Information on Punta Sal available from **Fundación Prolansate**, Apartado Postal 32, Tela *Tel./Fax 448-2042, Tel. 448-2035, E-mail: fprocans@hondutel.hn*
Access is by boat from Tela. **Garifuna Tours**, *Tel. 448-2904, E-mail: tours@honduras.com*, runs trips for $16 per person. There are trails in the most easily accessible sections, and a couple of isolated fishing villages offer supplies in a pinch. Highly recommended.

The park boasts two hidden bays, **Puerto Escondido** and **Puerto Caribe**, and a signed trail through beautiful tropical forest joining the two bays. Lots of birds, parrots, toucans can be spotted. Cappuchino and Howler monkeys are readily viewed from close distances. Dolphins and manatees can also be seen. Myriad tropical fruit trees, great shell hunting on white sand beaches.

The park has an area of 781 square km. Its buffer zone extends from the Garifuna hamlet of Miami to Tornabé and the nuclear zone of the park runs from Miami to Punta Sal. The peninsula of Punta Sal is some 3 km long and 1 km wide. Bring your own picnic supplies or you can purchase the fresh catch of the day fried up with a side order of beans and rice from the caretaker's wife on Playa de Cocalito. It is possible to camp at Punta Sal – get permission from Prolansate prior, or contact Garifuna Tours and bring all food, water and supplies. You will be rewarded with having literally the entire national park to yourself!

Nearby Laguna de los Micos

On the way to Punta Sal is **Laguna de los Micos**, a lagoon stretching for 15 kilometers along the seaside track. Los Micos is located within Punta Sal National Park. It is a birders paradise, with over 342 species recorded. Birders will appreciate the marine avian species, including herons, ducks, swallows and pelicans. You can tour the lagoon on your own or with Garifuna Tours (see above and Tela's *Excursions & Day Trips*).

El Triunfo

East of Tela, about seven kilometers, is the village of **El Triunfo de la Cruz**, reached by an unpaved road, site of one of the first Spanish settlements in Honduras. A bus leaves for El Triunfo from one block east of the main square of Tela. Don't walk the beach between Tela and Triunfo – robberies have been reported. Accommodations at **Caribbean Coral Inn**, *Tel 994-9806, E-mail: caribcoral@globalnet.hn, web: www.globalnet.hn/caribcoralinn*. Rustic cabanas on the beach, $50 for a double room.

In Triunfo de la Cruz is the **Playa Drive In Caracol**, with excellent Garifuna seafood dishes.

At **Punto Izopo National Park**, 12 km east of Tela, you can see abundant wildlife: monkeys, alligators, turtles, good birding. Entry is via sea kayak through mangrove forest. Garifuna Tours run trips to Punta Izopo. For more information, contact Fundación Prolansate (see above under Punta Sal).

A bus leaves for El Triunfo from one block east of the main square of Tela. Buses every hour 'till 5pm, 30 cents.

La Ceiba

La Ceiba, 107 km east of Tela, is **Standard Fruit's** town, a banana port where ships move in, and sailors move about, with all their traditional carousing – although today you will be hard pressed to locate any honest to goodness sailors strolling downtown as just about all shipping traffic has relocated to Honduras' main port, Puerto Cortes.

Hondurans say that "Tegucigalpa is where we think, San Pedro is where we make money, and La Ceiba is where we have fun." This is the only city in Honduras where Carnival is celebrated in the great fashion of the Caribbean islands. La Ceiba's *carnaval*, nominally in honor of San Isidro, takes place during the third week in May, with dances, parades, beauty queens, floats, and general fooling around.

In the annals of banana exploits, La Ceiba and Standard Fruit are known for developing the giant Cavendish variety of banana to substitute for the gros Michel, which is regularly laid low by Panama disease. Out in the market, Standard is better known by its brand name, **Dole**. Dole pineapples as well as bananas now keep the port busy. For visitors, La Ceiba is the main jumping-off place for the Bay Islands, La Mosquitia and a host of nearby ecotourism destinations such as Pico Bonito and Cuero Salado national parks, the Cangrejal River and the North Coast beaches.

Arrivals & Departures
By Air

Service is provided from **Golosón Airport** west of town (about $6 by taxi) by the following airlines:

Isleña Airlines, Av. San Isidro at the main square, *Tel. 443-0179, Fax 443-2632; Airport Tel 441-2521/22/50; Reservations 443-0179*. Their schedule is:
• La Ceiba - Roatan 6:25am, 9, 10,12,2pm,3:30,5:30, $35 round-trip
• La Ceiba - San Pedro 8am,9:45,2pm,3:50, $54 round-trip
• La Ceiba - Guanaja 10am, 4:30pm, $54 round-trip
• La Ceiba - Tegucigalpa 7:45am, 2pm,3:30pm,
• La Ceiba - Trujillo - Palacios 9:30am, $76 round-trip
• La Ceiba - Palacios 6am
• La Ceiba - Puerto Lempira 6am, $89 round-trip
• La Ceiba - Gran Cayman 10am, $300 round-trip
• La Ceiba - Utila 6am, 4pm, $35 round-trip

Aerolíneas Sosa, *Reservations, Tel 443-2519 Airport 441-2512, 440-0692, Fax 441-2513, E-mail: aerososa@psinet.hn or aerolinesosa@edured.net, web:www.aerolineasosa.com.* Their schedule is:
• La Ceiba - Tegucigalpa 7:30am,10,1:30pm, $76 round-trip
• La Ceiba - San Pedro Sula 7:30am, 10, 1:30pm, $ 58 round-trip
• La Ceiba - Puerto Lempira 6:30am
• La Ceiba - Ahuas 6:30am, $103 round-trip
• La Ceiba - Caquira 7:30am
• La Ceiba - Roatan 6:30am, 9,10,12:30pm,3:30pm, $39 round-trip
• La Ceiba - Guanaja 10 am,4pm, $58 round-trip
• La Ceiba - Utila 6am,3:30pm, $39 round-trip
• La Ceiba - Palacios 6:30am, $ 78 round-trip
• La Ceiba - Brus Laguna 6am

Atlantic Airlines, Edificio Plaza del Caribe, Ave La Republica, *Tel. 440-2343/46/47, Airport Tel. 440-1220.* Their schedule is:
• La Ceiba - Roatan 6am, 7:30, 9:45, 12:15pm,3:20,5:30, $ 39 round-trip
• La Ceiba - Utila 7:30am,3:30pm, $39 round-trip
• La Ceiba - Guanaja 7am,4:15pm, $58 round-trip
• La Ceiba - San Pedro Sula 6:30am, 8:30, $58 round-trip
• La Ceiba - Puerto Lempira 6:15am,3pm, $110 round-trip
• La Ceiba - Brus Laguna 6:15am, $98 round-trip
• La Ceiba - Ahuas 6:15, 3pm, $103 round-trip
• La Ceiba - Caquira 3pm, $126 round-trip
• La Ceiba - Tegucigalpa 6:30am, 1:15pm, $81 round-trip
• La Ceiba - Guatemala City 1:30pm, $205 round-trip
• La Ceiba - Belize City 6:30am, $205 round-trip
• La Ceiba - Managua 6:30am, $258 round-trip

Taca flies from La ceiba to El Salvador, Costa Rica,Guatemala, Nicaragua, Miami, Houston Los Angeles, New Orleans and New York. Their office location is Av. San Isidro in front of the Central Park, *Tel 443-3720, 443-1913.*

By Bus
The bus station is off Calle 11 at Blvd. 15 de Septiembre — go south, then west from the main square. Due to the distance, take a collective taxi to the bus station.Tupsa, Catisa, and City buses, direct to San Pedro Sula, depart every hour from 5:30am to 6pm. First class fare is about $6.
You can catch buses for Trujillo, Tela, Tegucigalpa and San Pedro Sula.
First class luxury buses to San Pedro Sula, Tegucigalpa and Copan Ruinas with **Hedman Alas**. Bus station at Supermercados Pueblo Carretera a Trujillo, *Tel. 441-5347.* Departs La Ceiba - San Pedro Sula at 5:15am, 10, 2pm,5:45pm. Connections to Tegucigalpa and Copan Ruinas. Highly recommended for

service and comfort. Best bet for those travellers wanting to travel La Ceiba-Copan Ruinas in one day in 1st class comfort, $13 one-way.

Viana Clase Oro 1st class La Ceiba - San Pedro Sula - Tegucigalpa, bus stop at Servicentro Esso Miramar Blvd 15 de sept, *Tel 441-2330.* Departs La Ceiba 6:30am, 3pm.

By Boat to The Bay Islands
The ferry terminal is quite a ways from downtown La Ceiba, taxi $6. There is daily ferry service to the Bay Islands from La Ceiba. Daily sailings on M/V Galaxy, *Tel 445-1796, 445-1250, 443-4633.* Their schedule is:
• La Ceiba - Roatan, 3pm, $25 round-trip
• La Ceiba - Utila, 9:30am, $23 round-trip

Orientation/Getting Around Town
La Ceiba is Honduras' fourth largest city with a population of about 115,000. It's low-lying and hot, but, despite its banana-port history, it's a surprisingly pleasant place. Streets are paved, and clean. Breezes blow through. Along the sea is a single great pier, culminating in a lighthouse, and, until repairs are made, severed neatly in two, a hurricane casualty. A canal with clean water cuts through, lined by the shady, broad-crowned *ceiba* trees (silk-cotton, or kapok) for which the city is named.

The summit of **Pico Bonito** (2580 meters, or 8464 feet) towers above La Ceiba. In the distance, the Bay Islands can be seen, and to the east and west of La Ceiba are miles of undeveloped white sand beaches and tranquil Garifuna fishing villages.

Car Rental
• **Budget**, *Tel. 441-1105, 441-2929, Airport 441-3398, web: www.budgethonduras.com*
• **Avis**, *Tel. 441-2802*
• **Toyota Rent A Car**, *Tel. 443-1975/76, Airport 441-2538*

Where to Stay
HOTEL LA QUINTA, *Tel. 443-0223, 443-3194, Fax 443-0226, lE-mail: laquinta@caribe.hn, web: www.hotellaquinta.com. 113 rooms. $30 single/ $48 double/$50 for four persons.*

Booming La Ceiba's most booming hotel is opposite the golf course, about ten minutes from the airport. La Quinta consists of motel-style rooms surrounding a pool, each air-conditioned, with carpeting, television with cable, and phone. Some rooms have refrigerators. The hotel is done up in an attractive colonial inspired design. Considered by many to be the best hotel in La Ceiba, good value. There's a Maya Rent A Car on premises, and you can play electronic slots at the Casino El Palacio, also on-site. Other amenities include bar, laundry service, souvenir shop, beauty salon, massage, and a safety security box in each room.

The restaurant is large, and there are conference facilities and protected parking. Two suites are also available.

GRAN HOTEL PARIS, *Parque Morazán (P. O. Box 18). Tel. 443-1643, 443-1662, Fax 443-1614, E-mail: hotelparis@psinet.hn. 63 rooms and suites. $35 double.*

The Gran is the oldest of the good hotels in La Ceiba, a secure, three-story office-type building overlooking Ceiba's main square. Rooms are clean and air conditioned, there is a nice, clean pool, and personnel are well trained and helpful. Take a room on the pool side, which is quieter. Coffee shop, good restaurant, parking. There's also a bar, tour operator, car rental on-site, and an excellent location in front of Centra Park – close to everything in downtown La Ceiba. A good choice, recommended.

GRAN HOTEL CEIBA, *Avenida San Isidro, 5 Calle. Tel/Fax 443-2737. 40 rooms. $25 double. MasterCard, Visa.*

This is a plain, modern hotel with an eighth-floor view terrace, air-conditioned rooms, bar, and coffee shop. Centrally located. Rooms have private bath and phones. Good choice for a mid-range hotel. Recommended.

HOTEL COLONIAL, *Av. 14 de Julio, 6/7 calles. Tel. 443-1953, Fax 443-1955, E-mail: hotel_colonial@hotmail.com. 60 rooms. $19 double.*

The hotel features a sauna, whirlpool, rooftop bar, restaurant, souvenir shop. Rooms have air conditioning, telephone and color television. Safe-deposit boxes available, protected parking. And as the name suggests, decor is wrought iron and dark wood.

There are numerous other small and cheap hotels downtown, and along the rail line that leads to the pier.

Where to Eat

RICARDO'S, *Avenida 14 de Julio at 10 Calle. Tel. 443-0468, E-mail: jirias@caribe.hn.*

This could be where you'll have your best meal in Honduras. Owned by a Honduran-American couple, Ricardo's offers air-conditioned seating, or dining on a very nice terrace, decorated with plants and protected from the rain. There is a variety of seafood, beef and pasta dishes, and a good selection of wines. Service is excellent. For what you get, it's not all that pricey, $10 per person or less.

RESTAURANTE LA PLANCHA, *located behind the El Estadio gas station, Tel. 443-2304.*

Excellent for grilled meats.

RESTAURANTE CHABELITA, *Barrio La Barra.*

Popular place for good seafood.

La Ceiba's Butterflies & Insects

For visitors interested in insects, the high point of La Ceiba will be a visit to the **entomology museum** (museo de entomología) at the **Regional University Center of the Atlantic Coast** (CURLA). More than a thousand specimens are on display, including many, many spectacular butterflies, and a rare homoptera known as the peanut head. Hours are 8am to 5pm during the week, and a free bus to the campus leaves every half hour from Manuel Bonilla Park, downtown.

There is also the **Museum of Butterflies and Insects**, Colonia El Sauce, 2nd Etapa, Casa G12, Calle Escuela Internacional, *Tel. 442-2874, E-mail: rlehman@gbm.hn*. This is a private museum with over 6,500 butterflies and moths from Honduras and 1,000 from around the world; 10,000 insects exhibited. Entry is Lps. 15. Hours: Monday-Saturday 8am-12, 2pm-5, closed Wednesday afternoon.

CAFETERIA COBEL, *7 Calle between Ave. Atlantida and 14 de Julio.*

This just could be the finest cafeteria in the entire country. Clean, efficient service, good hearty fare at reasonable prices, always crowded with locals. Breakfast, lunch and dinner. Heartily recommended.

Nightlife & Entertainment

For many visitors, and for many Ceibeños as well, night and dancing and drinking are what Ceiba is about. The *Zona Viva*, known as **Barrio La Barra**, is in front of the sea, with lots of bars, restaurants, and discos. It's especially busy on weekends. Cover charges of a dollar or so, more on weekends, are collected at most dance halls.

The hot places to dance and party at the moment are: **El Mussol**, with its open air beach front bar, air conditioned disco, very popular. **Cherrys** is one of the most popular places at the moment, open 8pm till dawn every night, **Africa Dance** is the place to hear authentic Garifuna music and see punta dancing, native drums, turtle shells, sea conch horn, highly recommended, open daily 9pm. **Crash** has a restaurant, bar, disco located in the zona viva.

For a taste of home, try:

EXPATRIATES BAR AND GRILL, *Final de la Calle 12, Barrio El Iman, Altos de Refricon.*

This is a fun place. Run by an American, you can get chicken wings, nachos, burgers, BBQ Ribs. Excellent spot to meet travelers and gringo residents of La Ceiba. Very pleasant in the evenings, open air rooftop setting, fine Honduran cigars sold. Closed Tuesday and Wednesday. Highly recommended, especially in evenings.

Excursions & Day Trips

As elsewhere along the coast, beautiful and near-deserted beaches lie to the east and west of town. At **Perú**, a fishing village about 10 kilometers east of La Ceiba, there are roofed shelters with barbecues and picnic tables available for day use, for a nominal fee.

Corozal, a Garífuna beach village about 15 kilometers east of La Ceiba, can be reached by hourly bus. Along the way is **Piedra Pintada** ("Painted Rock"), a greenish-yellow outcrop in an otherwise flat landscape. And there are other fishing villages with attractive and little-visited beaches in both directions from La Ceiba. If you want to stay overnight here, **Villa Rhina**, a mountain hotel, is located near Corozal, *Tel. 443-1222, Fax 443-3558, E-mail: villarhina@honduras.com, web: www.honduras.com/villarhina, $27 double.*

Esparta and **El Porvenir**, to the west, aside from their sands, are known for the so-called "crab invasions." In July and August, the creatures race through town in the thousands toward inland destinations.

Learn Spanish in La Ceiba

Centro Internacional de Idiomas offers certified Spanish instructors, conversation, reading, and grammar classes. Transfer credit available from US universities. Private and group instruction, family or hotel stay. Study in air-conditioned classrooms! Contact the school at Ave. San Isidro, Calle 13, Barrio Solares Nuevos, La Ceiba, *Tel 440-1557, E-mail: cii@laceiba.com, web: www.worldwide.edu/honduras/cici/.* In the US: IMC-TGU Dept 277, P.O. Box 025320, Miami, FL 33102-5320.

Try also the **Central America Spanish School**, Ave San Isidro 12 y 13 Street, *Tel 440-1742, 440-1707, E-mail: maya@ca-spanish.com or cass@laceiba.com, web: www.ca-spanish.com*

The **Cangrejal River** has excellent Class 2, 3, and 4 white water. Contact **Omega Tours**, *Tel. 440-0334, E-mail: omegatours@laceiba.com.* They offer rafting, kayaking, jungle and river hiking, horseback riding, La Mosquitia river expeditions. **Omega Jungle Lodge** has rustic, inexpensive lodging on the Cangrejal River, excluding meals, pool, free lodging with river trips. River guide Udo is from Germany is the Indiana Jones of Honduras. Recommended.

There's also **La Mosquitia Eco Aventuras**, *Tel. 442-0104, E-mail: moskitia@caribe.hn, web: www.honduras.com/moskitia.* Rafting on Cangrejal, hiking to Pico Bonito National Park, Cuero Salado. River guide Jorge Salaverri speaks Miskito and is the La Mosquitia river expert.

At **Sambo Creek**, a beachside Garifuna vilage, you can catch a bite at **La Champa** restaurant and beach bar and a nice view of Cayos Cochinos in the distance. You can also stay and eat at **Sambo Creek Restaurant**, food, 4 cabins for rent. Run by an expat American.

At **Rio Maria**, 8 km from La Ceiba, there's area hiking and swimming in this cool, clear mountain river.

Cacao Lagoon, 24 km east of La Ceiba, is an oceanside lagoon where you can go birding, see mangroves, and catch a view of Cayos Cochinos in the distance.

A new all inclusive resort, **The Barcelo Palma Real Beach Resort**, will open in 2002 on the beach of **Roma**, 22 km from La Ceiba. This will be Honduras' first international quality all-inclusive resort. Prices will be about $65 per person for a double and includes all you can eat and drink, and use of all facilities.

Practical Information

Banks

There are a number of banks downtown. **Credomatic** handles Visa, MasterCard, American Express. Located across the street from Gran Hotel Ceiba.

Churches

For English-language services, check the **Episcopal church**, Avenida Morazán 48, *Tel. 443-2641*.

Federal Express

Ave. San Isidro, *Tel/Fax 443-1219*.

Fiesta

La Ceiba's annual carnaval celebration takes place the third week of May, with parades, costumes, floats, all night dancing in the streets to some of Honduras' best bands. This is the only place in Honduras where carnaval is celebrated. This is Honduras' answer to Mardi Gras, with a wild crazy, party till you drop attitude. Only party animals need apply.

Internet

Hondusoft, Plaza Panayotti 2nd Floor, has internet access for Lps 30 per hour, US calls Lps 4 per minute, Europe Lps 15 per minute.

La Ceiba Tourist Train

Leaves every 15 minutes, 6am-7pm, across from Super Ceibeno Super-market in lovely Parque Sinfor.

Movies

Cine Tropical is half a block from Central Park, and **Cine Millenium** is in the Mega Plaza Mall.

Travel Agencies & Tour Operators

For Bay Islands travel, local tours or foreign travel contact:

• **Lafitte Travel**, Hotel Iberia, *Tel. 442-0115, Fax 443-1391.*

• **Caribbean Travel**, Hermanos Kawas building, Avenida San Isidro, *Tel. 4431361, Fax 4431360, E-mail: ctravel@caribe.hn.* Rents houses in Utila and arranges rafting trips on the Cuero and Cangrejal rivers. The cost is about $75 per person, including lunch and pickup at your hotel or at the airport.

• **Transmundo**, Hotel París, *Tel. 442-2820.* American Express Representative.

• **La Mosquitia EcoAventuras**, Ave. 14 de Julio, opposite Parque Bonilla, *Tel/ Fax 442-0104, E-mail: moskitia@caribe.hn, web: www.honduras.com/ moskitia.* They are the experts in treks to La Mosquitia. Cangrejal river rafting, Pico Bonito hiking, Cuero Salado. Whitewater rafting in La Ceiba, expeditions to Rio Platano in La Mosquitia, custom jungle expeditions. Tours to Pico Bonito Cloud Forest (see below for more details on Pico Bonito). The oldest and most experienced tour operator in La Mosquitia, speciality in ecotourism and sustainable tourism. Recommended.

• **Rios Honduras**, *Tel. 443-0780, rios@hondurashn.com, www.paddlehonduras.com.* Specializing in jungle river rafting on the Cangrejal River outside of La Ceiba. Full day trips on Class 3 & 4 rapids, US-certified guides, one-day package trips with airfare available from Roatan.

• **Omega Tours**, *Tel. 440-0334, E-mail: omegatours@laceiba.com.* The Cangrejal whitewater experts, also jungle hiking, and Mosquitia river expeditions. Recommended.

• **Tourist Options**, Lobby of Hotel Paris, *Tel 440-0265, 440-2999, E-mail: touristoptions@caribe.hn.* Rafting, hiking, Pico Bonito, Cuero Salado, Cayos Cochinos, Bay Islands air tickets, hotel bookings, good prices, very helpful. Recommended.

Cuero y Salado National Park

Cuero y Salado National Park, 33 km west of La Ceiba, takes in 85 square kilometers of coastline, river estuaries, and navigable canals lined by lush vegetation, and includes the major protected manatee habitat on the Caribbean coast of Central America. Spider, white-faced and howler monkeys, crocodiles and caimans, jaguars and many kinds of small mammals also inhabit the area. Plant species include water lilies an royal palms. Some 300 species of birds make their home in the park.

Access to Cuero y Salado is by hand-operated coconut railway cars (*burras*) from the village of La Unión, just off the highway — the park includes old coconut plantations, canals dug by United Fruit, and villages. Dormitories, campsites and trails are being developed. Limited sleeping and eating facilities are available at the moment. Admission is $10. The reserve boasts the largest population of West Indian Manatee (approximately 50) in Honduras. To get to Cuero Salado take a bus to la Union and then arrange for the hand-pushed train to take you to the reserve. Go early to see the most wildlife. Great close-up monkey viewing opportunities.

"Fucsa" – Fundacion Cuero y Salado – manages the national park and organizes overnight tours. Their office is in the Masapan district in the Standard Fruit Company complex, *Tel. 443-0329*. There is a cabin in the park for overnight stays, but bring food and water. Kayaks are available.

Near Cuero y Salado
Catarata del Bejuco (*Vine Falls*), about 15 kilometers southeast of La Ceiba at Las Mangas, cascades 80 meters into a dense vine-laden forest.

On the **Cangrejal River**, you can go white water rafting on Class 3 and 4 rapids. Swimming and hiking are also options.

Pico Bonito National Park

Pico Bonito National Park, south of La Ceiba, takes in 8025-foot (2433-meter) Pico Bonito mountain. In addition to high, mountainside tropical forest, the park includes lowlands with mixed deciduous forest (mahogany and Spanish cedar are characteristic trees), as well as jaguars, tapirs, deer, puma, white-faced monkey, spider monkey and a wide variety of birds. Pico Bonito contains 7 different ecosystems. Access to the park is usually with a guide, and by four-wheel-drive vehicle. Hiking trails are available.

Pico Bonito National Park is the largest park in Honduras, comprising 49,000 hectares (107,300 hectares including the buffer zone). The park is managed by the Fundación Parque Nacional Pico Bonito. There is a visitors center, located on the road from La Ceiba to Yaruca.

For more information, contact: **Fundación Pico Bonito**, Ave. La Republica, one block from San Isidro Church on the 2nd floor. *Tel/Fax 443-3824, E-mail: funpnapib@tropicohn.com.*

Entrance to the park is $2. Bilingual guides are available at $6 per day through the visitors center.

Where to Stay

THE LODGE AT PICO BONITO, *located ust outside of La Ceiba, 5 miles from the airport adjacent to Pico Bonito National Park, set in a lovely tranquil spot between the Coloradito and Corinto rivers. Tel 440-0389, 440-0388, Fax 440-0468, Reservations in the US toll-free 888/428-0221; E-mail: picobonito@caribe.hn; web: www.picobonito.com. $165-$220 double, meals extra, 22 rustic yet luxurious cabins.*

This is the finest ecolodge in Honduras. From the welcome cocktail upon arrival, to the gourmet meals served in the wood paneled dining room, to the tastefully furnished cabins, fluffy white towels and private porch where breakfast is delivered, no detail is too small and no request too large for the attentive and well-trained staff.

Trails wind their way throughout the 200-acre property, and there is plenty of wildife, especially birds, to satisfy the most ardent ecotourist. You'll enjoy wonderful views of Pico Bonito, the 8,000-foot mountain the national park is named for, and there's even an observation tower if the view from the ground doesn't suffice. The cabins, surrounded by coffe and cacao trees, are referred to as "rustic elegance," and that is a pretty apt description. Food in the restaurant is first-rate, and the wine list is extensive.

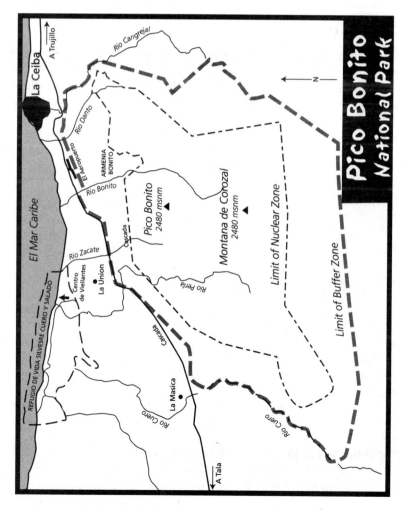

There's a butterfly garden (15-20 species are raised) and serpentarium (Boa, Hognosed Viper, Cascabel, Coral, Timbo and Fer de Lance, the most dangerous snake in Honduras) on the premises. Non-guests have to pay a small admission charge; it'sfree for guests. Contact James Adams for more information: *sibonxxx@hotmail.com*..

The lodge features excellent birding, guided hikes into the forest, river swimming, transfers included, tours to Cuero Salado, Cayos Cochinos, river rafting on Cangrejal, Punta Sal, Lancetilla and horseback riding. There's also a swimming pool and spa.

The Lodge is a mmeber of the prestigious Small Luxury Hotels of The World (*www.slh.com*).

Trujillo

Like other coastal ports, **Trujillo** languished between the colonial period and the twentieth century. The city was founded on May 18, 1825, by Francisco de las Casas at Punta de Caxinas, where Columbus had first sighted the mainland on his fourth voyage to the New World. Las Casas named the settlement for his home town in Spain.

Trujillo was the first seat of the bishop of Honduras, and for a time during the colony, was a shipment point for gold. Several forts were erected here to protect against pirates, though the town was intermittently sacked by Henry Morgan, among others, and for a time was abandoned. Late in the eighteenth century, Trujillo was a base for attacks against English trading posts in Mosquitia, to the east.

Remote Trujillo gave refuge to such outcasts as Black Caribs, deported by the British from the West Indies late in the eighteenth century. The one glorious note during the town's long decline came in 1860. The American adventurer William Walker, ousted from power in Nicaragua, supposing that English-speaking Bay Islanders chafing under Honduran rule would lend him support, gathered a new force and captured Trujillo. Britain, concerned about repayment of debts out of port revenues, induced Walker to surrender under a guarantee of safe conduct. In an act of treachery that is largely uncondemned, the British commander turned Walker over to the Hondurans. Walker was promptly shot, and buried in the Trujillo cemetery. His tomb may be viewed in the Municipal cemetary.

Trujillo saw some revival in the twentieth century as a banana terminal, and decline again as Panama disease hit the nearby plantations. More recently, its fortunes have climbed with the expansion of agriculture in the valley of the **Aguán River**, which flows to the south.

Trujillo is the Central American Caribbean at its best. A quaint, laid-back, untouristy town with plenty of local color, great beaches, plenty of eco-activities, great seafood and the opportuntity to see first hand the fascinating Garifuna culture. Trujillo is one of the few Caribbean towns left where it's still possible to get a feel for what life was like on the North Coast, say 50 years ago. It's a bit frayed around the edges, yet still has a special charm all its own.

Arrivals & Departures

By Air

Air service is provided by **Isleña Airlines** Monday through Saturday. Departs La Ceiba at 7am, $30 one-way. Connections in La Ceiba to San Pedro Sula, Tegucigalpa and The Bay Islands. Daily flight to Palacios, La Mosquitia.

By Bus

Cotuc run from San Pedro Sula direct to Trujillo, 7 & 8 Calle, 1 Ave, in front of the railway line, *Tel. 557-3175*, every 45 minutes from 6am- 4pm. From La Ceiba direct to Trujillo, Barrio Buenos Aires, Calle Principal La Ceiba a Tela, every 45 minutes, *Tel. 441-2199*. From Trujillo direct to La Ceiba & San Pedro Sula every 45 minutes, 1am-1pm. Road to Tocoa, Calle 18 de septiembre, *Tel 444-2181*.

Cotraibal run from Tegucigalpa to Trujillo, 7:30am, Barrio Concepcion, 7 Ave, 11 y 12 Calle, Comayaguela, *Tel. 237-1666*. San Pedro Sula to Trujillo from 6am-4pm, 1 Ave, 7 y 8 Calle, Barrio Medina, *Tel. 557-8470*. Trujillo to Tegucigalpa at 5am. Trujillo to San Pedro Sula from 1 am to noon, Barrio El Centro, *Tel. 434-4932*.

By Sea

For transport via sea to La Mosquitia, just ask around.

Orientation

Trujillo lies on the south side of a large bay, opposite the bend of the Cape of Honduras. With most of the modern fish-packing and shipping facilities going in at Puerto Castilla, on the opposite shore, Trujillo still maintains some of the romantic atmosphere of its turbulent past.

Visitors can walk through the **fortress of Santa Bárbara de Trujillo**, open daily from 8am to 5pm. The **San Juan Bautista church** was completed in 1809 (though its clock wasn't installed until 1899). The odd folk-Gothic church is worth a view, and the sleepy streets are ideal for strolling.

Trujillo lies about 100 kilometers east of La Ceiba by sea, or 240 kilometers by road, much of it in poor condition but currently being improved. Along the way are the **Balfate Falls**. The easiest access is by air from La Ceiba.

Where to Stay

VILLAS BRINKLEY, *Barrio Buenos Aires. Tel. 434-4444, Fax 434-4269, in the US: Tel. 412/791-2273. 20 rooms. $30 double.*

"The Brinkley" is quite suitable to the old atmosphere of the town, a bay-view complex of cottages in Spanish-colonial architecture on the hills above town, with pool and health-club facilities. Arrangements are made for fishing, boating, horseback riding and diving. Restaurant and bar with great panoaramic views. Air conditioning, two suites w/ full kitchenette, game room.

HOTEL CHRISTOPHER COLUMBUS, *located just off the Trujillo airstrip on the beach. Tel. 434-4966, Fax 434-4971, islena@caribe.hn. 71 double rooms, 2 suites. $47 double.*

Opened in February 1994, this is the most luxurious of Trujillo's hotels. An imposing concrete structure lacking in any Caribbean charm or atmosphere, the hotel nevertheless offers a pool, restaurant, bar, tennis courts, marina, air conditioning and cable TV. Same owners as Isleña Airlines.

LA QUINTA TRUJILLO HOTEL, *next door to Trujillo Airport, Tel 444-4732, Fax 444-4732, 25 rooms. $25 single/$30 double, children no charge. Visa, MasterCard. U.S. reservations Tel. 615/883-4770.*

Owned by the same owner as the Hotel La Quinta La Ceiba. Located just off the airstrip and 90 meters up from the beach. Air conditioning, cable TV, hot water, full service mini-mart. Boats available for rent, and fishing, car rental and diving arranged.

O'GLYNN HOTEL, *Tel. 4344592. $18 single/$25 double.*

Located in central Trujillo, air-conditioned rooms, cable TV.

HOTEL COLONIAL, *Tel/Fax 4344011. 20 rooms. $21 double.*

Centrally located, right on the Central Park and a short walk to the beach. Some rooms are air conditioned, and there is a decent restaurant, El Bucanero.

CASA CRISTINA, *located alongside rainforest. Tel/Fax 434-4545, E-mail: cristina@hondutel.hn.*

Small intimate hotel comprised of furnished apartments with kitchen, pool. English, German, Spanish spoken. Daily, weekly and monthly rates. Lovely view of town and Trujillo Bay. Recommended.

Where to Eat

Excellent seafood can be found in Trujillo. There are a number of thatched roof champas on the beach that serve up a tasty fried fish plate, shrimp, and seafood-based soups, at reasonable prices. In addition to the hotel restaurants mentioned above, try one of the following:

CAFE OASIS, *located across the street from Bancahsa.*

Run by a Canadian/Honduran couple, they offer vegetarian plates and daily specials. English is spoken and there is garden dining.

BAHIA BAR, *located on the beach, next to the airstrip, Tel. 434-4770.*
Best bar on the beach, good food and good music, popular gathering spot day or night.
ROGUES GALLERY, *located on the beach.*
Also known locally as Jerry's, an American, there's great gringo breakfasts and seafood specialties for lunch and dinner.

Nightlife & Entertainment

Barrio Cristales, a Garifuna neighborhood on the edge of Trujillo, is the place to check out some authentic Garifuna music and dancing. A must-see is *punta*, a rhythmic feast for the senses. Musicians play traditional Garifuna instruments like drums, conch, and turtle shells as dancers gyrate their hips to the African inspired beat; this is an experience not to be missed.
COCOPANDO, *in Barrio Cristales.*
The place to find authentic punta with live music and locals dancing up a storm. Weekends are best.
RINCÓN DE LOS AMIGOS, *located on the beach, open 9pm till dawn.*
Disco, restaurant, bar, live music every Saturday night, very lively.
DISCOTEQUE TRUXILLO, *located on the mountain.*
With views overlooking the bay, this is a very popular spot.

Excursions & Day Trips

Turtle Tours, based at the Hotel Villa Brinkley, *Tel 434-4444, Tel/Fax 434-4431, E-mail: ttours@hondutel.hn, web: www.turtletours.de.* Tours to sights in and around Trujillo (prices per person): Guaymoreto Lagoon $20, Rainforest Hike $15, 4WD Jeep Tour to National Park $20, Crocodile Reserve $20, Motorcycle rental $35 per day. Treks to La Mosquitia leaving from Trujillo, 3 days $290, 5 days $430 (minimum 2 persons).

Practical Information

Banco Atlantida can give a cash advance on Visa, Bancahsa cash advance on Visa, Banco de Occidente has Western Union and advances on Visa and Mastercard. Banco BGA.There's no ATM in Trujillo.
There is an internet shop nest door to Hotel Catracho.
The **Gari Arte** shop next door to Cocopando comes recommended for authentic Garifuna crafts.

Near Trujillo

Museo y Piscina Rufino Galan Caceres is a private museum with an excellent collection of artifacts from the Trujillo area. Pre-Colombian, colonial period, antiques, gadgets, very eclectic and interesting. Clean, clear, and cold natural river-fed swimming pools are located behind the museum. A visit to the museum and pools are highly recommended. Admission 5 Lps.

There are several Garífuna (Black Carib) villages nearby, clusters of high-peaked, thatched houses fronting beautiful white sand beaches. The most easily reached is **Santa Fé**, 12 kilometers west via an unpaved road along the sea. The **Campamento Hotel and Restaurant** *(Tel. 434-4244, cabanas, $25 double)* is located on a 38 acre working ranch. Located 4 km from Trujillo on the road to Santa Fe, right on a beautiful beach, excellent seafood, bar, open 7am-10pm daily.

Also in Santa Fé is **El Caballero** restaurant, also known as Pete's Place. This is one of the finest seafood restaurants on the North Coast. Continuing from Santa Fé, you pass through San Antonio and then Guadalupe, where the road ends. The stretch between Santa Fé and Guadalupe boasts lovely, untouched beaches.

To the east, off the road to Puerto Castilla, is **Guaymoreto Lagoon**, a wildlife refuge with lots of aquatic birds, caymans, turtles, mangrove forest. Entry is via launch from Trujillo. Turtle Tours organizes excursions.

Los Lirios Lagoon, to the south off the highway into town, also has varied bird life. On the northern, seaward side of the lagoon are stretches of nearly deserted beach.

Los Farallones are a rock formation on which waves produce thunderous and frightful sound effects.

Capiro y Calentura National Park, located on a mountain behind the town of Trujillo, covers a small forest area that includes two hills overlooking the bay, and includes some remains of ancient Indian cultures. Significant wildlife includes howling monkeys and macaws. Tropical rain forest, excellent hiking, views to The Bay Islands. You can get more information at the office of Fucagua, 2nd floor of kiosk in the Central Park, who manages the Reserve. Lovely waterfalls, excellent view of Bay Islands to the north and the Aguan Valley to the south. There is a road to the top of Celentura Mountain, where the US formerly operated a radar station.

Piedra Blanca (*White Rock*), east of Trujillo, is said to be perforated by caves, still unexplored.

Important archeological discoveries have been made in the **Cuyamel Caves**, which lie in hills about ten kilometers south of Trujillo. The importance of Cuyamel comes from the virtual absence of artifacts from the pre-Columbian nomadic hunters who lived along this part of the coast of Central America. Elsewhere in Honduras, and to the north, in Guatemala, pre-Columbian civilizations left cities that are in some cases virtually intact.

The appliqué and incised decoration on objects found at Cuyamel indicate a South American origin of the people who frequented the caves. But there are also indications of contact with Mexican and Mayan peoples during pre-Classic times. There is evidence that some of the inhabitants of the region practiced head hunting, and used alcoholic beverages in their rituals.

Interested in seeing crocodiles? **Hacienda El Tumbador Crocodile Reserve** boasts 12-foot crocs up close and personal. **Turtle Tours**, in the Hacienda El Tumbador, *Tel. 434-4431,* runs trips to the hacienda. Admission $5. Note: there are no signs indicating where to go.

East of Trujillo

Forty-four km to the east of Trujillo is **Santa Rosa de Aguan**, the largest Garifuna settlement on the Caribbean coast. Situated on the shore of the Aguan River, where the river meets the sea.

Northeastern Honduras is virtually trackless, barely populated by Miskito Indians along the coast, and Sumos and Payas inland. Sovereignty over much of the area was in dispute between Nicaragua and Honduras, until a 1960 decision of the International Court of Justice set the boundary for once and for all at the **Coco River** (also known as the Wanks, or Segovia). It was only in 1957 that the department of Gracias a Dios was established, taking in much of the region.

Coastal lagoons and rivers are the main transport routes, though a few dirt roads run inland from **Puerto Lempira**, on the Caratasca Lagoon in the far northeast. Only the most basic, frontier type of accommodation is available in Puerto Lempira and the villages along the road to the south. Planes operate regularly to Palacios and to Puerto Lempira, and irregularly to scattered airstrips in the region. It's also sometimes possible to ship aboard a dugout canoe, or simply hike along the bar, though there are many intervening waterways.

The Coco River was a gold-exporting route in the colonial period —gold was mined near the rapids at the source of the river, near the Pacific. But Spanish presence was usually minimal. **Brus Laguna** (Brewer's Lagoon) and **Black River** (Río Tinto, later Fort Inmaculada Concepción) were British trading posts and forts and timber depots in the nineteenth century. Black River, 25 kilometers from the coast, had a population that approached 4000.

But even after the British were expelled in 1782 there was little interest in the area by the weak central government. Under the remnants of British influence, and foreign missionaries, many of the inhabitants speak English, as well as their native languages. The Miskitos on both sides of the Coco River give allegiance to no government, and many of those from Nicaragua crossed over as refugees after disputes with the Sandinistas.

Inland from the mangroves and swamps of the coast are great stretches of sandy soil covered by Caribbean pine, and exploited in part for timber.

La Mosquitia

There are no guarantees about getting into, through, or out of Mosquitia. In La Mosquitia there is a saying which reflects the difficulties in transport, 'La Mosquitia – arrive when you want – leave when you can.' Often small planes will not be able to land due to inclement weather. Air transport in and out of La Mosquitia is really quite good, but waiting in a remote village for a day or two for the bush plane or dugout canoe to arrive is not an uncommon occurance.

There are only a few dirt tracks into the region that radiate from Puerto Lempira. Most transport is by water (unscheduled, of course), and hotels and pensions are difficult to find, or non-existent.

There is only one road in La Mosquitia from Puerto Lempira to Leimus and on to Ahuasbila, about 200 km distant; both are on the Rio Coco, which borders Nicaragua. In small villages travelers can always find lodging and simple but hearty meals with the very hospitable Miskito villagers. Within La Mosquitia, **Alas de Socorro** operates a bush plane service that works with the Moravian Missionary Hospital in Ahuas on the Patuca River. Alas de Socorro provides charter flights to backcountry villages. They can be contacted at their home base in Ahuas.

In recent years, tourism infrastructure has improved in La Mosquitia, especially near areas frequented by ecotourists. There are a number of small hospedajes in and around the Rio Platano Biosphere as well as an association of guides. Also prices for transport, accommodations and guiding services have been standardized in the Rio Platano Biosphere. In any village, accomodations and meals can be found simply by asking around. The Miskitos are very generous with what little they have and the custom of providing accommodations and meals to travelers is well entrenched. This also provides a wonderful first-hand look at Miskito culture and day-to-day life.

Be safe and take an antimalarial regime before embarking on a La Mosquita expedition.

Stocks of food in the few small general stores in La Mosquita are limited, so take your own reserve. Peanut butter, Nutella, canned sardines, tuna, and granola bars will come in handy. Insect repellant, water purification equipment, jungle camping equipment, tropical boots, rain protection and plenty of time, tolerance and patience will also come in handy.

If you arrive in La Mosquitia on your own you can always arrange transportation, a place to sleep and a meal. Usually all of the above may be set up with a local family, as restaurants, hotels and formal transport are all but non-existent in most parts of the region. The lack of tourism infrastructure means that travelers have plenty of opportunities to interact with the Mosquito people.

If you want to see Mosquitia with a tour group, contact: **La Moskitia Ecoaventuras**, Ave. 14 de Julio, opposite Parque Bonilla, La Ceiba, *Tel/Fax 442-0104, E-mail: moskitia@caribe.hn, web: www.honduras.com/moskitia*, offers ten- to fourteen-day low-impact adventures in Mosquitia, with emphasis on birding, wildlife viewing, and non-intrusive contacts with native peoples. This is the premier ecotourism outfitter running trips into La Mosquitia.

Arrivals & Departures

Isleña Airlines, Av. San Isidro at the main square, La Ceiba, *Tel. 443-0179, 441-2521, Fax 443-2632, E-mail: islena@caribe.hn.* Daily flight from La Ceiba to Ahuas (on the Patuca River), Puerto Lempira (the largest town in La Mosquitia, located on the Caratasca Lagoon), and Brus Laguna (on the Caribbean coast). The price for any of the three destinations is $117 round-trip.

Aerolineas Sosa, La Ceiba *Tel. 443-1399, 443-2519;* San Pedro Sula *Tel 550-6545;* Airport *Tel. 668-3223;* Roatan *Tel. 445-1154, 445-1658;* Guanaja *Tel. 453-4359;* Utila *Tel. 425-3161;* Puerto Lempira *Tel. 898-7467, 898-7432. E-mail: aerososa@psinet.hn.* Flight from La Ceiba to Puerto Lempira, $117 round-trip. Flight from La Ceiba to Brus Laguna, $117 round-trip. Brus Laguna, Ahuas, Cauquira and Palacios can be reached via radio from 5:30am-8am at 51234 LSB and from 8am-5pm at 6222.2 LSB.

Rollins Air, La Ceiba *Tel. 443-3206, 441-2172.* La Ceiba to Puerto Lempira, La Ceiba to Brus Laguna and Palacios, daily.

Atlantic Airline, Edificio Plaza del Caribe, Ave La Republica, La Ceiba, *Tel/ Fax 440-2343, Tel 440-2347, Airport 440-1220.*

Seeing the Sghts

The **Río Platano Biosphere Reserve (RPBR)** encompasses one of the largest protected areas in Central America with over 5,200 square kilometers. It was established as a United Nations World Heritage Site in 1982. It includes prime examples of lowland tropical rainforest, coastal lagoons, undisturbed beaches, mangroves, grasslands and patches of pine savannah. It is the home of members of the Miskito and Pech tribes as well as the Garifuna ethnic group which live in small communities on the coast and along the major rivers. You can visit anytime of the year but it is usually best to avoid the heavy rains during November, December, and January. The driest months are usually March, April, May, August, September and October.

Not many visitors have found the RPBR yet because access can be a bit pricey. No roads lead to this area so visitors must get there by other means. Flights on Isleña, SOSA and Atlantic Airlines go from La Ceiba to Palacios ot the edge of the reserve (about $170 round trip from Tegucigalpa or $85 from La Ceiba). Roads have been pushed to the edge of the reserve only recently. You can get a bus from La Ceiba to Tocoa for about $2. From the market in

Tocoa you would look for a pickup to Batalla for about $16 per person. In the rainy season your way will be blocked by several creeks so you take the pickup to Sangrilaya Creek, pay 10 Lempiras for a boat to take you across, then get another pickup on the other side. Repeat the process when you get to Tocamacho Creek. Once you get to Batalla you can cross the lagoon in a boat for 10 Lempiras to Palacios and continue from there. Another branch of the road from Tocoa leads to Sico but this a less safe and less desirable way to enter the reserve.

Some guidebooks talk about the possibility of catching a truck from Limon to Sangrilaya then walking along the beach and wading across rivers for a day or two to get to Batalla. While this is possible it is not recommended because of the heat, bugs and safety problems. Several commercial guides organize trips into the Rio Platano Biosphere Reserve and may be a good option for those with limited Spanish. Their all inclusive packages range from 3 to 14 days and cost about $100 per day. One of the best is La Mosquitia Ecoadventuras based in La Ceiba. In order to support the ecotourism program in the reserve you are encouraged to check out the tour operator you are considering to be sure they are working with local people in their operations as much as possible.

If you want to stay in Palacios, there are three hotels there. One is near the main boat landing and run by the Marmol family ($9), the other two are the **Hotel Mosquitia** ($7) and **El Centro** ($7 per person) located just off the runway. There is also a basic but clean place (called a hospedaje) across the canal in Batalla run by Doña Sulma (about $2.50). Most folks, though, usually head straight into the reserve to the coastal villages. Some basic visitor information may soon be posted on the wall of the Isleña airline office in Palacios.

Rivers, lagoons and inland waterways are the highways in the reserve and dugout canoes provide the public transportation. Once in Palacios, you can catch 'colectivo' boat transport at the landing near the Marmol hotel to travel along the inland passage to coastal villages inside the reserve such as Plaplaya, Raista, and Belen ($3 to $4, 1 to 2 hours). There is usually a boat to meet the airplanes that arrive in the morning. To return to Palacios the colectivos leave from several different coastal villages early in the morning (from 5:00am to 6:00am) and arrive in Palacios with sufficient time to make an outgoing flight. Hospedaje owners can assist you in arranging such trips.

If you miss the colectivo you will have to pay extra for a special trip ($7 to $15 depending on the distance). The boatmen are starting to get organized and may be posting a list of standard prices near the landing in Palacios in the future. The boat ride is a scenic introduction to the reserve as it passes through the watery habitat of a variety of bird species and past the stilted, thatch roofed dwellings that are typical of this area.

The Coastal Villages

A narrow strand of land divides the inland waterway and Ibans lagoon from the Caribbean. Along this pleasant setting lie a number of small native villages, starting with the Garifuna village of **Plaplaya** and continuing through the Miskito villages of Ibans, Cocobila, Raista, Belen, Nueva Jerusalem and Kuri. A trail connects all of these villages which makes for easy exploring. Vast expanses of unspoiled, white sand beaches can also provide an easy route for getting from place to place and the sea provides a wonderful way to cool off during the heat of the day. Ibans Lagoon is a beautiful body of water which fronts the Caribbean Sea on one side and the mountains of La Mosquitia on the far side. In the distance Mt. Baltimore rises majestically above the lagoon. Sunsets here are fantastic and the nearby Misquito villages are very hospitable and friendly.

There are several hospedajes to stay in while you are on the coast. One of the best is in Raista near the butterfly farm. They have clean rooms for $4 per person and Elma's Kitchen nearby serves some of the best food on the coast. Lodging in Plaplaya can be found at Sede's hospedaje ($3.50 per person), Yohanna's hospedaje ($7 per room - she also runs the boat to Limon), or Basilia's hospedaje, whose place is on the west edge of the village about a 15 minute walk from the center. In Belen there is the house of Doña Mendelia and in Kuri you can find lodging with Sixto George. Tourism is in its infancy in this area so facilities are pretty basic. Plan on pit toilets, no electricity and bucket baths. Some hospedajes have mosquito nets, some do not – you should bring one if you can. Most places are getting accustomed to serving water

The Miskito People

A word about the Miskito people. Due to their relative isolation, the Miskito have been able to endure as an indigenous group. Miskito is the first language for most residents; Spanish comes in a distant second. The Miskitos are extremely open and welcoming to visitors. The arrival of a visitor from afar is often reason enough to prepare a special dinner for the guest. Children in Mosquitia are a joy, curious and wonderfully friendly to travelers.

However, there are threats to the Miskitos' idyllic way of life. Campesinos from other parts of Honduras seeking land have settled in La Mosquitia, bringing with them a completely different culture and language and clearing large tracts of virgin tropical forest to make room for crops and pasture. Many Miskitos look to eco-tourism as a means to sustainably develop their homeland. La Mosquitia is rich in biodiversity and is the last great stretch of undisturbed tropical forest in Central America.

purified with chlorine but it is a good idea to bring a water filter or tablets to purify drinking water if you plan on camping away from the hospedajes. Feel free to ask if you are unsure. Meals are based on rice and bean dishes with yuca or plantains highlighted by chicken or the catch of the day ($2-$3). Be sure to bring a good supply of small denomination (50 Lempiras or less) bills with you to the reserve since few businesses have much change for larger bills.

Apart from relaxing in the slow paced life along the coast there are several interesting things to see and do in this area. The **butterfly farm** at Raista is closed at the moment but will hopefully reopen by mid-2002. It is a project in sustainable development that raises the colorful butterfly species of the area to sell to live butterfly exhibition houses throughout the world. They offered guided tours in Spanish for $2.

There is a wonderful project to protect the **leatherback** and **loggerhead sea turtles** that nest along the coast centered in Plaplaya. Each night during the breeding season (March to June) members of the village patrol the beaches to find nesting turtles, carefully gather the eggs and transplant them to a guarded area to be watched over until they hatch. Visitors can accompany them on their beach patrols for a small donation to the program. Last year they ensured that about 1800 of these endangered species hatched and made it back to the sea.

Occasionally, the Garifuna people of Plaplaya hold traditional dances which provide an interesting evening's entertainment. Check with Eddie Bodden in Raista to hire a boat and guide to take you on a day trip across Ibans lagoon to visit the rainforest of the Biosphere Reserve. These are wild areas rich in wildlife. You have a chance of seeing deer, tapir, macaws, jaguar, armadillo, sloth, monkeys, anteaters, manatee (in Ibans lagoon) and over 300 species of birds. Rain can come at any time of the year and trails can be muddy so be prepared. Efforts are underway to improve visitor services and infrastructure within the reserve to support a system of ecotourism that protects the reserve, provides benefits to the local villages and offers outstanding experiences for visitors.

Up the Río Platano

For those in search of a little more rugged adventure you should find a boat to take you up the Río Platano to **Las Marias**, a small Miskito and Pech village that is the last outpost of civilization in this part of the reserve. Ask at the place you are staying at on the coast for a good boatman who can take you upriver. They can also call on the marine radios that are found in many places to call one of several boatmen from Las Marias to bring their boat down to get you. In a pinch you can walk or catch a colectivo east to Kuri and look up Sixto George or Morgan Devis. Gasoline is very expensive in these remote areas (over $4 per gallon) and this is reflected in the high cost of transportation. The ride costs about $130 so it is best to put together a group of 4 or 5 people to share the cost. That price should get you a boat and boatman for 3 days to take you round trip from the coast with a day or two in Las Marias to look around. If you stay longer you should negotiate a fair price with the boatmen to cover his time if he comes up from the coast.

Be aware that there is great variation in the quality of the boats available for this journey ranging from small, unstable, leaky dugouts (pipantes), to larger, more comfortable boats with an outboard motor (cayucos). Even though the smaller boats can be cheaper it is worth it to find a more comfortable boat for the long journey (4 to 6 hours). Don't be afraid to ask the boatman for a brief rest stop or swim along the way to break up the trip. Bring food and water to enjoy along the way as well as a hat, sunscreen, repellent and umbrella or poncho in case it rains.

Along the river you will see **Miskito** and **Pech families** living as they have for centuries – planting rice, beans and yuca in the fertile soils in the river's flood plain and supplemented by what they can gather from the rainforest. Their small numbers and low impact techniques have not changed the reserve much over the years. In Las Marias, there are three basic but clean places to stay all priced at about $4 per night (in the hospedajes of Justa, Ovidio or Tinglas). All offer similar levels of service. Another small hospedaje is located a few hours upriver near the first petroglyphs.

Meals are available at the same places for about $3 each. The local women's group sells handicrafts, locally produced cocoa and sometimes baked goods which they bring around to the hospedajes. The residents have declared Las Marias to be alcohol-free so you are encouraged to respect their wishes and avoid bringing alcohol or drugs to the area. Please respect their wishes.

Once in Las Marias, you will be approached by a representative of the guides in the village to let you know what services are available and to help you make arrangements to suit your needs. A number of guides have been trained in Las Marias to deal with international visitors. They have formed a group, agreed on a set price structure and work to share the benefits of ecotourism with all of the guides and the village. The prices and rules are posted on the walls of all the hospedajes. This is ecotourism at its best, where income from visitors benefits local populations and gives them and economic incentive to protect the reserve.

Once you figure out what you want to do, the head guide will make all the arrangements for you. This service costs about $3.50. Typical guided trips include day hiking on trails around the village, a 3-day hike to scenic **Pico Dama** (very strenuous), a day trip by *pipante* upriver to see the **petroglyphs** at **Walpulbansirpi** left by the ancestors of the Pech, or multi-day trips upriver to visit other petroglyph sites and view wildlife in the heart of the reserve. Guides are required even for day hikes due to the possibility getting lost on the faint jungle trails and close encounters with very poisonous snakes. The cost for a guide for hikes is about $7 per day for groups up to 5. Overnight hikes require 2 guides. All prices include whatever food and equipment the guide should need. The cooks at your hospedaje can fix you a meal to take with you on your trip if you ask them. In the village, you are welcome to wander up and down river without a guide along the trail that connects different parts of the community. Since the trail goes along the river it is hard to get lost and the dangers are less. Chiggers and no-see-ums can be bothersome in Las Marias, so be sure to pack some insect repellant.

The trips upriver from Las Marias are an amazing adventure in the small, dugout canoes called pipantes. The river is too shallow in many places to use a motor so the boats are propelled as they have been for centuries by paddle and wooden pole. Pushing the boat upriver against the current, even through small rapids, is a labor-intensive chore that requires three guides per boat. Two visitors and their gear will fit in each boat with the guides. The trip can be wet so make sure your gear is waterproof or covered well. A day trip to the petroglyphs will have you in the boat most of the time, occasionally walking around difficult spots in the river.

An overnight trip will give you a fuller experience and give you the time to take some interesting hikes up side drainages, such as **Sulawala** or **Wahawala**. These small, clear streams offer a magical interlude to your boat trip. There aren't developed trails up these drainages but floods during the rainy season open enough room along the stream to allow for easy hiking with little fear of snakes. The jungle rises on both sides of you offering an opportunity to spot wildlife. You have to wade back and forth across the stream many times but this is a welcome relief from the tropical heat. A trip like this will cost about $25 per boat per day. This includes the boat rental, the 3 guides and their food. You will need to bring your own camping gear as none is available in the village.

You can buy basic food for a trip upriver such as rice, beans, yuca and plantains in Las Marias but it is better to bring it with you from the coast so you don't deplete the limited food stock available in the village. The guides will prepare this food for your group over an open fire as part of their duties. While sitting around the fire you can sometimes get them to tell you legends and tales of the creatures and spirits that inhabit the rainforest. No matter what impression you get from nature shows on TV, animals are hard to see even in a healthy forest. If you are hoping to see wildlife be sure to get an early start (like 6am), walk quietly and look carefully. The animals quiet down in the heat of the day but get more active in the late afternoon. Let your guides know you are interested in wildlife and they will make an extra effort to help you spot them.

A more detailed guide to the Rio Platano Reserve is being printed now and should be available by the end of the year. Along with basic logistical information it will have maps, photos, notes on the cultures of the area, a bird list, information on medicinal plants and more. Look for it in bookstores, tourist areas, from MOPAWI in Tegucigalpa or at some locations in the reserve. You can also write to the author for a copy at: Arden Anderson, 216 N. Colorado St. Gunnison, CO 81230, *E-mail: Arden_Anderson@co.blm.gov.* A "lost" city called **Ciudad Blanca** is also said to lie within the confines of the reserve, the remains of a vast city built by a mysterious ancient culture. While no individual metropolis has been found, any of the petroglyph sites could well have been the origin of the legend of the lost city. Some consider that the archaeological site known as Limonsito is, in fact, the lost White City.

Smaller reserves to the east include **Caratasca**, surrounding much of the Caratasca Lagoon, and the **Río Kruta** reserve, on the border with Nicaragua, where the rare harpy eagle is found.

Puerto Lempira is the largest town in La Mosquitia, located on the **Caratasca Lagoon**. Take a launch to Cauquira, a village located on the lagoon's north side. The lagoon has manatees, lots of birds, and abundant wildlife. **Ahuas** is a small town, a one hour walk to The Rio Patuca, where you can catch a *pipante* upriver to **Wampusirpe**, a lovely village set on the banks of the Patuca. You can get lodging and meals at Doña Irma Rivas' house right next to the river. From Wampusirpe it's a two hour walk to the nearby rainforest. Wampusirpe has a primitive grass airstrip, which receives flights from Mission Aviation Fellowship which flies out of Ahuas. From Ahuas to Wampusirpe it's a 6 hour ride in an outbord motorized canoe.

Continuing upriver from Wampusirpe, the terain becomes more mountainous, with beautiful vistas, virgin forest, and scattered friendly Miskito villages. Downriver from Ahuas leads to **Barra Patuca** on the sea. Barra Patuca is a racous, little seaside village locally known for its nightlife, seafood, and for being a cargo dropoff point where goods bound for the Patuca River region are offloaded from a La Ceiba-based freightor that makes a weekly sailing to Barra Patuca. *TukTuks* provide transport on major rivers like The Patuca. A TukTuk is a motorized dugout canoe (the name TukTuk is derived from the sound the engine makes).

Brus Laguna is an important seaside lagoon whose name comes from the pirate 'Bloody Brewer,' who made the lagoon his hideout. Look for the old cannons left by the British who occupied and fortified the island. Brus Laguna is located at the eastern edge of the Rio Plátano Biosphere. Motorized canoes are available for hire. Lodging is available at **Cabaña Bishop**, meals available.

This is one of the best places in the world for tarpon and snook fishing. The **Cannon Island Fishing Resort** offers packages that include full meals, tackle, guides, and lodging. This is the only true eco-lodge in the country, accommodating up to 70 people. The camp is in the lagoon. Access is via flight into Brus Laguna, launch will be sent from the resort to pick you up. Prices are $300 per person, per night, all inclusive. Contact **Caribbean Adventure Tours**, Richard Thompson, Brus Laguna, Gracias a Dios.

the bay islands

Chapter 14

Legally, constitutionally, formally, administratively, economically and institutionally, the Bay Islands form part of the República de Honduras. But more than a stretch of water separates mainland from islands. Mainlanders speak Spanish, while Bay Islanders speak English (sort of). Mainlanders are farmers. Islanders are fishermen and mariners and boatbuilders. Mainlanders are mostly *mestizos*, descended from Spaniards and native Americans. Bay Islanders are largely descended from Africans and Englishmen, from slaves and buccaneers and pirates.

And for the visitor, the Bay Islands are a world removed not only from the mainland, but from everywhere else in the universe, a paradise of beach and rainforested peaks in the sea, with few telephones, clocks, or cares, and some of the best fishing and diving in the hemisphere.

History

Before the Spanish came to the Americas, the Bay Islands were most likely populated by Paya Indians. Many old dwelling sites have been identified, and pieces of pre-Columbian ceramic are still occasionally found.

In 1502, Christopher Columbus, on his fourth voyage to the New World, landed on **Guanaja**, which he called Isla de los Pinos (Pine Island).

Discovery, as elsewhere, meant disaster for the natives. Though Columbus came in peace, Spaniards soon after carried off the inhabitants to slave in Mexico and the West Indies. Later, the islands were something of a breadbasket for the Spanish fleet, provisioning ships with fruits, vegetables and meat for the return voyage to Spain.

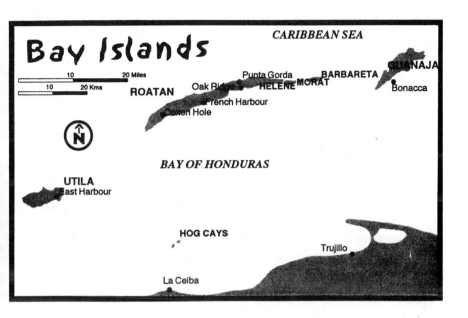

Bay Islands

CARIBBEAN SEA

ROATAN

Oak Ridge

Punta Gorda

BARBARETA

HELENE MORAT

GUANAJA

Bonacca

French Harbour

Coxen Hole

BAY OF HONDURAS

UTILA
East Harbour

HOG CAYS

Trujillo

La Ceiba

With their broken topography, swamps, and reefs blocking the approach from the sea, the Bay Islands attracted limited Spanish interest as sites for permanent settlement. But what repelled the Spanish is precisely what attracted buccaneers and pirates. Pirate ships could easily navigate shallow passages to harbors behind the reef, and lie safe from the larger and heavier vessels of the Spanish. And the islands were not far from Trujillo, whence gold was shipped to Spain.

Early English settlers came in peace. The Providence Company colonized Roatán in 1638 with Puritan farmers from Maryland. They called the place Rich Island, cut logwood trees for export, and grew tobacco and indigo, and cassava as a staple. Their colony, possibly located near today's Old Port Royal, lasted four years. In 1642, the Spanish threw out the Puritans, helpless and defenseless as civil war raged in England.

Spain followed a policy of keeping *everybody* out of the islands, so that no food could be grown, no shelter erected, that might be used by enemies. This policy turned many Indians into allies of the English pirates who continued to use the islands, despite the best efforts of the Spanish. A pirate camp at Port Royal was overrun by the Spanish in 1650, and all natives who could be found were exiled to the mainland. But pirates still returned to take on fresh water from island streams, hunt wild pigs, and dry turtle meat. Some say the loot from Morgan's 1671 raid on Panama is buried on Roatán.

Sometimes the borderline between pirate and merchant was hazy. Pirates cut logwood to ship home and sell, and the islands made a perfect base for trading cloth and manufactured goods to the Indians along the coast, in defiance of the Spanish monopoly.

In 1742, the British government moved to take the islands as part of a military campaign against Spain. New Port Royal on Roatán was fortified. Spanish attacks failed to dislodge the British, but diplomacy did the trick. The British evacuated in 1748.

When war between Britain and Spain broke out again in 1779, Roatán became a refuge for woodcutters displaced from the coast. Troops and refugees resisted bitterly at Fort George in 1782, but were obliged to surrender after two days. As many as 500 dwellings are said to have been burned. The fort was destroyed, and the black survivors sold into slavery.

The islands were nearly deserted once again, but not for long. In 1797, Britain marooned 5000 Black Caribs on the Bay Islands. The unfortunates, descendents of Carib Indians and shipwrecked African slaves, had rebelled against British rule on the island of Saint Vincent. Spain, still maintaining a no-go policy, obliged the Caribs to move to the mainland near Trujillo, by that time virtually abandoned due to repeated British attacks; though some managed to stay on at Punta Gorda on Roatán's north shore.

The modern culture of the Bay Islands really dates to Central American independence. After 1821, Central America maintained a garrison in the islands, but the weak, decentralized country was no longer able to defend its territorial claims. White Cayman Islanders, fearful of black domination after the abolition of slavery, began to migrate to the Bay Islands, which some knew from fishing and turtling expeditions.

After 1838, a new wave of black Cayman Islanders began to arrive, as their indentured service during the transition from slavery ran out. The new settlers came into conflict with the Central American garrison, and with the aid of the British superintendent at Belize, packed the soldiers off to Trujillo.

Most of the modern towns in the Bay Islands were established during this period. The islanders built the kind of houses they were familiar with, on stilts, above the range of insects. They lived from fishing and from garden crops.

In 1849, the residents applied to be governed by the authorities in Belize. A local 12-man legislature was established, and in 1852, England formally annexed the Bay Islands. The new British expansion caused a fury, however, especially in the United States, despite the long tradition of British involvement in the islands and along the coast. In 1859, Britain gave in to U.S. pressure, and ceded the islands to Honduras.

For many years thereafter, despite the abolition of English-language schools under Honduran administration, and the settling of small numbers of mainlanders, the islanders were mostly ignored by the distant government in Tegucigalpa, and continued to live lives apart from the mainland mainstream.

The Bay Islands developed an export agriculture of coconuts and plantains long before the mainland. When a hurricane destroyed many of the plantations in 1877, many turned to service on U.S. merchant ships.

The Bay Islands Today
Today, many islanders are still merchant seamen and skilled boatbuilders. And fishing, for the dinner table or for the market, remains the most important occupation. Though tourism is fast becoming the mainstay of island life, and migrants from the mainland are becoming a more and more significant part of the population.

Arrivals & Departures
By Air
Guanaja has a dirt airstrip, while the runways on Roatán and Utila can handle jets. Approximate schedules from La Ceiba, San Pedro Sula and Tegucigalpa to the islands are given elsewhere. From Tegucigalpa, the roundtrip fare to the islands is about $120, from La Ceiba, about $50. Runways on Guanaja and Utila have no lighting. Roatán boasts a recentlybuilit airport (the best in the country), very modern and comfortable.

If there is an evening delay in your connection, you could be "forced" to overnight on the mainland at San Pedro Sula or La Ceiba before continuing to the islands the next morning. If you have a confirmed connection, the airline picks up the tab, and you get to see more of Honduras than you might have otherwise.

Private planes must land and clear customs first on the mainland, most conveniently at La Ceiba.

TACA, *Tel. 800/535-8780,* flies direct to Roatán from New Orleans on Friday; direct to Roatán from Houston on Saturday; and direct to Roatán from Miami on Sunday. There are daily international flights into San Pedro Sula with connections to Bay Islands.

American, *Tel. 800/433-7300,* has a daily flight from Miami to San Pedro Sula.

Continental, *Tel. 800/231-0856,* has a daily flight from Houston to San Pedro Sula.

Isleña, *Tel. 443-0179,* has flights from La Ceiba to Utila at 6am and 4pm, $39 round trip; La Ceiba to Roatán at 6:25am,9:00,10:00,12:00,2:00,3:30 and 5:30pm, $39 round trip. La Ceiba to Guanaja at 10:00am and 4:30pm, $56 round trip.

Sosa Airlines, *La Ceiba Tel. 443-1399, 441-2512, Fax 4443-2519, E-mail: aerososa@psinet.hn or aerolineasosa@edured.net, web: www.aerolineasosa.com,* has flights from La Ceiba to Utila at 6am, 9:15am, 3:30pm, $29round-trip. La Ceiba to Roatán at 7:30am, 9am, 10am, 12:30pm, 3:30pm, $44 round-trip. La Ceiba to Guanaja at 10am, $56 round-trip.

Atlantic Airlines, *Tel 440-2343/46/47*, flies La Ceiba to Roatán at 6:00am, 7:30,9:45,12:15,3:20,5:30pm, $39 round trip. La Ceiba to Utila at 7:30am and 3:30pm, $39 round trip. La Ceiba to Guanaja at 7:00am and 4:15 am, $58 round trip.

By Boat

Yachties and others of that ilk can consult the *Cruising Guide to the Honduras Bay Islands*, available from Wescott Cove Publishing Co., P O Box 130, Stamford CT 06904. Fuel is available at the larger towns. Seas are generally choppy, with steady south-southeast winds of about 15 knots.

If you don't sail down, you can find a sailing vessel for hire in the Bay Islands. Start your search by contacting **Roatán Charter**, Box 877, San Antonio, FL 33576, *Tel. 800/282-8932, Fax 904/588-4158, E-mail: info@Roatán.com, web: www.Roatán.com* . One of the vessels they represent is the 46-foot sloop *Honky Tonk*, currently for hire at $900 per person and up on a weekly basis, including beach barbecues and nights spent in ports and coves throughout the Bay Islands.

The **M/V Galaxy** *(Tel. 446-1796, 446-1250, 443-4633)* sails daily. La Ceiba-Roatán 3:00pm, Roatán-La Ceiba 7:30am. La Ceiba-Utila 9:30am, Utila-La Ceiba 11:00am. Fares: La Ceiba-Utila $23 round trip, La Ceiba-Roatán $24 round trip.

Bay Islanders are famed boat builders. Many craft are *dories*, elongated and similar to sailboats, and now often fitted with rudders, though traditionally they have had none; and dugout *cayucas*, canoe-like vessels made from hollowed logs.

Mainland Excursions

Since the Bay Islands are the principal tourist destination in Honduras, a whole network of inland treks, tours and ventures has developed as adjuncts to diving packages. Samples of add-ons that can be booked through hotels in the Bay Islands, or when arranging your dive package:

• **Copán Ruins**, from $125 day trip, from $160 overnight.
• **Banana plantation tour**, from $40 day trip, $65 overnight.
• **Trekking in Cusuco Cloud Forest**, with camping, $435 for three nights.
• **River adventure in Mosquitia**, with camping, $810 for eight nights.

Orientation

Located about 60 km offshore, the islands, running in a 125-km arc, are the tips of undersea mountains that extend out from the mainland's Omoa ridge. Their peaks, rising as high as 400 meters (1300 feet), are covered with oak and pine and cedar and dense, broad-leafed undergrowth, and studded with caves and cliffs. Coral reefs, often within swimming distance of shore, virtually surround most of the islands, forming natural breakwaters, and creating ideal, calm pools for diving, fishing, swimming and sailing.

Roatán is the largest of the Bay Islands, with the major towns, though there are also settlements on **Utila** and **Guanaja**. The smaller islands are **Morat, Helene** (Santa Elena) and **Barbaret** (or Barbareta). With more than 60 smaller cays offshore, the Bay Islands cover about 92 square miles.

Population

About 22,000 persons inhabit the Bay Islands altogether, about 15,000 on the main island of Roatán, about 5500 on Guanaja, and 1500 on Utila. In addition to fishing and boatbuilding, some make a living harvesting and drying coconut meat, or copra, and many keep gardens of root vegetables, especially cassava. Local cuisine is heavy on fish, of course, but also on coconut, as in coco bread.

Most residents are Protestant and English-speaking and live right along the water. But there have long been a couple of small inland settlements of Spanish Hondurans, at Juticalpa and Corozal on Roatán, where the inhabitants grow corn and beans and live just like mainland farmers.

In recent years, as tourism has presented opportunities not available on the mainland of Honduras, the numbers of Spanish-speaking residents has been rising. Meanwhile, the close-knit, church-centered life of English-speakers has been hard hit by the ways brought not only by visitors from the outside, but also by satellite television, and a government and educational system, once semi-autonomous, that now operate in Spanish and are administered by mainlanders.

Sports & Recreation
DIVING

What can you say about the diving? First, diving is what the Bay Islands are most known for. Second, the water is warm. Temperatures range between 79 to 84° F (26° to 29°C). Third, underwater visibility is good. The water is not as clear as in Bonaire, but it is crystalline nevertheless. Visibility can vary with the weather. The sea is calm within the fringing reefs, and there are practically no drift currents along the south side of the islands.

And if you like **coral reefs**, you'll find the corals around the Bay Islands spectacular, intact, and very much alive (coral can get silted up and damaged by hurricanes, among other things).

The islands are each surrounded by coral reefs, from 20 to 40 feet down. Almost all of the coral types specific to the Caribbean can be found in the reefs off the Bay Islands. One of the most unusual and characteristic types is pillar coral, which reaches several feet in length. Others are elkhorn, star, lettuce and brain coral. And there are multi-hued rope, vase, finger and barrel

Diving High Points
Major points to consider about diving in the Bay Islands:
• Decompression chamber available on Roatán and Utila
• Wall diving a major feature
• Several wrecks to dive
• Easy diving from shore — unlimited at a number of resorts
• Excellent variety of coral and fish
• Lowest package diving prices in the Caribbean
• Diving available on opposite shores of Roatán — sheltered diving off the south when winds are up on the north side.
• Live-aboards available
• Minimal travel time to dive sites—minutes in many cases.
• Many small resorts and representative agencies willing to answer visitors' questions before money is put down

Diving Low Points
• Sand flies are a nuisance on shore
• Limited entertainment and other non-diving resort amenities

sponges, flittering sea fans, and schools of rainbow colored fish, indigo hamlets, parrot fish, rock hinds, chromis and others that favor the reefs, seahorses, sea urchins, anemones, polyps, and more ordinary snappers and jacks and groupers and sea turtles. In deeper waters are manta rays.

The underwater landscape features wandering clefts and caverns, sheer walls, cracks, tunnels, caves and ledges, reverse ledges, and dropoffs of 100 to 200 feet. Walls start as little as twenty feet under the surface, which affords more natural light than is usually available in wall diving.

Famous sites include **Mary's Place**, off Brick Bay, a huge crack in the ocean floor (called the Grand Canyon of wall diving, and currently off limits because of over-visitation); **Bear's Den**, a formation that in earlier times was a waterfall, until the shifting of continental plates submerged it; the **Enchanted Forest**, planted with black coral and sea fans; **West End Wall** and **CoCo View Wall** off Roatán, and **Captain's Crack**, off Guanaja.

Wrecks include the *Prince Albert*, off CoCo View Resort on Roatán, and the *Jado Trader*, off southern Guanaja, and there are proprietary wrecks near some of the resorts. Others, reputed to be from colonial times, are only discussed in whispers.

I'm told there are few sharks, and, for what it's worth, I haven't seen any.

Most of the resorts that offer diving make life easy. The diving equipment and compressors are on the dock, right at the diving boat. There is nothing to lug, and no loss of time. Diving sites are usually no more than 20 minutes away. Many hotels have interesting coral formations and submarine landscapes within easy range of shore dives.

Waters are generally clearest for diving during the periods when there is the least rain: mid-February to mid-September. The onset of hurricane season and winds can churn up the waters during the late months of the year. But the same conditions help to distribute the nutrients in the water, and encourage growth of undersea life.

You *must* be certified to dive at Bay Islands resorts. If you're not, you can arrange to take courses for PADI or SSI certification.

Airlines have the usual baggage limits of about 70 lbs. per piece on checked pieces.

Diving Live-Aboards

Terrific diving is within easy reach of almost any hotel on the Bay Islands, even if you just wade out from shore. Absolutely superb diving, at sites where the sea creatures are not yet accustomed to seeing masked humans, is a little farther out. To reach a number of such sites requires dragging your gear to the dock every morning, setting out for a long ride, returning for lunch, setting out again, and returning to your hotel, followed by repeated packing up and unpacking as you move on to your next diving base.

Or, you can live aboard your dive boat, and roll off the dive platform shortly after you roll out of bed.

Live-aboards come at a price. A week-long trip, with six days of diving, runs from $1000 to $1500, based on double occupancy. And the diving can be tougher. You'll spend more time in the water, probably at greater depths than if you dive from a shore base, sometimes in uncharted seas. Medical help in an emergency is *not* at hand.

But live-aboards also come with amenities: sundecks, video libraries for evening entertainment, good-sized rooms, and often photo-processing facilities. And since the diving is usually limited only by decompression tables and safety considerations, the cost *per dive* can turn out to be even more reasonable than from a land base. As many as five daily dives are scheduled.

Some of the live-aboards currently operating in the Bay Islands are:

The **Bay Islands Aggressor**, 110 feet, carries 18 passengers in air-conditioned cabins (two to four persons each). Showers and toilets are shared. Features include sun-and-shade deck, video entertainment, bar, equipment and underwater cameras for rent, and on-board slide processing. Certification and specialty courses are available. The rate is about $1400 per person for a weekly trip with five-and-a-half days of diving throughout the islands and the

Hog Cays, with discounts available from September to February. Resort and certification courses are available on board. Contact **Aggressor Fleet**, *P O Drawer K, Morgan City, LA 70381, Tel. 800/348-2628 or in Honduras contact Romeo's Resort, Tel. 4451127, where the boat docks.*

The **Isla Mia**, 75 feet, takes 14 divers in seven air-conditioned cabins, each with private bathroom, to sites around Roatán, Morat and Barbareta. Also on board are sundecks, slide-viewing tables, video player, two compressors, and a small library. The ship avoids using anchors on reefs, and offers naturalist seminars during selected weeks. The cost of an eight-day, seven-night package with unlimited diving is $1000 at any time of year, slightly more during seminar weeks. Guests are expected to be certified, in order to avoid excessive guiding.

For information, contact Isla Mia, 1315 Post Office St., Galveston, TX 77550, *Tel. 800/874-7636 or 409/765-1776, Fax 409/765-1775.* In Roatán, contact the French Harbour Yacht Club, *Tel. 445-1478, Fax 445-1459.*

The **Maid'en Desert** is a 60-foot air-conditioned sailing ketch with just three double rooms and compressor, available at a weekly rate of $900 to $1250 per person. For bookings, contact Roatán Charter, Box 877, San Antonio, FL 33576, *Tel. 800/282-8932, Fax 904/588-4158.*

Costs

Diving in the Bay Islands is almost always part of a package included with your hotel booking, and if you compare prices, you'll find that a week of diving will cost several hundred dollars less than in Belize. Partly, this is because Honduras is a real country, that grows its own food and provides many of the services that must be imported for visitors elsewhere in the Caribbean.

Here's a listing of prices from the **Utila Dive Center** to give an idea of rates. Remember that diving on Utila is quite a bit cheaper than Roatán and Guanaja. 1 tank dive $20, 2 tank dive $30, night dive $25, 10 dive package $125, discover scuba course $85, open water course $159, advanced open water course $159, rescue diver $159, dive master $500, instructor development course $995, night diver $145, deep diver $145, wreck diver $145, naturalist diver $125, navigation $135, search and recovery $145. Seven nights at a dedicated dive resort in the Bay Islands will run $800 for 7 nights which includes lodging, all meals, 3 boat dives daily, 2 night dives/wreck dives, all equipment, welcome coctail and airport transfers.

What to Bring

When resorts talk about inclusive dive packages, they generally mean that air tanks, weights, guides, and boat transport to dive sites are provided. Bring your own regulator with tank pressure gauge, buoyancy compensator, depth gauge, fins, masks, and, optionally, booties, gloves (to protect against abrasions), underwater light and dive watch. Anything you don't bring can be rented. And don't forget your certification card.

FISHING

This is the how most resident islanders make their livings, either directly or indirectly. Traditionally, fish have been caught and kept fresh in pens made of closely placed stakes driven into the shallow seabed offshore, then transported to markets in La Ceiba and elsewhere on the mainland. But commercial catches of lobster and shrimp for export are becoming increasingly important.

Sport fishing isn't quite as developed as in some other Caribbean locales, though not for the lack of resources. Among the species found in the shallows near shore are bonefish and permit, which are caught all year, and grouper, snook, and all sorts of snapper, including yellowtail and red. Tarpon has a more limited season, generally from February through June.

Deeper waters have mackerel (king and Spanish), bonito, blackfin tuna, and wahoo, kingfish, and, seasonally, marlin, while jewfish are caught around the Hog Cays. Commercially fished are shrimp and lobster, red snapper, and conch ("conk," or sea snail), a somewhat tough species that is consumed locally but not much exported.

A typical offshore or flats fishing package of 7 nights lodging, 5 days of offshore or flats fishing, tackle and bait, all meals, welcome coctail, beer and soda while fishing (and airport transfers) runs $1,200 per angler.

Tournaments

An annual **billfishing** tournament operates out of the Fantasy Island Resort and Marina on Roatán, usually at the end of September or beginning of October. The fee for participation has recently been just $50 per angler, and the winning fish in 1992 was a 400-pound marlin. Boat rentals can be arranged with registration.

For information, contact Fantasy Island: *Tel. 800/676-2826 in the U.S., or 445-1222 on Roatán.*

Lodging & Fishing Packages

Hotels offering fishing facilities usually quote a price inclusive of boat, equipment, and guide. See hotel listings in the pages that follow.

Fishing Gear

Choice of equipment can be limited, however. For bonefishing in shallow waters, a light spinning rod is suitable, with 200 yards of four- to six- pound test line (or eight-pound line, according to some anglers), and light lures. Heavier line and tackle are suitable for casting from shore, or for trolling. Take an assortment of lures to suit different conditions, jigs (hair, nylon, white, yellow, pink), hook sizes 1-0, and tipped leader 20- to 30-pound test, 18 to 20 inches long.

Basic Information

Beasts, Bugs, Bites, & Bonks

There are no poisonous snakes or dangerous wild animals in the islands, though sandflies ("no-see-ums") are placed by some in the latter category. I should say that this is without justification. There are some sandflies, but if there is even the slightest wind, they will not be a problem. On a still day, it would be hard to stay for very long on the beach unless you have insect repellent, so come prepared with your favorite brand. Residents place their houses on stilts above the level of molestation.

Hikers and treasure hunters venturing into the hills need have no particular concerns about wildlife, such as deer, lizards, rabbits, and parrots. And don't nap under coconut palms on the beach. Plummeting coconuts can cause serious injury or death. In a storm, do not shelter under a coconut palm. Ample fallen palms are evidence that they don't have much of a supporting root structure.

Costs

Things cost more in the Bay Islands than elsewhere in Honduras, but it's still possible to live cheaply in the towns. Everything depends on where you stay. At Anthony's Key, the price of a beer is triple the price at the best hotel in La Ceiba. But this is not how things are everywhere.

Island Talk

Open belly? It's just how you say diarrhea in the local language, which is English, sort of, with many, many modifications. Bay Islands sayings have been collected in a fascinating illustrated booklet entitled *Wee Speak*, by American resident Candace Wells Hammond, which you'll find on sale here and there. Black Caribs, or Garifunas, speak their own language, and a perfectly intelligible version of English.

Standard English is also understood and tolerated. And since the Bay Islands have been part of Honduras for the last hundred years, you'll find that some people speak Spanish as well, though residents of Hispanic origin usually have to learn some English in order to get along.

Land

Oddly, the entire area of the Bay Islands is classified as urban, which, among other things, allows foreigners to own land along the water (prohibited in rural areas). Real Estate develpers have moved in, in a big way, and you can buy a piece of the islands from one of them. Can time-sharing be far away?

The following realtors offer land and homes on the islands:

RE/MAX Bay Islands: *tjlynch@remax.net, jefft@remax.ne, halliday@hondusoft.com, remaxbi@hondusoft.com, web: www.roatanbayisland.com*
Parrot Tree Plantation/Century 21/J. Edwards Real Estate: *jedwards@globalnet.hn, web: www.hondurasrealestate.net*
Luna Beach: *TLC@globalnet.hn, web: www.lunabeachresort.com*
Roatán Properties: *lizl@globalnet.hn*
Ocean View Estates/Coldwell Banker: *weissman@coldwellbanker.com*

Protecting The Environment

The **Bay Islands Conservation Asociation** has a number of projects in the Bay Islands. Their main office is: *Edificio Cooper, Coxen Hole, Roatán; there is also an office on Utila.* The **Inter-American Develpoment Bank Environmental Project for The Bay Islands** is a 5 year, $24 million project to protect the fragile Bay Islands ecosystems. Information: *Tel. 4451559, Fax 4451635*

Lethal Yellowing, a disease which hits coconut palms, has arrived in Roatán. Previously, Lethal Yellowing has struck in The Yucatán, Jamaica, and Florida. Measures have begun to be taken in The Bay Islands to save the palms. Lethal Yellowing has now taken hold on the mainland Caribbean coast. Plans are under way to establish nurseries where resistant palm trees will be grown. It is expected that the problem of palm tree die-off will get worse before it gets better.

For more information, contact The Bay Islands Conservation Association.

Souvenirs

Avoid picking, carrying, harvesting, buying, or otherwise acquiring to take home the following: coral (black or otherwise), fish, shells, and pre-Columbian artifacts (in plentiful supply, and commonly known as *yaba-ding-dings*). It's either illegal to take these out of Honduras without a license, or illegal to bring them back to your own country, or both, and it doesn't help to conserve what you came to see and do. This leaves T-shirts and hardwood carvings.

Weather

If you like rain, come in October or November or, with less certainty, in December — 50% of the yearly total falls just in these three months. If you have just a week of vacation, and don't want it spoiled by rough seas or airplane delays, come from January to September. The best months are March to August.

Expect to see some rainfall at any time of year, as storms blow through the Caribbean. Average rainfall in October and November is about 450 mm (almost 18 inches). The lightest months are March, April and May, with under 75 mm (less than three inches) of rain. January and February — when the islands are heavily visited — see moderate rainfall of about 200 and 125 mm (8 and 5 inches) respectively.

Temperatures are generally perfect in the Bay Islands. The yearly average is about 27.5°C (81°F). The coolest month is January (25.8°C, 78°F), the warmest month is August (28.8°C, 84°F). With a sea breeze usually blowing, it's not hard to take.

On average, a serious hurricane strikes every 20 years.

Utila

Utila is the nearest of the Bay Islands to the mainland, just 35 kilometers from La Ceiba. Measuring about seven miles long, and almost three miles wide, it is the smallest of the three main Bay Islands and sees only some 15,000 tourists per year. It is only nineteen miles off the Honduran coast. The average temperature ranges between 79°F-85°F year round, with the water being nearly the same. The population of Utila is about 2,500. People here are very different than on the mainland. They are mostly fair skinned and speak a heavily inflected Island-style English that takes getting some used to.

The island's geography is low-lying, something like an atoll, and the central portion, taking up a good two-thirds of the surface, is mangrove. A fringe of dry land surrounds this near-lake. Most of the high ground is at the east end — the absolute high spot is 200-foot Pumpkin Hill in the northeast, a walk of less than an hour from town. A canal through the mangrove bisects east-central Utila.

Utila is where most of the white Cayman Islanders settled after 1830, and to this day, most of the inhabitants are fair-skinned.

You don't find any big resorts on Utila. Even the most expensive all inclusive dedicated dive resorts (Laguna Beach Resort and Utila Lodge are small, family-owned and run operations).

But these "disadvantages" for big-time tourism make Utila a great place to go and rest and hang out, away from the crowds, and from touristy expectations. People are friendly, and there are small stores, bars and restaurants where you can get to know them. Prices are lower than elsewhere.

Utila is famous for offering the cheapest diving and dive courses in the entire Caribbean. A PADI open water course costs $159 and a 2 tank fun dive costs $30. Budget travellers take note: most dive schools on Utila are offering free accommodations at local hotels with all dive courses. This inexpensive diving, combined with cheap hotels and meals, has converted Utila into a major stop on the Central America Gringo Trail.

Utila's reefs are of the close-hugging, fringing type referring to their close proximity to shore. Utila lies at the edge of the continental shelf with some sheer walls dropping from twenty feet to more than a thousand feet. Offshore sea mounts start in thirty-five feet of water hosting a myriad of soft corals and offering frequent sightings of hawksbill and green turtles, schooling spade-fish, horse-eyed jacks, and yellowtail snappers. The majority of dive sites are excellent for snorkelers.

A large number of European and, to a lesser degree, American backpack-ers make up the majority of Utila's visitors. Utila has a very funky, international atmosphere, kind of what the Caribbean must have been like in the 1950's before the hordes of package tourists and Club Meds took over.

Arrivals & Departures
Arriving by Boat
The **M/V Galaxy** leaves La Ceiba at 9:30am for Utila. It leaves 11:00am from Utila-La Ceiba, $23 round trip.

Arriving by Air
Isleña, *Tel. 441-2521, 443-0179.* Flights from La Ceiba-Utila at 6am and 4pm, $39 round trip.

SOSA Airlines, *Tel. 441-2512, Fax 425-3161 (Utila), E-mail: aerososa@psinet.hn or aerolineasosa@edured.net, web: www.aerolineasosa.com,.* Flights from La Ceiba-Utila at 6:00am and 3:30pm, $39 round trip.

Atlantic Airlines, *Tel 440-2343/2347 , 425-3241(Utila).* Flights from La Ceiba-Utila at 7:30am and 3:30pm, $39 round trip.

Passengers on diving packages will be met at the airport. A truck meets incoming planes and will take you into town for $2 or so, or you can walk in — it's under a mile.

Orientation
There is one road, running a few hundred yards from the airport to East Harbour (identified on maps as the town of Utila), and two to three cars have been occasionally reported on it. Other settlements are on Pigeon Cay and Suc-Suc Cay, offshore to the southwest, connected to each other by an over-water walkway; and at West End.

Most of the patch coral reef near the island is between these two places — the small offshore cays are surrounded by coral, making for good diving. There are some good walls and slanting reefs, though most dive sites are farther from shore than those off Roatán.

Where to Stay
LAGUNA BEACH, *Tel/Fax 4253239, U.S. reservations Tel. 800/668-8452, www.utila.com.*
West of town, the resort has packages catering to divers. They offer a full

service dive operation, 3 dives daily, night dives, unlimited beach diving, plus fishing, volleyball, kayaking, snorkeling, cabañas, restaurant and bar. This is Utila's newest and most luxurious resort. Bungalows feature private decks, hot water and air-conditioning. All-inclusive 7 night dive package runs $795 per person.

UTILA LODGE, *Tel. 425-3143, U.S. reservations Tel. 800/282-8932, E-mail: ulodger@hondutel.hn or utl@roatan.com, www.roatan.com/utilalodge.htm. 8 rooms. $50 double.* Week-long dive package $800 per person including airport pickup, three daily boat dives and two night dives per week, tanks, weights, belts; non-diver $700. Week-long fishing package with five days of fishing from $1,150 in the flats to $1,395 offshore. Heavy tackle included for offshore fishing; bring your own light tackle.

Located in the village, built right over the water on two levels. Each air-conditioned room has a ceiling fan, front and rear porch entry, a single and double bed, and equipment closet. Personal gear is *not* available for rent — bring your own, or make arrangements beforehand for rental through a local dive shop.

Utila Lodge is one of the few hotels in the Bay Islands ready, willing and able to receive sport fishermen. There are two fully equipped diesel-powered boats, and the specialties are marlin in the deeps, tarpon and permit and snook closer in, and bonefish in the flats. Marina facilities are available, with 14 slips on a 130-foot dock.

VICKY'S ROOMS, *Suc-Suc Cay, $4 night.*
Basic lodgings at very cheap rates.

MANGO INN, *Tel 425-3335, E-mail: mango@hondutel.hn, web: www.mango-inn.com. 23 rooms, air conditioned cabin $45 double, double with private bath $25, double with shared bath $15.*
Highly recommended by this writer, clean, comfortable, friendly management. The best mid-priced hotel on Utila. Excellent restaurant on premises, Cafe Mango is one of the best restaurants on the island, with great food and wonderful atmosphere especially in the evenings. Diving available with Utila Dive Center.There's 24 hour power and cable TV.

MARGARITE VILLE, *ocated at the edge of town on the path to Blue Bayou Beach. Tel 425-3366, $13 double.*
Plain simple rooms, clean, nice views of town. Best budget hotel in town. Across the path is the Driftwood Restaurant perched out over the bay.

Other Lodging
Utila specializes in inexpensive, basic accomodations. The island and its dive schools fill with budget travelers and backpackers from a dozen nations in search of low cost diving, accommodations, food and funky Caribbean atmosphere.

There are lots of very basic houses, apartments and rooms for rent. Most are rented by the young international diving crowd. For the price of a week at Club Med, one could settle down on Utila and dive for the entire winter season.

Where to Eat

Food is served in any number of small eateries in East Harbour, much of it is of the junk food variety; burgers, sandwiches and such. Fish, of course is your best bet, fresh but always fried or in a soup. You'll also find Caribbean style pastries *(pastelitos)* and wonderful coconut, baked fresh daily.

THOMPSONS' BAKERY is the best place in town for breakfasts; great pancakes, cinnamon rolls, pies and cakes, eggs, funky decor. The Johnny Cake Biscuits are superb. Highly recommended.

ISLAND CAFE in front of Coco Loco, recommended for seafood.

SUSAN'S RESTAURANT, *at Suc-Suc Cay.*
Good inexpensive food.

MERMAIDS CORNER, *on the main drag.*
Probably the biggest and most popular restaurant on the island, good pastas, bar, lunch and dinner.

DELANY´S KITCHEN, *located at Coopers Inn.*
Good pizzas and lasagna.

MANGO CAFÉ, *located at the Mango Inn.*
One of the best restaurants on the island, great atmosphere at night, bar.

Other places include **Marios**, zero decor but good fish plates at $4 and fish burgers at $3, free soup appetizer; **Munchies**, as the name says, the place in town to see and be seen munching out – sit on the porch looking out on the main strip, shakes, sandwiches, burgers; and **RJ's**, open Wednesday, Friday and Sunday, known for its BBQ.

Bars
Popular bars are **Coco Loco**, **Mango Cafe** and the **Bush Bar**.

Seeing the Sights

The **Iguana Research & Breeding Station**, *www.utila-iguana.org or www.cyclura.com*, is home to the Wishwilly de Suampo or **Swamper Iguana** (Ctenosaura bakeri) which is only found on the island of Utila. The Swamper is threatened due to encroachment of habitat and over-hunting by local residents. The **Utila Iguana Conservation Project** seeks to ensure the reproduction of the Utila Iguana as well as surveying the flora and fauna of the island. There's a Visitors Center, live captive iguanas exhibit, and community environmental education programs.

Volunteers are welcome to work at the Breeding Station. Up to eight volunteers at a time live at the station for 1-3 months. The volunteer program is open to graduate students and anyone who wants to actively engage in species conservation and preservation. The project is sponsored by the Frankfurt Zoological Society and the Senckenberg Nature Research Society, with assistance from sponsors and individual donors.

Sports & Recreation

There are a large number of dive shops on Utila and competition is great amongst them. This has resulted in Utila gaining fame as the cheapest place in the world to learn to dive.

Walk the main drag in town and visit with a number of dive centers before settling on one. Among them are:
• **Underwater Vision**, operating out of Hotel Laguna del Mar, *Tel. 425-3103*
• **Utila Dive Centre**, *Tel. 425-3326, E-mail: info@utiladivecentre.com, web: www.utiladivecentre.com*
• **Captain Morgan's Dive Center**, *Tel. 425-3161*
• **Utila Watersports**, *Tel. 425-3239*
• **Bay Islands College of Diving**, *Tel. 425-3143, E-mail: bicdive@hondutel.hn, web: www.dive-utila.com*
• **Alton's Dive Shop**, *Tel. 425-3108, E-mail: altons@hondutel.hn, web: www.divealtons.com*
• **Gunter's**, *Tel. 425-3350, E-mail: ecomar@hondutel.hn*

Diving is unregulated in Honduras, and unless you go through a hotel that offers dive packages, you can't be sure of what you're getting. Great snorkeling from a dock is available at **Blue Bayou**, a 1/2 hour walk from the village. There's a small charge of $1 and a restaurant. It's a popular spot with snorkelers.

You can also visit a cay. At **Miss Trudy's**, for example, you can arrange to be dropped off for a day of snorkeling, and picked up, box lunch included, for $10 per person or less. It's like having your own private island for the day. Make arrangements a day in advance.

Water Cay, off the southwest of the main island, has great snorkeling off the south shore. Water Cay is an idyllic speck in the midst of some fantastic coral reef. There are no services on the Cay, but there is a caretaker who will charge $1 per person. Bring all supplies you might need or want like food and water with you, although fresh cut coconuts are available from the caretaker. You can spend the night on the Cay, but bringa tent, sleeping bags, and plenty of food and water. If spending the night, arrange with your boatman to pick you up at a prearranged day and time. Highly recomended.

Captain Morgan's Dive Center will take you out to Water Cay for the day for $9; you'll get snorkeling gear, a hammock, and a barbeque lunch. Or, from town, walk out and snorkel off the airstrip. Interested in deep sea fishing? Charters are available aboard **The Huntress**; call Utila Lodge, *Tel. 425-3143.*

Also found, without too much difficulty, are caves both over water (especially on **Pumpkin Hill**) and under water; **Blue Lagoon** along the south side of the island; waterways through the mangroves to explore by canoe; and trails across the island's interior. You can hike up Pumpkin Hill, the island's highest point and only 'mountain.' From there, you can view the entire island as well as Roatán in the distance.

There are a number of privately owned cays which can be rented. **Bell Key** has a small lodge. **Morgan Key** and **Sandy Key** can be rented. Contact George Jackson, who lives on Pigeon Key.

Snorkeling gear can be rented at any dive shop for about $3 per day.

Practical Information

Services in East Harbour include a couple of banks (BGA and Banco Atlantida for VISA withdrawls) and several Protestant churches.

The **Bay Islands Conservation Association** has an office on the main street. They're a good source of information on wildlife, iguana protection program, reef ecology – and they have great T-shirts for sale. BICA also has information on the Utila Dive Safety Association, a group of Utila dive shops that have joined together to monitor and ensure adherence to international safety standards.

There is a Spanish School on Utila. Contact **CA Spanish School**, *E-mail: edu@ca-spanish.com, web: www.ca-spanish.com.*

Bay Islands Originals, located on the main street, is without a doubt the best souvenir and crafts shop on the island.

There are two cinemas in town: **Reef Cinema** and **Bundu Cinema**, movies change nightly, $2.

Internet is available at Henderson's Cafe and The Internet Cafe.

Roatán

Roatán is the largest and most developed for tourism of the Bay Islands, roughly Cuba-shaped, stretching about 40 kilometers long and no more than three kilometers wide. Separated by a passage almost narrow enough to step across, at the eastern end, is the island of **Helene** (or Santa Elena), and slightly beyond are **Morat** and **Barbaret** (Barbareta).

If you like sun, beaches, swimming, a nice island away from it all, genial people, you'll find all that on Roatán. It is everything that you might hope for from a perfect Caribbean island, and it is not yet too commercial.

If you like diving, you might as well call it paradise.

And that's not the end of it. If you're a birder, you can see a wealth of tropical birds. And to round things out, there is even a lot of barely touched forest, for seafaring, rather than agriculture, has been the heritage of the islanders.

Landscape & Seascape

There is a long, irregular mountain ridge inland on Roatán, with hilltops reaching up to 235 meters, but these are just the peaks of the mountains that lie below the waters. Beaches and cliffs punctuate the north shore.

It was the inlets and bays on the south, some with deep water, all protected by reefs, that attracted the first European pirates and loggers, and, in modern times, divers.

Reefs line the north coast, a few hundred meters from shore; along the south, coral formations are, in many places, within just steps of the beach. With easy diving, hotels, frequent air service, towns, and even a small road network, Roatán is what most people think of when they think of a vacation in the Bay Islands.

With the exception of a couple of "Spanish" settlements inland at **Corozal** and **Juticalpa**, the people of Roatán live right along the coast —many in white clapboard tin-roofed stilt houses set right above the water that is their highway and disposal system. Most are English-speaking blacks, though Black Caribs inhabit the village of Punta Gorda on the north side of the island. Inland, much of the hardwood forest in the hills has been virtually untouched since English woodcutters and their slaves took timber more than 150 years ago. Hikers occasionally find pieces of pottery made by the Paya Indians who lived here in pre-Columbian times.

Versions differ, but the name of the island might be a corruption of "rattan," from the vines of the island's forests, or a derivative of the Nahuatl expression for "place of women."

Arrivals & Departures

By Air

Isleña Airlines, *Tel. 445-1550/1387/1918,* has six flights per day between La Ceiba and Roatán. The flight takes about 20 minutes, the fare is about $18 one way. La Ceiba-Roatán daily at 6:25am, 9, 10, 12, 2pm, 3:30 and 5:30.

Aerolíneas Sosa, *Tel. 445-1154, 445-1658, E-mail: aerososa@psinet.hn, aerolineasosa@edured.net, web: www.aerolineasosa.com.* Five flights per day La Ceiba-Roatán at 6:30am, 9am, 10am, 12:30pm, 3:30pm. Fare is $18 one-way.

Atlantic Airlines, *Tel 445-1179.* La Ceiba-Roatán, six flights per day at 6am, 7:30, 9:45, 12:15, 3:20, 5:30pm. Fare is $18 one-way.

The modern, newly completed airport is located two km from Coxen's Hole. A hotel reservations desk is located in the terminal. They will reserve hotel rooms on Roatán, La Ceiba, and Copán Ruinas. Local transport around the island is quick, efficient, and downright reasonable. A minibus ride from Coxen Hole to West End runs 70 cents. A taxi on the same route will charge $1 per person. A taxi (which holds up to 5) from the airport to West End is $10. A taxi (for 5) from West End to West Bay will run $10. The very popular West End to West Bay Beach water taxi runs $1.25. As on the mainland, everything (and I mean everything!) is negotiable if you've got the stamina.

By Boat

Trip time is 2 hours, fare $6 one way. It is advisable not to eat or drink much prior to sailing; the up and down motion of the boat may cause a bit of seasickness in more than a few passengers. There is a brand new , very nice passenger terminal in La Ceiba, accesible via a 10 minute taxi ride ($6 per taxi). The **M/V Galaxy** leaves La Ceiba for Roatan at 3pm and leaves Roatan for La Ceiba at 7:30am. Fare $28 round-trip.

Getting Around

Unlike the other islands, Roatán has some significant roads, generally in excellent condition.

A single paved road runs northward across the island from Coxen's Hole to West End; and eastward from Coxen's Hole to French Harbour.

An unpaved road runs from Coxen's Hole west to Flowers Bay. From French Harbour, a dirt road continues inland through the hills, with branches to Oak Ridge and Punta Gorda.

If you plan on getting around the island and dislike taxis, renting a car is a good option. **Sandy Bay Rent A Car**, *Tel. 445-1710, airport Tel. 445-1300*, has offices in Sandy Bay, West End, and at the airport, and rents 4 wheel drive Samurais for $42 a day. If you plan to drive the back roads of Roatán, for example, Punta Gorda to Paya Bay, a 4 wheel drive is definitely recommended. Heavy rains often make these unpaved roads impassable. If you stick to the paved roads, a 4 wheel drive is not necessary. Weekly and monthly rates.

Toyota Rent A Car has a desk at the airport, *Tel. 445-1936, 445-1729, E-mail: trac@123.hn, web: www.123.hn/trac*. **Captain Van's**, West End, rents jeeps, vans, bicycles, mopeds, and rafts. **Avis** is also at the airport, *Tel. 445-0122*.

And finally, there's **Caribbean Rent a Car**, *Tel. 455-5648, 445-1430, E-mail: caribeanrentacar@hondusoft.com, web: www.caribbeanrentacar.com*.

By Bus or Boat

Small buses and minivans operate in either direction from Coxen's Hole. There is usually no waiting, as one minibus leaves the next one arrives. To get

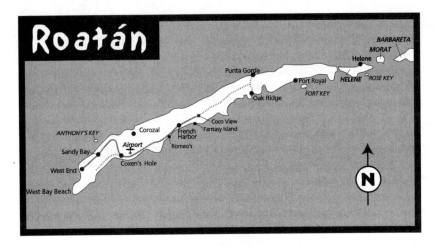

around, just flag down the minibus and pay the *ayudante* (the driver's helper), usually about a dollar on most routes. Some destinations, for example West Bay Beach, are best reached by water taxi. Small launches go back and forth all day long and charge $1.25.

Diving, Fishing, & Charter Boats

Most of the resorts mentioned below have diving boats, and some have fishing boats. In addition, the **Bay Island Aggressor**, a cruising boat designed to accommodate 20 divers, is based at Roatán. You arrive by plane, and off you go from one dive spot to another, sleeping on board.

The following boats are available for Charter:
• **Maid'en Desert**, which sails to Cayos Cochinos, Barbaretta, Utila, Guanaja. Information at Mermaid Marina in Brick Bay, *Tel/Fax 445-1620.*
• **Far Tortuga Charters' Trimaran, Genesis**, is docked at Half Moon Bay in West End. Information: Rick Biddle at Roatán Dive & Yacht Club, *Tel/Fax 445-5233*, half-day sail costs $25 per person.
• **Capt. Douglas** charters a 57 ft. yacht; 8 days will cost you $900. Information in the U.S.: *Tel. 800/432-5828.*
• The **Caribbean Sailing Club** in Brick Bay rents boats.
• **Casablanca Charters** rates from $20 perday, per person. Information at Rick's American Cafe in Sandy Bay, *Tel. 445-1461, 445-2163, 445-1614*

The following gentlemen provide fishing charters: Roy Gibson, *Tel. 445-1461*; Randy French, *Tel. 445-2163*; Arthur Johnson, *Tel. 445-1614*.

In the mood for a glass bottomed boat ride? The **Coral Reef Explorer**, *Tel/Fax 445-1402*, is a semi-submarine where passengers are seated in the glass enclosed hull which is submerged 5 ft. below the surface of the water.

It's air conditioned and there's a bilingual guide. Daily sailings commence at 11:00am and 2:00pm. The fare is $20 per adult, children $12.

Orientation

The Towns of Roatán

There are hotels on Roatán that price everything in U.S. dollars, though Lempiras will be accepted. Generally, these are the resorts outside of towns, though there are exceptions, which are noted.

Roatán towns that are covered in the pages that follow include: Coxen's Hole, Sandy Bay, West End, West Bay Beach, French Harbour, Oak Ridge, Punta Gorda, and the remains of the Old Port Royal fortresses.

Coxen's Hole

Coxen's Hole is the capital of the islands, but, with just a few thousand inhabitants, effectively conceals any self-importance.

Arrivals & Departures

From La Ceiba or anywhere on the mainland, you buy a ticket for Roatán, but once you arrive at the town's airport and are talking to locals, ask for **Coxen's Hole**, the local name, which recalls Captain John Coxen, a pirate of past days.

Orientation

Coxen's Hole has an attractive, small central plaza, and clapboard houses and small general stores and lumber depots and outboard motor repair shops, and one or two larger general stores that style themselves "supermarkets." The wharf can be lively, with the landing of the catch, and processing and re-loading for export to the United States. If you like fish, it's enough to whet your appetite.

Coxen Hole is busy, noisy, and crowded. It's a good place to stock up on supplies and groceries before going to your hotel. But there's really no reason to spend a night here.

Where to Eat

QUE TAL CAFE, *located at the Sandy Bay exit of Coxen Hole, Tel. 445-1007, E-mail: quetal@globalnet.hn.*
Internet cafe, coffee, sanwiches, baked goods.

Practical Information

Banks

Use **Credomatic** for ATM machine and Visa, Mastercard, American Express, at Edificio Cooper Calle Principal, *Tel. 445-1196, 445-1724.* There are a number of banks downtown for cash advance and changing dollars.

Gift & Book Shops & Other Stores

Being the island metropolis, Coxen's Hole has more amenities, shops, and services than are found elsewhere in the islands, including several souvenir shops. One, the **Traveller's Rest Gift Shop**, in the Bay Islands Company building (across from the airline offices) sells maps and books, and has a xerox machine.

Mahchi is a nice gift and crafts shop in a gallery-like setting in the Galindo Building. **Librería Casi Todo** arranges tours of Roatán, Cangrejal River rafting tours, Copán Ruinas, and boat charters.

IMAPRO, *located next to the airport, Tel 445-1945*, sells Honduran crafts, and beautiful handmade mahogony doors for export.

HB Warrens Supermarket has the largest and best selection on the island and an old fashioned '50's style cafeteria. Open Monday-Saturday 7a.m.-6p.m. Next door to Que Tal is **Libreria Casi Todo**, *Tel 445-1944, E-mail: casitodo@globalnet.hn,* which sells paperbacks and is a good place for information. Discovery Tours located here too.

Post Office & Phone

There is a post office and a Hondutel office for international phone calls.

Other Information

A good source of information on Roatán is **BICA** (Bay Islands Conservation Association), *Cooper Building, Coxen Hole, Tel. 445-1424.* Good information on reef and ecosystem protection projects.

Sandy Bay & Environs

This area is known for good scuba diving and snorkeling.

BAY ISLAND BEACH RESORT, *Tel/Fax 445-1425. 10 rooms. $125 double with daily diving, $90 non-diving. U.S. reservations Tel. 800/4ROATÁN or 708/537-2381, Fax 708/520-3908. Week-long diving package: $695, including three daily boat dives, meals, transfers, and one night dive. Non-diving package, $595.*

An intimate resort offering excellent diving at north shore sites. Rooms are either individual or two to a cottage, fairly soundproof, air-conditioned, with sea views. Good for getting away from the crowd.

ANTHONY'S KEY RESORT, *Sandy Bay, Tel. 445-1003, Fax 445-1329. 50 units, E-mail: akr@gate.net. U.S. office: 1385 Coral Way, Suite 401, Miami, FL 33145, Tel. 800/227-3483 or 305/858-3483, Fax 305/858-5020. 56 cabañas, air-conditioning. Weekly dive packages from $775 to $975 per person, including three one-tank boat dives daily and two night dives per week, dolphin encounter and dolphin dive, and all activities. Additional nights $132 to $139 single/$310 double with meals and diving. Non-diving rate, $140 single/$240 double. Children 3 to 11, $45. About 15% lower in summer.*
Everything about Anthony's Key can be described in superlatives. The landscaping alone makes it a paradise. The resort flows down a slope, and across to a small cay. Structures, plantings and terrain are all integrated, and there is a great respect for the environment. There are units in the lodge on a hill, bungalows set into the foliage on the slope, and slat houses along the edge of the cay, on stilts in the water, reached by a 60-second boat ride. Macaws and hummingbirds flap and gyre about. Rooms are clean and somewhat sparse, but easy on the senses. Meals are simply prepared, and hearty. The bar is quite expensive.

The emphasis is on diving, as elsewhere on the island, with many boats and good instructors and equipment. Numerous groups come here. The location near the west end of the island allows easy access to diving spots on both shores. (Northers might churn up the sea in front of Anthony's Key, while the south shore remains calm.) Rates are higher than elsewhere, but Anthony's Key has a lot more: horseback riding, weekly beach picnic, swimming with dolphins, a dinner party on the key, island-style entertainment, crab races, tennis, and use of canoes, kayaks, pedal boats and small sailboats are included in the daily rate (non-guests can use the sailboats for a fee).

There are also a wildlife sanctuary with trails on nearby Bailey's Key; the Museum of Roatán, housing an excellent, well-presented display of a variety of artifacts from the mainland and Roatán, admission $4; a decompression chambe; a doctor on-site; and secluded beaches. Fishing can be arranged, and snorkeling equipment is available for rent. Also available: resort diving courses, PADI instruction, underwater photo courses, and videos in which you can star. The souvenir shop has a good assortment of trinkets, and a photography shop offers processing, and rentals of cameras and underwater equipment. There's even the Casino Royal, if you're interested in gambling between dives.

OCEANSIDE INN, *Sandy Bay, Tel. 445-1552, Fax 454-1532. 8 rooms. $60 single/double. U.S. reservations, Tel. 407/855-5517, oceanside@globalnet.hn. Package price from $390 per person for seven days, including airport pickup, meals, picnic, and night out in French Harbour. Dives cost an additional $20 each, $22 with equipment, even less (!) for a package of ten dives.*
Located alongside Anthony's Key (and right next to their dolphin pen), Oceanside Inn has good-sized hardwood-panelled rooms, all upstairs with sea view, steady breeze, and ceiling fans. Food is said to be quite good,

emphasizing seafood prepared American-style—lobster, shrimp, pan-fried grouper, etc., served in a breezy dining room. The hotel also has two sun decks, a patio bar, and gift shop.

The owners of Oceanside are Hondurans who have returned after successful business careers in the States, so they know the worlds of both the islands and their guests.

THE INN OF LAST RESORT, *oceanfront location. Tel. 445-1838, Fax 445-1848, lastresort@globalnet.hn. US reservations Tel. 800/374-8181. 30 rooms. $100 double.*

Popular among divers. Bar and restaurant.

SUNNYSIDE BED & BREAKFAST, *on the beach, Tel 445-0006, E-mail: iomalzer@magnet.at. $50 double.*

Snorkeling and diving off private dock at Spooky Channel. Also beach front house for rent, sleeps 6, fully equipped kitchen, air conditioning, ceiling fans, private pier with 16 foot skiff and 40horsepower engine, weekly and monthly rates. Recommended.

Where to Eat
RICK'S AMERICAN CAFE, *Tel 445-0123.*

Spectacular setting and views, located high up on a hill top. Best steaks and burgers on the island. Saturday night prime rib special, happy hour 5-6pm, bar, satellite TV with all sports. Open from 5pm daily except Wednesdays, Sunday brunch during NFL season from 11am.

OCEANSIDE INN, *next door to Anthony's Key.*

Well known for its excellent seafood, you can eat on a deck looking at over the bay.

ANTHONY'S KEY has a deck restaurant open to the public.

Seeing the Sights
Gardens, Institutes, & Museums
Carambola Botanical Garden, across the road from Anthony's Key Resort, *Tel. 445-1117*, has plantings of native and exotic species, including spices, elephant ear, hibiscus, bird of paradise, six different varieties of bananas, breadfruit, starfruit and cacao. Wildlife includes the yellow headed parrot and green iguana and many, many others. There are nature trails and the locale is excellent for birding. The hilltop, reached via a 20-minute hike, offers a good sea view. This is the only private botanical garden in Honduras, and is Roatáns' most extensive orchid collection. Open daily from 7am-5pm. Highly recommended.

The **Institute for Marine Sciences** (IMS), in Sandy Bay, uses the facilities of Anthony's Key to care for, train and investigate a dozen or so bottle-nosed dolphins. Visitors are invited to swim with the dolphins in limited numbers ($65 guests, $75 non-guests; Dolphin Dive, $75 guests, $100 non-guests. A three day Dolphin Specialty Course runs $160.)

IMS is also a sanctuary and rehabilitation center for ailing marine mammals, sea turtles and birds. IMS offers classes on marine mammals and coral reef biology, and, of course, the reef surrounding Roatán makes for a superb field laboratory. Students, according to their resources, stay at Anthony's Key Resort or at the Institute's dormitory. Degree credits may be available in cooperation with various universities. For information, contact the Anthony's Key office in the States, or Anthony's Key directly (see above). Entrance fee is $4 if you are not a guest at Anthony's Key Resort.

The **Roatán Museum**, in the same building as the Institute for Marine Sciences, houses exhibits on the ethnology of the Bay Islands. Displays include Paya and Mayan artifacts, and a video presentation on the islands' past and prospects. Entrance fee is $4 if you are not a guest at Anthony's Key Resort.

West End

West End is a quiet town on the north coast of Roatán, opposite and west of Coxen's Hole, about ten kilometers away. There are beaches and palm trees, and for the visitor, things are cheap. Rooms may be rented by asking around of locals. The going rate is $10 per person per night, or less. You can always find a place, except at Easter week. The reef off West End is protected as part of the **West End Marine Sanctuary**.

West End is the place on the island to get an excellent meal, a good room, and enjoy the mellow island nightlife – Roatán style. There are a number of new restaurants and hotels, all moderately priced, and of good value, many owned by expats. The white sand beaches are just steps away from the unpaved main drag that winds its way through town. West End is laid back, tranquil, and definetely running on 'island time.'

A minibus ride from Coxen Hole is 70 cents, taxi fare is $1. Taxi from the airport is $10.

Where to Stay

LOST PARADISE INN, Tel. 445-1306, Fax 445-1388, E-mail: paradise@simon.intertel.hn. 34 rooms, $68/double, including three meals and airport transfer.

Beachfront cabins at the end of West End.

HALF MOON BAY, Tel. 445-1075, Tel/Fax 445-1241, E-mail: paradise@globalnet.hn. US Contact: 5364 Ehrlich Rd. #35, Tampa, FL 33625 Tel. 800/989-9970. $45 double with fan, $60 double with air conditioning.

There are 14 natural wood bungalows, bar, restaurant, beachfront, very popular, one of the best hotels in West End. Diving offered with Scuba

Romance, a 33-foot dive boat with fresh water shower, toilet and sun deck. Costs are $20 per dive, 10 dive package $150; trips to Cayos Cochinos and Barbaretta. German operated.

PURA VIDA, *Tel. 445-1141, E-mail: puravida@hondutel.hn, web: www.puravidaresort.com. 12 rooms, $30-$40 dbl with fan, $50-$60 dbl with air-conditioning, fan, private hot water bath, cable TV.*

Owned and operated by Giacomo and Adriana, an Italian couple who also run the excellent Italian restaurant of the same name in front of the hotel. Sparkling clean, nicely decorated, good value, just steps from the beach. Recommended.

POSADA ARCO IRIS, *Half Moon Bay, Tel/Fax 445-1264, E-mail: roberto@hondutel.hn, web: www.roatanet.com/scuba/posada.htm. 8 apartments with kitchen, 4 rooms, air-conditioning, weekly, monthly rates. $20-$30 without kitchen, $28-$35 studio with kitchen, one bedroom apt with kitchen $35-$40, two bedroom apt with kitchen $50-$60.*

Owned and operated by Andres and Valeria, an Argentine couple. Private, hot water bath, ac, fan, cable TV. Clean, comfortable, steps from the beach on Half Moon Bay. Ideal for long term stays. New addition, apartments and rooms. Restaurant & cafe with Argentine grilled specialties, Copan coffee, Recommended.

CHILLIES, *Half Moon Bay next door to Arco Iris, Tel. 445-5365. 7 rooms, $7.50 per person in shared room, $15 for private dbl room, 20% discount for monthly stay, communal kitchen facilities, shared bath.*

Good value, clean rooms. Coming in 1999: two studio apartments with kitchen, two bedrooms, private bath, $30 per night, $400 per month. Steps from Half Moon Bay. A backpacker favorite. Recommended.

COCONUT TREE #1, *Tel. 445-1648. 11 cabins, $50double.*

MERMAID BEACH CABINS, *Tel. 445-1335. 10 rooms, $50 double.* Decent place, porch on ocean.

PINOCCHIO, *located on a hill just off the main street, 4 rooms, restaurant, low season $35 double high season, otherwise $30 double.*

Lovely view of the bay from here. Recommended restaurant.

SUNSET INN, *Tel. 441-1925, E-mail: oceandivers@globalnet.hn, web: www.Roatánet.com/sunsetinn. 16 rooms. $20 double with fan and shared bath, $35 double with private bath, apartment $40.*

Large motel-like setting. Popular with the young diving crowd.

GEORPHI'S TROPICAL HIDEWAY, *Tel. 445-1794, Fax 445-1205, US: Tel. 508/8569432. 9 cabins. Single $50/2 persons $61/3 persons $74/4 persons $80. Low season prices are half off. Also Dorm style rooms for $10 per person, sleeps 6.*

Friendly, helpful management. Recommended. The best breakfasts in West End at Rudy's next door – same owners.

KEIFITTOS PLANTATION, *located on a hill overlooking West Bay. $30 double.*
Secluded location, access via launch from West End.

LUNA BEACH, *Tel 445-0009, E-mail: TLC@globalnet.hn, web: www.lunabeachresort.com. 8 rooms, $90 double.*
Excellent restaurant, fully furnished renatal units.

Where to Eat

FOSTER'S RESTAURANT, *located on pillars in the water, just across from Foster's Hotel.*
Open Friday nights only for a big come one come all party over the water.

SALT & PEPPER, *located at Coconut Tree Cabins, at the entrance to West End. Open for breakfast, lunch, and dinner.*
Chef Paul Clevland, a British chap, cooks up a different cuisine each evening. Cable TV (only satellite dish in town), best spot to catch all your favorite sports events.

RUDY'S, *located in front of Georphy's Tropical Hideway.*
Absolutely the best breakfasts in town. Banana pancakes, (ask Rudy for a copy of her famous Banana Pancakes recipe), french toast, omeletes, breakfast sandwiches. Lovely shaded, open air sitting area. Recommended.

HALF MOON BAY has a very nice restaurant, with a lovely view of the bay from their beach front deck.

PURA VIDA, *located on the main drag in West End, steps from the beach at Half Moon Bay.*
Italian owners Giacomo and Adriana cook up authentic Italian cuisine in this bright, airy, seaside bistro. Great pizza, $9 medium, $12 large, homemade pasta, shrimp, squid, fish. Great service and view of the beach. Recommended.

EAGLE RAY'S, *located on the water on top of Sueño del Mar dive shop.*
Great views, cool breezes. Fish burger and fries $4, whole fried Snapper $6.50, big screen TV. Sunset happy hour from 4-7pm.

BOULANGERIE, *on the main drag.*
Bakes up a yummy assortment of French goodies, baguette, croissant. Breakfasts and light lunch served, sandwiches $2. Recommended.

TONY'S, *on the main drag.*
According to the locals, this place has some awesome, authentic Italian food, cooked up by its Italian owner.

PINOCCHIO, *just off the main drag.*
Another locals favorite. Recommended.

POSADA ARCO IRIS, *Half Moon Bay.*
Just opened in 2002. Grilled Argentine specialties, Copan coffee. Recommended.

LIGHT HOUSE RESTAURANT AND LOAFERS, *on the water.*
Good place to sip beers and tropical coctails.

Sports & Recreation

There are a number of dive shops at West End: Tyll's Dive Shop, West End Divers, Ocean Divers, Scuba Romance, Bottom Time, Reef Gliders and Sueño del Mar.

There are a number of ways to view the reef without getting wet. Among the options are: **Underwater Paradise**, a new semi-submarine, $20 per person, $10 child; **Coral Reef Explorer**, half-sub half-boat, operates out of its dock on West Bay Beach, complimentary water taxi from West End, $20 per person, $12 child; and **Belvedere´s Glass Bottom Boat**, $8 per person.

Deep sea charter fishing trips can be arranged in West End. Horseback riding can be arranged in West End, just ask around. Options include riding along the beach or up into the forested mountains.

West Bay Beach

Some of the best beaches on the island are here. White sand, palm trees, crystal clear waters — a tropical fantasy come true. But be on guard for sunburn!

The snorkeling is excellent 100 meters from the beach, where the water is only five feet deep. There are coral and fish in all sorts and varieties, and when the weather is good, there are no currents at all.

There are some excellent hotels, bed & breakfasts, and beach homes for rent. Dining on West Bay Beach is limited, but luckily West Bay boasts one of Roatán's best seaside restaurants. Excellent diving courses can be arranged with Bananarama or at the newly opened Wet 'n Wild at the Las Rocas Resort.

Beaches & Supplies

The beach at West End is very nice, but the best beaches are three kilometers away at **West Bay Beach**, near the very tip of the island. Just ask for a boat near Foster's Restaurant. Just ask for a water taxi at Foster's Restaurant. You can walk along the beach in about an hour, or take a glass bottom boat trip over the reefs. The road from West End to West Bay is now paved. Taxis cost $6, you can bargain at night.

The best supermarket in town is **Woody's Groceries**, located on the road to Half Moon Bay.

Where to Stay & Eat

COCONUT TREE #2, *on the beach. Tel. 445-1648. 5 cabañas, 1 with kitchenette/$80 per night, studio cabañas/$70 per night, discount for week stay.* Cabañas have microwave, air conditioning, hot water, maid service.

FOSTER'S COVE, *on the beach. Contact Maya Tours International in US, Tel. 800/392-6292, E-mail: info@mayatour.com. 2 bedroom $665, 1 bedroom $525 per week.*

Rental beach house. Fully equipped (sheets, towels, gas range, refrigerator, kitchen utensils, purified water). Maid service, lovely beachfront location, and nearby dock. Close to restaurants and excellent close in snorkeling.

CABANA ROATÁNA, *Tel. 991-5659, E-mail: paradise@globalnet.hn. 6 beach front rooms. $60-$80 low season, $75-$95 high season. High Season in Roatán is from Dec 15 through Easter Sunday. There is a $5 per day discount for a stay of 3 nights, a $10 per day discount for a stay of 7 nights, and a $15 per day discount for a stay of 15 days.*

Proprietors Liz Mathias have a nice place with hot water, refrigerator, microwave, toaster and fan in each room. Snorkeling, restaurants, and dive shop nearby. Laundry service, scuba and fishing trips arranged. Air conditioning costs an $10 extra per night.

BANANARAMA, *located just off the beach. P.O. Box 134, Coxen Hole, Tel. 992-9679, Fax 445-1205, E-mail: bananarama@globalnet.hn. 3 double cabañas, 1 quad cabaña, hot water, fan. Double $45, triple $59, quad $69, rate includes full breakfast. Special rates during low season.*

Part bed & breakfast, part dive resort, part rustic beach lodge, Bananarama offers the best of all worlds. Simple, wood paneled private cabañas with private bath, yummy homemade breakfasts, and in-house dive shop make this lodge an excellent choice.

On-premises full service dive operation offering dive packages and PADI Dive Courses. The Open Water Dive Course runs 4-5 days, $220; Advanced Open Water Dive Course is 2 days, $160; Rescue Diver Course is 3 days, $200; Divemaster Course is $700. Equipment and certification included, instruction in English or German. Dive rates: Beach Dive $20, Boat Dive $25, Two tank boat dive $39, Night Dive $25. Equipment rental is $5. Five dive package is $110. Ten dive package is $200.

Dive packages: 3 days, $145; 7 day package, $275. Package includes 2 boat dives daily, 1 night dive. Nikonos camera rental and snorkel gear rental are available. Waterskiing, horsebackriding and fishing tours can be arranged. Prices are reasonable by West Bay standards and service is excellent and very personalized. Recommended.

LAS ROCAS RESORT, *located on West Bay Beach, Tel/Fax 445-1841, E-mail: info@lasrocasresort.com, web: www.lasrocasresort.com. 3 single story cabañas, 3 multi level cabañas. Single story cabaña for 2 guests, $80; multi-story cabaña, 3 guests $100, 4 guests $120, 5-6 guests $140. Air-conditioning, fan, private hot water bath, continental breakfast included in rate, airport pickup and drop-off included. Free launch service to West End.*

Located on a a rocky point at the entrance to West Bay, La Rocas is an attractive wood paneled resort. Salt water pool on beach, lush tropical gardens, great restaurant next door. Run by a trio of young Italian chaps. A great place to relax. Wet 'n Wild has a Dive Shop at the resort, newly opened in 2002. PADI, brand new Mares equipment, new boat, 3 dives daily, 1-2 night dives per week, and dive courses. Recommended.

ISLAND PEARL, *on the beach, P.O.Box 116, Coxen Hole, Fax 445-1241, islandpearl@globalnet.hn, www.Roatánet.com. 4 multilevel beachfront homes with 2 bedrooms each, full kitchen, balcony with view of sea. Bar, restaurant, commons area, dive shop, fishing. 2 guests $130, 3 guests $150, 4 guests $180. 20% discount for walk ins.*

Owners Pascal Accard and Lainie Cohen have created an exclusive, intimate dive resort. Wonderfully furnished and artfully decorated, beautiful details abound. Recommended. Try the Chez Pascal restaurant here.

WEST BAY LODGE, *on a hilltop just up from West Bay Beach, P.O. Box 189 Roatán, Tel. 991-0694, E-mail: westbaylodge@globalnet.hn, web: www.stic.net/Roatán/Roatánonline. 1 room in main house, 2 cabañas, $40/ double, $35/single, low season rates $35double, $30 single. Full Breakfast included. Dive packages, 7 days, 10 boat dives, 1 night dive $450; 6 days PADI Open Water Course, $390.*

West Bay Lodge is a small, intimate bed & breakfast run by Maren and Reinhard Gnielka from Germany. Lovely view of West Bay Beach below. Tranquil location. Maren is a licensed massage therapist with her studio on the premises. Airport transfers.

CARIBBEAN DREAM, *just up from the beach, near West Bay Lodge, Tel. 445-1059, E-mail: paradise@globalnet.hn, web: www.roatanet.com/ caribbean. 6 rooms, air-conditioning, fan, $40/double without kitchen, suites available with kitchen.*

Owned and operated by Augusto Alfano from Italy and his Honduran wife Candida Flores, this is a large Caribbean-style home that has been divided up into guest rooms. There are nice views of West Bay, and diving is available with Island Pearl. Rooftop shower, good homestyle atmosphere, and the personal attention of Don Augusto.

MAYAN PRINCESS BEACH RESORT, *on the beach, Tel 455-5917, E-mail: info@mayanprincess-roatan.com, web: www.mayanprincess-roatan.com. 16 rooms, $125-150 double, bar & restaurant. Dive packages available.*

Set on a pretty white coral sand beach with palm trees, the Mayan Princess offers good snorkeling and diving. A swimming pool with swim-up bar and hot tub is under construction and may be open by the time you read this.

BITE ON THE BEACH, *on the water at West Bay, next door to Las Rocas Resort and the Coral Reef Explorer dock.*

This could just well be the best seafood restaurant in the whole darned country. Excellent, tasty, well prepared seafood, courteous, friendly and attentive service. Wonderful seaside location on a deck built out over West Bay.

The menu varies daily. Specialties include the absolutely best fish burger I have ever had the privlege to munch on, huge slabs of blackened or grilled tuna steak that barely fit into the bun, served up with a side of salad and fries, all for $5. Fresh fillet of fish, baked, fried or grilled, beautifully prepared with all the fixins', runs $7. A hearty bowl of fresh fish soup (guaranteed to rid one of even the most awesome island hangover) is $2. Lobster tails, out of the shell, served up with a truly awesome tomato and garlic based sauce (rumored around West Bay to possess not so subtle aphrodisiacal properties) is $8. To top it all off, a truly four star example of Key Lime Pie, tart, sweet and oh so yummy, is $2.

Ted & Laura are the new proprietors of what has become a West Bay institution.

Other Places to Eat

If none of these places is to your liking, the Italian-owned **Henry Morgan IGV Beach Resort** has an all you can eat Italian buffet. You can also try the **Hemingway Bar & Restaurant** (a la carte) on the beach.

East of Coxen's Hole – Brick Bay

ROMEO'S RESORT, *Brick Bay, Tel. 4451518, Fax 4451645. 30 rooms. About $96 per person daily with meals and diving, $88 non-diving. U.S. reservations: Tel. 800/535-DIVE or 305/633-1221, Fax 305/633-1102. Weekly dive package from $670 to $840 per person, lower in summer, including three daily boat dives and two night dives per week.*

This is a quiet place off the road between French Harbour and Coxen's Hole, in a sheltered cove, run by the same Romeo who managed Romeo's Restaurant in French Harbour. Most rooms are in a long concrete building, the central section of which (with terrace restaurant, front desk and gathering areas) has a soaring roof that suggests the South Seas. The whole place is pleasant enough, with luxuriant vegetation all around and views everywhere to the mangrove-lined waters. And Brick Bay (English Harbour) is a good place to anchor: Romeo's is the closest hotel to Mary's Place, one of the most famed dive spots in the islands.

Standard rooms have two double beds, ceiling fans, balconies, and lagoon views. Deluxe rooms on the lower level are air conditioned. A hillside house, Casa Pepe, can be reserved for groups. Facilities include a pool with wooden deck, pavilion dining area, bar, sea kayaks, dockside gear storage, slide film processing, and several dive boats. Onshore amusements include volleyball, Ping Pong, and island trips. The current management, the Silvestri family, has worked hard to develop this hotel (which formerly was a yacht club) as a complete dive and vacation center, and they personally look after the needs of guests in the best innkeepers' tradition.

THE MERMAID MARINA AND TAVERN, *located near Romeo's, Tel. 455-5525.*

The Mermaid has a restaurant, bar with happy hour, deli with sub sandwiches (imported cold cults and cheeses), and also offers diving, sea kayaking, and moutain bikes for rent.

French Harbour

French Harbour is about ten kilometers up the south coast to the east of Coxen's Hole. Nobody here speaks French (I was disappointed to learn my first time out). The bay is quite big, and you will find a large processing and packing operation for shrimp and lobster traveling on to the States.

The town itself is a small concentration of houses built on pillars over the water, which serves as transport route and disposal system. I wouldn't go out of my way to visit the place, but you'll pass through getting to some of the resorts nearby. Bus service is frequent from Coxen's Hole.

Where to Stay

ROATAN DIVE & YACHT CLUB, *Tel. 455-5407, E-mail: yachtclub@hondusoft.com, web: www.roatanyachtclub.com. 20 rooms. $35 single/$60 double.*

Overlooking the harbor, the hotel has docks, motor boats and dinghies, and a bar, a short walk away. Maybe it's for yachties who want to sleep ashore. You have good views in any case, on a hilltop, traditional, tin-roofed island house, with verandas, and a six-acre buffer zone. And it's clean. Rooms come with hot showers and fans, each with one double and two twin beds, air conditioning, and a television. The location is on the main road, eight kilometers from the airport, a half-kilometer from town.

The hotel has a restaurant, bar, internet cafe, and dive shop. Totally renovated in 2001.

Near French Harbour

FANTASY ISLAND, *Tel. 455-5222, Fax 455-5268, E-mail: fantasyislandresort@bonnebeach.com, web: www.fantasyislandresort.com. U.S. reservations: 304 Plant Avenue, Tampa, FL 33606, Tel. 800/676-2826, Fax 813/251-0301. 75 rooms. $100 single/$130 double/$150 triple; $40 per child. Daily diving (3 dives), $50. Visa, Master Card, American Express. Package rates with three meals per day, $150 to $170 single/$228 to $250 double/$414 triple. Week-long dive packages $1300 single/$2100 double/ $2900 triple, including three boat dives daily and one night dive per week.*

This is a marina-diving-beach complex with some of the most comprehensive facilities. From a distance, it looks like condominiums in ski country, two stories of attached clapboard units with peaked roofs. Up close, you'll espy the palm-shaded verandas, and a dining area with soaring roof and cupola.

Rooms come with ceiling fans, air conditioning, carpeting, refrigerator, shower and tub, artificial plants, satellite t.v., and private balconies. There are three bars, and plenty of loud music to accompany your time at the crushed-shell beach (if that's what you're looking for).

The resort is located two kilometers east of French Harbour on a small (15-acre) cay, about 500 feet offshore. The last stretch of road is unpaved. As at some of the other Bay Islands resorts, they try hard at Fantasy island, though in a country without a strong resort tradition, some things still don't come together perfectly at meal time, or in room furnishings.

For diving, Fantasy Island offers the most modern facilities on the island, with a dive gazebo, camera rentals, film processing, a fleet of custom dive boats, and easy access to both sides of the island. There is good snorkeling, and canoes and windsurfers are provided. And Fantasy Island also has tennis courts and a marina. Less expensive packages are available during the slow season, from September 15 to December 15.

COCO VIEW RESORT, *French Cay, Tel. 455-5011, 455-1013, E-mail: info@roatan.com. 25 rooms (9 beach rooms, 4 luxury bungalows, 12 over-water cabanas). About $130 per person daily with diving and meals, $110 for non-divers ($110 diver, $90 non-diver after one week). U.S. address: Box 877, San Antonio, FL 33576, Tel. 800/282-8932, Fax 904/588-4158. Weekly dive packages from $725 per person with all meals, transfer from airport, two daily boat dives and unlimited beach and night diving; non-diver packages from $625.*

This is considered by knowledgeable folks to be *the* place for divers. Located on a peninsula on the south shore, it was a wild, remote place, when you could only reach it by boat from French Harbour. Now, it's just beside Fantasy Island, more accessible, but still quite nice. You don't sleep in an aquarium, but aside from that, everything is diving.

Units, all with overhead fans (no air conditioning) and hot showers, are in two guest houses, and in individual roundhouse bungalows (extra charge $50 per person on a weekly package) and cabanas built on stilts over the water. It's not luxurious, and the price is appropriate, a good balance between budget and comfort. The resort is ten minutes by boat from Old French Harbour (just east of French Harbour), and transportation from the airport is included in the rate.

There is spectacular wall diving 100 yards out, and there are reefs and channels nearby, accessible on two dive boats. The wreck of the *Prince Albert*, a 140-foot freighter, deliberately sunk in 1985, is directly in front of the resort, in 65 feet of water. Tanks, backpacks and weights are provided and stored at dockside, and other equipment can be rented. Processing for E-6 slide film is available.

Instruction capabilities include resort, certification and specialty courses. Landside diversions include kayaks, board games, Ping Pong and picnics on a private islet. Sailing and fishing can be arranged. Coco View comes highly recommended by guests for its excellent service and magnificent diving operation.

Also available are rental houses at **Playa Miguel**, the development adjacent to the hotel, at about $800 per week. These have two or three bedrooms, full kitchen and sundecks. For four persons, the rate is $2700 to $2800 with diving and meals, or $1785 to $2000 for non-divers; and live-aboard boats with air-conditioned quarters, at about $650 per person per week. Children are not encouraged to come except during a specific family week in July.

Sherman Arch, a native islander, runs a unique **Iguana Breeding Farm** on his property in French Key. His project seeks to save the islands' iguana population through captive breeding. Iguanas in Honduras are prized for their meat, which could lead to the destruction of the species. The iguanas are very tame and can be held (not for the faint at heart)! From Coxen Hole take the bus to French Harbour, get out at entrance to French Key. The farm is one mile down road. Admission is $1.

Where to Eat

CASA ROMEO'S RESTAURANT, *French Harbour. Tel. 455-5518, Fax 455-5645.*

One of the oldest and best restaurants on Roatán, specializing in crab. Or, you can stop just for drinks, over piers lapped by Caribbean waters.

GIO'S RESTAURANT, *located across from Dixon Plaza, French Harbour. Tel. 455-5214, Fax 455-5536.*

Famous for crab and seafood.

Nightlife & Entertainment

Bolongo's Disco, at the entrance to French Harbour, is currently the disco of note on the island of Roatán. If you stay anywhere nearby for a few days, you're likely to spend at least a few hours here one night for reggae and salsa. Saturday nights are the big nights.

Oak Ridge

Oak Ridge, located on the southern end of the island, is 22 km up the coast from Coxen's Hole, an hour's drive away. Beyond Oak Ridge is Roatán's oldest, most untouched part of the island. The best way to see Oak Ridge is via a dory ride through the mangrove channels.

Officially, the town is called José Santos Guardiola, after the national hero/dictator/president of Honduras at the time the Bay Islands were recovered by Honduras; but nobody in the islands calls it by anything but its real name. A tongue of land wraps around a bay here, and most of the houses sit on stilts in a semicircle above the water.

Meals and snacks can be purchased at watering holes in the village, as well as at the hotels in the vicinity of the town that specialize in diving. Or take a break from diving to explore the mangroves by boat and listen to and look for birds.

Where to Stay

REEF HOUSE RESORT, *Oak Ridge, Tel. 4352297. US Tel. 800/328-8897. 3 bungalows, 12 other rooms. $120 single/$180 double per day with diving and three meals, $90 single/$160 double without diving, including meals. U.S. address: P. O. Box 40331, San Antonio TX 78229, Tel. 800/328-8897, Fax 210/341-7942. American Express, Visa, Master Card. Week-long diving package $625 to $750 per person, including two boat dives daily, meals, one night dive per week, unlimited shore diving. Fishing packages run $200 per day single, $225 per day double with meals and boat.*

This is a nice resort, with serious dive packages. A wide, sea-view passageway connects the large rooms, each with louvers, sea breeze and overhead fans for cooling. The long, shallow sea area in front of the hotel is perfect for swimming, and there are beaches nearby. Food is usually served buffet-style, with an emphasis on fish, and there are an open-air bar and terrace, and an indoor dining and reading area.

Reef House has one main diving boat, the 37-foot diesel-powered *Henry Morgan*, and several smaller boats for fishing and cruising. There's a wall diving site right in front of the hotel. Of the many, many dive sites nearby, some of the most notable are Calvin's Crack, a cleft in the reef; Crab Wall, encrusted with sponges; and Church Wall. A diving trip to Barbareta Island, with beach picnic, is often included with weekly packages. Resort and certification courses are available.

Snorkeling equipment is provided for guests at no additional charge, and you can snorkel right from the hotel—the reef is just outside your door. Windsurfers, sailboats, kayaks, and a water bicycle are available to guests. Fishing packages provide a 14-foot skiff for every three to four persons. Bring your own tackle.

The detailed price list for extras for diving equipment rentals, and for persons not on dive packages, includes: $25 per single tank dive, $35 per two-tank dive, $30 per night dive, $75 for a resort scuba course, $350 for full certification. Daily tank rental $7; regulator $10; buoyancy compensator, $8; masks, fins and snorkel, $7; dive light, $5.

HOLE IN THE WALL, *in Jonesville near Ok Ridge.*
Run by expats Bob & Rhonda, boasts a bar on the water. Access via boat only (water taxi from Oak Ridge).

If you want to stay in a **private home** for rent, contact Richard and Betsy Watson at P.O. Box 1040, Port Aransas, TX 78373, U.S, *Tel. 512/749-4152. E-mail: 102403.3500@compuserve.com, web: http://cyberrentals.com/sa/chuhon.html.*

Near Oak Ridge & Punta Gorda

PAYA BAY BEACH RESORT, *located on the northeast corner of the island. Tel/Fax 435-2139, web: www.payabay.com, US Toll free Tel. 888/662-2466, or 888/430-5874.*
The resort is situated in a spectacular setting on the highest rock cliffs on the island. Cabins are very nice, and there's an excellent restaurant with a large deck featuring a 360 degree view overlooking Paya Bay and the beach below. To reach the resort, take the road going east from the Oak Ridge-Punta Gorda detour; the road is in good shape. There are also some lovely solitary beaches in nearby Camp Bay.

Punta Gorda

On the north shore of Roatán, opposite Oak Ridge, **Punta Gorda** is a Black Carib village. This is where the paved road ends. From here the road continues west to Camp Bay and Port Royal. The village is very beautiful, with undeveloped beaches and no services, so pack in all necessary food, water, and supplies.

Unlike Creole Bay Islanders, Caribs build their houses right on the ground, and use traditional, locally available palm thatch for floors and roofs. Superficially, Black Caribs look like other islanders. But you see just from their bearing and dress that they are different, more relaxed. People here are very friendly.

An **annual carnival** is held each year, April 8-12, which celebrates the arrival of the Garifuna to Roatán in 1796. Punta Gorda is the only majority Garifuna community on the island, and is also the oldest established community on the island. It was home to the first Garifuna settlement in Central America.

Where to Stay

HENRY'S COVE RESORT, *Tel. 435-2187. 34 rooms. $70/double*
Rooms come with air conditioning and hot water. There's a pool, bar, and restaurant.

Old Port Royal

Old Port Royal is not a town at all in modern times, but it was the site of pirate encampments in the seventeenth century, and English fortifications in the eighteenth century. The last great battle here was fought offshore at Fort George in 1782. The English were ousted after a two-day battle, though not for the last time.

The remains of four different forts still exist, two on Roatán, and two on Fort Cay offshore, and there are some vacation houses in the area, which is otherwise uninhabited. Wood from wrecks found offshore has been dated to before the arrival of Columbus, suggesting that Europeans visited this area earlier than is generally acknowledged.

Boats on diving and fishing excursions will sometimes stop to let visitors walk around the old fortifications; or you can hire a boat for a trip out from Oak Ridge. A trail reaches Port Royal from the end of the island road east of Punta Gorda — it's a hike through the hills to reach the site.

Port Royal Park and Wildlife Reserve protects Roatán's water supply, and not incidentally, is a haven for birds and small mammals, such as the opossum and agouti. The park is the largest highland reserve on Roatán. For information, contact BICA, Bay Islands Conservation Association, in Coxen's Hole, *Tel. 445-1424.*

There are no services in Port Royal. Beaches on this part of the island are devoid of tourists, in large part because you have to haul in all supplies (food, water, etc.).

Barbareta

Barbareta, three km from Helene (the island that adjoins Roatán), is a five-by-two-km island covered with forests and fringed with coconut palms. Spring water is abundant, and a hotel has sometimes operated here. The island is a private nature reserve. Hiking trails, beaches, diving, sport fishing, snorkeling and caving are all available.

Barbareta Marine National Park, covering Barbareta, Morat, and the eastern part of Roatán, protects **Diamond Rock forest**, the last remnant of tropical rain forest on the island, as well as coral reef and the largest mangrove area. Day trips to Barbareta are available from Guanaja resorts.

Guanaja

Columbus called **Guanaja** the Island of Pines (he landed at El Soldado beach on the north shore when he discovered it during his fourth voyage in 1502). The island measures about 18 by 6 km, and much of it is green and hilly and is covered mostly by Caribbean Pine. The highest point on the Bay Islands at 1,400 feet is here. There are more Spanish-speaking people on Guanaja than elsewhere in the Bay Islands.

If you like Roatán, you'll love Guanaja. It's like an earlier version of Roatán — no real roads, only a few resorts, but of the best type. And the people are genuinely friendly and glad to have you around. The north side of the island is very hilly and forested, the south side has many small cays and also the main settlement of Bonacca. The north side has lots of wonderful white sand beaches and crystalline blue water.

The dive spots are excellent, with clear water and spectacular formations — walls, caves, channels, ridges, tunnels — certainly as good as Roatán's, or, according to local enthusiasts, better. The main diving is off the reef and cays that border the southern shore, and the walls that drop in the depths of the Bartlett Trough.

The tourists that I've met that have vacationed here all seem to love Guanaja because of its natural setting, desolate beaches, reefs that aren't full of dive boats and great drinking water. It's an island that they've imagined about but didn't know existed. It's refreshingly undeveloped: no roads, no cars and all transport is via the sea. All resorts are small, funky and full of island charm. Guanaja is one of the last remaining unspoiled islands in the western Caribbean, and is a safe haven with virtually no crime to speak of and plenty of local color.

Guanaja has a wonderful climate, cool breezes, white sand beaches and crystal blue waters. Removed from the confines of civilization, visitors to Guanaja can roam the miles of unspoiled beaches and lush volcanic mountains covered with jungle fauna and birds. Scuba and snorkel on virgin reefs, circumnavigate the island, or paddle out for a leisurely day in a state-of-the-art sea kayak, sail a Hobie Cat, take a swim in the tropical waters or just relax in a beach hammock and enjoy a tropical drink.

You can get a free Guanaja Tourism Kit available from the Guanaja Tourism and Hotel Association, *Tel/Fax 453-4443*.

You can fax the Hondutel office in Bonacca *(Fax 453-4146)*, useful for contacting just about anyone on the island.

Arrivals & Departures

Guanaja has a small, primitive airstrip. There is an entry fee of $10 at the 'airport' to fund environmental protection programs on the island.

Isleña Airlines, La Ceiba *Tel. 441-2521*, Guanaja *Tel. 443-0179*, has the following flights: La Ceiba-Guanaja at 11am and 4pm, daily, $56 round-trip. The airstrip is right next to the canal that cuts across Guanaja about a third of the way across the island, from its southwest tip. If you have a reservation, you'll be fetched and taken to your hotel.

Sosa Airlines, *La Ceiba Tel. 441-2512*, has a La Ceiba-Guanaja flight at 10am daily, $56 round-trip.

Rollins Air, *La Ceiba Tel. 443-4181*, has flights that leave La Ceiba at 10:30am and 3:30pm.

There is regular ferry service from La Ceiba- Guanaja, aboard the **M/V Tropical** and **M/V Galaxy**, *Tel. 445-1795, 455-5056*, departs La Ceiba on Sunday and Wednesday at 8am, $19 one way.

If you are arriving with a reservation at one of the hotels or resorts, they will have a water taxi waiting for you at the small dock next to the air strip. If arriving without a reservation, a water taxi can be hired at the dock. Miss Vivalee comes highly recommended. There are no cars on the island.

Orientation

The town of Guanaja is the official name of the main settlement on the island, though locals call it **Bonacca** or **El Cayo**. Bonacca is also known as the Venice of Honduras, and the similarity is genuine not only in the presence of canals, but also in their aroma. The architecture of Bonacca is not quite as grand as that of its Italian cousin. The majority of Guanaja's 10,000 inhabitants live in Bonacca and it's the only real town on the island.

Bonacca sits on Hog Cay and Sheen Cay, half a kilometer offshore, where Cayman Islanders settled and constructed stilt houses over the water. With time, new houses were added in outlying sections, and connected by walkways on stilts. Eventually, fill was dumped around the houses, dry land was built up, trees were planted, and some of the canals were closed off. Today, Bonacca is a labyrinth of zigzagging pathways and walkways, its houses built close one upon another.

Where to Stay

Bonacca & Environs

HOTEL ALEXANDER, *on Hog Cay. Tel. 453-4326. $40 double.*

There are 15 seafront rooms with private baths, and, unexpectedly, 24-hour satellite television. At about $40 double facing the sea, less inside, it's probably the closest to a vacation hotel that you'll find right in Bonacca. There's a slightly higher charge for air conditioning.

HOTEL HILLTON, *next to the airstrip. Tel 453-4299. $50 double.*

This is not a part of the Hilton Hotel chain, but it is run by Captain Al, a good source of information on everything that's happening on the island. There's a restaurant on-site. Convenient if catching an early 6 am flight to La Ceiba.

HOTEL ROSARIO, *Tel. 453-4240.*

This is the best of the inexpensive hotels. Rooms cost about $22 double, more if you require a television and air conditioning. None of these, given the congested surroundings, can really be called a resort destination. A Caribbean houseboat, **Red Sky Over Paradise**, can be hired. It sleeps four and rents for $99 per night. Contact: Jo Wahl, Fruit Harbor Bay, *Tel. 453-4368.*

Elsewhere Around the Island
POSADA DEL SOL (Inn of the Sun), *Tel. 4534186. U.S. Reservations: 1201 US Highway One, Suite 210, North Palm Beach, FL 33408, Tel. 800/642-DIVE, Fax 561/624-3225, E-mail: posadadel@aol.com, web: www.posadadelsol.com. 23 rooms, $170/double, $210/single for divers, $120/double, $150/single for non-divers (based on double occupancy), children under 12 half diver rate. American Express, MasterCard, Visa.*

Weekly dive package (six nights, seven days), $900/double, $1,125/single, including three daily boat dives, unlimited shore diving, and two night dives per week; all-inclusive non-diver rates, $700/double, $1,025/single. Off-season specials from $1400, including airfare. Land Air Special: $1,199, 7 nights/8 days, includes airfare, transfers, room, meals, diving and scheduled daily activities.

Posada del Sol is a classy, tan-colored, palm-shaded villa on a good-sized estate at the base of the hills on Guanaja's south side. Rooms have beamed ceilings, sea views, and tiled floors — in solid Spanish genre, rather than the usual island stilt style. There are also four detached hillside units, each with two rooms. The owners are former commercial divers.

The site is very nice and relaxing. There are lots of good diving places in the area and on the eastern side of the island, and the resort owns its own beach on the north side where picnics are staged. Aside from the usual compressors and the three diving boats with water-level platforms and instruction facilities, Posada del Sol has a hillside pool with hardwood deck and adjacent bar, tennis court, gift shop, exercise equipment, processing for E-6 film, underwater video camera rental. Deep sea fishing can be arranged (bonefish, permit and snook can be caught in the flats right in front of the hotel) and guest boats can be accommodated.

Relaxed dining in dining room or pool deck with great food. 'Good Morning Coffee' or juice served to your room or terrace (truly wonderful!) each morning. Scheduled weekly activities include archaeological hike, Beach Party and BBQ, Bonacca Town tour, Tuesday evening Night Dive, Michael´s Rock Day trip, Barbaretta Island Dive Trip, Sunset Rum Punch Cruise (my favorite – I'm sure it has something to do with Posada's famous rum punch !), and a mountain hike.

Recreational activities include massage, light tackle fishing (bone and permit) and sea kayaking. You can also arrange a private picnic catered by the resort, complete with hammocks, champagne, beach blanket and gourmet food.

Posada del Sol is in a class with Anthony's Key and Fantasy Island as one of the Bay Islands' top resorts – well designed, attentively staffed, with very good food, and recommended.

EAST END LODGE, *Tel. 453-4443. 4 rooms and beach house.* Located near the northeastern tip of Guanaja, twenty minutes by boat from the airport, East End is more modest than the other resorts on the island. The lodge accommodates guests in 2 cottages built on stilts, on grassy plots, just a few feet from the coconut-palm-shaded beach. All face the water, and have private bath and porch. Amusements are limited to a bar, taped music and radio, and a VCR. Diving, sailing and fishing are arranged, and fishing guides are available.

East End is run by Julius and Sandy Rensch, who head up the Guanaja Tourism Association. They are very knowledgeable about Guanaja.

CASA SOBRE EL MAR, *Tel. 453-4269. U.S. Tel. 800/869-7295 or 615/443-1254. $170 double.*

On Pond Cay, off the main island, a private house with three guest rooms, built on concrete piles directly over the water and the coral reef (ideal for snorkeling right from the door). Each room has private bath. Spring water is piped from the mainland. Casa Sobre el Mar has its own compressor, and supplies tanks, boat, and guide for diving. There's a wreck right off the dock, 80-feet down, which is recommended for night diving. The package rate, with meals and dives, is $600 per person per week. A small extra charge is made for fishing, to cover fuel.

NAUTILUS RESORT, *Tel. 453-4389. US Tel. 800/535-7063, nautilus@caribe.hn. 6 rooms. $80 single/$130 double with meals, $105 single/$180 double/$240 triple with diving. One-week diving package with two daily boat dives, one night dive, unlimited shore dives, meals and airport transfers from $600 per person; non-diving from $450.*

On Guanaja's south shore, within view of Bonacca Town, Nautilus resort is a former private retreat totally renovated in 1992. The concrete guest house, with generous balconies and overhangs, is set well back from the beach, with just three guest rooms on each level, furnished and decorated with Mexican and Central American crafts. Two rooms are air conditioned. Extras include a television and video, and the balcony has commanding sea views.

Set on 60 hillside acres and reached by boat, the hotel has a thousand feet of beachfront, and a fast dive boat to reach the best spots quickly, along with a compressor, ample tanks, and rental equipment. Courses from certification to rescue diving are available. There are also trails through the forest nearby, and horseback riding, fishing and sailing can be arranged. The wind is steady, and is said to help control the sand flies on the beach.

BAHIA RESORT, *Tel/Fax 453-4212. U.S. reservations: 7903 Gardner Dr., Naples, FL 33942, Tel. 800/504-0035, Fax 305/567-1585, www.mayanet.hn/ bahia, bahia@mayanet.hn. $160 double.*
Nice bungalows welcome you to this relaxing place. The restaurant serves Italian cuisine, and there's a bar as well. Other services: paddle boats, pool, diving, certification classes, snorkeling, and hiking.
EL FIN DEL MUNDO RESORT, *US contact: 1205 Newton St. #2, Key West, FL 33040. Tel. 305/292-1993, Fax 305/292-2127, web. 5 duplex cabañas.*
Rooms are 2 bedroom, 2 bath cabañas which sleep 6, fully equiped. The resort has a restaurant, bar, PDIC Dive Center, watersports rental, marine taxi and boat dockage. There are lovely views of the bay from their deck. Great place, highly recommended.
MANATTEE, *Tel. 453-4182, 5 doubles, single/$35, double/$58, not including diving or meals; $20 for 3 meals daily, bar.*
Simple, rustic wooden structure, German owned and operated.
TERRY´S LIGHTHOUSE INN, *on Pond Cay near Bonacca Key, Tel. 453-4119. 3 rooms, $120/double.*
Fishing and diving can be arranged; rooms are air-conditioned.
ISLAND HOUSE, *Tel. 453-4299, Fax 453-4146, duplex cabañas, $160/ double.*
WEST PEAK INN, *US Tel. 408/377-2714, Fax 408/377-2716, wpi@vena.com, www.vena.com/wpi. 6 cabins, bar, restaurant, private bath, $35 per person per day, includes meals, sea kayaking, $875 per week, $95 per person per day, camping available, $28 per person per day, includes 3 meals and even supplies the tent.*
Located on the western end of the island, in a very isolated and beautiful spot, with a view of Barbareta and Roatán in the distance. Three miles of white sand beach, good snorkeling right off the beach. Very rustic and simple resort.
JODIS´SEASCAPE, *jodis@together.net, www.jodis.com.*
JoAnna and Richard Sheridan packed up their lives in the States and are building a B&B, with 2 cabins and a main house. Should be ready by 2000.
HENDRICKS KEY, *located on the southeast side of the island on a small cay, Tel. 453-4368. 3 bedroom guest house, private bath, refrigerator, 3 meals per day, $79 per person per day, 1 day deep sea fishing excursions $120 per person, $390 per boat, bonefishing right off Key.*
Run by Hans Glanegger, this is the place to stay for those interested in bonefishing (see below).

Where to Eat
I'd recommend the following places: **The Pirates Den** on Bonacca, **End Of The World** on Michael's Rock Beach, **Posada del Sol**, and **West Peak Inn** on West End.

Seeing the Sights

Guanaja Marine National Park covers 90 percent of the island and surrounding reefs. Sea Cave, along the south of the island, is a rock that rises 80 feet from the Caribbean, and is said to have been a headquarters for William Walker when that American adventurer was trying to take over Honduras more than a hundred years ago. You'll find good hiking, lovely views, and pretty waterfalls.

Nightlife & Entertainment

The best places to party on the island are **End Of The World** on Michael's Rock Beach, **West Peak Inn** on West End, **The Tucan** on Bonacca, **Dina's Reef House Lounge** on Pelican Ree,f and **Casetta 2000** on Michael's Rock Beach. The best discos on the island are **The Tucan** on Bonacca, **Pirates Landing** at Savannah Bight, and **UI's Disco On The Water** at Pelican Reef.

There are two scheduled BBQ's each week, weather permitting: **West Peak Inn** on Sunday's all summer, and **End Of The World** every Sunday all summer (after October every Saturday).

Sports & Recreation

Diving & Snorkeling

Guanaja was formed by volcanic activity that produced a barrier reef similar to small Pacific islands. There are 35 moored diving sites around the island. Diving and snorkeling from the beach are very popular and accessible. Weather conditions permit diving 95% of the time throughout the year. During the rainy season, which begins in late October and continues through January, the visibility is rated good with a range of approximately 80 feet. The remainder of the year the visibility ranges from 80-120 feet, with water temperatures averaging 84-88°F. Guanaja harbors a large variety of virgin dive sites beginning with shallow lagoon reefs, walls, wrecks, pinnacles and a volcanic vent system with caves.

The *Jado Trader* is a wreck deliberately sunk off southern Guanaja in 1987, to form an artificial reef. The 260-foot ship remains intact in 90 feet of water, making for the premier wreck dive in the Bay Islands. This is one of the Bay Island's most famous dive sites, with an abundance of fish and coral.

Snorkeling trips to offshore cays and points around the island are organized on an ad-hoc basis from most of the hotels, usually at $10 per person or so.

Fishing

Fishing can be arranged with various skippers if your hotel doesn't have the capability. This is a good place for deep sea fishing for marlin and wahoo. Day trips run $120 per person, or hire the entire boat for about $400 per day.

Guanaja has some of the best bonefishing in the Caribbean. Hendricks Key has some of the best bonefishing on the island. Bonefish average 2 pounds, but can run up to 11 pounds. They are caught with fly as well as hook and bait. They make bad eating and put up a big fight. Best bonefishing is from October -May. For more info on bonefishing contact, Hans Glanegger on Hendricks Key. Guanaja's waters are plentiful with Bonefish and Permit. Anglers are successful with both cast or fly rigs and can either fish from a boat or wade in the flats.

Deep Sea fishing is also available. Full day charters aboard completely rigged vessels troll for Sailfish, Marlin, Wahoo, Cero, Barracuda and Mahi Mahi. Charters are all-inclusive: boat, captain, mate, poles, bait, tackle and lunch are provided. Cook will prepare the catch for dinner. Surf fishing and fishing from the dock is provided free of charge. Commonly caught fish are Snapper, Pompano, Jacks and Grouper.

Sea Kayaking
The **End of the World** is the premier sea kayaking outfitter in the Bay Islands providing the best state-of-the-art equipment. New 17-foot Eclipse single person sea kayaks and Warner Furer extra light fiberglass paddles, spay skirts and life jackets are included.

Practical Information
Bonacca has two banks, **Banco Atlantida** and **Bancahsa**, several general stores, a pharmacy, and a cable television system.

Hog Cays (Cayos Cachinos)
The **Hog Cays** are off the coast of Honduras, 20 kilometers to the northeast of La Ceiba, and 30 kilometers south of Roatán. Consisting of two main islands and thirteen smaller cays, they have coral reefs, coconut palms, small mountains, and hardly any inhabitants but for a few Garífuna (Black Carib) fishermen. The entire mini-archipelago is a marine reserve, **Santuario Marino Cayos Cochinos**. For more inforamtion, contact the Cayos Cochinos Biological Reserve, *Isla Cochino Pequeño, Cayos Cochinos, Tel. 4434075*.

Big Hog (Cochino Grande) and **Little Hog** (Cayo Pequeño) are the two major islands, the former U-shaped, providing a sheltered anchorage, and covered with hardwoods, palm, and cactus.

The Smithsonian Institution of Washington, DC, has undertaken a 50 year scientific study of the Cayos Cochinos reef ecosystem, with an eye towards developing a sustainable management plan that will permit tourism development and protecting the fragile marine ecosystem. No commercial fishing is permitted nor anchoring off the reef. An environmental research station is located on Cochino Pequeño.

In addition to diving and snorkeling, there is excellent birding and hiking on these cays.

Arrivals & Departures

Rene Arzu takes visitors out to the Cayos on his 20 foot dugout canoe with diesel motor. It's a 1 1/2 hour trip; wrap all gear in plastic bags to keep out ocean spray, wear swimsuits, and expect to get wet. A one day trip costs about $30 per boat. Recommended for the high spirited only. Boat leaves very early am from Armenia.

Where to Stay

It is possible to obtain rustic accomodations with the Garifuna fishermen on Chachauate Key. Otherwise, try:

PLANTATION BEACH RESORT, *Mailing Address: Apdo. Postal 114, La Ceiba. Tel. 442-0974 – this is the only telephone on the island. U.S. address: 8582 Katy Freeway, Suite 118, Houston, TX 77024, Tel. 800/628-3723, Fax 713/973-8585, pbr@hondurashn.com. 10 rooms. Weekly dive package $750 to $900 per person, including three daily boat dives and night dives; non-diver $700.*

To really get away from it all, book a week at Plantation Beach on privately owned Cochino Grande, the largest island in the group — all of a mile across, and once a pineapple plantation. Guests stay in mahogany-and-stone cottages, with hammocks and decks, four rooms with sleeping lofts to each. There are also two small separate houses. It's an all inclusive resort. There is a 5 pm Saturday resort boat from La Ceiba. The boat returns 1 week later .

In addition to diving at some of the less-visited (and even unexplored) sites in the islands, there are hiking trails, a beach, snorkeling, windsurfing, sea kayaks, and sailboats available for charter.

The resort handles a maximum of 20 divers, with three boat dives daily and unlimited shore and night diving. An annual music festival is held at the resort at the end of July.

western honduras

Chapter 15

We've gone from Tegucigalpa to the north, along the coast, and out to the Bay Islands. Now we'll head back south along the western edge of the country.

Western Honduras is mountainous, curving along the borders of Guatemala and El Salvador. It is fairly densely populated for Honduras (though it doesn't seem so), with the highest concentration of Indian inhabitants, some living in villages virtually isolated from modern life. There are few roads, most of them are unpaved, rutted, and little traveled.

The Road to Copán

Copán, site of the most important pre-Columbian ruins in Honduras, is just 225 kilometers by air from Tegucigalpa. But there are no scheduled flights, and the roads that meander out this way in a roughly direct route from Tegucigalpa are so poor, that most travelers go all the way to San Pedro Sula from the capital, then cut back to the south, a trip of close to 500 kilometers. An option is to take the **Maya Mountain Route**: San Pedro Sula (or Tegucigalpa)-Lake Yojoa-Santa Barbara-Copán Ruinas. It's a pleasant paved mountain highway through spectacular scenery.

The road to Copán from San Pedro Sula follows the **Chamelecón River**, twisting and turning, and gradually gaining altitude. The banana fields of the lowest of the lowlands fade out, gradually replaced by pasture, corn fields, and tobacco. All of the route between San Pedro Sula and La Entrada has been resurfaced. The driving time is approximately an hour and a half.

La Entrada, 135 kilometers from San Pedro Sula, is a hot, dusty, and bustling commercial junction, a transit point for visitors heading to the Copán Ruins and west to Santa Rosa de Copán. Most traffic continues to Santa Rosa de Copán (when getting directions, always specify Copán Ruinas – not Santa Rosa de Copán). If you stay the night, the best hotel town is at the turnoff to Copán Ruinas, **Hotel San Carlos**, *Tel. 661-2228*, has air conditioning, TV, hot water, and the best restaurant and bar in town.

Past La Entrada, you'll notice tall, single-story structures. These are used for curing tobacco grown locally. They're painted black to absorb the maximum amount of solar heat.

El Puente Archaeological Park

The **El Puente Archaeological Park** in **La Jigua**, a few kilometers out of La Entrada, is Honduras' second most important Mayan archaeological site after the ruins of Copán. To reach the site, take the signed turnoff about 10 minutes outside of La Entrada on the road to Copán Ruinas. From the turnoff, it's 5 km down a newly paved road to the site.

El Puente was first visited and reported on by Danish explorer Jens Yde in 1935, who wrote a detailed description of the site and elaborated a schematic map of its principal structures. In 1984, Japanese archaeologists began exploratory investigations and mapping. The 4 acre site is made up of 210 structures, of which only the main group has been restored. **Structure 31**, located to the extreme east of the main group, shows the remains of two living quarters in its upper part and a stairway on the west side. **Structure 1** had six construction phases, large amounts of archaeological material, ceramics, and a grave. The structure is the tallest at the site at 11 meters. The east and west facades have an imposing staircase. This structure is the only one with a vaulted ceiling which indicates it served as a funerary temple.

Structure 10 is located on the southern part of Plaza A. A burial tomb was discovered under one of the older construction phases. The steps on the north side of the structure have been restored. In addition, a tunnel has been dug to allow the visitor to view ancient walls that were buried and built upon by the Maya. **Structure 204** is located to the extreme southwest of Structure 10. Two tombs were found inside.

Structure 3, located on the northern end of Plaza A, had nine construction phases. The south staircase has an interesting archaeological element, an *alfarda*, a decorative inclined plane. The north facade has elaborate masonry, excellent stone carving, and the remains of a stucco covering. There is a tunnel constructed by archaeologists that gives visitors a view of ancient stonework. **Structures 4 and 5** are considered to have been housing for the elite. Structure 5 is well preserved; there's a stuccoed bench with molding and two small side rooms have been restored. Under the structure you can see a drain built by the Maya to channel water out of Plaza A. The site boasts a lovely, colonial-inspired visitors center housing an **Archaeology Museum**. A small peninsula formed by the Chinamito River on the far western side of the site is a lovely spot to relax and have a picnic lunch.

The site and museum are open daily from 8:30am-4:00pm, including holidays.

La Jigua also contains a restored colonial church. From Florida, farther along the road, a branch track leads for 10 kilometers to **Cerro Azul National Park**, covering 150 square kilometers along the Guatemalan border (only nine square kilometers are an absolute reserve — the rest is farmed with some restrictions). The protected area includes caves, cloud forest and recovering forest. The lake atop Cerro Azul mountain, known as **Laguna de los Pinares**, is frequented by migrating birds. Its outlet is a waterfall.

Copán Ruinas

This town, also known at times in its history as San José de Copán, is quaint and small, with a population of bout 7,000. It's in a lovely valley surrounded by gentle mountains, not too cold, and not too warm, at an altitude of about 600 meters. The streets are cobblestoned, many buildings have tile roofs, and the plaza has a colonial air — all in all, a pleasant place just for resting and walking around. The ruins that give the town its name are a kilometer away.

Copán has an average yearly temperature of an almost perfect 78°F.

Arrivals & Departures
By Bus
From San Pedro Sula, the **Casasola** bus has daily direct service in a first class bus with cushioned reclining seats. Bus leaves San Pedro Sula at 2pm, from the corner of 6 avenue and 6 street. Fare is $4. Travel time is 3 hours. Bus leaves Copán Ruinas at 7am in front of Hotel Paty for the return trip to San Pedro Sula.

Hedman Alas has direct first-class buses from La Ceiba, Tegucigalpa and San Pedro Sula to Copán Ruinas daily. Buses depart San Pedro Sula bus terminal (Barrio Guamilito 7 y 8 ave 3 calle, *Tel. 553-1361*) for Copán Ruinas at 7am, 9:50am, 2:30pm. San Pedro Sula-Copán Ruinas is $6, takes 3 hours, and you're in a comfortable first-class bus, with a movie, bathroom, and good service. Recommended. Copan Ruinas terminal is at the the San Lucas Visitors Center, 2 blocks north of the Central Park, *Tel. 651-4106*. Buses leave Copán Ruinas for San Pedro Sula at 5:30am, 10:30am, 2:30pm. Connections in San Pedro Sula to La Ceiba and Tegucigalpa.

The **Gama** bus offers daily direct service, leaving 6 avenue and 6 street in San Pedro Sula, at 3pm. The bus leaves Copán Ruinas at 6 am daily, from in front of Hotel Paty. Travel time is 3 hours, fare $4. There's also a bus leaving Copán at 8am for San Pedro Sula, returning 1:30pm from San Pedro Sula.

Transportes Toritos and Copanecos has buses departing hourly from San Pedro Sula - Santa Rosa de Copán. To reach the ruins of Copán, take this bus as far as La Entrada (two hours), then catch the bus for Copán Ruinas on the main road in front of the bus terminal, departing about every 40 minutes until 4:30p.m. It's still a ride of another two to three hours or so from this point. To shave some time off your trip, catch the San Pedro Sula-Santa Rosa de Copán direct bus. There are two, 8:30a.m. and 2:00p.m.; the bus makes one stop at La Entrada, where you then hop off and change for the bus to Copán Ruinas.

The stretch of road from Copán Ruinas to the Guatemalan border at El Florido has been partially paved; construction should eventualy be completed all the way to the border. On the Guatemalan side, the road from El Florido to Chiquimula is paved and excellent.

Travel Tips

Information for bus travel from San Pedro Sula is given above. I recommend taking the bus only if you are going to stay for a few days (which is highly recommended). It is impossible to try to arrive, visit the ruins and museums, and leave in one day by public transport. Even a drive on the winding roads will be quite tiring. It's a six-hour round-trip drive from San Pedro Sula - Copán Ruinas.

Most Honduran tours depart from San Pedro Sula, rather than from Tegucigalpa, at prices ranging upward from $130 for an overnight stay.

From the Bay Islands, one-day trips operate to Copán for about $125 per person, overnight trips for about $165 per person. Arrangements can be made through most hotels, or when booking a dive package in the Bay Islands.

To Guatemala

Guatemala is just 12 km away from Copán, but anyplace interesting in Guatemala is farther removed, and transport from the border area is poor.

Pickup trucks leave Copán Ruinas for the border at El Florido all day long, starting about 6am. Leave early in order to make onward connections. Beware of overcharging by pickup drivers. The greatest problem arises for those traveling from El Florido (Guatemalan border to Copán Ruinas). Since this is a very isolated crossing and there is no town of any consequence nearby, pickup drivers often charge an extremely high fare for the trip. The locals in the truck will pay about $1, tourists are charged a lot more. Don't bother asking the locals what they are paying, because they play along with the drivers and will tell you an exaggerated price. Travelers who refuse to pay the exorbitant fare will be left stranded at the border, or they can choose to hitch a ride (be advised there's not much traffic on this road) or hike the 7 miles to Copán. Your best bet is to stand firm and negotiate a reasonable fare. The last bus from El Florido to Chiquimula leaves at 3:30pm. The trip takes 2 1/2 hours and the fare is $1.50. Onward bus from Chiquimula to Guatemala City leaves every 1/2 hour; it's a 3 hour trip, fare $3.

Travelers entering Guatemala pay about 80 cents to leave Honduras and about $2 to enter Guatemala. To leave Guatemala, travelers pay about $2 and to enter Honduras the fee is $1.50. It is possible to enter Honduras with a special one-night visa at a cost of 75 cents.

You can buy quetzales (Guatemalan currency) with dollars or lempiras, but exchange rates at the border are lower than elsewhere. It is recommended to exchange just enough for your bus, food, etc. Upon arrival in Chiquimula or Guatemala City, you can exchange at a much better rate.

Monarcas Travel, two blocks from Central Park across from Hedman Alas bus terminal, *Tel. 651-4361, E-mail: monarcas@honduras.com, web: monarcas@conexion.com.gt*, offers direct minibus service to Rio Dulce, Quirigua, Guatemala City and Antigua with connections to Panajachel and Chichicastenango. The minibus leaves Copán daily at 2:30pm, $25 one way from Copán to Antigua; the bus leaves Antigua at 4 am daily back to Copán Ruinas. Highly recommended.

Where to Stay

A number of new hotels, in all price categories, have opened in recent years, and many older ones are refurbishing and adding new rooms, so finding comfortable lodging is not a problem. Most hotels have a local phone number in Copán Ruinas and the better establishments have fax, E-mail, and a San Pedro Sula office. If you cannot reach the hotel of your choice by phone, sending a telegram within Honduras is quick and very inexpensive.

These hotels are all on the main square, or just a few blocks away:

HOTEL MARINA COPÁN, *Tel. 651-4070, 651-4071, 651-4072, Fax 651-4477, E-mail: reservations@hotelmarinacopan.com, web: www.hotelmarinacopan.com. 40 rooms. $69 single/ $80 double/$90 in suite, $11 per extra person, less in older rooms. Visa, Master Card, American Express. Add $25 for three meals.*

This gracious establishment, located on one side of the main square, is a great place to stay, a complex that has grown from a simple, inexpensive village inn to a luxurious, colonial-inspired hotel complex with pool, air conditioned rooms, sauna, meeting facilities, restaurant, bar, cafe and souvenir shop. The wings of the new section are built in traditional ranch style with covered outdoor passageways, adobe tile roofs and redtile floors, and surround quiet, interior gardens. Rooms are large and comfortable and have cable TV.

HOTEL POSADA REAL DE COPÁN, *Km. 164, Highway from San Pedro Sula to Copán Ruinas, Tel. 651-4480-98, Fax 651-4497, E-mail: hotelposadareal@sigmanet.hn, web: www.mayanet.hn/posadareal. 80 rooms. $72 double.*

The Posada is a 5 minute drive from the village of Copán Ruinas on the road to La Entrada. The hotel is on a large hill overlooking the Copán Valley. Amenities include air conditioning, cable TV, direct dial phone in each room, pool, jacuzzi, restaurant, private dining room, bar, convention facilities. You should have your own vehicle if staying at The Posada, as it is too far to walk to the ruins or the village from the hotel – unless you want to rely on the hotel's shuttle bus service to town and ruins.

HACIENDA EL JARAL, *P.O. Box 1006, San Pedro Sula. Tel. 552-4457, Tel/Fax 552-4891, 552-5067, E-mail: hotel@haciendaeljaral.com, web: www.haciendaeljaral.com. 26 rooms. $56 double.*

Located in Santa Rita de Copán, 11 kilometers before Copán Ruinas on the road from La Entrada to Copán Ruinas. Lodging in colonial, country style cabins with hot water, cable TV, porch, hammocks, air conditioning, and country ranch atmosphere. The Copán River passes through the resort, and there's a private lake, peddle boats, horseback riding, bird watching, hiking, river tubing, playground for children, swimming pool (open to the public) and restaurant. Very quiet and peaceful, popular with families and tour groups. Transport to ruins and town available.

Next door to El Jaral is a Tourist Mall and theater complex. First run films are shown every weekend, and there's a food court too.

HOTEL LOS JAGUARES, *located on the north side of Copán's Central Park. Tel. 651-4451, 651-4075. 10 rooms. $25 double.*

Rooms have air conditioning, cable TV, and parking is available.

HOTEL CAMINO MAYA, *near the village museum at the south corner of the central park. Tel. 651-4646, 651-4518, E-mail: hcmaya@hondutel.hn. 23 rooms. $50 double.*

Offers pleasant rooms, right on the Central park, hot water, interior courtyard and restaurant. Bar, restaurant, internet access, swimming pool and disco nearby.

HOTEL MADRUGADA, *located one block from the square near the bottom of the steps. Tel. 651-4092, Fax 557-8830, E-mail: mayatt@netsys.hn, web: www.mayatropic.com. 15 rooms. $24 double.*

Colonial inspired architecture, balcony with pleasant view. Owned and operated by a San Pedro Sula tour operator.

HACIENDA SAN LUCAS, *at the site of the Los Sapos Archaeological site. Guest Center is 2 blocks north of Copán's Central Park. Tel. 651-4106 E-mail: sanlucas@copanruinas.com, web: www.geocities.com/sanlucascopan. 2 double rooms, private bath, meals.*

Opened in 1999 by Dona Flavia, San Lucas is a 100 year-old

hacienda high in the hills, 3 km from the village of Copán Ruinas. Lovely views of the valley, village and main archeological site below. Horseback riding, birding, hiking. A lovely, tranquil spot in a spectacular setting.
HOTEL PLAZA COPÁN, *located next to the Cathedral on Copán's Central Park. Tel. 651-4508, 651-4278, Fax 651-4039, E-mail: servicio@hotelplazacopan.com, web: www.plazacopan.com. $32/double.*
   The Plaza Copán has 20 air-conditioned rooms, cable TV, pool, restaurant, bar, hot water, underground parking, and a souvenir shop.
HOTEL ACROPOLIS MAYA, *Tel/Fax 651-4118. $42/double.*
   Ten air-conditioned rooms, cable TV, hot water, underground parking.

Bed & Breakfasts
   LA CASA DE CAFÉ BED & BREAKFAST INN, *Barrio Las Vegas, three blocks west of Restaurant Llama del Bosque and Tunkul. Write to: Casa de Café, Barrio Las Vegas, Copán Ruinas, Tel. 651-4620, Fax 651-4623, E-mail: casacafe@hondutel.hn, casadecafe@mayanet.hn, web: www.todomundo.com/casadecafe. 10 rooms. $35 single/$45 double/$53 triple. Protected parking.*
   Copán's first B&B offers 10 comfortable rooms in an authentic colonial setting. Wood framed picture windows, lace curtains, handcrafted pine furniture, writing desk, ceiling fan, private hot water bath, garden with spectacular view of the Copán River Valley and distant mountains of Guatemala. Common area has color TV with cable, VHS, reference library with books, magazines, and videotapes on travel, archaeology, and culture in Central America. Breakfast is included in rate – waffles, banana pancakes, country omlettes. Export quality coffee is ground fresh each morning.
   The inn is run by a lovely Honduran-American family. English, Spanish and Miskito are spoken. They are a good source of Honduran travel information and can arrange local tours to a coffee plantation, hot springs, or horseback riding. This is a very good value for your vacation dollar. Brochure available upon request.

Budget Choices
   BRISAS DE COPÁN, *located just west of the entrance to town up the hill. Tel. 651-4118. 18 rooms. $22 double.*
   Good moderately priced and centrally located hotel. Rooms come with fan and hot water. Parking is available.
   HOTEL ACROPOLIS MAYA, *Tel. 651-4634, same owners as Brisas de Copán across the street, $36 double.*
   Cable tv, underground parking.
   HOTEL PATY, *located at the entrance to town just west of the soccer field. Tel. 651-4021, 651-4473, Fax 651-4109. 18 rooms. $13 double.*
   Rooms have hot water and fan. Parking is available. Owner offers direct minibus shuttle service to San Pedro Sula Airport, Tela, and La Ceiba.

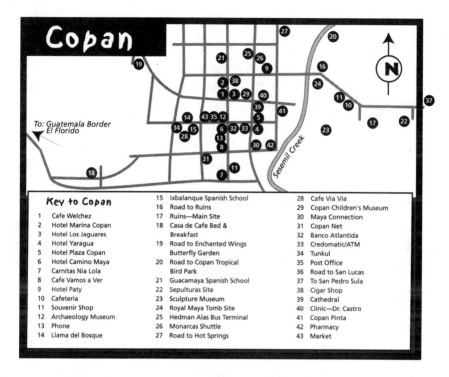

Copan

Key to Copan

1 Cafe Welchez
2 Hotel Marina Copan
3 Hotel Los Jaguares
4 Hotel Yaragua
5 Hotel Plaza Copan
6 Hotel Camino Maya
7 Carnitas Nia Lola
8 Cafe Vamos a Ver
9 Hotel Paty
10 Cafeteria
11 Souvenir Shop
12 Archaeology Museum
13 Phone
14 Llama del Bosque
15 Ixbalanque Spanish School
16 Road to Ruins
17 Ruins—Main Site
18 Casa de Cafe Bed &
   Breakfast
19 Road to Enchanted Wings
   Butterfly Garden
20 Road to Copan Tropical
   Bird Park
21 Guacamaya Spanish School
22 Sepulturas Site
23 Sculpture Museum
24 Royal Maya Tomb Site
25 Hedman Alas Bus Terminal
26 Monarcas Shuttle
27 Road to Hot Springs
28 Cafe Via Via
29 Copan Children's Museum
30 Maya Connection
31 Copan Net
32 Banco Atlantida
33 Credomatic/ATM
34 Tunkul
35 Post Office
36 Road to San Lucas
37 To San Pedro Sula
38 Cigar Shop
39 Cathedral
40 Clinic—Dr. Castro
41 Copan Pinta
42 Pharmacy
43 Market

POPUL NA, *located 1 block south of Central Park. Tel. 651-4095. 7 rooms. $11 double.*

Rooms have hot water and fan. A good budget option.

VIA VIA TRAVELLERS CAFÉ, *next door to Tunkul. Tel. 651-4652, E-mail: copan.honduras@viaviacafe.com. 4 rooms. $12 double.*

Rooms come with private bath, hot water, fan, breakfast included. Nice bar and good restaurant with cafe style sitting area out front.

HOTEL BELLA VISTA, *located a few blocks north of the Central Park up the hill. Tel. 651-4502. 18 rooms. $14 double.*

HOTEL YARAGUA, *on Central Park. Tel. 651-4050, E-mail: hotelyaragua@yahoo.com. 14 rooms. $20 double.*

Centrally located on a corner of the Central Park, rooms come with fan and hot water. There's a pleasant interior courtyard, reception area with color cable TV. Good mid-range hotel.

Where to Eat

GLIFOS, *restaurant of the Hotel Marina, Tel. 651-4070.*

This is the most sophisticated and upscale restaurant in town. The names means "glyphs." Offers the most extensive menu in the village, with everything from a club sandwich to Mexican-style chilaquiles (chicken, peppers and fixings served with sauce on tortillas) to steaks to chicken cordon bleu. Breakfast at the Marina costs about $4, lunch or dinner $10 or so for a complete meal.

LA LLAMA DEL BOSQUE, *a block and a half from the museum and 2 blocks west of Central Park. Tel. 651-4431.*

The "flame of the forest" is a favorite among travelers and locals, featuring large portions of hearty Honduran fare, shish kabob, steaks, chicken, tacos, salads. Open for breakfast, lunch, and dinner, the prices are very reasonable: a full meal will set you back $5. Popular with tour groups. Newly remodeled, great decorations and atmosphere,this is one of the best restaurants in town. Recommended is the 'parillada copaneca,' a mountainous feast which feeds 4-6 hungry tourists.

TUNKUL, *located in front of Llama del Bosque above. Tel 651-4410.*

This is one of the most popular spots for eating and drinking in town, serving beef, chicken, vegetarian dishes, spaghetti, and salads. A meal runs about $6. Best happy hour in Copán, half-price drinks from 7pm-8pm. Popular hangout for travelers, tour guides, archaeologists and locals. Another plus is the good music playing here – they have the best tape collection in town. Great grilled burgers – the best in town.

CAFE VAMOS A VER, *one block south of the Central Park.*

Run by a Dutch couple, Gerard and Diny, specialties include homemade bread, Dutch cheeses, Italian salami, great sandwiches, huge salads and daily specials like lasagna, madras chicken, quiche, soup of the day. Open three meals daily. Good music. Full meal runs $5. Heartily recommended.

CARNITAS NIA LOLA, *one block down the street from Vamos A ver. Tel. 651-4196.*

Simple country atmosphere and reasonable prices make this a good budget choice. Good beef dishes and *anafres* (a ceramic pot filled with hot coals and covered with another ceramic dish filled with refried beans, stringy cheese, and sausage, it all melts into a gooey, wonderful mess; you eat it with fried tortilla strips – sounds wierd but it's really good). Pleasant open air dining area/bar. Good place for happy hour drinks and typical foods.

VIA VIA COPÁN, *next door to Tunkul. Tel. 651-4652.*

This is a restaurant, bar, and café. Breakfast, lunch, dinner at reasonable prices. Via Via Copan is owned by a Belgian tour operator which has similar traveler's cafes in Belgium, Spain, Senegal, and Indonesia. They seek to create cultural meeting points for travelers around the world. There's a pleasant outdoor cafe-style sitting area fronting the street.

CAFE WELCHEZ, *overlooking the Central Park, located next to Hotel Marina Copán. Tel. 651-4477.*

This is a very nice café, offering light meals, desserts, and speciality coffees in a lovely colonial setting fronting the Central Park.

ELISAS CAFÉ, *next door to Hotel Camino Maya.*

Nice atmosphere, good food.

Among inexpensive places to eat are the following: **Comedor Isabel**, 2 blocks west of Central Park, popular with tourists and locals, reasonable prices. Try also **Licuados Juda**, for good fruit shakes and light snacks.

Nightlife & Entertainment

Nightlife in Copán Ruinas consists primarily of eating and drinking heartily. Recommended nightspots include **Carnitas Nia Lola** and **Tunkul**. For dancing, **La Piscina** is a pool, restaurant, and disco complex a few blocks south of the Central Square, open weekends only. Also on weekends, **Las Vegas** is the after-hours hangout for local cowboys out for a good time (not recommended for single women or women in groups).

Seeing the Sights

Less than a kilometer from the modern town of Copán Ruinas is the **UNESCO World Heritage Site of Copán**. Thirteen hundred years ago, it was one of the great cities of Classic Mayan civilization, and today is one of the most esteemed and important archaeological sites in the world. Harvard University has been working at Copán on and off for more than 100 years. More recently, archaeological and conservation projects have been carried out involving scholars from the University of Pennsylvania, Tulane University, Penn State University, Northern Illinois University, University of Houston, University of Queensland (Australia), University of New Mexico, Smithsonian Institution, Getty Foundation and the Honduran Institute of Anthropology and History.

Visitors will find a great number of restored ancient buildings at Copán, including monumental temples and palaces, both in the site center — the Principal Group — and in nearby areas of the ancient city, such as the area of Las Sepulturas.

Archaeology Museum

The **Regional Museum**, on the town square, is well done, and gives a good presentation of ancient Mayan history at Copán. Jade, shell and bone jewelry are housed here, as well as some of the more valuable altars and monuments from both the main ceremonial center and outlying areas. You can see the reconstruction of a tomb, the jewels of a governor, the dried blood of an ancient sacrifice, a skull with jade-filled teeth, a very male bat from Temple 20, an expressive sculpture called "the melancholy woman," and clay figurines. The museum is well worth a visit. Hours are 8am to noon and 1pm to 4pm, admission is $2.

Copán Sculpture Museum

This new museum, inaugurated in August 1996, houses the most beautiful and important stone sculptures found at Copán to date. The museum is the only one of its kind anywhere in the world and has become a must-see sight on the Mundo Maya Circuit. The museum building was constructed to reflect the central concepts of the Maya worldview. The entrance is a stylized mouth of a mythical serpent, symbolizing a portal from one world to the next. Entering the serpent, the visitor walks through a winding, subterranean tunnel where the sense of entering another time and place envelops the visitor.

Emerging from the tunnel, you come face to face with a truly awesome sight: a full-scale reconstruction, in colorful splendor, of the temple nicknamed **Rosalila** by archaeologists. Found in 1991, Rosalila was so sacred to the Copán Maya that it was left intact, including its roof crest, before being carefully buried within the core of Structure 16, the central building of the Copán Acropolis. Local artisans have made highly accurate reconstructions of the elaborate colored stucco reliefs that adorned all sides of Rosalila.

The temple, dedicated in the year A.D. 571 by Copán's 10th ruler, Tzik Balam (Moon Jaguar), represents a mountain; a place of creation, a source of life giving water. For the first time, visitors to Copán can get a glimpse of what Copán might have looked like during the glory days of the Classic Period (400-900 AD). The first floor of the museum contains some of the best original stelae, which were moved inside the museum for reasons of conservation.

Altar Q, one of the most celebrated monuments of Copán, is now located on the museum's first floor. Originally located on the West Court of The Acropolis at the base of the staircase of **Structure 16** (where a replica has now been placed), Altar Q depicts the 16 rulers of Copán. Each ruler is seated above his name glyph, starting with the first and going chronologically clockwise around the monument. On the second floor, the world of the living is represented by pieces from 18 different buildings, including seven complete facades reconstructed by archaeologists.

The museum is located at the parking area of the main ruins site and is open 7 days a week from 8am 4pm. Admission is $5 and well worth it.

Panoramic Views

For a panorama of the town of Copán Ruinas and the valley stretching beyond, walk up to the **Cuartel**, also known as Fuerte José Trinidad Cabañas, the remains of an old army outpost, on the hill four blocks directly north of the square — follow the road that passes the museum. Though of centenary appearance, with massive walls and corner towers, it only dates from 1946.

Learn Spanish!

The **Escuela de Español Ixbalanque** ("Ish-ba-lan-keh" Spanish school) offers one-on-one instruction in Spanish for four hours a day, five days a week. Students board with local Spanish-speaking families, or have the option of staying at a hotel. All teachers are government-certified.

Since Copán Ruinas is pretty much a backwater town without the hordes of resident foreigners present in other Spanish-language study centers (Antigua, Guatemala, or San José, Costa Rica), students have ample opportunity to experience the language in an extemporaneous manner. Which is to say, you can talk a lot in Spanish with real people in real-life situations. To contact the school: *Tel. 651-4432, E-mail: Ixbalan@hondutel.hn.*

Academia de Espanol Guacamaya is another Spanish school that comes highly recommended. One to one teacher student ratio, 4 hours per day instruction, room and board with family, located a half-block norh of Central Park. Contact them at: *Tel. 651-4360, E-mail: Director@guacamaya.com, web: www.guacamaya.com*

Excursions & Day Trips

M.C. Tours, working out of the Hotel Marina, *Tel. 651-4454, 552-4549, E-mail: sales@mctours-honduras.com, web: www.mctours-honduras.com,* arranges package stays in Copán and excursions in the area. Offerings are a horseback tour of the coffee farm of the Welchez family, who owns the Hotel Marina; a visit to hot springs; a cloud forest hike; and a horseback visit to outlying ruins are available. Prices range from $25 to $35 per person. They also offer tours throughout the country: Celaque Cloud Forest and Gracias, overnight $162 per person; Copán, overnight $150 per person; Copán and The Caribbean Coast, 4 days/3 nights $239 to $339 per person; and The Lenca Highlands, 5 days/4 nights $360 per person. MC Tours is one of the largest and most professional tour operators in Honduras. A full color catalogue of trips is available upon request.

Go Native Adventure Tours is next door to Ixbalanque Spanish School, *Tel/Fax 651-4432, E-mail: Gnative4@hotmail.com*. Rene Hernandez is practically a legend in and around Copán Ruinas. He specializes in budget trips to the Rio Platano Biosphere in La Mosquitia as well as running local trips to hot springs, horseback riding, mountain bike trips and caving. Destinations include Pico Bonito cloud forest, Cuero y Salado wildlife refuge, the forests, rivers and lagoons of Mosquitia, and a beach walk from Puerto Cortés to Tela. Rates vary according to number of participants and the trip – about $150 to visit two reserves, including an overnight stay, $450 for a five-day trip through Mosquitia. They also conduct local tours to hot springs, waterfalls, horseback riding, caving, archaeological ruins.

Shuttle Yax Kuk Mo, *Tel. 651-4021*, operates out of Hotel Paty, direct minibus service to San Pedro Sula, Tela, and La Ceiba.

Bob 'The Butterfly & Bird Guy' Gallardo is a naturalist, bird guide and expert on Honduran flora and fauna. He offers birding and nature trips around Copán. To date Bob has recorded 283 species in the Copán area. Bob has published the first-ever *Guide To The Birds of Copán*. He offers a Copán River Walking tour, 3 hours, 40-50 species of birds can be seen, hotel pickup at 6am, includes use of spotting scope and free entry to Butterfly Garden, $25 per person. His Miramundo Trip offers birding at 1,800 ft, tour of a coffee plantation, excellent birding, 7 hour trip, hotel pickup at 6am, $25 per person, free entry to Butterfly Garden. Contact him at: *Tel 651-4133, E-mail: rgallardo32@hotmail.com.*

Yaragua Tours specializes in local adventure tours. Horseback riding $15 per person, 3 hour trip up into the hills above Copán, caving, hot springs, coffee plantation tour. Run by Samuel Miranda Yaragua Tours are fun, well run and he charges a fair price. *Tel 651-4645*, located a half- block south of the Cathedral.

Practical Information

Art Classes

Copán Pinta is a local group run by Carin, a young Dutch woman. Art classes for local children, art studio, crafts shop, painting and drawing classes and other cultural events are held year round. Donations of art supplies and funds are always welcome. Located one block from Hotel Gemelos.

Cigars

Tobaccos y Recuerdos, half a block north of the Central Park, across from the Hotel Marina, has a good selection of fine Honduran cigars.

Emergency Assistance, Ambulances & Medical Help

Paramedics For Children runs an excellent volunteer ambulance and paramedic service in Copán Ruinas. Contributions and donations of supplies are always welcome. Contact Rodger Harrison: *E-mail: rodger@Copánruinas.com, web: www.parmedicsforchildren.com.*

A recommended English speaking doctor is Dr. Castro, a few doors down hill from Banco de Occidente, 8:30-12:00am, 2:00pm-5:00pm.

Exchanging Money

The free market for currency exchange is near the bus terminal in front of Hotel Paty. However, most visitors to Copán exchange their money at one of two local banks: **Banco Atlantida** (cash advance on Visa) and **Banco de Occidente** (cash advance on Visa and MasterCard), both on the Central Park. It is recommended that you exchange Guatemalan quetzales in Copán or at the El Florido border, as it will be extremely difficult to exchange Guatemalan currency anywhere else in Honduras. **Banco Credomatic**, next door to Banco Atlantida, is the Honduras representative for MasterCard, Visa and American Express. The bank boasts Copán's first ATM.

Note: Banco Atlantida offers a better exchange rate than Banco del Occidente.

Phone & Post

The **Hondutel** office has telephone and fax service. It is located a half-block from the central park, next door to café Vamos A Ver. The **post office** is next door to the village museum.

Internet

Maya Connections, two locations, next door to Hotel Los Gemelos and one block south of Copán Museum, has internet, e-mail, fax and telephone service, *E-mail: mayaconn@hondutel.hn*. **Copán Net** offers internet and e-mail serivce at: *E-mail: copannet@hondutel.hn*. **Hotel Camino Maya** has good rates on internet access.

Laundry Service

Copán Ruinas is also the cleanup center for traveling grungy gringos. Maya Connections has laundry service.

Immigration

The immigration office is located in the old Colegio building on the Central Square. Hours are Monday through Friday 7am-4:30pm.

Massage

Dona Tona offers massage in her studio just across the street from Llama del Bosque.

The Copán Ruins

Beginnings

Copán has been referred to as the Athens of the Maya world, a place where art, science and religion flourished between A.D. 426 and A.D. 820. Maya cities larger than than Copán did exist at this time farther to the north, in present-day Mexico and Guatemala, for example at Calakmul and Tikal, respectively. However, at Copán, there are more carved monuments and inscriptions than at any other ancient Maya center, including *the longest hieroglyphic inscription ever found in the Maya area*, carved into the risers of the Temple 26 Hieroglyphic Stairway. The intricate, swirling, decorative art at Copán is widely considered to surpass not only that of other Maya cities, but also that of all other civilizations in the Western Hemisphere before the arrival of Europeans.

Copán might have been settled as early as 2000 B.C., and there is good archaeological evidence linking Copán to the Olmec culture sphere (of Mexico) at around 1200 B.C. The valley was fertile and well watered. Over time, harvests became more and more abundant, with the perfection of corn agriculture and of a calendar to guide planting. More organized societies developed in Copán and the neighboring areas among the people that are today called the Maya.

Copán developed in much the same way as other Maya cities. Simple thatched houses on foundations evolved into temples on substantial masonry platforms. Ironwood, or chicozapote, substituted for less sturdy materials used for lintels and wall supports. Great stones were rolled down from nearby hills, carved with glyph figures representing names, dates, and events, and erected in the plazas as stelae.

This stone was a relatively soft volcanic rock—made of compressed ash deposits more than 18 million years old—was quarried from a local, still-visible hillside (north of the Great Plaza); it was cut and carved using harder rock. Household implements were made of wood, stone, and clay; as techniques improved, pottery became more complex, and was used for larger and more elaborate ceremonial purposes. Newer, more complicated and probably more beautiful buildings were erected right on top of older ones. The custom developed of memorializing rulers and royal families and recording history on buildings and monuments and in tombs.

The Rise ...

None of this happened in isolation. The Copán River, which flows into the Motagua in present-day Guatemala, probably served as a link to other Maya centers, and as a route for trade in cacao, obsidian, and many other perishable materials for which archaeologists find little or no evidence. There are some artistic similarities between Copán and Quiriguá in Guatemala, which could have been reached overland and by water, and the same language was used for writing throughout the Maya area.

The Classic Era at Copán spanned just a few hundred years, from approximately A.D. 400 to A.D. 900, though the first and last dates are as cited above: A.D. 426 and A.D. 820. During this period of recorded history, construction, reconstruction, astronomical reckonings, and artistic expression were most intense. Despite the general air of mystery that surrounds Copán, the names of some of its rulers are known, and much of its written history has been uncovered and deciphered.

For example, the 12th ruler, 'Smoke Jaguar,' lived to the ripe age of 82, and was succeeded by in A.D. 695 by Waxak Lahun Ubah K'awiil, popularly known as '18 Rabbit,' who broke the tradition of destroying monuments with each change in rulership, until he was captured and sacrificed at the hands of the ruler of Quirigua in A.D. 738. The 15th ruler, K'ak Yipyah Chan K'awiil, popularly referred to as 'Smoke Shell,' completed the Hieroglyphic Stairway that was begun by 18 Rabbit. Several other rulers have been identified, and their architectural programs and life events can today be read almost as literally as Copán's scribes would have intended more than a thousand years ago.

... and Fall

But the creative impulse and energy of Copán were not to last forever. The city covered all of the valley floor and all of the foothills north of the river, probably to well over 15,000 inhabitants. Having depleted the forests and exhausting the soils, Copán lost its self-sufficiency, and thus became vulnerable. For some reason – perhaps a combination of political and social decline, disease, drought, famine, and environmental destruction – building programs ceased, no more dates or histories were inscribed, and urban maintenance came to a halt.

Some social activity persisted, especially in the northern foothills, but after A.D. 1000, non-Maya people resettled the valley floor, bringing with them new forms of social organization and material culture. After a short time, these people departed the Copán Valley as well. The forest gradually renewed itself and grew onto the plazas and onto the temples; earthquakes tumbled buildings; and after centuries of abandonment the ruins of the city became obscured by dense vegetation. Some people continued to live in the vicinity of Copán, up to and beyond the arrival of the Spanish in the 16th century. However, the traces of Classic Maya civilization were consumed by time and lost to all but the most distance memories.

In the 1800's, the newly independent and newly opened Central America began to draw interest from potential trading partners. American diplomat John Lloyd Stephens, accompanied by the famous artist Frederick Catherwood, visited Copán in 1839. They later published a description of the ancient ruins, along with illustrations, in the book, *Incidents of Travel in Central America, Chiapas and Yucatan*. This book is still available today. Stephens was so impressed with Copán that he bought the site for $50.

Reviving Interest in Copán

Alfred P. Maudslay, arriving from England in 1881, was the first of a stream of the true archaeologists to study Copán. For a time, the Carnegie Institution of Washington took charge of the ruins, between about 1937 and 1946. The Instituto Nacional de Antropología e Historia assumed control in 1952. New excavations have been carried out in recent years. With ongoing work, interpretations of life at Copán, and of the Maya in general, are constantly being revised.

The main ceremonial center of Copán covers about 30 hectares, or 75 acres, but this is only a small part of the residential, administrative, and ceremonial area that was built at Copán. Some of these, like the northern foothills, are not yet integrated into the National Archaeological Park. However, other areas can—and should—be visited, such as the nearby regions known as El Bosque ("the forest"), to the southwest of the Principal Group (accessed by trails through the forest), and Las Sepulturas ("the burials"), to the east (accessed by simply walking east along the highway, ten minutes).

While the vast majority of Copán's temples and stelae are located in the Principal Group, these areas show much of the diversity in building styles and spatial patterns that defined the ancient city. A number of impressive stelae, belonging to the 12th ruler, remain situated in outlying areas of the Copán Valley, and can be accessed by foot, car, or by horseback.

Orientation

The ruins are a ten-minute walk from town, about a kilometer away. You can follow the road, or, more pleasantly, take the stone path that runs just to the side of the road, right alongside some mounds and carved monuments, or stelae.

The visiting hours at the site are from 8am to 4pm. Entrance fee is $10. The visitors' center is well organized and well maintained. There are some exhibits, and a model of the site, photos, pottery (including pieces of Olmec and Teotihuacan origin), sculptured pieces of bone, and jade pendants. Time-line charts show the rise of the Maya relative to contemporary civilizations. Take a good look before you go out among the ruins. Several guide booklets are available for sale, including one in English published by the Instituto Hondureño de Antropología e Historia.

There is a cafeteria on the west side of the parking area. Next to the cafeteria is a very good shop that specializes in Honduran crafts; they carry many hard-to-find items from remote parts of Honduras. Across the street from the parking area is a simple comedor with a souvenir shop next door. There are also picnic tables in a forested area on the trail to the ruins.

Hiring a Guide

Guides can be hired on-site. They have a lot more information, especially in the way of local lore, than is provided in this book or in the booklets you can buy at the site; and though some of what they tell you may be strictly anecdotal, and may conflict with published descriptions and analyses, I strongly recommend that you hire one in order not to miss anything. Expect to pay a guide about $20 for a 3 hour tour of the main site and sculpture museum. The Copán Guide Association has a table set up in the visitors center where qualified bilingual guides can be hired.

Seeing the Ruins

From the **reception center**, walk across the old airstrip, now a fledgling grove of trees. You approach the ruins via a wide trail lined with towering tropical trees. Be forewarned about two things:

1. You can be heavily fined if you destroy or damage anything at the site — stone, plant or animal — or if you try to take home any souvenirs. Or you can go to prison for several years. Or both.

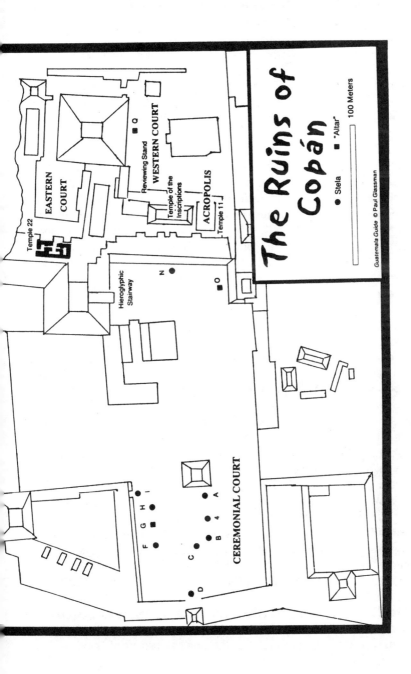

The Ruins of Copán

EASTERN COURT
Temple 22
WESTERN COURT
Reviewing Stand
Temple of the Inscriptions
ACROPOLIS
Temple 11
Hieroglyphic Stairway
CEREMONIAL COURT

● Stela   ■ "Altar"

100 Meters

Guatemala Guide © Paul Glassman

2. There are irritating plants, sometimes ten feet high, which can cause a severe reaction. They have pale-green leaves and small spines.

The **Great Plaza**, is the long open area that you reach first, at the northern extreme of the Principal Group of ruins. This space would have been the physical and conceptual center of the ancient city; it is defined by a U-shaped architectural complex, with a four-sided, "radial pyramid" (Structure 4) located in the open, southern end of the 'U'. All of the exposed masonry was once covered with lime stucco, and painted. Perhaps the most notable feature of the Great Plaza is the presence of many carved stelae, most of which date to the reign of the 13th ruler. These were erected over 25 years and celebrate important calendrical and historic events. The ruler is depicted figurally, with symbols of power and lineage. Elaborate glyphs explain dates and history. Symbols and inscriptions are exaggerated—with respect to proportions, for example—and interlace in a manner similar to that found in Asian art.

All of the stelae in the center of the Great Plaza depict this 13th ruler. He stands straight with feet together, his short arms crossed in front, holding a serpent bar, and he bears a flamboyant accoutrement upon his head. Additional figures and symbols fill the front of the block, while glyphs on the sides and back relate the story of his ritual events.

Stela A, dating from A.D. 731, is located beside the radial pyramid (Structure 4). The stela includes the glyphic names for Tikal, Palenque, and Calakmul, all large and important cities in the 8th century, and indicates a knowledge of and contact with these other renowned Maya centers. The chamber underneath this and other stelae was cruciform and held offerings of ceramics.

Stela 4, just north of Stela A, dates to five years earlier than Stela A, demonstrating that one of the important events was the passing of five-year intervals in the Maya calendar round. In front of Stela 4 is a large stone, about four feet high, perhaps used to sacrifice captives from warfare. The head of the victim might have been placed on a depression in the surface; the channels then would have carried off the blood.

Stela B, to the north of Stela 4, commemorates the accession of the 13th ruler (Wakaklahun Ubah K'awiil). Symbols of power include the macaws' beaks at the top, miniature heads, and the detailed headdress.

Stela C is unusual because it has a figure carved on the back, instead of glyphs, and shows traces of red paint, which might once have covered other monuments as well. The two figures on this stela, one young and one old, are thought to represent the ruler and his father, the 12th ruler, respectively. Beside this stela lies a turtle-shaped stone.

Stela D, next to the steps at the north end of the plaza, dates to A.D. 736 and shows a double column of glyphs on the rear side. Sea shells and figures of deities appear on top. The figures on the altar before it are of Chak, the deity of rain.

Along the east side of the plaza, Stela F, to the north, also with the remains of paint, shows a figure whose robes extend from the front around the sides to form a frame for the glyphs on the back. A representation of the sun is similar to those on stelae C and 4, and the same artist might well have carved all three.

Next comes **Altar G**, a double-headed serpent with a glyph that indicates a date of A.D. 800. This is one of the latest dates inscribed at Copán, and is from the period of the 16th ruler, Yax (pronounced 'yash') Pasah.

Stela H shows the ruler in an elaborate skirt, which probably refers to the ruler donning the garb of the great Maya maize god, or corn god. A gold figurine was found in the vault beneath this stela, that must have come from lower Central America at some time after the 9th century; this may suggest that people were still carrying out devotional ceremonies at the Great Plaza for some time after the abandonment of Copán.

Stela I, set into a niche in a stairway on the east side of the plaza, shows a masked figure, probably Smoke Jaguar, who ruled from 628 to 695 A.D. This stela was likely left in place by the 13th ruler, Smoke Jaguar's son, as a means of commemorating and integrating his father's memory and being.

East of Structure 4, the radial pyramid, beyond the Great Plaza, is **Stela J**. This monument is covered completely by glyphs, especially on the back side where they form the pattern of a mat, the symbol of rulership. The only similar Maya stela is found at the site of Quiriguá, a fact which draws further attention to the many associations between these centers in antiquity.

The main **Ball Court** is just south of the Great Plaza. Ancient Maya ball courts characteristically have a long, narrow space bound by dramatically sloping walls. This ball court was dedicated in A.D. 738, the same year the 13th ruler was killed by the ruler of Quirigua, and bears the carved stone heads of large macaws. The macaw was a sacred bird for the Maya of Copán; and you'll see plenty of scarlet macaws around Copán today, especially on the fence at the entrance to the site. This ball court sits atop two earlier structures, the first built in the fifth century. The players probably had to hit markers along the side with a rubber ball. In the 16th century, the Spanish reported that many different types of ball game were played in what is today Mexico and Central America, and they report that the losers often were decapitated.

The main Ball Court is closed to foot traffic, and more and more areas of the site are being closed to casual visitors, as it becomes painfully clear that exposing ancient structures to the elements and to the footsteps of visitors only hastens their deterioration. For a closer inspection of a ball court at Copán, one should proceed to Ball Court B in the El Bosque zone of the Archaeological Park.

To the south of the main Ball Court is the most spectacular of Copán's treasures: the **Hieroglyphic Stairway**. More than a 2000 glyphs set in the 63 steps — together constituting the longest known Mayan inscription — relate the history of Copán's later rulers, up to 755 A.D., and cite the burial of the powerful 12th ruler, interred beneath the stariway's crowning temple. The structure was dedicated by the 15th ruler, K'ak Yipyaj Chan K'awiil, popularly known as Smoke Shell. Unfortunately, the inscription as a whole can barely be read, since all but the lower third of the stairway collapsed in antiquity. The Carnegie Institution replaced the blocks to the best of their ability in the 1940's, but this reconstruction nowhere approaches reality. However, Barbara Fash of Harvard University, in cooperation with the Getty Foundation and the Honduran Institute of Anthropology and History, currently is carrying out a large scale project involving conservation and re-analysis of the stairway. In time, we may have a much better sense of what how the text, in its entirety, would have been read.

Visitors will notice that along the center of the stairway are four male sculptures; a fifth is preserved in a climate-controlled environment at the Peabody Museum of Harvard University, having been shipped there from Copán more than one hundred years ago. An altar at the base of the steps shows a head inside the jaws of a monster; its companion stela depicts the 15th ruler who finished the stairway project.

Adjacent to the Hieroglyphic Stairway is **Temple 11**, at the base of which is Stela N, the inscription of which provides a date of 761 A.D. The human faces on each side extend to the edges, almost as a precursor to a statue. Serpents and indications of the cardinal points can be seen on top.

In the southern area of the Principal Group of ruins, south of the Hieroglyphic Stairway, is an architectural complex known as the **Acropolis**. This is not a true acropolis, or "high city," in the sense of ancient Greece, but rather is an area which has experienced a dozen or more successive building phases over the course of five centuries. The result is a relatively high and isolated part of the Principal Group that accommodated some of the most sacred and meaningful temples and buildings anywhere in the ancient city.

It is divided into two functional areas that archaeologists now refer to as the East Court and the West Court. The **West Court** is defined by two hugely monumental structures: Temple 11 on the north and Temple 16 on the east. Temple 11, with its staircase Reviewing Stand portrays huge snails and deities, as well as symbols of the religious concept, Ik, associated with wind and life. Inside the temple, seen in the entryway, for example, are fine hieroglyphic panels that are organized in accordance with cosmological precepts.

Temple 11 was built during the reign of Yax Pasah Chan Yooat, who ruled from 763 A.D. until his death in 820; he sponsored the last major construction phases at Copán, which include Temple 11 and 16.

Temple 16 is perhaps the greatest monument of Yax Pasah's reign and it was built on a sacred axis. Many of the most important buildings in the history of Copán were built on this axis, including (as mentioned) the now-famous structure known as Rosalila, constructed in A.D. 571 and excavated by the Honduran archaeologist, Ricardo Agurcia. During the tunnel excavations conducted by the University of Pennsylvania, many important tombs have been found beneath the Acropolis. In 1993, a tomb was discovered on the above-mentioned axis that several archaeologists now believe is that of the dynastic founder, Yax Kuk Mo. Known only through references in the inscriptions, Yax K'uk Mo is understood as the 5th century ruler from whom was born Copán's royal lineage. Situated at the western base of Temple 16, Altar Q depicts the royal lineage of Yax Pasah, the 16th ruler. Four ancestral rulers are shown on each side of the square block, each sitting on a name gylph which acts as a royal cushion, and organized in a reverse chronological order (moving counterclockwise). There are sixteen altogether, and on the west face Yax Pasah can be seen receiving his right to rule from Yax K'uk Mo himself.

The last major area of the Principal Group is the **East Court** of the Acropolis. Like other open areas, this plaza was slightly sloped, and an ancient drain still channels rain water. **Temple 22**, on the north side, built under the reign of "18 Rabbit," the 13th ruler who ruled from 695 to 738 A.D., is another spectacular example of Maya architecture. The doorway to the structure at the top is flanked by sculpture that shows it to be monstrous serpent's jaws. At the corners are figures of Chak, the long-nosed god of rain. These motifs are indications of influence from Maya areas farther to the north in the Campeche and Yucatan areas of modern Mexico. The inner doorway of Temple 22 (the original of which is housed in the sculpture museum) shows themes from Maya cosmology, including death's heads at the base. Along the sides, deities known as Bakabs hold up the heavens, with a two-headed serpent above. On the west side of the East Court is the Jaguar Stairway, with stone jaguars flanking the steps. Their eye sockets, now empty, were once filled with polished obsidian.

Temple 20, now largely destroyed by the undercutting of the Copán River below, is on the eastern side of the court. **Temple 18**, on the extreme southern end of the East Court, is thought by some to have been the burial place of Yax Pasah. It is an interesting building, not least because the tomb chamber strongly resembles an ancient building tradition from the Guatemalan Peten, the heartland area of the Classic Maya. The river was successfully re-routed in the 1950's to forestall further damage. Some protective work is still going on. The stratified layers, visible on the eastern damaged side of the Acropolis (best viewed from below) neatly illustrate how successions of building and plazas were built one over the other during the course of nearly 500 years.

Nature Trail

Adjacent to the ceremonial center is a trail through a section of the subtropical forest that has been protected from agricultural development. The trail runs for about a kilometer, taking one to Ball Court B and several other landmarks southwest of the Principal Group. Copán's protected forest is a sample of leafy mid-level rain forest, with its vegetation determined by elevation, rainfall, and temperature. It's a seasonally dry forest, since rain falls mostly from May to November, and the trees shed their leaves during dry periods to conserve energy. Much of the relatively dense forest seen today has grown back only over the last 50 years. The majority of the valley's forest around the ruins was clear-cut since the 1850's when agriculturalists moved into the area from Guatemala.

Just at it must have taken many centuries for full regeneration of the original diversity and complexity of the forest after the collpase of Copán, a considerable amount of time will be required to achieve the lush environment that would have existed prior to 1850. This may never happen, as agriculture has taken away the habitat of many of the original species. Over many centuries, and continuing today, the forest penetrates the ancient stone mounds built by the Maya, and deliberately, steadily and inevitably demolishes their work — unless held back by consolidation teams. The nature trail is low-lying, and can be waterlogged during the rainy season. Nineteen numbered stopping points indicate particular features of the forest, such as Maya mounds, humus, and secondary growth. Species of interest include:
• Matapioja ("lice-killer"): the root of which forms a shampoo effective in treating lice.
• chichicaste: a thorny plant often seen on roadsides
• anona (custard apple): one of many trees with edible fruits. Others are the ramón or masica (breadnut), still occasionally used as a food source, with shiny leaves similar to those on coffee bushes; and the guanacaste, or earpod, with its brush-like leaves.
• ceiba (silk-cotton): one of the massive trees of the tropical forest, with great buttress roots to support its weight in the shallow soil
• guarumo (cecropia): a tree swarming with ants that feed on its sap and lay their eggs in its trunk.
• matapalo (strangler fig): which climbs, entangles, penetrates, overwhelms, and eventually murders many a tropical tree that provides its initial support.

Once you get to know many of the trees along the nature trail, you'll be able to identify them among the ruins. The ceiba in particular grows on many temples, able to support its massive trunk with buttresses and roots that penetrate the cracks between stones.

Las Sepulturas
About one kilometer east of the Principal Group, the ancient ceremonial and residential area of Las Sepulturas has been studied intensively only in the

last twenty years. Some of the buildings were modest, but others had multiple rooms and sculpted facades and benches. Many tombs and burials were found in this area, some of which some yielded magnificent ceramic vessels and jade objects.

One of the most notable burials from Las Sepulturas, known as **El Brujo**, was found beneath the surface architecture of Plaza A and is on exhibit at the museum in town. This important personage, and the prestigious burial rites provided him, show that this area of Copán was significant during the early Classic period, before A.D. 600. This should not seem surprising since the earliest datable archaeological deposits at Copán also have been found in this area of Las Sepulturas: a cemetary dating to approximately A.D. 1000 was found directly beneath Plaza A and Structure 82 on the south side.

Structure 82, also known as the Scribe House and as the House of the Bakabs, is the crowning example of the importance of this area late in the archaeological sequence. It dates to the reign of Yax Pasah and the inscription on the building's interior bench suggests that the lineage at Las Sepulturas had long-standing ties with rulership. Thus, the architectural settlement of Las Sepulturas is considered to have been an integral part of the ancient city during its florescence. The site has lovely walking trail through its neighboring forest that will take you to other groups of restored architecture. It is uncrowded and very peaceful, a great place for a picnic. Just behind the site is the Copán River, a great place to relax or splash around in the cool waters.

Access to Las Sepulturas is via horseback, walking from the main site, or by car. The admission to the main site, purchased at the Visitors Center, enables visitors to tour the Sepulturas site as well, so hold on to your ticket. Hours here are also from 8am to 4pm.

After Copán?

After visiting the ruins of Copán, the choices for most travelers are to continue to Guatemala or return to San Pedro Sula. Another possible route is to take the turnoff to Santa Barbara on the La Entrada-San Pedro highway, passing through rugged mountains and emerging near Lake Yojoa.

Another option is the **Honduran Highlands Loop**: Copán Ruinas- La Entrada-Santa Rosa de Copán-Gracias/Celaque National Park-La Esperanza-Siguatepeque-Lake Yojoa-San Pedro Sula.

Side Trips

There are **hot springs** located about 20 km from Copán Ruinas, about a one hour drive over a decent unpaved road. Catch a ride with local villagers heading home in a pickup or hire a pickup to drive you. The springs are located in the village of **Agua Caliente**, which takes its name from the hot waters. There are two man-made pools for swimming, or you can ford the shallow river and soak at the spot where the hot water tumbles down the hillside into the river. By adjusting the position of rocks and your sitting position, you can regulate the temperature of your bath.

You can hike up the hill through a coffee plantation to view the source of the thermal waters. There's a picnic area, grills, and soft drinks and beer sold. Admission is 75 cents and it's a secure place for camping.

You can go horseback riding in **Los Sapos**, an archaeological site in the nearby hills about 4 km from Copán. You can catch lovely views of Copán's main site and the Copán Valley below. There are a number of large carved stones at the site which bear a likeness to frogs. Archaeologists theorize that this site was used for fertility rites and ceremonies. For the Maya, the frog was a symbol of fertility. Access is via hiking about one hour or via horseback; about a 3 hour round-trip costs $15 per person. This is a secure place for camping.

Just down from the old finca house at the entrance to Los Sapos is a beautiful *mirador* (lookout), with extraordinary views of the Copán River valley and the village below.

Rubi Waterfall, located in the hills above Santa Rita, is about 8 km from Copán Ruinas. From Santa Rita it's about a 45 minute hike. I'd suggest hiring a local guide to take you, beacuse the trail is not marked at all. There is a lovely 10 meter high waterfall and a deep natural pool in which to swim directly under the falls. Hiking above the falls will lead you to additional waterfalls, but this is for the truly adventurous only.

Peña Quemada Forest Reserve is excellent for birding, located 22 km from Copán near Rio Amarillo. The Copán area has approximately 200 species of birds.

There are a number of **caves** which can be explored in the Copán area; The **Cueva Especial**, a 500 meter long cave, is easily accessed from Copán. The **Cueva Boqueron**, 20 km from Copán, has stalactites and stalagmites and an underground river. Ask locals for information on additional caves in the area.

For a truly special experience, visit the **Chortí Maya Villages**. There are some 4,200 Chortí Maya Indians living in a number of small villages near Copán Ruinas. The Chortí are considered direct descendents of the Copán Maya. The Chortí language has all but died out on the Honduran side of the border, but it is still spoken on the Guatemalan side of the frontier. Villages include: **Shonco**, 8 km west of Copán; **Chilar**, 8 km south of Copán; **La Laguna**, 6 km east of Copán; and **Carrizalito**, 5 km from Copán. Villages can be reached via pickup for about 50 cents, or by horseback.

El Jaral is where about 5,000 white herons return to the lake at El Jaral at about 5pm each evening to spend the night in the trees. This is a lovely spot to view the herons as they fly up the Copán River Valley.

Copán is also one of Honduras' finest coffee growing regions, with the surrounding mountains home to mostly small family owned coffee planta-tions. Tours to the plantations can be arranged. The best time is during the

275 WESTERN HONDURAS 275

harvest season from November through February, when the picking and processing can be viewed.

A number of outlying stelae can be visited. **Stelae 12** is located east of the main ruins 2 1/2 km from Los Sapos, built in 652 A.D. by 12th ruler Humo Jaguar. Access is via horesback or hiking. **Stelae 10**, located west of the main site, was also erected in 652 A.D. This is a spectacular setting on top of a mountain, with an awesome view of the Copán Valley and village below. April 12th is the best day to visit Stelae 10, because on this date, if you stand in front of Stelae 10 at sunrise, in the distance you will see Stelae 12 with the sun rising directly behind it. At sunset, the sun will set directly behind Stelae 10. This phenomenon coincides with the start of the corn planting season.

South Toward Santa Rosa de Copán

From La Entrada, where the branch road forks toward Copán Ruinas, the main highway of the west continues toward the regional center of **Santa Rosa de Copán**. Along the way, at **San Nicolás**, are ponds formed by the Chorro de Carrizal and the Chorro del Callejón, artesian geysers.

At **Trinidad** are some partially explored caves, in the hill of the same name, and **Zapotal Lake**.

Santa Rosa de Copán

Santa Rosa de Copán is 170 km from San Pedro Sula, at the near-perfect tropical altitude of 1100 meters. With a church nearly 200 years old, cobblestoned streets and tile-roofed houses, Santa Rosa has a pleasant colonial air, though it was founded only in 1802, not long before independence.

The town is laid back, unhurried, untouristy and has a pleasant colonial inspired downtown which bustles with shoppers who come in from the surrounding villages to pick up provisions. The climate here is decidedly fresh and cool so pack a sweater.

Santa Rosa is at the center of the Honduran Highlands Loop: Copán Ruinas–Santa Rosa de Copán–Gracias–La Esperanza. The area boasts Honduras' highest mountain, hot springs, the indigenous Lenca culture and fine examples of colonial architecture.

Arrivals & Departures
By Bus

Connections to north, south and west are very good from Santa Rosa de Copán. There are buses about every hour to Nueva Ocotepeque, to the south, connecting with small shuttle buses for the Guatemalan border at Agua Caliente. Trade and religious pilgrims follow this route to Esquipulas, just inside

Guatemala. Buses for San Pedro Sula also depart at least every hour, passing the junction for Copán Ruinas at La Entrada. The bus station is on the highway outside of town, a short ride by local bus or taxi. There are also buses to the El Poy border crossing with El Salvador.

Agua Caliente (Guatemala border crossing) to Santa Rosa de Copáan via Nueva Ocotepeque. From Honduran side of customs and immigration checkpoint: Seven departures/day, $2.50, travel time 2-3/4 hours.

Copán Ruinas to Santa Rosa de Copán via La Entrada. From Hotel Posada Honduras: Two departures/day, $2, travel time 3 hours.

Gracias to Santa Rosa de Copan. From central plaza: departures every 90 minutes, US$1, travel time 45 minutes

Nueva Ocotepeque to Santa Rosa de Copán. From Terminal Congolon, main street: Six departures/day, US$2, travel time 2-1/2 hours

San Pedro Sula to Santa Rosa de Copán. From Terminal Toritos y Copanecos, 6 Ave, 8 y 9 Calle, *Tel. 553-4930*: Departures every 30 min, $2, travel time 3-1/2 hours. Four express departures/day, $3.50, travel time 2-1/4 hours

From Terminal Congolon, 8 Avenida 9-10 Calle S.O., *Tel. 553-1174*: 5 departures/day, $2, travel time 3-1/2 hours.

San Salvador, El Salvador to Santa Rosa de Copan via Nueva Ocotepeque. From the King Quality gate at the Puertobus bus terminal: One express departure/day (6:30 a.m.), $23, travel time 5-1/2 hours. This is a through bus to San Pedro Sula, but the driver will let ou off at Santa Rosa by request.

Tegucigalpa to Santa Rosa de Copán via San Pedro Sula From Terminal Sultana, 8 Avenida 11-12 Calle, Comayaguela: Five departures/day, $6, travel time 7-1/2 hours. Transportes Sultana.

Where to Stay

As a stopping point on the main route to Guatemala and the jumping off point to the Western Honduran Highlands, Santa Rosa de Copán has a good supply of reasonably priced rooms.

HOTEL ELVIR, *Calle Real Centenario. Tel. 662-0103, 662-0805, E-mail: hotelelvir@hondutel.hn, web: www.hotelelvir.com. 41 rooms, 2 suites. $15 single/$22 double.*

Newly renovated, restaurant, air-conditioning, bar, pool, cable TV. Next door is the Flor de Copán Factory Outlet Cigar Store.

HOTEL SANTA ROSA, *on main highway near bus terminal, Tel 662-2368, 25 rooms. $26 double.*

New, secure parking.

HOTEL VIP COPÁN, *near the old market, Tel 662-2284, $ 20 double.*

Newly remodled, very nice.

Where to Eat

PIZZA PIZZA, *four blocks east of central plaza on Calle Centenario. Tel 662-1104.*
Besides offering up tasty pizzas, proprietor and American expat Warren Post is a good source of travel information. This is the best place to eat in Santa Rosa. Internet cafe and book exchange on premises. Playground for families traveling with children.

FLAMINGOS, *1/2 block south of the Central Park. Tel. 6620654.*
This restaurant/bar serves beef and seafood at moderately prices. Newly remodeled, this is the place to impress your date in Santa Rosa.

EL RODEO, *1 1/2 blocks south of the Central Park.*
This is the place to eat beef in town as well as the best spot for nightlife with live music most nights.

LILY'S RESTAURANT, *1/2 block west of central plaza.*
French cuisine in a pleasant courtyard.

Seeing the Sights

Tobacco has long been a major crop in the area and world class cigars are made in town. The **Flor de Copán factory** produces some of the world's finest cigars. Cigars are available for sale at the Flor de Copán **Cigar Factory Outlet Store** located two blocks west of the Central Park in the old historic cigar factory building. The new factory is located four blocks east of the bus station. Guided tours in Spanish are available 7:30am-11:30am and 1:30pm - 4:30pm Monday - Friday. There is a charge of $2 per visitor. You can view the entire process of how a handrolled cigar is made. Cigars from this factory are exported to the US and Europe. Among the labels produced here are Don Melo, Sta Rosa, Zino, Mouton Cadet, Petrus and Encanto.

You can also visit a coffee processing facility. The **Beneficio Maya** factory may be visited. Contact Sheri Dunaway, *Tel. 662-1605, 662-0484, Fax 662-0467, web: www.cafecopan.com.* They produce Café Copán and Café San Marcos, of which San Marcos is of superior quality. A pound goes for about $3. For true coffee aficionados, whole bean coffee can be purchased in bulk.

Just as Santa Rosa is famous abroad for its cigars, it is known among Hondurans as a center of cultural activity. The city cultural center, **Casa de la Cultura**, 1/2 block south of the central plaza offers a library, frequent exhibitions, performances, readings, and concerts. Ask about upcoming events. Volunteers are welcome.

Ten minutes outside of town on the road to Gracias is the village of **La Montanita**. There you will find **Doricentro**, a privately operated park mwith water toboggan, swimming and wading pools, light snacks and beverages, picnic areas, and music. An entrance fee of $1.50 includes use of the toboggan and pools. Doricentro is open weekends and holidays.

Further along the road to Gracias is **Las Tres Jotas** (75¢), another private park that is also a working tobacco farm and fishery. Have the bus driver point it out, as the sign on the highway is easy to miss. Aside from picnic areas and wading pools, Las Tres Jotas has the freshest fish you'll eat. Las Tres Jotas is open daily and welcomes overnight campers.

A special time to visit Santa Rosa is during **Easter Week**. During the week before Easter, Santa Rosa presents some of the best processions in the nation. Six in all, the processions are full dress street theater reenactments of the different parts of the Easter story daily beginning Holy Thursday. There's the Incarceration Procession, the Holy Cross Procession, the Funeral and Mourning Processions, the Resurrection Procession, and more.

The most spectacular is undoubtedly the **Holy Cross Procession**, or Via Crucis, on Friday morning. Bearing cross and under guard, Jesus makes his way through the heart of Santa Rosa's historical district along a two kilometer route beautifully decorated with carpets of flowers and colored sawdust in the streets. Because the carpets are ruined by the passage of the procession, you will want to arrive well before the 9am starting time to admire the handiwork of the many Copanecos who have labored since dawn on the decorations.

Another good time to visit Santa Rosa is during the **annual fair** in the last two weeks of August. Dedicated to the local patron saint, Santa Rosa de Lima, there are religious observances, a beauty pageant and coronation, street carnivals, a rodeo, cultural performances, and more.

Lenca Land Trails, in the lobby of Hotel Elvir, *Tel. 662-0805, Tel/Fax 662-0103, E-mail: lenca@hondutel.hn*, is a Santa Rosa-based tour operator who is developing the Western Honduran Highlands as a tourism destination. They can arrange trips to Lenca Indian villages and national parks.

Practical Information
Banks

Banco BGA, one block west of the central plaza on Calle Centenario, changes American Express travelers cheques and provides cash advances on Visa cards. **Banco Atlantida**, facing the central plaza, has an automatic teller machine (ATM) that accepts Visa and Plus cards. Both banks will change U.S. currency to Honduran lempiras.

Doctor

English speaking doctor: Dr. Sohel Rajabian, Clinica Medica Las Gemas, 1/2 blocks north of Hotel Elvir, *Tel. 662-1428.*

Immigration

One block north of central plaza. Tourist visas may be renewed here with much less trouble than in larger cities.

Internet

Cybercafe at Pizza Pizza is a full service Internet cafe offering e-mail and Internet access. Located four blocks east of the central plaza on Calle Centenario, it is open daily except Wednesday 11:30am - 9:00pm. These websites offer a good look at Santa Rosa:

• Guide to Santa Rosa de Copán: *http://sites.netscape.net/srcopan/*
• Santa Rosa de Copán's historic downtown: *http://www.santarosahistorica.org/*
• Cultural center and library: *http://www.srcbiblioteca.f2s.com/*

Laundromat

Laundromat Super Lavanderia Florencia, four blocks west of the central plaza. Closed Sundays.

Post Office & Phone Service

The post office, **Honducor**, faces the central plaza. It is open Monday through Friday 9am to 4pm. A letter or post card bound for the US typically requires two weeks for delivery. The telephone company, **Hondutel**, is next door to the post office. Long distance calls can be placed daily; a three minute call to the US costs $4. Faxes can be sent Monday through Friday.

Spanish Language School

Santa Rosa de Copán Language School, 1 1/2 blocks south of central market. *E-mail: starosalanguage@yahoo.com.*

Travel Information

Your best source of up to date 'gringo trail' travel info is with US expat Warren Post at Pizza Pizza.

Nueva Ocotopeque

Nueva Ocotopeque is just 15 kilometers away from both Guatemala and El Salvador, in piney highlands along the **Lempa River**. The Lempa rises in Guatemala and forms part of the border between Honduras and El Salvador. This area is very beautiful, with lots of pine-clad forests, small isolated villages – but is lacking in tourist services of any kind. To trek out here, come prepared with a 4-wheel drive vehicle, a full tank of gas, a warm sweater and a sense of adventure.

There is a border crossing to El Salvador at El Poy and a border crossing to Guatemala at Agua Caliente. Just on the other side of the Guatemalan frontier is the town of Esquipulas, which houses the most important Catholic religious shrine in Central America – The Black Christ of Esquipulas, which is visited by multitudes of the faithful.

The original town of Ocotepeque was founded in 1830 — its Nahuatl name means "pine hill" — and destroyed by floods on the Marchala River in 1934. Nueva ("new") Ocotepeque was founded the following year, on the site of the village of Sinuapa.

In the short, bitter war of 1969, the army of El Salvador quickly captured Nueva Ocotepeque, but was obliged to retire soon after, under diplomatic pressure.

Montecristo-Trifinio National Park, near Ocotepeque, extends into Guatemala and El Salvador, including the border-marking peak of Montecristo (2419 meters) covering 54 square kilometers of regenerating forest. The absolute reserve above 1800 meters covers 20 square kilometers, most of which is regenerating forest.

The park is currently in a state of development. Access on the Honduran side of the park is dificult; there is better access to the park from the Salvadoran side near the town of Metapan.

Arrivals & Departures
By Bus
Buses leave frequently for the Guatemalan border, and it's also possible to cross to El Salvador and continue to San Salvador, 100 km distant. Guatemala has a consulate in Nueva Ocotepeque.

Where To Stay
HOTEL MAYA CHORTÍ, *Tel. 653-3377. $21 double.*
A full service hotel with all the conveniences.

HOTEL SANDOVAL, *Tel. 653-3098, E-mail: hotelsan@hondutel.hn. $25 double.*

The Sandoval offers cable TV, hot water, pool, sauna & jacuzzi, and a restaurant.

Gracias

Gracias, high in the pine country of southwest Honduras, was founded in 1536 by Gonzalo de Alvarado, brother of the conqueror of Guatemala, and for a time was the base from which the valley of Comayagua was subdued. The name of the town is a shortened form of the phrase of thanksgiving, "*gracias a Dios.*"

Gracias saw its moment of glory several hundred years ago. In 1544, the Audiencia de los Confines, then the governing council for all of Central America, was briefly based here. But Gracias soon lost all importance. The trade route from Guatemala passed to the west. The silver mines were in

Tegucigalpa to the southeast. And the regional capital settled in Comayagua, to the northeast, once the rebellious chief Lempira was subdued.

This early loss of face, though, had the effect of preserving some of the town's colonial heritage. Three colonial churches survive, along with the Casa de los Leones, one of the first buildings in Gracias, named for the heraldic lions that decorate its doorway. Old fortifications above the town can be visited as well, and there are some excellent **hot springs** nearby, about 6 km (15 minutes by pickup or taxi, $5 one-way, $9 round-trip per car load; one hour walk) outside of Gracias. There is no regular transport to the springs, which are open from 6am-8pm. Admission is $1.25 cents. There is a restaurant here selling light snacks.

And overlooking Gracias from the west is the peak of **Celaque** ("cold water" in Nahuatl, the language of the Indian allies of the conquistadors), at 2849 meters (9350 feet) the highest mountain in Honduras.

Arrivals & Departures

By Bus

Gracias can be reached via frequent buses from Santa Rosa de Copán, 2 hours, hourly from 5am - 4:30pm. Direct buses to Santa Rosa de Copán from San Pedro Sula with Toritos y Copanecos. Direct bus from Copán Ruinas to Santa Rosa de Copán or take direct bus from Copán Ruinas to San Pedro Sula, get off bus at La Entrada and catch the San Pedro Sula to Santa Rosa Bus (Toritos y Copanecos) as it makes a stop in La Entrada.

There are no buses to La Esperanza. Pickups leave every hour from the bus terminal in Gracias, 1 block south of main square and go as far as San Juan which is 1/2 way to La Esperanza. From San Juan there are less regular pickups to La Esperanza. It's no problem to reach La Esperanza in one day if you leave early in the morning. By car it's 2 1/2 hours on a good dirt road.

Where to Stay

HOTEL GUANCASCOS, *3 blocks south of bus terminal at the foot of San Cristobal Fort, Tel/Fax 656-1219, E-mail: fronica@tutopia.com. 11 rooms, $20 double.*

Private hot water bath, large windows, telephone and TV in room, garden, restaurant/bar, secure parking, travel info, credit cards accepted, camping gear for rent, English, Spanish, Dutch spoken, Dutch-owned. Recommended.

POSADA DE DON JUAN, *half- block down from Banco de Occidente. Tel. 6561020, 23 rooms, $20 double. Secure parking.*

Rooms come with hot water, cable TV, air-conditioning.

HOTEL PATRICIA, *1 1/2 blks west of main square, Tel. 656-1281. 6 rooms. $20 double. secure parking.*

Private hot water bath, TV, air-conditioning.

ECO LODGE VILLA VERDE, *8 km from Gracias at the border of Celaque National Park, get information at Hotel Guancascos.*
Two basic comfortable cabins.

Where to Eat

GUANCASCOS RESTAURANT, *located at Hotel Guancascos.*
The best place to eat in town. International and typical foods, bottled water used for cooking, great view over town, breakfast, lunch, dinner, bar, reasonable prices, great atmosphere.
LA FONDA, *on main square.*
Typical foods
LA GALERA, *next to Hotel Patricia.*
Typical snacks.
VILLA DE ADA, *500 meters from hospital.*
In a beautiful spot, the house specialty is farm-raised fish. Lunch and dinner served. Recommended.

Nightlife & Entertainment

Gracias is a laid back, untouristy kind of place. For nightlife the only place in town is **K'Nelos**, which does triple duty as a disco/restaurant/bar.

Excursions & Day Trips

Celaque National Park takes in the largest cloud forest in Honduras on Celaque mountain, and also the richest, its diversity protected by the steep slopes that have resisted cut-and-burn agriculture over the centuries. Among endangered mammals that inhabit the park are ocelots, peccaries, pumas and jaguars. Quetzals and linnets are among resident bird species. There is even wild cattle.

The park is developed for visitors. Trails, visitors center, campsites. Information at Hotel Guancascos. The main trail is well marked. A recommended day trip involves 5 hours of hiking, 3 hours up and 2 hours down, passing small streams and pine forest. Hike to the cloud forest involves heavy hiking, 5 hours up and 3 hours down. Recommended to start hike early, by 7am. Hike to the top of Mt Celaque is a 2-day trip, there are two campsites on the way up, pack in all supplies, camping gear rental at Hotel Guancascos. Transport to park from Gracias, $2-$10 per person depending on number of passengers in pickup, or walk, 1 hour. Meals available at Dona Alejandra's at the visitors center.

The most direct access route to the park is from Gracias along the road to the hydroelectric station; there is also a trail to the peak from Belén Gualcho, to the west. Celaque mountain is the highest point in Honduras at 2,849 meters. The hike to the summit is rough and takes about 6 hours. Pack in all supplies. Temperatures get cold and rain is frequent at higher altitudes, so this is a trip for the adventurous and those in good shape.

The mountain village of **La Campa** is 16 km from Gracias. With its beautifully rugged, mountain setting, La Campa is famous for its rustic ceramics, which still enjoy day-to-day use in the mountain villages of the Lenca Highlands, and its lovely colonial church. **San Manuel Colohete**, 16 km beyond La Campa, boasts a beautiful colonial church as well. This is a very remote and friendly area of the Highlands, seldom visited by tourists.

There is a **visitors center** 8 km from Gracias, a half-hour walk inside the park, with a good topographic map on display. You can also stay overnight here; there's a dorm available with 7 beds, cooking facilities, and shower. You need to bring food, sleeping bag, and all supplies. Warm clothing is recommended.

Mt. Puca, at 2,300 meters, is close to Gracias. You can hike up to see cloud forest and wildlife.

Special interest tours are available to coffee farms, sugar cane mills, milk processing, and bee keeping. Check with Candido at Hotel Guancascos, *Tel/ Fax 656-1219*.

La Esperanza & Intibucá

La Esperanza is the administrative center of the department of Intibucá. Adjacent is the town of **Intibucá**, for the most part populated by Lenca Indians who still maintain their traditional ways: communal land ownership, and *guancascos*, exchange visits of saints at town fiesta times, among other customs.

La Esperanza and Intibucá are located at over 1600 meters, on a plateau that is still partly forested, and timber is one of the main products of the region. The cool climate and old adobe houses with thick walls lend a remote, old-time air. Sunday is the traditional market day, when country people come to town to sell their wares, much in the manner of Indian villages in Guatemala.

La Gruta, once a penal colony, contains an altar to the Virgin of Lourdes. Nearby are public swimming areas. A few kilometers out, at **La Posona**, is a dam with fishing, and boats for rent.

Arrivals & Departures
By Bus
La Esperanza is 86 kilometers by gravel road from the main Tegucigalpa-San Pedro Sula highway at Siguatepeque. There is usually one daily bus from the capital (4 Calle, 8/9 Avenidas, Comayagüela), and one from San Pedro Sula. Buses leave at the break of day for Tegucigalpa, San Pedro Sula and Comayagua.

Marcala

Marcala, 35 km southeast of La Esperanza on the way to El Salvador, is one of the centers of coffee growing in Honduras. Some of Honduras' finest SHG (Strictly High Grown Coffee) is grown here.

It's a pleasant center with a main square shaded by full-grown trees. The ridge of mountains to the east shelters several communities of indigenous Lenca who have maintained their traditional ways over the centuries.

Chapter 16

South to the Coast

Southern Honduras has been all but ignored by tourists. If you are seeking an off-the-beaten-track destination, the South Coast may be for you.

You leave Tegucigalpa on a road through hilly country, climbing to **Sabana Grande**. There are good views of high plateaus. The vegetation changes to pines, and it is fresh and windy as you gain altitude. From the heights, before long, you can see the Gulf of Fonseca in the distance, as you begin to wind down through hilly and broken terrain toward the Pacific Ocean.

Once in the low country, you follow the course of the Nacaome River. At **Pespire**, right along the river, there is a church with silver domes, impressive and unexpected. Pespire ("pyrite river") is an old town, founded in 1640.

You reach the Pan American Highway at **Jicaro Galán**. Here you can stay at the **Turicentro Oasis**, *25 rooms, Tel. 881-2220, $25 single/$30 double, $40 for four persons.* A full-fledged motel and highway resort, getting on in years but well maintained, with air-conditioning, pool, restaurant, and cable television. Arrangements can be made for horseback riding, and fishing in the Gulf of Fonseca. The restaurant here serves a range of seafood and steak main courses, as well as sandwiches and salads, at a top price of about $7. If you're driving through the area, you can stop and use the pool at a charge of a dollar or so a person; or for free, if you order something in the restaurant.

A right turn there takes you to **Nacaome** ("double flesh," signifying two founding Indian nations), six kilometers onward on the way to El Salvador. Nacaome officially dates from 1535 as a town, though it was a major indigenous settlement long before. Nacaome is on a strategic invasion route: in 1844, the Honduran army defeated the Nicaraguans here. There is a colonial church in Nacaome, and there are two hot springs within walking distance.

Goascoran is the town near the border of El Salvador — El Amatillo lies on the other side. Silver was once mined nearby. Goascarán has the most basic of accommodations. Buses run frequently to the border from the Belén market in Comayagüela.

The Gulf of Fonseca

Five kilometers onward from Jícaro Galán toward the east is the intersection for **Tigre Island**. Three volcanoes are visible, one each in Nicaragua and El Salvador, and one on Tigre Island itself (see below).

Namasique, near the gulf, was a field of battle in the 1907 war with Nicaragua, and saw the first use of machine guns in Central America.

The Gulf of Fonseca, famous for its extensive coastal mangrove forests, is the huge inlet of the Pacific Ocean bordered by El Salvador, Nicaragua and Honduras. Of 288 islands in the gulf — most of them Honduran, some awarded to El Salvador in a recent border arbitration — **Zacate Grande** ("tall grass") is the largest, adjacent to the mainland and reached by bridge. **Isla de Pájaros,** "bird island," has what you would expect: lots of birds. And the treasures of Sir Francis Drake and other pirates are buried along the many beaches in the gulf, if you believe what people say.

The area under and around the gulf seethes with volcanic activity, and the great Central American volcanic ridge marches right across the water. Cosigüina Volcano, nearby in Nicaragua, 859 meters high, erupted spectacularly in 1838. On the Salvadoran side is Conchagua Volcano, 1243 meters high. **El Tigre Island**, between the two, is a volcano.

Amapala

Amapala, on El Tigre Island, reached by motor launch from the end of the road, was for most of the history of Honduras the major Pacific port of the country, and once the locale of major intrigue. Britain occupied El Tigre Island in 1849 to make a point about debts owed by Honduras, an action that stirred the ire of the United States, not to mention that of the locals.

Now that modern container facilities have been built near San Lorenzo, off the Pan American Highway, Amapala is on the way to becoming a ghost town, with some of the lost-in-time atmosphere that clings to the old mining towns near Tegucigalpa. Amapala's **beaches** are sticky, dark volcanic sand, and little-frequented, except at holiday times.

The ascent of the island-volcano is relatively easy as volcano-climbing goes. There are magnificent views on the hike up, all the way to El Salvador, Nicaragua, and mainland Honduras – all three nations can be seen at once. The views of distant volcanos in El Salvador and Nicaragua are awe inspiring. Sunsets over the Gulf of Fonseca are spectacular, some of the best anywhere.

Arrivals & Departures

To reach Amapala, take a bus from Tegucigalpa toward Choluteca, and get off at the road junction before San Lorenzo. Pickup-taxis take passengers to the strait at El Coyolito, where skiffs can be hired for the short trip across to the island.

There are irregular launches to La Union in El Salvador. Another possibility is to ask around with local fishermen and hitch a ride (for the truly adventurous ony). There is an immigration office in Amapala.

Where to Stay

Accommodations are limited, but try one of the following:
HOTEL PLAYA NEGRA, *Tel. 898-8580, Fax 238-2457.*

This is the best hotel on the island. Rooms have air conditioning. There's a pool and restaurant.

Other budget possibilities include **Hotel Playa Blanca**, **Hotel Al Mar**, and **Pensión Internacional**, which also offers meals.

Moving East

Oxcarts appear from the fields. Huts are primitive. It all seems out of the Middle Ages, until suddenly you are at the impressive suspension bridge at the entrance to Choluteca over a muddy river.

Choluteca

Choluteca is the major city of the south, 142 kilometers from Tegucigalpa, with a population of over 50,000. The Cholula Indians of Mexico might have known or settled the area, lending their name to the city. Spanish dispatches mention Choluteca as early as 1522, for the wealth of its mines. The city was renamed in 1585 as Jérez de la Frontera de Choluteca, after a city in Spain, and had nicknames that referred to tamarind-sized gold nuggets mined nearby. It was also an indigo-producing center around the time of independence, until that market collapsed with the development of synthetic dyes.

Choluteca lies on a vast alluvial plain guarded by mountains, which, like few other parts of southern Honduras, is suitable for large-scale agriculture.

You'll see herds of cattle guided by cowboys. Sugar cane is also evident. The dry and hot area also produces excellent melons. The rainy season here is mainly from May to September. Cultivated shrimp farming has also become a major industry in the area in recent years. The **Granja San Bernadino**, 10 miles from Choluteca, may be toured.

Though there are no particular activities in town for visitors, Choluteca is clean and pleasant enough, a transit point with good accommodations. It used to be the main base for dove hunting, but no longer – the sport is now prohibited at all times.

Arrivals & Departures
By Bus
Service is very efficient between Tegucigalpa and Choluteca. There are hourly buses throughout the day, until 6pm. Some buses continue to San Marcos de Colón, to the east. From there, you can pick up another bus to the Nicaraguan border, and continue to Managua, if you happen to be headed that way.

From Tegucigalpa, buses leave from the Mi Esperanza station, 6 Avenida, 24/25 Calles, Comayagüela, *Tel. 238-2863*. Service is every hour from 6 a.m. The ride takes about three hours, the ticket costs less than $2.

There are several other companies as well that serve this route, including **Transportes Dandy**, 20 Calle, 6/7 Avenidas, Comayagüela, with departures every two hours. In Choluteca, the Mi Esperanza station, one block from the Pan American Highway, has a restaurant and hotel, neither especially recommendable.

These buses will also drop you at the turn for Cedeño beach.

Where to Stay
HACIENDA GUALIQUEME, *on Pan American Highway at entrance to Choluteca. Tel. 882-2760, 8823620. $65 double.*
Without doubt the best hotel in town. Pretty gardens, restaurant, horseback riding, tennis, racketball.

HOTEL PIERRE, *Avenida Valle, Barrio El Centro, Tel. 882-0676. 29 rooms. $12 single/$17 double with fan, $20 single/$25 double with air conditioning.*
Centrally located, very clean, opposite the market downtown. Friendly personnel, well-maintained and recommended. Protected parking.

HOTEL LA FUENTE, *Pan American Highway, Tel. 882-0263, 882-0253, Fax 882-0273. 45 rooms, $29 single/$42 double. American Express, Master Card, Visa.*
This is the best-known hotel in Choluteca, with a nice interior garden with pool. Rooms are air-conditioned and clean, and there are a bar and restaurant, but facilities and furniture are getting on in years, with doubtful maintenance. If you stay elsewhere in town, you can use the pool and garden here for a

minimal fee. Some rooms get the noise of the Restaurant Charley, a popular local hangout.

Where to Eat

There aren't too many places to eat here. At the **Hotel Pierre**, the coffee shop is clean, and provides honest meals for $4 and less. Nearby is **Pizza Taste**, run by the owner of the Pierre. The restaurant in the **Hotel La Fuente** is somewhat more elaborate. And the **Charley Restaurant**, next to Hotel La Fuente, a beer garden (*jardín cervecero*) serving grilled meats accompanied by music, is the in place in town, open only from 7pm to 11pm.

The **Camino Real hotel** on the eastern outskirts is a favorite meal stop for drivers. There's a sheltered dining patio, as well as an air-conditioned restaurant. Seafood and sandwiches are served, with most dishes priced under $4 — a good deal, indeed. And the fruit drinks are refreshing in the local heat.

Seeing the Sights

Newly restored is the house of **José Cecilio del Valle**, one of authors of the declaration of independence of Central America, near the Cathedral opposite Valle Park. There's a cultural center in the colonial church of La Merced, which dates from 1643, with some exhibits, usually by local artists. Construction of the suspension bridge over the Choluteca River was started in 1935 and completed in 1937. And there is also a correspondence university in town.

Directly east of Choluteca, at **El Corpus**, about 15 kilometers down a dirt road, is the **Poza de Ocampo**, a noted local swimming hole.

Cedeno

Cedeño is located along the Gulf of Fonseca about 35 km from Choluteca. The gulf has unlimited beaches, the waves are not too big, and the water is warm. And there are no dangerous currents, as at the more exposed beaches elsewhere on this coast. The village and beach are crowded on weekends, especially on Sundays. The beaches here are of dark volcanic sand and the surf is rough.

Cedeño is more a fishing village than the beach resort (*"balneario"*) that it is claimed to be. There are some hotels, but all are dirty. If you want to stay here, you'd do better to camp outside of the village. Ask permission of the owner of any desirable site.

Many small eateries serve fresh fish and shrimp at a myriad of small, beachside *champas* (thatched roof shacks). It's really pleasant to enjoy your meal and look out to the fishermen landing the catch in narrow boats. People around here are of more Indian descent than others in the interior of the country. Houses along the beach are on stilts, and everything looks ready to fall down.

Arrivals & Departures
By Bus or Taxi
Buses run from the Choluteca market to Cedeño about every hour, and the trip takes about 90 minutes. Or, you can go in a taxi for about $15 for as many passengers as will fit in. From Tegucigalpa, there are direct buses from the Mercado Mayoreo (wholesale market) at 3:30am and 1:30pm. These take about three and a half hours.

By Car
By car, Cedeño is about 33 kilometers off the Pan American Highway, via a paved, flat road. Along the way you get a view of oxcarts, melon and sugarcane fields, sugar processing plants, and salt pans, where sea water is evaporated.

Punta Ratón Wildlife Reserve
Up the gulf, reached by a road that branches from the road to Cedeño, is the **Punta Ratón Wildlife Reserve**, just south of the village of Punta Ratón. Giant sea turtles nest here from August into November.

Other wildlife sighted in the dense forest and along the narrow strip of beach and overhead includes sea birds, parrots, doves, pelicans, and iguanas.

Guasaule
Guasaule is the town on the Pan American Highway at the border with Nicaragua. There are no accommodations of note. Local buses run from Choluteca. Arrive by 3pm if planning to continue into Nicaragua.

San Marcos de Colon, to the northeast of Choluteca, is higher up, at an elevation of almost 900 meters. About ten kilometers to the east is **El Espino**, on the border of Nicaragua.

From Tegucigalpa, buses for San Marcos leave from the Mi Esperanza station, 6 Avenida, 24/25 Calles, Comayagüela, about every two hours.

East of Tegucigalpa
What with Contra training camps and border skirmishes, the road to **Danlí**, 108 kilometers east of Tegucigalpa, was little traveled except by those

with a military stake in the area, and foreign journalists. With the outbreak of peace in Nicaragua and along the border, there is now no reason for others to stay away. There's a beautiful colonial church here. Danlí is the most important cigar-producing town in Honduras, with many fine brands made here.

The road to Danlí passes **San Antonio de Oriente** and **El Zamorano**, both easily reached on day excursions from Tegucigalpa. Zamorano is home to a world famous agricultural school. Their installations can be toured and it is possible to spend the night.

Yuscaran, "place of the house of flowers" (in Nahuatl), off the Danlí highway to the south, is an ex-mining town, picturesque like other, similar towns that have been left behind economically. Founded around 1730 as a base for exploiting the Quemazones and Guayabillas mines, it retains some old buildings, including the Fortín house, a nineteenth-century residence open daily to the public. Yuscarán is the home of the famous *guaro* distillery. For the unititiated, *guaro* is the Honduran version of distilled 'white lightning.' Tours of the factory can be arranged, just stop in and ask.

Monserrat Cloud Forest Reserve is located near Yuscaran. **Güinope**, to the southwest of Yuscarán, is known for its orange groves.

Danlí

Danlí ("sandy stream" in Nahuatl), founded in 1667, is the major town of the area directly east of Tegucigalpa, where sugar, tobacco and coffee are produced. Located at an altitude of 700 meters, about four hours from the capital by bus, it offers fair accommodations, and surroundings of piney hills. Danlí's corn festival is celebrated the last week of August to honor the staff of life in Central America, with corn stew (*pozole*), corn beverages (*atol*), corn hooch (*chicha*), corn tortillas, and corn cakes, along with rodeos and bull-fights.

Danlí is the center for Honduras' flourishing cigar industry. High quality tobacco is grown nearby and there are a number of factories turning out fine hand-rolled cigars for export. Tours of cigar factories can be arranged by just showing up.

The road south from Danlí heads toward Estelí in Nicaragua.

Arrivals & dDepartures

Buses of the **Discua Litena** company, *Tel. 232-7939*, serve Danlí from the Jacaleapa market in Tegucigalpa, on the road to Colonia Kennedy, about five km from downtown. Also **Emtraoriente**, 6 Calle, 6/7 Avenida, Comayagüela, *Tel. 237-8965*, 6 departures from 6:30am to 4:30pm for Danlí and Paraíso, farther south.

Transportation is available several times an hour to the Nicaraguan border at Las Manos, about 30 km to the south.

Facilities in Danlí include several banks (Banco Atlántida, Banco Central de Honduras, Banco Sogerin).

where to stay

GRAN HOTEL GRANADA, *Tel. 883-2499, Fax 883-2774. 36 rooms, $12 per person.*

A motel on the way out toward Tegucigalpa. Bar and restaurant, air-conditioned rooms, pool.

Northeast of Tegucigalpa

The **Olancho Highway** runs north from Tegucigalpa through mountains, and then northeast through hills in the vast grasslands of Olancho department. **Cedros**, 85 km from Tegucigalpa, on a spur from the Olancho road, is a mining town where the first constitutional congress of Honduras was held in 1824.

Juticalpa

Juticalpa ("place of snails" in Nahuatl) is the major town of Olancho department. The first Spanish settlement in this part of Honduras, it was founded by refugees from the original settlement of San Jorge de Olancho, which was destroyed by a volcanic eruption in 1611 (other refugees founded Olanchito, farther to the north).

Juticalpa and environs are the Wild West of Honduras, a sparsely settled frontier area with its own traditions. Horseback riders use a peculiar saddle with heavy, shoe-like stirrups to which a lasso is tied. Gold has been mined since colonial times, and panned along the Guayape River. In addition to cattle ranches, sugar and grains are planted.

If you arrive around Easter Week, you'll see the **Miss Coyol Pageant**, celebrating the season of Coyol, which is a local drink made from the sap of the Coyol palm native only to the Juticalpa area.

Nearby is the **La Muralla Los Higuerales Wildlife Reserve**, located near La Union, south of Juticalpa (one of Honduras' most spectacular national parks). It's a quetzal habitat and has lots of wildlife and virgin tropical forest. There's a visitors center to help you get oriented.

Arrivals & Departures

Juticalpa is about three hours by bus from Tegucigalpa. **Empresa Aurora** buses depart about every hour from 8 Calle, 6/7 Avenidas, Comayagüela. Ask also about the new Discovery bus service in town, which is said to have more modern buses.

The main road continues northeast from Juticalpa to Catacamas and Dulce Nombre de Culmí, and up to the Caribbean lowlands, reaching the coast at Iriona. Another road heads to the northwest, then runs almost parallel with the former road, before turning to the northwest to terminate in Trujillo. At least one bus runs daily along this route – a full day's journey away. Another track runs to the northwest, over wild, sparsely inhabited mountains and down toward Olanchito and the department of Yoro.

Catacamas

Catacamas, site of a government agricultural school, has a few plain hotels, among them the **Juan Carlos**, the **Central**, and the **Catacamas**. Some buses from Tegucigalpa for Juticalpa continue to Catacamas.

Further East

Sierra de Agalta National Park lies 50 km northeast of Juticalpa and about 20 km north of Catacamas. Included in the park's boundaries are the Agalta Ridge, with peaks as high as 2500 meters, one of the largest expanses of dwarf forest in Honduras, and numerous caves. Unique to the park is the *choloepus hoffmanni*, a species of two-toed sloth.

Dormitories, trails and campsites are being readied. For information on the current state of facilities, inquire at COHDEFOR, the forestry department, in Juticalpa.

The **Talgua Cave**, undeveloped for visitors, lies five km from Catacamas along the main highway. Also known as The Cave of The Glowing Skulls, it's currently closed to visitors while archaeologist James Brady undertakes exploration of the site. The cave and the surrounding area is the largest pre-Maya site found to date in Honduras, dating from 3000 to 3,500 years ago.

Dulce Nombre de Culmi, on the edge of the northeastern wilderness of Honduras, was a colonial settlement, from which the Spanish attempted to raid the English trading post at Black River on the Caribbean.

h o n d u r a s   m i s c e l l a n y

Chapter 17

Billiards

This can seem to be the national entertainment. There are *billares* in every city and town. Billiards is a men's game – women are not tolerated in pool halls.

Fiestas

In addition to national holidays, every town has its own local celebration day, usually in honor of its patron saint. In some Indian towns of the west, fiestas are rich in religious tradition. Elsewhere, they are revelry with no excuses, a break from humdrum existence, with beauty contests, dances, and always lots of drinking. Itinerant purveyors of mechanical games, cotton candy and religious trinkets eke out a living by following the fiesta route from town to town.

Here's a compiled list of town fiestas, usually giving the main day, though festivities can last for up to a week. Many of these towns are not mentioned elsewhere in this book. The department (*departamento*, or province) is listed to help you find each place.

January

1: Dulce Nombre de Culmí, Olanchi. 6: La Unión, Copán; Fraternidad, Ocotepeque. 14: San Juan, La Paz; San Antonio de Oriente, Francisco Morazán; 15: Cedros, Francisco Morazán; Esquías, Comayagua; El Triunfo, Choluteca; Liure, El Paraíso; San Lucas, Paraíso; Intibucá, Intibucá; San Juan, Intibucá; Opatorio, La Paz; San Juan, La Paz; San Manuel Colohete, Lempira; Esquipulas del Norte, Olancho; Guayape, Olancho; Gualala, Santa Bárbara;

Langue, Valle; Jocón, Yoro; Victoria, Yoro. 18: Morocelí, Paraíso. 20: San Sebastián, Comayagua; Pespire, Choluteca; Alauca, Paraíso; Danlí, Paraíso; Marale, Francisco Morazán; Ojojona, Francisco Morazán; Reitoca, Francisco Morazán; Colomoncagua, Intibucá; Erandique, Lempira; San Sebastián, Lempira; Aramecina, Valle; Olanchito, Yoro. 20: Santa Lucía, Francisco Morazán; 21: Jesús de Otoro, Intibucá. 25: Cedeño, Choluteca; Siguatepeque, Comayagua; Soledad, Paraíso; Ceguaca, Santa Bárbara.

February

2: Tegucigalpa: Virgin of Suyapa, Patron Saint of Honduras; Duyure, Choluteca; Comayagua, Comayagua (Virgin of Candelaria); Humuya, Comayagua; El Corpus, Choluteca; Jacaleapa, Paraíso; Sabanagrande, Francisco Morazán; Villa de San Francisco, Francisco Morazán; San Antonio, La Paz; Yarula, La Paz; Candelaria, Lempira; Cololaca, Lempira; Sesenti, Ocotepeque; Salamá, Olancho; Santa María del Real, Olancho; San Francisco de Ojuera, Santa Bárbara; Sensentí, Ocotepeque; Goascarán, Valle. 9: Concepción del Sur, Santa Bárbara. 11: Veracruz, Copán; Choloma, Cortés; Ilama, Santa Bárbara. 14: San Matías, Paraíso; La Campa, Lempira. 24: San Jerónimo, Copán. 28: Santa Fé, Ocotepeque; Concordia, Olancho.

Third Saturday: Paraíso, Paraíso (coffee festival).

March

4: La Unión, Lempira. 7: Concepción del Sur, Santa Bárbara. 8: Mapulaca, Lempira. 19: San José de Comayagua; Copán Ruinas; Florida, Copán; Morolica, Choluteca; San José, Choluteca; Oropolí, Paraíso; San José, La Paz; Piraera, Lempira; Ocotepeque, Ocotepeque; Lucerna, Ocotepeque; San José de Colinas, Santa Bárbara; Nacaome, Valle; Alianza, Valle; Barrio Buenos Aires, Tegucigalpa. 25: San Elena, La Paz (Dance of Los Negritos). 25-April 2: Intibucá (provincial fair).

Moveable: Holy Week.

April

18-23: French Harbour, Bay Islands. 23: San Jorge, Ocotepeque. 25: San Jerónimo, Copán; San Marcos de la Sierra, Intibucá; Dolores Merendón, Ocotepeque; San Marcos, Ocotepeque; San Marcos, Santa Bárbara; Taulabé, Comayagua.

May

3: Tela and Triunfo de la Cruz, Atlántida (Holy Cross); Trinidad, Copán; Santa Cruz de Yojoa; San Miguel Guancapla, Intibucá; San Pedro Tutule, La Paz; Guarita, Lempira; Santa Cruz, Lempira; Sinuapa, Ocotepeque; El Rosario, Olancho; Manto, Olancho; Atima, Santa Bárbara; Gualala, Santa Bárbara; Amapala, Valle. 8: Macuelizo, Santa Bárbara. 13: San Francisco de la Paz,

Olancho. 15: La Ceiba, Atlántida (May 8-23) (major Carnival celebrations, with fireworks, music, and general mischief); Concepción de María, Choluteca; Tocoa, Colón; San Isidro, Choluteca; Güinope, Paraíso; Lepaterique, Francisco Morazán; San Isidro, Intibucá. 20: Concepción del Norte, Santa Bárbara; 22: Sabá, Colón; Santa Rita, Copán; Santa Rita, Santa Bárbara; Morazán, Yoro; Santa Rita, Yoro. 28: La Trinidad, Comayagua; Ojos de Agua, Comayagua; Trinidad, Copán; Trinidad, Santa Bárbara. 25: El Corpus, Choluteca. 30: San Fernando, Ocotepeque; Omoa, Cortés. Yuscarán, Paraíso (mango fair);

June
3: Nueva Armenia, Francisco Morazán; San Isidro, Choluteca. 6: Fraternidad, Ocotepeque. 13: Tela, Atlántida; Minas de Oro, Comayagua; Villa de San Antonio, Comayagua; Cabañas, Copán; San Antonio, Copán; San Pedro, Copán; Veracruz, Copán; San Antonio de Cortés; San Antonio de Flores, Choluteca; San Antonio de Flores, Paraíso; La Venta, Francisco Morazán; Maraita, Francisco Morazán; San Antonio de Oriente, Francisco Morazán; Masaguara, Intibucá; San Antonio, Intibucá; Erandique, Lempira; Vallodolid, Lempira; Ocotepeque, Ocotepeque; El Níspero, Santa Bárbara. 21: Balfate, Colón (Garífuna); San Luis, Comayagua. 24: El Porvenir, Atlántida; La Entrada, Copán; Trujillo, Colón (Garífuna); La Unión, Copán; Nueva Arcadia, Copán; San Juan de Opoa, Copán; Yuscarán, Paraíso; Paraíso, Paraíso; San Juan de Flores, Francisco Morazán; San Marcos de la Sierra, Intibucá; La Paz, La Paz; San Juan, La Paz; San Juan Garita, Lempira; La Labor, Ocotepeque; Juticalpa, Olancho; Guarizama, Olancho; Quimistán, Santa Bárbara. 29: San Pedro, Copán; San Pedro Sula, Cortés; Apacilagua, Choluteca; Nuevo Celilac, Santa Bárbara; Yorito, Yoro.

July
15: San Buenaventura, Francisco Morazán; 16: Santa Fé , Colón; La Virtud, Lempira; San Francisco, Lempira; El Negrito, Yoro. 20: Magdalena, Intibucá. 22: Oak Ridge (José Santos Guardiola), Bay Islands, discovery of America. 22-29: La Esperanza, Intibucá (potato festival). 25: La Jigua, Copán; Camasca, Intibucá; Santa Elena, La Paz; San José, Ocotepeque; Lepaterique, Francisco Morazán; Santiago Puringla, La Paz; Lepaera, Lempira; Piraera, Lempira; Yoro, Yoro. 26: La Ceiba, Atlántida (milk festival); La Libertad, Comayagua; Meambar, Comayagua; San Marcos de Colón, Choluteca; Santa Ana de Yusguare, Choluteca; Yauyupe, Paraíso; Santa Ana, Francisco Morazán; Santa Ana, La Paz; Campamento, Olancho; Guata, Olancho. 31: Roatán (Coxen's Hole), Bay Islands.
Third Sunday: Yuscarán (mango and zapote festival)

August
2: San Ignacio, Francisco Morazán. 10: Alubaren, Francisco Morazán; San

Lorenzo, Valle. 15: Esparta, Atlántida; Jutiapa, Atlántida; Sonaguera, Colón; Corquán, Copán; Santa Rita, Copán; Pimienta, Cortés; Puerto Cortés, Cortés; Marcovia, Choluteca; El Porvenir, Francisco Morazán; Utila, Bay Islands; Opatoro, La Paz; Santa María, La Paz. 21: La Iguala, Lempira; Arada, Santa Bárbara; Chinda, Santa Bárbara; Naranjito, Santa Bárbara. 24: Namasigüe, Choluteca; Talgua, Lempira; Villanueva, Cortés. 28: San Agustín, Copán. 30: La Masica, Atlántida; Santa Rosa de Aguán; El Triunfo, Choluteca; Santa Rosa de Copán; La Lima, Cortés; Guaimica, Francisco Morazán.
Last Saturday of August: Danlí, Paraíso (Corn festival);

September
8: San José del Potrero, Comayagua; Erandique, Lempira. 10: San Nicolás, Copán; El Progreso, Yoro. 11-17: Olanchito, Yoro. 12: Dulce Nombre de Culmí, Olancho; Dulce Nombre, Copán. 24: Veracruz, Copán; Aguanqueterique, La Paz; Mercedes, Ocotepeque; San Esteban, Olancho; Arenal, Yoro. 16: San Manuel, Cortés; 28: San Jerónimo, Comayagua. 29: Tegucigalpa, Francisco Morazán; Potrerillos, Cortés; San Miguelito, Francisco Morazán; Dolores, Intibucá; San Miguel Guancapla, Intibucá; Marcala, La Paz; San Rafael, Lempira; Macuelizo, Santa Bárbara.

October
4: San Francisco, Atlántida; Dolores, Copán; Texiguat, Paraíso; Orica, Francisco Morazán; Reitoca, Francisco Morazán; Cabañas, La Paz; Cane, La Paz; Chinacla, La Paz; San Francisco, Lempira; Santa Cruz, Lempira; Tambla, Lempira; San Francisco del Valle, Ocotepeque; La Unión, Olancho; San Francisco de Becerra, Olancho; Azacualpa, Santa Bárbara; San Francisco de Yojoa; Tatumbla, Francisco Morazán; Valle de Angeles, Francisco Morazán; Catacamas, Olancho. 8: El Rosario, Comayagua; El Rosario, Olancho; Belén, Lempira. 17: Amapala, Valle (fish festival) 18: San Lucas, Paraíso. 19: Piraera, Lempira.

November
4: Paraíso, Paraíso; La Paz, La Paz. 24: La Libertad, Francisco Morazán; 24; Mercedes, La Paz. 30: Orocuina, Choluteca.

December
4: Las Flores, Lempira; La Virtud, Lempira; Santa Bárbara, Santa Bárbara. 8: Limón, Colón; Lamaní, Comayagua; Teupasenti, Paraíso; Concepción, Copán; Cucuyagua, Copán; Concepción de María, Choluteca; Choluteca, Choluteca; Yuscarán, Paraíso; Potrerillos, Paraíso; La Esperanza, Intibucá; Concepción, Intibucá; Gracias, Lempira; Gualcince, Lempira; San Manuel Colohete, Lempira; Tambla, Lempira; Concepción, Ocotepeque; Juticalpa, Olancho; Santa Bárbara, Santa Bárbara; Yoro, Yoro; El Progreso, Yoro; Sulaco,

Yoro. 12: Comayagua, Comayagua; Comayagüela (Virgin of Guadalupe); La Labor, Ocotepeque. 13: Gracias, Lempira; Santa Lucía, Francisco Morazán; Santa Lucía, Intibucá; Yamaranguila, Intibucá; Virginia, Lempira. 18: Lejamaní, Comayagua; Tomala, Lempira. 19: Caridad, Valle. 25: Lamaní, Comayagua; Puerto Lempira, Gracias a Dios; Brus Laguna, Gracias a Dios; Belén Gualcho, Ocotepeque; 25-28, Minas de Oro, Comayagua.

Fireworks

Fireworks are great toys in Honduras for children of all ages. They're sold to kids to play with, and some devices are as big as dynamite sticks, with equivalent sounds. You don't want to be around when one explodes, but sometimes it's hard to avoid. You'll hear explosions at night and think that a bank robbery or revolution is going on, but it's only play or a celebration.

In Honduras, fireworks are set off to celebrate birthdays, Christmas, New Years', town festivals and religious festivals.

Military & Security

Security is everywhere in Honduras. There are guards at every hotel of any pretension, at stores, at banks, at restaurants and parking lots. But in my travels through Honduras, by plane and bus and on bicycle, I have never felt afraid, or exposed to any untoward danger.

Of course, you don't want to go looking for trouble. Display appropriate deference to people in uniform and cooperate if you're asked for identification or stopped for some other reason.

Movies

Movie theaters in San Pedro Sula and Tegucigalpa are modern and comfortable. The price of tickets is about $3.

In small villages, video halls, usually located in back of small restaurants, have replaced itinerant projectionists. Up to 30 persons are seated in front of a t.v., and the latest Mexican thrillers are shown at a charge of a few cents per person.

Salaries

A laborer on a coffee or banana plantation might make up to Lps 60 a day, about $4 at the current exchange rate. A typical middle class salary is approximately Lps 6,000 or $400 per month.

Sexual Roles

"Nice" women — I'm talking from the local point of view — don't smoke or drink in public, and those who do are considered to be of doubtful virtue.

Much depends on the social class of the woman in question. Women from the upper classes have their own cars, go out to bars, clubs, and discos, where they will smoke, drink, and engage in other typically 'manly' behavior – at least in the eyes of the average Honduran.

But despite some old-fashioned ideas about morality, legal marriage is not always the rule in Honduras. A church wedding costs money that many do not have, or would rather spend on other priorities. So many working-class couples, and even solid middle-class couples, simply live together without legal blessing, and without the support of liberal and liberated ideology.

Tipping

Although tipping is not quite so frequent in Central America, it is recommended that you leave something if the service was good. Often young girls will toil all day long waiting on tables for a few lempiras, and many must support young children on this wage. In better restaurants, a service charge (tip) of 10% is often included on your bill automatically.

Weights & Measures

Mostly, Honduras follow the metric system: kilometers (equivalent to .62 miles), kilograms (2.2 pounds), and liters (1.05 U.S. quarts). However, you'll also find some U.S. measures in use, especially gallons, along with old Spanish measures. The *quintal* is equal to 100 pounds, the *arroba* is 25 pounds, the *vara* is about nine-tenths of a yard, and the *manzana* is a square measurement equal to about 1.72 acres or 0.7 hectare.

Honduras Guide

i n d e x

Things Change!

Phone numbers, prices, addresses, quality of food, etc, all change. If you come across any new information, we'd appreciate hearing from you. No item is too small! Drop us an email note at: Jopenroad@aol.com, or write us at:

Honduras Guide
Open Road Publishing, P.O. Box 284
Cold Spring Harbor, NY 11724

travel notes

travel notes

travel notes

If you're traveling elsewhere in the region beyond Honduras, check out these other Open Road travel guides to Central & South America:

$16.95

$17.95

$21.95

$18.95

$17.95

$18.95